CANADY:

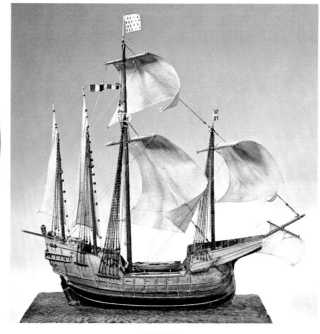

The Discoverers

An Illustrated History by Leslie F. Hannon

McClelland and Stewart Limited
Toronto/Montreal

0-7710-3867-4

The Canadian Publishers
McClelland and Stewart Limited
25 Hollinger Road, Toronto 374

Other books
by Leslie F. Hannon:
Maclean's Canada (ed.)
Canada at War
Forts of Canada

The Discoverers was designed
by Frank Newfeld and David John Shaw.
The type was composed
by Moore Type Foundry Limited.
The book was lithographed and bound
by Evergreen Press Limited.

Printed and bound in Canada

Contents

THIS BOOK
is offered as a token
of gratitude to those
several of my colleagues
at *Maclean's* magazine,
in Toronto, 1949-62, some now
dead and some now famous,
who first intrigued a wayfaring writer with the
complex past and challenging
present of Canada, and then
gave shape and purpose to
his life by making him
one of themselves,
totally seduced to the
waking dream of the
magnificent Canada of
the future.

Hec Insula habet .30. millia
popul. et amplius
Hec habitat Deus.
Insularum

BALENA

ORCA

The Great Captains

THIS is a book about the truly remarkable men who discovered the Canada we know today. These are the great and heroic captains who first marked out the dimensions of the huge improbable land, eventually sliced east-to-west across a continent that, according to all natural laws, should be integrated north-to-south. The present work attempts, in popular terms, to lift out of the grey monotony of historical dates and diagrams the very human stories and personalities of the men – Scandinavian, Irish, Scottish, Italian, French, Spanish, Portuguese, English – to whom the dimly perceived territory in the western ocean was either a place to plunder or a promised land.

It has been argued that the discovery of the New World was the greatest event in the history of the Old, the crowning achievement of the Renaissance. Navigators representing half a dozen nations set out into the Atlantic, confident they would not fall over the edge of a global earth. These men took back news of the discovery of ample lands above the Tropic of Cancer, lands which the atlas now lists as the Dominion of Canada and the United States of America. But – did they really *discover* these lands? Can you *discover* something that has already been discovered?

The very word "discovery" may require redefinition.

The word brings to mind the ancient mariner on a far ocean, sighting unknown lands. But every continent – with the exception of Antarctica – was inhabited before the arrival of European explorers. Africa had its Negroes; Australia its Aborigines; and in Canada, fifty tribes of a brave and infinitely resourceful people had adapted to this demanding environment during 25,000 testing years. The Indians were sparse, it's true – never more than a sprinkling of humanity on the earth's second-largest land mass. They were, moreover, unwisely hospitable to the rapacious men from the narrow fields and short horizons of Europe. The intruders everywhere put forward a putative friendship, but it was quickly backed with ready cannon. The metal goods they offered in trade, the woven cloths, the wondrous coloured trinkets, were seductive beyond resistance. And the darker gift of firearms brought a passing advantage to the lucky recipient tribe, but soon a fatal hardening of the patterns of tribal conflict.

But "discovery" also means this: "To disclose to knowledge, to make known." And that, finally, is what the heroes of these pages did. In an era when men still believed in Isles of Demons, in great sea monsters that could pull a ship into the depths, in ocean whirlpools from which there was no escape, they slowly brought into focus a new world: first, a brooding cape or two; then a span of coastline offering wood and water (and a bounty of cod); sheltering harbours; and soon a thousand coves, islands, inlets, bays, gulfs, river mouths, shoals, and beaches which later hands would tame to charts that captains-to-come could follow with ease. One by one, the mythical Straits of Anian and Isles of the Blest took the shapes we know, or were reluctantly erased from the maps.

The recognized "discoverer" was not always the first man on the scene. After Jacques Cartier (and most likely even *before* him) there were venturers into the St. Lawrence whose names are lost to history – or were never known. James Cook was not the first European to see the mountain backdrop of the Pacific coast. Samuel Champlain was, indeed, part sea discoverer and part overland explorer; but in his time, the inland reaches of Canada were as unknown to Europeans as were any ocean. These men are, however, those who brought the country into the cognition of the outside world, and their courage, devotion, and ability to record and communicate – their sheer survival – give them the honour of discovery.

The motives for discovery were almost always commercial – this is a nation owing its birth and being to free enterprise. The riches in furs so featured in the school texts were by-products to merchant princes who wanted, above all, a water route to China and the Spice Islands which would cut the long haul around the southern tip of South America. The profit on one voyage to the Moluccas for nutmeg and peppers could make a man rich for life. Some expeditions were, of course, concerned in expanding national grandeur; when the seemingly incessant wars of Europe allowed, kings hankered to boast of foreign dominions. But only the Spaniards found gold and silver for the taking; none of the Canadian captains died in wealth.

By a curious coincidence, all the major discoverers of Canada were men whose names begin with the letter "*c*" – Cabot, Cartier, Champlain, Cook. By an equally unlikely chance, they were all humble men, men of the people, at a time when the leaders of most expeditions were nobles serving their kings or seeking land and riches for their private treasuries. It is destiny's subtle rejoinder that the nation which grew within these coasts is the egalitarian mirror of its discoverers, reflecting their solid strengths – and, inevitably, their limitations. One has the comfortable feeling that, although they lived across three centuries and spoke different languages, they would all have settled into the same wardroom in respectful propinquity.

L.F.H.   *Belleville*

Scoured by harsh winds and battered by high seas, the rugged rocks of Canada's east coast held little appeal for even the bravest of mariners. But as desolate and forbidding as they were, these sea-swept shores were the threshold of a vast and varied land. Indeed, in the eyes of the men who first discovered Canada, these were

The Shores of a New World

Land of Sea Mists

When Viking prows first penetrated the mists of the North Atlantic and probed the Canadian littoral, they no doubt skirted the coast of Labrador. A silent, desolate land, Labrador fronts the sea along more than seven hundred miles of changing coastline – ranging through sandy beaches, granite flatlands, and thrusting sea cliffs. In the barren boulders of its Precambrian bedrock we can see the Helluland of Lief Eriksson, the Vikings' "land of flat stones." And in the fog-shrouded forests of the coastal range, we can see the valued Markland, source of much-needed timber. But whatever role it played in the history of Norse explorations, Labrador certainly hosted a wide variety of early seafarers – not least of whom was João Fernandes, *llabrador* of the Azores, whose rediscovery of far northern lands yielded a name for Canada's northeast coast.

Spit, Sand, and Shoal

Of all the articles of trade in fifteenth- and sixteenth-century Europe, fish was one of the most important. To a people who relied heavily on agriculture as a chief source of sustenance, salted fish was an essential food during the lean months of winter and spring. It is not surprising, therefore, that John Cabot's discovery of seas teeming with cod was regarded as being at least as important as his discovery of unknown lands to the west. Cabot's reports were confirmed by the findings of Portuguese seafarers such as João vaz Corte-Real and Alvarez Fagundes. And the later voyages of Estevan Gomez for Spain and Giovanni da Verrazzano for France made the Newfoundland

fisheries a matter of international concern. The wealth of the fisheries is to be seen in the fact that in the long run, the Portuguese earned more from their catch on the Grand Banks than the Spanish gained from their South American treasure ships, and they earned it without the benefit of slavery. Yet the fisheries were also renowned as a nursery of ships and seamen. For the vessels which dared to venture into Arctic seas, the expeditions which began the settlement of America, the Dutch and English fleets which defied the might of Spanish sea power – these were manned, to a large extent, by men who had acquired their courage and their skills in the demanding school of the fisheries.

Nova Scotia

With its bold coastline abounding
in snug coves and fine harbours, it
is not surprising that Nova Scotia
was an appealing landfall for Europe's questing captains. On a
manuscript map of 1544, the label
"Prima terra vista" points to Cape
Breton as the land first sighted by
John Cabot. But in the legend of
Henry Sinclair, the adventurous
Earl of the Orkneys, it seems that
the Bay of Fundy was the site of an
earlier landing–as far back as
1398! The first to settle on Nova
Scotian soil were the French colonists of De Monts' Port Royal, a

hardy group of men who had suffered severely in their winter stronghold at the mouth of New Brunswick's Saint Croix, then crossed, in
the spring of 1605, to the haven of
the Annapolis basin. But as with
other regions of Canada, the Nova
Scotia of today is a land of varied
heritage. In 1621, the arrival of
Scottish colonists under Sir William
Alexander provided the province
with the second of its founding
peoples. It also provided the province with a new name–"New
Scotland" in place of the original
French "Acadia"–with the name
as we now know it deriving from
the Latin phrasing of Sir William's
charter.

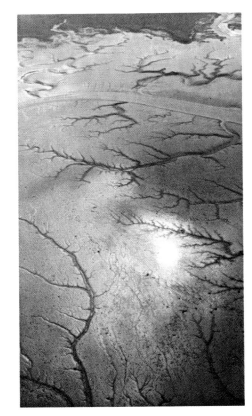

Gateway to the Interior

After wandering for weeks in the vast Gulf of St. Lawrence, Jacques Cartier slipped out through the Strait of Belle Isle and set his sails for St. Malo. He had seen much of the Maritimes in that summer of 1534–the prominent peaks of Newfoundland's Monts des Granches, the lush trees and meadows of Prince Edward Island, the wooded slopes of New Brunswick's Baie de Chaleur, and the singular *roche percé*

off the craggy coast of Gaspésie. But despite his patient and painstaking efforts, Cartier failed to detect the way to the west–the mighty River of Canada. One year later, he resumed his westward search and this time discovered the broad waterway which leads far inland. It was, to say the least, a monumental achievement–one which served to open the way to the founding of French colonies in Canada.

Through the Wilderness...

Flanked as it is by mountains to the north and by rolling woodlands to the south, the Ottawa River has a certain beauty about it. But the beauty of the Ottawa bears little relation to its features as a route to the interior. For the Ottawa is not a free-flowing, easily-navigated stream. It is, rather, a series of pleasant lakes and stretches of peaceful river – linked together by dozens of fierce rapids and treacherous waterfalls. Yet it was up this very river that Champlain made his way – not once, but twice – surviving countless hazards and enduring

endless hardships. In the first of his ventures up the Ottawa, Champlain was as much lured by the lies of Nicolas Vignau as he was driven by his own desire to find a way to the Orient. According to Vignau – one of the earliest of the *coureurs de bois* – there lay to the north an open sea, which he himself had seen. Champlain set out for this "sea of the north" in the summer of 1613, but he was doomed to disappointment. For on an island in Lake Allumette, he learned from Algonquin Indians that Vignau had never passed beyond their encampment. Though frustrated in his first attempt, Champlain returned to the Ottawa two years later, this time pressing on to Lake Nipissing and thence to the shores of Georgian Bay.

to the Inland Seas

From stone shores the restless waters stretch away to the west and northwest, for as far as the eye can see. Here, at the edge of Georgian Bay, Champlain gave up his search for a way to the Orient. He seems to have sensed that the "sweetwater seas" were an obstacle he could not surmount, and from this time forward he devoted himself to New France–leaving exploration to other men.

Part I
Out of the
Sea Mists

There is a legend that St. Brendan, coming to what he thought was an island, pulled ashore, and began to say a mass. The island proved to be a whale. Clearly the artist knew of whales only from hearsay.

CHAPTER ONE

From Island to Island

THE discovery of Canada and of all the Americas was the eventual outcome of the westering search for the fabled Fortunate Isles, the Islands of the Blest, by a few fearless men from Europe. Steppingstone by steppingstone, island by island, they pushed out into the Atlantic Ocean in northern and central latitudes. Storms that swept the early square-rigged craft far away from known landfalls, fog and cloud that made all sight of the heavens impossible for days on end—these also added accidentally to the sum of discovery. But the seamen were more skilled than the traditional texts suggest, and in most cases, they were following in the wake of other travellers now lost to history.

The venturers were propelled by overpopulation in narrow valleys at home, by the threat of merciless raiders, the urge for religious freedom, the hunger for metals precious and durable, for silks and spices, and by the simple but powerful urge to seek beyond the horizon. When the earth was still believed flat by most, when the sun turned men black in tropic lands and would doubtless consume those who ventured too far south from the safe womb of the Mediterranean, when horrendous serpents swallowed whole ships, and towering ice and sucking whirlpools waited at the edge of the abyss—surely all lands where a voyager could find even wood and water were fortunate and blest!

It is today universally accepted that the forbidding eastern cliffs of what is now Canada were first seen and scaled by Europeans centuries before Christopher Columbus saw Watling's Island in the Bahamas in 1492. The Viking voyages of the tenth and eleventh centuries are acknowledged, and Erik the Red and his son Lief acclaimed as discoverers, almost totally on the basis of the fistful of fading vellum pages that constitute the Atlantic sagas of the Norse. Yet these accounts—as vague, controversial, and often baffling as they are—refer to western voyages and settlements in what can only be North America long years before the Viking ships leapfrogged from Norway to the Faeroes, to Iceland, to Greenland, to Canada. And there is an extensive literature of pre-Columbian Atlantic discovery—one recent book lists nineteen expeditions—in which fable and folk tale are no doubt mingled inextricably with fact as recorded on parchments by monks and scribes of ancient royal households until the whole story is shrouded by mists as changing and often impenetrable as the sea mists that held Canada secret, except to the boldest of men.

The precursors of the early voyagers were, of course, the earlier masters of the Mediterranean—those Egyptians who sought myrrh in the Land of Punt in cedar ships from about 2500 BC; the bold Cretans of King Minos; the Phoenicians of Tyre and Sidon who first ventured out into the Atlantic between the Pillars of Hercules (today we call it the Strait of Gibraltar) and founded Gades, the port that still thrives under the name of Cadiz; the roving and reckless Carthaginians; the Greek emigrants who built their Massilia (today's Marseilles) at the mouth of the Rhône; the restless voyagers from the Greek lands celebrated in *The Odyssey*—all these and others probed into far waters, widened the boundaries of the known world, and improved the seaworthiness of ships. The open ocean, with all its legendary terrors, now beckoned irresistibly.

Pliny the Elder reported briefly the four-month journey of Himilco, son of Hamilcar, about 525 BC. The Carthaginian coasted north to Oestrymnia seeking the source of the highly valued tin that was finding its way down the Rhône to the Mediterranean. Oestrymnia was, in all probability, England; and Himilco found the tin in Cornwall after a series of adventures which has been suitably embellished in the folk tales. The sea monsters he reported were probably whales, then common in the Bay of Biscay.

Most learned men at that time laughed to scorn the theory of Pythagoras that the earth was round: his school at Crotona depicted a spherical cosmos in which ten smaller spheres, including the earth, moon,

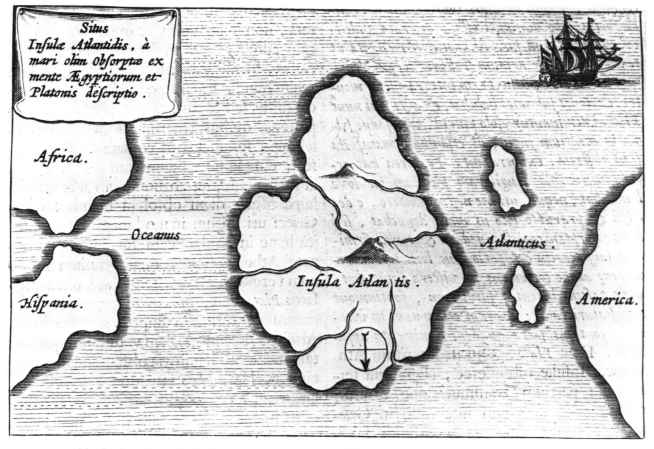

Atlantis, the mythical island believed to lie west of the Strait of Gibraltar, was originally a concept of the Egyptians.

and sun, circled "the hearth of the universe." It was another century and a half before Parmenides stated publicly that the earth was a spinning ball, and yet another century before Plato and his contemporary, Eudoxus, proved the matter. The latter estimated the circumference of the earth at 35,000 miles. His method was brilliantly correct, even if the mileage was somewhat in error. The Greeks, though, still liked to believe that Titan held up the heavens and Poseidon ruled the deeps.

It was Pytheas, a middle-aged mathematician of Marseilles, who took the next giant stride in the fourth century BC. The powerful traders of Carthage had guarded Gibraltar and refused passage to the ships of other city states, mostly to try to maintain their monopoly. For the same reason, they kept a blanket of secrecy over their explorations and spread hair-raising stories of the dangers of the ocean—techniques that other nations would follow in the centuries ahead. Thus, it's entirely possible that certain countries were "discovered" several times. Coin finds on Corvo, the most westerly isle of the Azores, seem to confirm that the Carthaginians were already 1,000 miles towards the American mainland. Some enthusiasts believe that they made the full journey.

Pytheas either slipped through Gibraltar undetected and turned north around the Iberian peninsula or first went up the Rhône and down the Loire to the At-

lantic. Either way, his great voyage is reasonably well documented past modern Brest, to southern England, Ireland, Scotland, the Hebrides, the Orkneys, then "six days over the sea to Ultima Thule, the outermost of all countries." Some argue that Thule was in what is today Norway, around Trondheim, but the weight of opinion favours Iceland. Pytheas' own books have not survived; but as his genius was slowly recognized, quotations from them were included in other classical writings. He sailed "a day"—that is, 100 miles in the vessels of the time—west of Iceland and reported that to the north of Thule the sea turned solid and the sun never set in the summertime. He was probably halfway to Greenland and may have glimpsed its icy mountains. Among his travel notes was the fact that the Britons had already become addicted to warm beer, made from fermented barley.

On his return to Marseilles, Pytheas tried to convince the Greek world of the relationship between moon and tides. (Unfortunately, along the tideless Mediterranean the concept was too wild for general belief.) He is also credited with being the first known navigator to apply astronomy to geography as a means of fixing specific locations. He went into an eclipse of his own when the geographer Strabo, in the early years of the Christian era, won acceptance for his theory of a world of five zones—two habitable by man, one (the equatorial) too hot for life, and the others too cold. Since the Arctic zone began at approximately the tip of Scotland, no man or plant could survive where Pytheas claimed to have sailed. Strabo was, in effect, calling Pytheas a liar. He also breezily contradicted Eratosthenes' near-perfect measurement of the circumference of the earth (24,662 miles) and substituted his own: 18,000 miles. The correct figure is 24,899 miles.

While the Mediterranean seafarers were coasting Africa and exploring the Indian Ocean, there is a suspiciously long gap in the literature of Atlantic discovery. The next figure to emerge with some substance from the shadows of legend is the Irish monk, St. Brendan of Clonfert, in the sixth century. There are, however, plenty of romantics who will insist that during the hiatus not only Phoenicians but also Romans and even Chinese discovered our continent. The Romans in question are said to have been Christians fleeing Nero's atrocities. Certainly the Romans had ships capable of any ocean journey. When Caligula took from Egypt the obelisk that stands today in Rome he obviously had a ship capable of carrying the 130-foot stone needle, which weighs 1,300 tons. The Greek writer Lucian left a description of the *Isis*, a Roman grain freighter on the Alexandria run that was 180 feet long with a hold 44 feet deep. Its displacement must have been over 2,500 tons. Often, the hulls of such ships were sheathed in lead with a tarred insulation between the metal and the planking of cedar or fir. They were partly decked and driven by banks of oarsmen and square sails—some of these dyed purple—which could provide about seven knots in a fair wind. The trireme, a "three decker" of up to 165 feet in length, had a crew of two hundred. For sheer size, these vessels would have dwarfed Columbus' *Santa Maria* or Cabot's *Mathew*.

The Celtic ascetic known as Brendan the Bold certainly had nothing as sturdy. The Irish sea-going craft was the curragh, a ribbed boat covered with three thicknesses of tanned and greased hides, carrying a triangular lugsail of hide, and capable of transporting up to sixty persons. Like all ocean-going vessels until comparatively modern times, they operated only in summer seas.

There is no surviving contemporary account of Brendan's voyages, but the tales of his exploits were handed down for several centuries and were then drawn together in the Middle Ages into the *Imrama*, one of Ireland's most popular sagas. He is the Celtic Sinbad, and it is possible, of course, that the most interesting and daring deeds of several men were accredited to him. But there is more than sheer legend to support the case of an Irish discoverer before the Vikings. Brendan was firmly an historical Christian figure, born on the Dingle Peninsula in Kerry, southwest Ireland, in 484. He went to school in Limerick, learning Latin, Hebrew, Greek, Gaelic, mathematics, and astronomy. Ireland was one of the few sanctuaries

Pythagoras of Crotona advanced the idea that the world is round.

Pytheas of Marseilles perceived the relationship of moon and tides.

Above: The Greek geographer Strabo was both traveller and writer.
At right: Phoenician biremes were able to make long sea voyages.

of learning in the Dark Ages, escaping the ravages of the barbarians, but many of the most deeply devoted priests itched for martyrdom and sought it as hermits in crude stone "beehive" huts on sea-swept islets in the Atlantic. Others cast themselves adrift in boats and gave themselves up entirely to God's winds and currents. Brendan is said to have done this in a curragh in 545 with fourteen other monks, praying loudly that their combined devotions would bring them safely to the Fortunate Isles–here, a concept of heaven. Another source insists that the key date was March 551.

As far as is known, the Brendan saga was not written down until about the time of the Norman invasion of England, but since then more than eighty studies– some serious, some scoffing–have been published. Manuscript versions of the chronicle exist in French, Swedish, German, Italian, and English. On Martin Behaim's globe, unveiled at Nuremberg in 1492, a "St. Brendan's Isle" was included among the lands west of the Canary Islands, and later expeditions were sent to look for it from both Spain and Portugal. Since Behaim was in the service of the King of Portugal, it's open to speculation whether Columbus knew of "Brendan's Isle" before he sailed from Palos on August 3, 1492. The Azores, the Madeiras, and the Canaries were then well known, but several fifteenth-century maps also show a vague but large island called "Antilla" across the western ocean. Brasil, another name for the Fortunate Isles, and Atlantis, the land of a forgotten civilization mentioned by Plato, were somewhere in those far seas, towards the exotic Indies, Cathay, and Marco Polo's Cipango (today's Japan).

Mythical St. Brendan's Isle, shown here on a map of 1367, was believed to be a reality until the eighteenth century.

Brendan, ordained at twenty-six, founded a monastery on a mountain near the Bay of Tralee (on modern maps, Mount Brandon, 3,127 feet) and built a church at Inishtooskert, the most northerly of the Blasket Islands. He was entering his sixties when his voyage – or series of voyages – began. Accepting the basic fact of a major journey, but trying to sift out the fanciful embellishments, there is an itinerary which touches on St. Kilda in the Hebrides, and on the Shetlands and the Faeroes (the "Sheep Islands"), where a fiord is known as Brendansvik. Then the course was set west for forty days until the monks saw, in a sudden clearing of the fog, their first iceberg – described as being "the colour of silver, as hard as marble, and of the clearest crystal." Brendan is then thought to have been in the region off Newfoundland, where the waters from Davis Strait carry down the bergs "calved" from the Greenland glaciers.

It follows that he closed on Newfoundland's eastern coast – or possibly Nova Scotia's – amazed by the strange shore creatures with "catlike heads, boar's tusks and spotted bellies" (*i.e.*, walruses, once common on the northeastern coasts). Coasting America, driven by errant winds, dodging waterspouts, the next landfall is proposed as the site of modern Hamilton, Bermuda.

Here the travellers found an aged Irish monk who reported that he was the last survivor of a group of twelve that had reached the island many years earlier. (Another devout party of voluntary castaways?)

Eight more days' sailing brought the monks to land again – presumably in Florida, either at St. Augustine, in one version, or at what is today Miami, in another. The legend describes the land in terms that must have suited the monks' anticipation of the Fortunate Isles: "This paradise . . . odorous, flower-strewn, blessed. A land many melodied." Once more, Brendan was greeted by an old monk, given the name of Festinus, who announced that he had been there thirty years. After a five-week exploratory expedition ashore, with the autumn approaching, Brendan sailed back to Ireland on the prevailing westerlies. The saga tells us they had reached a land far to the west where, on wild vines, "all the branches were borne down to the ground by the weight of grapes." (Vinland, perhaps?)

This kind of sympathetic sifting of the Irish chronicles could still be swept aside as extravagant allegory were it not for the persistent reference in the accepted Viking sagas to an earlier Celtic presence in America. The Norsemen were proud, even boastful, and it seems most unlikely that in recounting their tales of Vinland they would give needless credit to Irish predecessors.

When the Scandinavians began to settle Iceland in the ninth century, they found the Irish already in possession. Picts from Scotland had probably been there even earlier. The *Landnamabok* (the twelfth-century Icelandic book of the settlers) states: "There were here the people whom the Norse call Papar [sometimes given as 'Papas']. They were Christians with…books, bells, croziers, and other things which show they were Westmen [another term for the Irish living west of homeland Norway]." By this time, most of Ireland and northern Scotland was in the hands of the pagan Vikings. So the Celtic pioneers in Iceland had no choice but to push further westward, across the Denmark Strait.

When Erik the Red first reached Greenland in 982 during his exile from Iceland, he too found Irishmen – small pastoral settlements of religious communities. It seems likely that the appearance of the dreaded dragon ships in Greenland's western fiords would cause the Celts to move once again, pushing desperately westward – by curragh, or even by coracle – onto the North American land mass. Vilhjalmur Stefansson, the Canadian explorer and Arctic historian, noted that once in Greenland, a man can walk the rest of the way to the North American mainland. In 1963, Quebec historian Gustave Lanctot presented the case for an Irish colony on the Gulf of St. Lawrence in the ninth century.

In fact, no indisputable archaeological evidence of an Irish presence in Greenland has yet come to light. But experts are at pains to propose that the incoming Norse probably took over existing buildings – they would be no more than simple stone huts – or used them as foundations for their own structures. With genuine Norse emigrants having melded into some Celtic environments for upwards of two centuries, it is extremely difficult to be sure of the origins of certain remains. One Icelandic history says that Erik's men found "habitations both east and west, broken hide boats, and stone smithery." Determined to prove the feasibility of an Irish discovery, a red-bearded Irishman named Bill Verity sailed the Atlantic alone in 1968 in his square-rigged craft, *St. Brendan*. He landed in the Bahamas.

The next milestone is the story of Ari Marsson – one of the most carefully documented of the early Icelandic tales. Ari was related to Erik the Red by marriage. It is told in the *Landnamabok* how Ari, about 970, was driven by storm for several days past his intended port of Reykjavik (such a storm would likely carry him to the southwest) until he reached Irland Mikkla, or Greater Ireland. The sagas also refer to this country as Albania and Hvitramannaland ("White Man's Land"). It was reported as lying "westward in the ocean adjacent to Vinland the Good." The key reference is that Ari was taken prisoner on Irland Mikkla "and there he was baptized." So he must have come upon a Christian community and that could only mean an outpost of the far-flung Celts. Ari's fate was first related by Rafn,

a Viking trader out of Limerick, and therefore it seems likely that Rafn also touched at Greater Ireland – unless he got the news from an escapee from Ari's ship.

Who baptized Ari? Where exactly was Greater Ireland? It is argued that a group of Irish monks known as the Celi Dei – the "Servants of God," usually called the Culdees – fled before the Viking raids on the Irish homeland about 795 and island-hopped to the North American mainland as the Norsemen pursued westward. They were a breakaway sect from the growing religious power of the Church of Rome, introduced in Ireland by St. Patrick. Historian A. B. Scott wrote: "Their appetites were subordinated to the longing of the soul and the Celi Dei had disciplined their bodies to endure the severest hardships. They possessed no personal property except the clothes they wore, a scanty store of food and the area of ground covered by their hut or cave." Quite large communities may have sprung up, first in volcanic Iceland and then in Greenland, as yeomen farmed the coastal strips of these misnamed islands. Iceland's capital actually enjoys a winter temperature like that of Milan and there are certainly more fur coats in Regina than there are in Reykjavik. Greenland, on the other hand, was given its name (like the "Sunny Acres" developments of today) mainly to entice new citizens to its glaciered slopes.

Four days' sail could have taken the fleeing Culdees to the shore of Canada-to-be, somewhere in the vicinity of the Strait of Belle Isle. This far, the story can be supported by crude logic, in a sympathetic interpretation. Beyond this, however, it moves into the realm of sheer – and most spirited – speculation. Ari Marsson could easily have been storm-tossed as far as the Labrador or Nova Scotia coast and that could, indeed, be "adjacent to Vinland the Good" (assuming there is general agreement that the Wineland of Leif Eriksson was somewhere between Cape Cod and Cape Bauld). American writer Charles Michael Boland unhesitatingly places Greater Ireland in Massachusetts, and Canadian writer Farley Mowat is just as certain that it was in Greenland.

Christianity was not adopted by the Icelandic Norse until 1000 AD, but it is safe to assume that a traveller such as Ari was familiar with the Westman religion and would be willing to submit to baptism, especially if it was his sole means to survival in captivity. Another mention in the sagas reports, indeed, that Ari "had become a chieftain in the land."

The Norsemen were, without question, closing on the new continent. The violent and moody Erik Rauda had established his colony in Greenland in 985, losing eleven of the twenty-five ships in his settlement expedition. He had already crossed Davis Strait to the Cumberland Peninsula of Baffin Island, and the stage was now set for the veil of the sea mists to be torn aside by the courageous men of the north.

CHAPTER TWO

The Shore of Wineland

THE Viking discovery of the eastern Canadian shore–the firm footprint of the European in the New World–is one of the most stirring and, at the same time, one of the most controversial episodes in the history of questing man. Today, nearly a thousand years after the event, scholars, journalists, and historical novelists are still sending articles and books to press arguing every page (and even phrase) of the Norse sagas that record the voyages. Tempers still rise as dates and venues are debated, and once-friendly colleagues cut each other icily in the groves of academe. At least fifty theories can be studied and the fruitful Vinland the Good of Lief Eriksson has been "located" in at least twenty places–from Labrador to the Carolinas. It has been placed inland on the Great Lakes, on Hudson Bay, and on the banks of the St. Lawrence River. There was even a time when it was thought to be an extension of Africa.

Apart from these lively matters, the sagas offer tales of sheer luck, wild storms, one-legged men, cruelty and bloody murder, incredible endurance and resolution, and, finally, an account of how the European discoverers were initially repulsed by the Asiatic nomads who had, in a much earlier era, taken the continent for their own.

The details and dates that are still indefinite are now likely to remain so, unless fresh archaeological evidence is turned up that a majority of the quarrelling scholars will accept. Still, it is not seriously disputed anywhere that the Vikings found this continent, attempted to settle it, and were familiar with its northeastern shores almost five hundred years before John Cabot appeared on the scene. Bjarni Herjulfsson, Erik Thorvaldsson, his sons Lief and Thorvald and his daughter Freydis, Thorfinn Karlsefni and his wife Gudrid–these are the Norse discoverers whom we know by name. There were, of course, many others: Lief the Lucky had thirty-five men in his crew, and Karlsefni sailed with perhaps as many as one hundred and sixty.

Only patient and devoted scholarship by savants of several lands has won acceptance of the main outline of the sagas. These accounts, or histories, covering a thirty-year period, were passed solely by word of mouth from generation to generation in Greenland and Iceland before being committed to paper as late as three hundred years after the event. Unlocking their puzzles has required the skills of both the expert geographer and the literary detective.

The Danish historian, Carl Christian Rafn, first brought the sagas to the attention of the modern world in his *Antiquitates Americanae*, published in 1837. This classic work included all of the relevant sagas which have since absorbed both expert and layman and which caused significant shrinkage in the glory and glamour of Columbus. Selection in these matters is essential, since there are more than two hundred known sagas. The late Dr. Tryggvi Oleson, a professor of history at the University of Manitoba, himself of Icelandic descent, confirmed that the two chief sources of the Viking voyages with which we are concerned here were the *Graenlendinga Saga*, written about 1200, which recorded six voyages, and the *Eiriks Saga Rauda*, of later date, which included only three. Both sagas deal with the epic journeys made to Vinland by the family of Erik the Red, or by those who were closely connected with that lusty group of frontier aristocrats. But Professor Oleson has warned us that the accounts were irreconcilable on many points and that each must be treated with caution.

To further complicate matters, the original transcripts of these sagas were lost and we must now be content with the versions which were included in two later compendiums, the *Flateyjarbok* and the *Hauksbok*. A fourteenth-century scholar, Jon Hakonarsson, of Flat Island, in Breidafiord, western Iceland, had all that he deemed significant or worthy of posterity transcribed by two priests into a single large vellum volume known as the *Flateyjarbok* (literally: "Flat Island Book"). The book was given to the King of Denmark in 1647 and now rests in the Royal Library in Copenhagen. The

Hauksbok was written by three men, among whom law-yer Hauk Erlendsson was the leading spirit. It can be dated only as having been completed before 1334, when Hauk's death was recorded. This book is in the library of the University of Copenhagen. The *Flateyjar-bok* concerns itself mostly with Erik and Lief and the other Greenlanders; the *Hauksbok* concentrates on the men of Iceland, particularly that great captain, Karl-sefni.

Together, these collected works are comprehensive enough for our present purpose, particularly since Hauk Erlendsson–a descendant of Karlsefni's–care-fully noted that he had drawn his materials mostly from two earlier histories of Iceland and Greenland, the *Landnamabok* and the *Islendingabok*, both of which had been written in the twelfth century by Ari Thor-gilsson (known in literature as Ari the Wise). "I took from each book whatever it had more than the other," Hauk stated, "but to a great extent they contained the same matter." Unless otherwise noted, the quotations from the sagas that follow are drawn from these sources.

The first reference in Western literature to the Viking discoveries in the New World is contained in a history written by Adam of Bremen before 1076. He was quot-ing Sveinn Ulfsson, King of the Danes: "He spoke also of yet another island of the many found in that ocean . . . It is called Vinland because vines producing excellent wine grow wild there. That unsown crops also abound on the island we have ascertained not from fabulous reports but from the trustworthy relation of the Danes." It can be added that in medieval times, the word "island" was often used interchangeably with the word "land." Adam of Bremen may indeed have been a bit of a romancer, but in this instance he was dealing with the world's hottest piece of news. It was nearly half a century later before a casual mention of "Wineland" cropped up in Icelandic literature.

The irresistible thrust across the western seas had been given impetus by the visitation of the Viking scourge on all of Europe. The dreaded longships, with their carved figureheads and their barbaric, helmeted warriors, penetrated from the British Isles to the Med-iterranean and Caspian seas, and for three centuries the Vikings held most of Europe's coasts to ransom at the point of their iron broadswords. They ventured boldly as far upriver as Rouen and Paris and once crucified more than a hundred Frenchmen as sacri-fices to Woden. The raids began about 750 and within fifty years Scotland, Ireland, and the isles to the north were never free of threat. Some of the Christian popu-lations of these islands fled to Iceland and were even-tually pursued there by the Vikings when easy pickings became scarce on the European littoral.

The shallow-draught longships of war were not suit-ed to the open ocean, and the raiders had to adapt the slower but sturdier trading vessel, the knorr. This craft measured as much as one hundred feet, and carried up to forty tons of cargo. It was propelled by banks of oarsmen (up to thirty a side) and by a square sail of reinforced woollen fabric mounted on a single 60-foot mast. The knorr was guided by a steer-board mounted on the right side of the stern (that side has been called "starboard" ever since). According to some modern seamen, the knorr could sail within five or six points of the wind, but others believe that the craft could make little headway against adverse winds. There was a small foredeck and an afterdeck, a drum windlass of hard-wood, and rigging of oiled walrus hide. Two small ship's boats were carried on the larger *knorrir* for close shore work. There was no galley and no cabin. These were the ships of the iron men who dared the spuming sea cliffs of Canada.

As the Norse followed their Celtic quarry westward, they took Iceland, first as conquerors then as settlers (there were 40,000 there by 930 AD), and were soon made aware by mariners who had been blown off course that another "island" lay into the setting sun within easy reach. In fact, from halfway up Iceland's Old Woman Mountains, the Kerlingarfjoll, you can see the peaks of Greenland on a fair day. When Erik Thorvaldsson–red-haired, red-bearded, and often red-handed–was banished from Iceland for three years for murder, he decided to carve himself a new domain in the partly known land beyond. Gunnbjorn, an earlier seafarer, had reported the existence of Greenland pos-sibly as early as 877, and the *Landnamabok* included an account of a voyage to northeastern Greenland by Snaebjorn Hog about 980.

In Professor Oleson's chronology of the early voy-ages (noting his warning of a possible margin of error), Erik set out in 982 with twenty men, and some sheep and cattle to provide fresh meat. Crossing Denmark Strait, he rounded Cape Farewell and explored the fiord area of Julianehaab, which he named Osterbyg-den ("Eastern Settlement") and coasted further along the western coast to the Godthaab district where he placed Vesterbygden ("Western Settlement"). Now he chose the name "Greenland" for the huge ice-capped island, for he felt that "men would be more readily persuaded to go there if the land had a good name." In the spring of 986, he returned with his own colonizing expedition.

According to the Swedish historian, Count Eric Oxenstierna, Erik's twenty-five ships carried perhaps as many as seven hundred men, women, and children, plus stocks of wood, farm implements, cattle, goats, chickens, and horses. Fresh water was carried in skins. Only fourteen of the *knorrir* arrived and the fate of the remainder is uncertain–some may have been blown back to Iceland. For his own estate, Erik established Brattalid at the head of a fiord in the Eastern Settle-ment. His house had sod walls up to twelve feet thick and included a "great hall" fifty feet long by fourteen feet wide. It also had running water piped into a stone basin from a small spring.

Among Erik's colonists was Herjulf Bardarsson, a

RÓST

LOFFOET

This sixteenth-century woodcut shows the fearsome Vortex dragging down ships and sea monsters alike.

steady trader and farmer, descended from one of the best-known Scandinavian families. Although he was in his sixties, he was eager to begin trading in the new land and immediately established the port of Herjulf-ness, near Cape Farewell. His son Bjarni handled the maritime side of the family business, making regular trips to Norway with Icelandic cloth, dried fish, cheese, and walrus tusks. He wintered there and returned early the following summer with a cargo of metal tools, timber, pottery, and weapons from the homeland.

When Bjarni reached Iceland in 986, he learned that his father had already left with Erik, the new Jarl (Earl) of Greenland. Bjarni – described as "a most promising young man, a keen traveller abroad who had prospered both in purse and in general reputation" – immediately decided to follow his father to Greenland, and his crew stuck with him. "They sailed for three days before losing sight of land. Then their following wind died and north winds and fogs overtook them so that they had no idea where they were going. This continued over many days.

When the sun broke through the fog, Bjarni saw a strange coast and sailed close in. When he saw that the land was tree-covered and not mountainous, he realized it did not fit the picture he had of Greenland. "He kept the land on his port side and coasted northerly." Two days later, he made another landfall – but again, he decided it wasn't Greenland. His crew were now eager to go ashore, but Bjarni refused – even though the men argued they were running short of food and water. A third coastline rose to view and once again Bjarni rejected it and "set the stern towards the land and held out to sea with a fair wind . . . They now sailed for four *doegr* [one *doegr* was the equivalent of about 120 nautical miles] and saw land on the fourth." This time, the expected towering icy mountains and glaciers flowing to the sea were clearly visible and Bjarni said: "This most resembles what I was told about Greenland and so we may steer to this land." They landed at ebb tide below a cape, very close to the spot where Bjarni's father was anxiously awaiting the firm's shipment of cargo.

Bjarni's western journey merits a larger recognition in the long epic of Canadian discovery. He was the first man in recorded European history to see the main-land of North America. It's true, of course, that his discoveries were made by sheer accident and that he didn't set foot ashore. But he left behind for the saga-men a straightforward, unembroidered mariner's account that has enabled experts to name, with near certainty, the lands he saw – in order from the south – as Newfoundland, Labrador, and the southern tip of Baffin Island, about Frobisher Bay. Another thing: he had squelched the tall tales of the *hafgerdingar*, the whirlpool said to await the foolhardy who ventured into the fog-shrouded western sea. This fabled vortex looked "as if all the waves and storms of the ocean had been collected into three heaps . . . These so surround the whole ocean that no openings can be seen any-where . . . They are higher than lofty mountains."

Bjarni didn't receive any laurels in his own day either. He settled down at Herjulfness for several years and is next mentioned at the court of the ruling Jarl of Norway about 1000 AD. He was derided, in fact, for not having landed on the newly discovered lands. He must have returned to Greenland for the saga picks up the tale: "There was now [in Greenland] much talk of land-seeking voyages. Lief, son of Erik the Red of Brattalid, went to visit Bjarni Herjulfsson and purchased his ship."

Jarl Erik and his wife Thorhild had three sons, Lief, Thorvald, and Thorstein, and the family tree sheltered one acknowledged illegitimate daughter, Freydis. Lief had been only fifteen at the time of Bjarni's epochal journey, but he was now grown hard and tall. He is described as "a large man and strong; a temperate, fair-dealing man." Like all Greenlanders, he wore a tight woollen undershirt, a tunic tied at the waist, skin leggings, and a type of heavy sandal secured at instep and ankle. A hood of skins covered his head against storms. On combat missions, he would don the famous horned helmet. He is reputed to have made a first voyage from Greenland to Norway, where King Olaf converted him to Christianity and ordered him to carry the faith back to his western homeland. But this tale is now considered an invention by some authorities.

Enlisting a crew of thirty-five, Lief sailed in Bjarni's proven knorr in the spring of 1001. He had asked his father to lead this expedition to claim the lands beyond the sea mists, but the chieftain decided against it. One of the crew was Tyrkir, a "southern man" who spoke German, who had been "like a foster father" to Lief for many years. Lief's plan – no doubt thoroughly discussed with Bjarni – was to sail the known course in reverse.

"They sailed out to sea when they were ready," the saga runs, "and they came first to that land which Bjarni and his people had come to last. They cast an anchor and put off a boat and went ashore, and could see no grass there. The background was all great glaciers and up to the glaciers ran a single slab of rock. 'I shall now give the land a name,' said Lief, 'and call it Helluland [Flatstone Land].' After which they returned to their ship." That's how today's Baffin Island was first named. The Vikings repeated their actions at the second sighting of land and when they noted the heavy forest cover of the Labrador coast (in the vicinity of Hamilton Inlet), Lief called the place Markland (Wood Land).

The next step would seem, at a glance, to be a simple progression in this uncomplicated sailor's log to Bjarni's first landfall – the third for Lief and his crew. But the next leg of the journey is, instead, a giant leap into heated controversy. It took the Greenlanders to the land that Lief named "Vinland." To reach beyond conflicting Canadian and American interpretations, here is the relevant passage from the saga as presented by Professor Gwyn Jones of the University of Wales, a past president of the Viking Society for Northern Research:

From there [Markland] they now sailed out to sea with a northeast wind and were at sea two days before catching sight of land. They sailed to land, reaching an island which lay north of it, where they went ashore and looked about them in fine weather, and found that there was dew on the grass, whereupon it happened to them that they set their hands to the dew, then carried it to their mouths, and thought they had never known anything so sweet as that was. After which they returned to their ship and sailed into the sound which lay between the island and the cape projecting north from the land itself. They made headway west round the cape. There were big shallows there at low water; their ship was aground, and it was a long way to look to get sight of the sea from the ship. But they were so curious to get ashore they couldn't wait for the tide to rise under their ship, but went hurrying off to land where a river flowed out of a lake. Then, as soon as the tide rose under their ship, they took their boat, rowed back to her, and brought her back up into the river, and so to the lake, where they cast anchor, carried their skin sleeping bags off board and built themselves booths [shelters]. Later, they decided to winter there and built a big house. There was no lack of salmon there in river or lake, and salmon bigger than they had ever seen before. The nature of the land was so choice, it seemed to them that none of the cattle would require fodder for the winter. No frost came during the winter, and the grass was hardly withered. Day and night were of a more equal length there than in Greenland or Iceland. On the shortest day of winter, the sun was visible in the middle of the afternoon as well as at breakfast time.

Bringing out further clues, the saga continues:

One evening, Tyrkir was missing and Lief took a dozen men to look for him. But when they had got only a short way from the hall, there was Tyrkir coming to meet them. His welcome was a joyous one. Lief could see at once that his foster father was in fine fettle. "Why are you so late?" Lief asked him. Tyrkir held forth a long while in German, rolling his eyes and making faces. Then after a while he spoke in Norse, "I have found vines and grapes . . . I was born where wine and grapes are readily found."

Not to mince matters, Tyrkir was drunk on wild grape juice which he had squeezed and allowed to ferment. After an easy winter in this snowless land, Lief loaded his ship with timber and dried grapes (berries, perhaps?) and sailed home to Eriksford. On the way, he rescued a shipwrecked Viking named Thorir. On treeless Greenland, Lief's single load of timber made him a wealthy man.

Mainly on the evidence as stated here, the competing experts have jousted to claim Vinland for their chosen "sound which lay between the island and the cape" where "a river flowed out of a lake." Staunch

Britishers have argued that Newfoundland could indeed have "no frost during the winter" and would abound in juicy berries that would make a wine to befuddle anyone. In his book *Westviking*, Farley Mowat makes a spirited case for Tickle Cove in Newfoundland's Trinity Bay. Yankee patriots put Lief's winter house right in Plymouth, Massachusetts (where the Pilgrim Fathers later landed), on the Bass River off Nantucket, even in Georgia and Florida. James W. Curran, then editor of the Sault Ste. Marie *Daily Star*, wrote a book in 1939 arguing that Vinland lay on the Great Lakes, by way of Hudson Bay, the Nelson River system, and lakes Winnipeg and Nipigon.

Professor Gwyn Thomas writes: "The facts of geography, strung out as they are over thousands of miles of varied coastline, can all too easily be made to fit very different interpretations of the evidence...It is easy to deny the notions of others, hard to establish a more durable case of one's own...We must at all times remember that there is no theory of the Vinland voyages of discovery reconcilable with *all* the evidence." Thomas himself plumps for Newfoundland's northernmost Cape Bauld as the *Promontorium Vinlandiae* marked on the earliest maps. And he designates the general area of Sacred Bay—where exciting archaeological finds have been made at l'Anse aux Meadows by the Norwegian, Helge Ingstad—as Lief's main encampment. At the same time, however, Thomas suggests that "maybe it was as a result of far-ranging voyages to coasts below the Promontorium that tales of grape clusters and warm winters enriched the Norse tradition of Vinland."

Surely there is no compulsion to fix Vinland on this bay or that, as though it were a village or a town? In other words, Lief's Wineland might well have come to denote a long and varied territory reaching perhaps from Newfoundland to New England. In *National Geographic*, Helge Ingstad wrote: "I never doubted that Norse voyagers might also have made long cruises southward." Or as Professor Oleson put it: "All that is certain is that this land lay south of Markland." Vilhjalmur Stefansson allots Vinland to "the St. Lawrence-Newfoundland-New England region." The Vinland map, drawn by a Swiss monk about 1440 and unearthed in 1957, shows a *Vinlandia Insula* that appears to stretch from above Hudson Strait to well below the Gulf of St. Lawrence.

Erik the Red died shortly after the return of the first Vinland expedition and Lief took his place as leader of the clan. The Greenland settlement now included several hundred farmers, hunters, fishermen, and traders. The first Christian church—built to the order of Thorhild, Erik's consort—was thriving. The island population reached about four thousand at its peak.

Thorvald, the second son, now borrowed Lief's knorr and sailed for Vinland in 1004 with a crew of thirty. The saga mentions no incident on a journey direct to the *Liefsbodarna*, Lief's wintering place. Thorvald sent parties to explore first to "the land to the west" and then he "followed the coast to the northward." The

Dr. Helge Ingstad, seen here at l'Anse aux Meadows, has found archaeological evidence that the Vikings actually reached Canada.

next major event in the Viking discovery was near at hand. After a stay ashore to replace the keel of his ship, which had been broken in a storm (they named a nearby cape "Kjalarnes"–Keel Cape), Thorvald's party "saw three mounds on the sands up inside the headland. They walked up to them and could see three skin boats there and three men under each. So they divided forces and laid hands on them all, except for one who got away. The other eight they killed."

Thus the Vikings greeted the first Canadians–they called them *skralingar*, or skraelings–in traditional brutal style. This time, though, the Norse had met their match. Shortly afterwards, a warning shout sent the Greenlanders rushing for their ship, and "there came from inside the fiord a countless fleet of skin-boats and attacked them." Thorvald took an arrow in the ribs and was buried on a cape called "Krossanes" (Cape of the Cross).

Whether the skraelings were Eskimos or Indians is another of the conundrums that bedevil the chronicle. Professor William L. Morton of Trent University, in his history *The Kingdom of Canada*, says that they were "a primitive and dwarfish folk ... presumably Eskimos." Count Oxenstierna thinks that they were Indians –"skin boats" could denote bark canoes, as the Norse had no knowledge of the use of tree bark as sheathing. Professor Thomas suggests that the Norsemen encountered both Eskimos *and* Indians, noting that about 1000 AD the Eskimos were to be found much further south than their present limits. One saga reference insists that the man who shot Thorvald was a uniped– one of the one-legged men of fable.

When the expedition returned to Brattalid, the third brother, Thorstein, set out with his wife, the desirable Gudrid, and twenty-five men–ostensibly to bring back Thorvald's body. Thorstein's knorr, however, was caught by storms for the whole summer and limped back to Greenland's Western Settlement, near the present capital city of Godthaab (Good Hope), as winter closed in. Thorstein died that winter and a newcomer from Iceland, Thorfinn Karlsefni, "a man of great wealth," quickly wooed and won the young widow Gudrid (he was, in fact, her third husband).

Karlsefni now took up the discovery crusade of the House of Erik. In 1011, accompanied by Gudrid, he set out for Vinland in three ships, apparently with every intention of settling in that land of wood and wines. They carried "a good supply of livestock of all kinds [including a bull]." They encountered no noteworthy difficulties on their journey to the *Liefsbodarna* and a stranded whale fed them well on arrival. "Soon they were able to supplement this diet with grapes and game which they found in abundance." The next summer, the skraelings appeared–"swarthy, evil-visaged men"–and offered to trade packs of furs for weapons. Karlsefni, however, forbad the exchange. (The saga says that he got the furs for milk from the expedition's cows.) Remembering the attack on Thorvald, the

Norsemen built a fort, a high stockade around Karlsefni's house. Gudrid had by now given birth to a boy, counted as the first European child to be born in North America. They called him Snorri. When a thieving skraeling was killed by one of Karlsefni's slaves, the leader expected a major retaliatory attack. The battle took place where "there was lake on one side and forest on the other," but seems to have been inconclusive.

The variations in the sagas that tell the story of Thorfinn Karlsefni force the impartial reader to pick his way carefully. The *Eiriks Saga Rauda*, for instance, adds that the skraelings used some kind of a huge slingshot–a primitive form of artillery–against Karlsefni's men and had almost routed them, when Freydis, Erik's bastard daughter, saved the day. Seizing a sword from a fallen Viking, she "pulled out her breasts from under her shift and slapped the sword on them, at which the skraelings took fright and ran off to their boats."

After three years in Vinland, during which a long coastline (perhaps 1,000 miles) was thoroughly explored, the settlement broke up and returned to Greenland. One version has it that the men fell to quarrelling over the favours of the few women; but most references blame the relentless hostility of the natives. Perhaps there were only enough survivors to require one ship.

The formidable Freydis, with her husband Thorstein, returned to Vinland in 1014 with two brothers, Helgi and Finnbogi, who had recently arrived in Greenland from Norway. They were to share equally in any profits. This expedition added nothing to the record, except the blackest deed ever perpetrated by a woman on this continent. Most sagas agree that Freydis ordered the slaughter of all members of her partners' groups–about thirty men–and when her assassins were reluctant to kill the five women, Freydis took an axe and butchered them herself. Then she had all the ships loaded with Vinland's precious timber and sailed back to Greenland. She swore she would kill any man who denied that the Helgi-Finnbogi party had decided voluntarily to stay in Vinland, but the story leaked out and Freydis was "shunned by all who knew her."

From this time onwards, the Viking contact with the Canadian mainland began to slip back under the shroud of the sea mists. In 1121, the Icelandic annals report that Bishop Erik Gnupsson of Greenland went in search of Vinland, and Paul Knutsson was sent forth in 1354 by King Magnus of Norway. Other vague references dot the ancient histories, but following the Black Death in Europe, few ships sailed westward. The entire Norse settlement in Greenland vanished in the early fifteenth century, creating one of the world's deepest mysteries. Helluland, Markland, and Vinland retreated into the shadows of history to await a new discoverer.

VIKING

THE LONG SHIP
A Northern Design

The Viking ship we admire grew from
a crude, light-ribbed craft of overlapped
boards fastened together with thongs. In
time a boat evolved with curved stern and
stem fixed to the bottom beam, its planks
joined by iron rivets. So far it was intended
only for oars. Next came a broader
ocean-going vessel such as crossed the
Arctic seas, whose bottom plank was
taking on the aspect of a true keel. When
the Oseberg ship was built about 800 AD,
a sail was used when wind and water conditions were right. This ship had the
shallow draft of a raider, but was a poor
sailor owing to its high prow and low
gunwales. But within fifty years, improved
boats like the Gokstad ship (another
burial vessel) were making extended voyages safely. The planks of the high
sides, tied to the ribs with spruce-root
ropes, shifted flexibly with the ship's
movement; a more efficient mast and the
Norse starboard-oar rudder were used. A
replica of this ship, crossing the Atlantic
in 1893, made 223 nautical miles in a day.

*Above, a manuscript shows the rudder side of a knorr.
At right, the famed Oseberg burial ship, seen in Oslo.*

WEAPONS
Made the Man

A warrior, especially one who decided to go *viking* (adventuring), was a well-accoutred man in the great era of the Norsemen. He wore a woollen undergarment and trousers (either tight or loose), a shirt of chain mail, leather shoes, and sometimes a cloak fastened on the right shoulder. His helmet was a conical metal cap with a noseguard. For weapons he had a damascened sword – steel and iron wires hammered together for strength – for hand-to-hand fighting; a broadaxe to fell man or horse if he fought on foot; a bow or perhaps a javelin for the first attack; or an iron-headed spear if he was a horseman. Most of this gear had been adapted from earlier Norse weapons, or even from enemies, such as Franks or Huns. Some items, such as the swords, were imported from skilled metalsmiths. Add to this the early desire for plunder, or the later need for land for an expanding population, and a ruthless disposition, and Viking terror takes human form.

Above, Thor, god of thunder. His symbol was a hammer. Left, swords were often named for their efficiency.

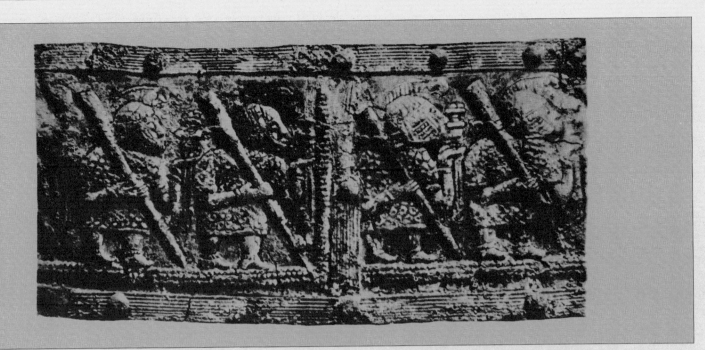

Warriors dressed in mail, armed with swords and carrying staffs, march eternally around the edge of a Viking helmet from Sweden.

Wooden shields centred by a bronze or iron knob went to sea hanging in rows outside the gunwales – a twofold protection for the rowers.

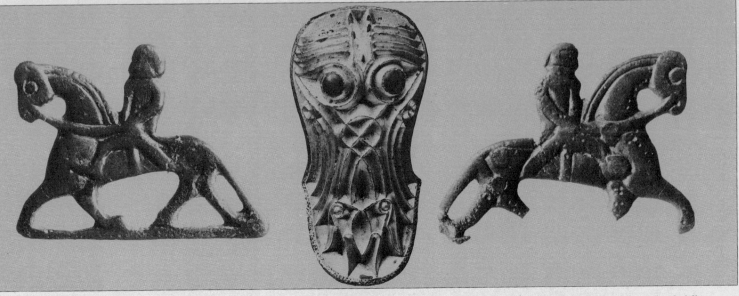

A Viking knight might have his spurs, harness, and even his horses buried with him. The masklike ornament perhaps adorned a bridle.

THE CULTURE THEY CARRIED

Most Norsemen lived by farming, fishing, and hunting. Others traded to Russia, Byzantium, France, Britain, Ireland, and Iceland and lived in towns such as Birka and Hedeby. Necessary articles – clothing, brooches, utensils, sledges, wagons, and furniture – were made in the home or by local artisans. Luxury goods were imported or plundered in raids: jewellery, drinking glasses, swords, silks. Mead, in quantity, was the popular tipple. The Viking religion, centring round the gods Thor, Odin, and Freyr, was bloody and superstitious, demanding human sacrifice, honouring the lucky. Those who fell in battle were escorted to Valhalla by the Valkyries. *Skalds*, the court poets, hymned these heroes in the metaphorical *Eddas*.

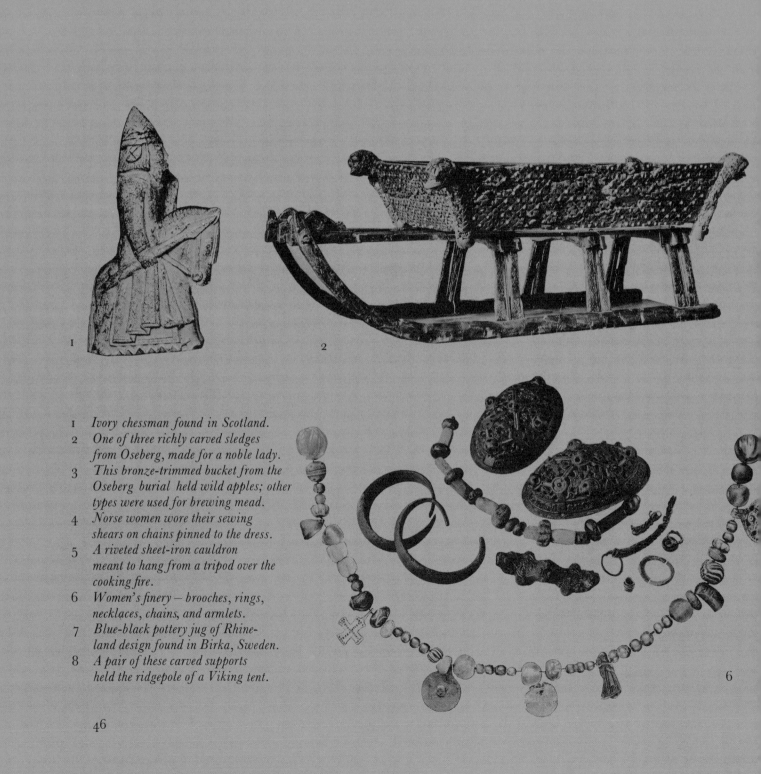

1 *Ivory chessman found in Scotland.*
2 *One of three richly carved sledges from Oseberg, made for a noble lady.*
3 *This bronze-trimmed bucket from the Oseberg burial held wild apples; other types were used for brewing mead.*
4 *Norse women wore their sewing shears on chains pinned to the dress.*
5 *A riveted sheet-iron cauldron meant to hang from a tripod over the cooking fire.*
6 *Women's finery – brooches, rings, necklaces, chains, and armlets.*
7 *Blue-black pottery jug of Rhineland design found in Birka, Sweden.*
8 *A pair of these carved supports held the ridgepole of a Viking tent.*

6

3 4 5

7 8

47

Stones carved with characters in the Runic alphabet were usually set up to mark graves, but some may have been memorials of events or pious acts. Over three thousand of them have been found in Scandinavia, a few in Britain and Russia, but none deemed genuine in North America. Important for fixing locations of inhabited places in Viking times, the stone might also show a warrior's death or record the name of one for whose soul it was set up. In European countries that they conquered and settled, the Vikings were quickly absorbed by the natives. Their own language soon disappeared and they became Christians—the Normans of 1066 spoke French and were great cathedral builders. Only in Iceland did much of their culture linger. The Greenland colonies hung on until the fourteenth century, then died out. Beginning about 800 AD, the Viking era ended after little more than two centuries. In Canada, the legacy was mostly one of legend.

CHAPTER THREE

To the Smoking Hill

THE Nova Scotian—a modest and secure man steeped in the rockfast virtues that seem to thrive within sound and smell of the sea—is usually content to leave the boasting of big deeds to those from inland Babylons who struggle for elbow-room in stifling cities. Yet, if the mood strikes, he can spin tales of the discovery of Canada that surge with the excitement of the fifty-foot tides of Fundy. His land, that peninsula thrust like a sledgehammer into the northern ocean, its 350-mile profile deep-etched by the art of the sea, knew the earliest of the westering adventurers.

There is the salty smack of controversy to many of the chronicles that are told of men and events still only partly known to us, and they are treated with proper reserve by precise academics. Like the reports of Ultima Thule by Pytheas of Massilia, like Marco Polo's Cipango, the first accounts of Acadia may have to await an even later date to emerge from the shadows of fable and ancient hearsay and enter the pages of formal history. Some of the tales just might, of course, be sheer inventions. But it goes against the grain of intellect to accept the half-millenium of darkness that the provable written record demands from the last of the Norsemen to the first of the Renaissance rovers. To stand on the sea cliffs of Cape Breton at dawn, braced to the wind lifting spindrift from the incoming rollers from Cabot Strait, looking into the path of the new sun, is to be open to persuasion on the probability of more pre-Columbian voyages than the standard texts accept.

At any rate, the Viking knew the Nova Scotian shore and the striped sails of their ships probably caused wonderment to the Micmac Indians along the fiord where Halifax was to rise—the Norse seldom failed to penetrate promising inlets on all their discovery voyages. The regional Indian legends are rich with tantalizing tidbits which refer to all-powerful white beings who "came from the east, far across the great sea." The earliest unlettered fishermen from Bristol and Brest, Cadiz and Lisbon (the unsung heroes of the entire saga of the western sea) hauled the teeming stockfish from the Grand Banks and some then ran for shelter into the Nova Scotian harbours when busters blew out of the northeast. The great French fortress of Louisbourg was later built on such an inlet, called Havre a l'Anglais with obvious thankful reason.

Solidly within the written record, Nova Scotia nurtured the first permanent settlement on the American mainland north of the distant Spanish lands, the Port Royal of De Monts and Champlain, by today's Annapolis Royal. This frontier fort through the dramatic doorway of the Digby Gut was the first to stand, but it was by no means the first attempt to colonize the Canadian shore. The French alone had made three previous efforts. It must be counted as likely that there were still others earlier, and there is a fascinating but barely-known literature which spiritedly contends that a Scottish prince late in the fourteenth century spent at least a year in Nova Scotia, establishing a claim to the discovery of America almost a full century before Columbus and Cabot. He was Prince Henry Sinclair, Earl of Orkney, Regent of the Shetlands and Faeroes, favourite envoy and ally of the paramount King of Norway. In this story the name, the "New World," appears for the first time.

The Sinclair claim turns on a plot that most fiction writers would abandon with a sigh. Yet many years of investigation by a few scholars of several nations and a handful of dedicated laymen with foxhound instincts have pieced together one of the world's most intriguing might-have-been accounts. The basic text on which the structure stands was published as Volume 50 of the works of the Hakluyt Society in London in 1873. This society honoured the name of Richard Hakluyt, the famed English geographer who collected and published in the last two years of the sixteenth century "the prose epic of the English people"—*The Principal Navigations, Voyages, Traffics, and Discoveries of the English Nation*. The volume published by the society in the nineteenth century, in both Italian and in an English translation, was *The Voyages of the Zeno Brothers*.

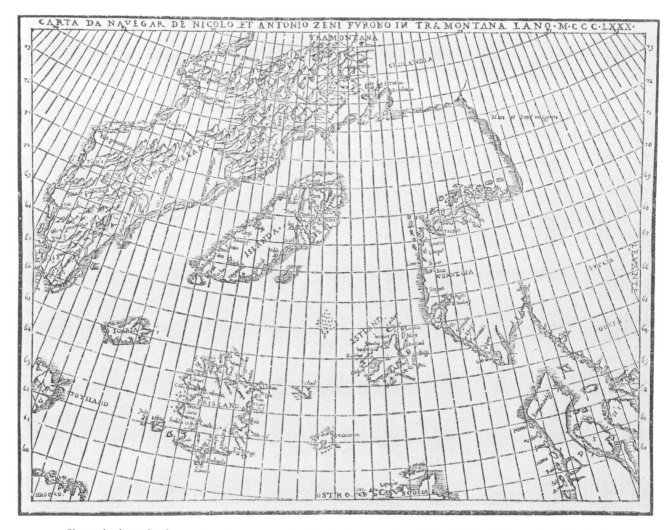

CARTA DA NAVEGAR DE NICOLO ET ANTONIO ZENI FVRONO IN TRAMONTANA LANO·M·CCC·LXXX·

Shown clearly on the above map are the names mentioned in the Zeno narrative: Frisland, Estland, Engronelant, Estotiland and Icaria. Printed in Venice in 1558, the map accompanied and illustrated the story of Prince Henry Sinclair.

Who exactly were the Zeno brothers? The scene shifts swiftly, like the picture slide in an old stereopticon, to the Venice of the early sixteenth century. A young boy, a rich kid in that floating city of memories, wiled away a long afternoon by rummaging in the attic of the family *palazzo*. His name was Nicolo Zeno. He came upon some dusty letters written 140 years earlier by his wayfaring great-great-great-grandfather, also a Nicolo Zeno, and by *his* brother Antonio. The boy puzzled at the old-fashioned fourteenth-century script, tore up some of the letters wantonly, then tired of the sport and drifted away.

When young Nicolo reached early manhood, he read of the great discoveries by the seekers of Cathay and recalled the seafaring history of his family–and, particularly, the torn letters in the attic. Another of his forebears had been Admiral Carlo Zeno, "Carlo the Lion," who had introduced cannons into naval warfare and had thus helped the Venetians to beat off the invading Genoese. Nicolo now pasted together the fragments that remained of the letters–it was virtually a literary jigsaw puzzle–and in 1558 he published a narrative with this resounding designation: *The Dis-*

covery of the Islands of Frislandia, Eslanda, Engronelanda, Estotilanda, and Icaria; Made by Two Brothers of the Zeno Family, Namely, Messire Nicolo, the Chevalier, and Messire Antonio. With a Map of the Said Islands.

The book created a sensation in Europe. At first accepted as whole truth, it was then denounced as a crude Venetian attempt to steal credit for the discovery of the New World. And although more than four centuries have since passed, some professors are still devoting time to proving it preposterous, while other men–perhaps recalling that history is but "a fable agreed upon"–are not quite so sure. The book recounted voyages said to have been made by the Zenos in the North Atlantic, both to Greenland (Engronelanda) and to Drogio (America) under the command of the mighty Prince Sinclair. Acceptance of the narrative demands, for instance, that the name "Sinclair" can be deduced from "Zichmni," the name by which the hero of the chronicle is known. Contemporary believers–notably the astute Frederick J. Pohl, author of *The Lost Discovery*–have patiently doped out ingenious ways in which Sinclair's name might have been distorted (first by the fourteenth-century Zeno and then by his sixteenth-century namesake) to read "Zichmni." They have also shown how the many puzzles in the narrative can be translated into a recognizable itinerary from the Orkneys to Newfoundland to Nova Scotia and New England, and back again. Even a firm date for the arrival on Canadian soil has been proclaimed: Sunday, June 2, 1398. The place: Guysborough Harbour, Chedabucto Bay.

The stalwart *Prencipe* Zichmni was first deduced to be Sinclair by Dr. John Reinhold Forster in 1786, and the renowned German explorer and scientist, Baron Humboldt, also accepted the general accuracy of the Zeno voyages. For many years, maps and globes showed "the Zeno islands." The American historian, John Fiske, included the Hakluyt Society's text–which had been prepared by an official of the British Museum– in the important 1892 volume, *The Discovery of America*. A few years later, Britisher F. W. Lucas tore the Zeno story to shreds in a weighty book of his own. Sharp Danish criticism was also published. The pendulum swung back briskly in the 1940's when a retired professor of geology at the University of Michigan, Dr. William H. Hobbs, took up the Zeno torch and pinpointed the Pictou area, on the Northumberland Strait side of Nova Scotia, as the main site of the Sinclair visit. Others have since proposed further confirming evidence.

The timing of such an expedition would jibe with our knowledge of the day. For the most part, the Viking sagas were being collected and transcribed during the fourteenth century and the knowledge of Vinland had no doubt spread quickly by word of mouth among the sea-faring peoples of the British Isles. Scattered groups of early Britons had been to Iceland and beyond even before the Norsemen, and travel across the northern seas was now routine. The white falcon of Baffin Island was already highly prized as the hunting bird of kings following the diplomatic gifts made by the rulers of Norway. Even live polar bears were presented to important monarchs. From the European coast, the Portuguese were probing ever westward from the reign of Alphonse IV (1325-57), gingerly testing the fringes of the Torrid Zone, still thought by most to be uncrossable. The Canary and Madeira islands, known to the Phoenicians, were firmly rediscovered, and Henry the Navigator was a wide-eyed boy listening to the legends of Prester John.

According to Antonio Zeno, the idea of an oceanic voyage to find the new lands under the setting sun grew in the mind of Prince Henry Sinclair in the Orkneys some time before 1397. Henry heard firsthand the report of a fisherman, the sole survivor from three ships blown onto Estotiland (believed to be Newfoundland), that his life had been spared because he showed the natives how to fish with nets. The island, he said, was "rich and abundant in all the good things of this world." The fisherman told of spending twenty-six years in the new lands, visiting Drogio and other southern lands where cannibals dwelt. He also re-

Within decades of the purported voyage of Henry Sinclair, Henry the Navigator was sending Portuguese ships down the coast of Africa.

ported gold, beautiful cities, and a king who had Latin books in his library. The territory to the south of Estotiland was "a very large country and, as it were, a new world"–*un nuovo mondo* in Zeno's phrase.

Sinclair was then about fifty-two. His father was William, Baron of Roslyn, descended from Normans who had come to Britain with William the Conqueror. Their family seat was Roslyn Castle, near Edinburgh. Through his Norwegian mother, Henry inherited the Earldom of Orkney–this title was confirmed after a protracted struggle with another branch of the family. At eighteen, Henry was married to an infant daughter of the King of Denmark, but the girl died in childhood. He then married Janet Halyburton of Dirleton Castle and they had three sons and three daughters. (Sir Walter Scott would later claim descent from the family.) Henry's princedom–it included 170 islands in the waters north of Scotland–would be his only when he could enforce his rule, and he was engaged in that difficult task in the summer of 1390 when he met *Messire* Nicolo Zeno on Fer Island (the Frislandia of the narrative), halfway between the Orkneys and the Shetlands.

It was, at the least, a lucky meeting for Zeno, as the

Among the animals known to explorers of the northern seas were the "sea horse" or walrus, the seal, and the polar bear.

islanders were about to massacre the crew of Venetians and seize the fine vessel that chance had thrown onto their rocks. Nicolo Zeno, brother of Carlo the Lion, was a man of learning and substance in Venice, blown north of his intended destination in England – a frequent fate in the early days of sail. Rescued by Prince Henry, Zeno convinced the Lord of the Isles that he was well versed in naval matters (he had captained a war galley against the Genoese) and Henry put him in charge of his fleet of thirteen ships. When Henry had pacified his scattered realm – he became known in the legends as "the Sea King" – he gratefully conferred a knighthood on Nicolo and gave valuable presents to the Venetian crewmen.

The narrative continues that Sir Nicolo now (in 1391) sent to Venice asking his younger brother, Antonio, to join him in Henry's service. Voyages to Eslanda (Iceland) and Greenland followed and during the latter, Nicolo became ill from exposure – he claimed to have reached 74° north latitude on the east coast of Greenland – and died soon after his return to Kirkwall, the site of Sinclair's castle in the Orkneys, in 1395.

Antonio Zeno succeeded as admiral to Prince Henry, and his letters make up the remainder of the chronicle. Following the report by the returned fisherman, Henry "determined to make himself master of the sea" and provisioned a fleet for a great western journey. Antonio reported: "I set sail with a considerable number of vessels and men but I did not have the chief command, as I expected to have, for Zichmni [Sinclair]

went in his own person." The old fisherman had been retained as a pilot, but he died before the expedition sailed from Kirkwall.

After a revictualling stop in the Shetlands, the fleet pushed through an eight-day storm to a harbour on Estotiland, where the inhabitants showed such hostility that the Scots decided not to land. Another ten days in stormy waters raised another coastline and "by God's blessing, the wind lulled and there came a great calm. Some of the crew went ashore in a small boat and soon returned with reports that they had found a fine country. We brought our ships to land and when entering an excellent harbour we saw in the distance a great hill that poured forth smoke, which gave us hope that we should find some inhabitants ... Sinclair sent one hundred soldiers to explore and bring back an account of what sort of people the inhabitants were." While they were gone, the others caught a lot of fish and snared wildfowl; birds' eggs were available in great numbers (a point made by almost all of the earliest voyagers).

"While we were at anchor here," Zeno wrote, "the month of June came in and the air in the 'island' was mild and pleasant beyond description. To the harbour we gave the name of Trin." Assuming that "Trin" was short for "Trinity," and knowing that discoverers often named geographic features for dates in the Christian calendar, Frederick Pohl deduced that Sinclair went ashore in Guysborough Harbour, at the head of Chedabucto Bay, on Trinity Sunday – which, in 1398, fell on June 2. Almanac research convinced him that no other year suited the various references in the narrative.

Sinclair's infantry returned after eight days and reported that "the smoking hill" was a natural phenomenon. There was fire burning deep in the base of the hill and pitch, or asphalt, was running from a cleft into the sea. The literary detectives carefully weighed each of the related points and came up with the conclusion that the hill of fire was across the body of the Nova Scotian peninsula, at the coalfields of Stellarton, close by today's New Glasgow. A seam of coal has burned there on several recorded occasions and it was once doused by diverting into it the East River. The length of time the soldiers had marched jibed with the distance from the head of Guysborough Harbour to Stellarton (fifty miles). There is no flowing pitch today at Stellarton, but there is an old railway flag stop called Asphalt. And there is the local folk memory of a spongy deposit of tarlike material – "many people in the neighbourhood dug it up and used it in their stoves like the peat they knew in the Old Country." Michigan's Dr. Hobbs determined that at only four places in the Western Hemisphere were there natural pitch deposits: California, Venezuela, Trinidad, and Stellarton, Nova Scotia. Only the Canadian site was feasible.

The soldiers also reported that "the smoking hill" was by a large river and that there was a safe harbour.

The East River and Pictou Harbour certainly fill that bill – landlocked Pictou is the best harbour on Nova Scotia's north shore and resembles the fiords and inlets beloved of the Northmen. "When Sinclair heard this," the Zeno narrative continues, "he decided to establish a settlement." The presence of natives at the new site suggested the hunting would be better than around the uninhabited Chedabucto. At this point, some controversy seems to have arisen in the Scottish camp and Prince Henry split his forces. He sent Admiral Zeno back to the Orkneys with part of his fleet and led the remainder personally through the Strait of Canso into George Bay and via Northumberland Strait to the snug base of Pictou. Antonio Zeno's personal record of the expedition ends with his safe arrival in the Faeroes. He returned to Venice and died in 1406, presumably before he could fulfil his ambition to write "the life and exploits of Sinclair, a prince as worthy of immortal memory as any that ever lived."

Was it all a dream from a long-stemmed ivory pipe? If not, what did Prince Henry do after the departure of Antonio Zeno? Is there no other wisp of evidence to mark his stay in the land that would, coincidentally, be named New Scotland? History records briefly that Henry died defending his Orkney Island princedom from the invading English in 1404, and he lies today beneath the cold stones of Roslyn Church. The legend thus gives him room to have spent a year or more in Drogio, that land of air "mild and pleasant beyond description."

Two theories have sprung up to fill the vacuum. One is that Sinclair, who "explored the whole of the country with great diligence," became the Glooscap of Micmac legend – the "culture hero" whose fabled career can be followed in the several translations of the Indian tales and who established his home near Parrsboro, in the Minas Basin. He travelled overland through the Annapolis Valley to the site of today's Liverpool. In this happy tale, with its many obvious supernatural touches, Glooscap sailed away on the ebbing tide of the Bay of Fundy on his "floating island" – that is, perhaps, his decked ship with tree-like masts.

The second proposition is that Prince Henry was carried by a nor'easter to the New England shore, where he landed to await a fair wind for his return journey. Here, he and his knights mounted a 500-foot hill – now Prospect Hill, at Westford, Massachusetts – which offered a view of the coastline for fifty miles. The support for this "second discovery" is an outline of holes on a rock ledge on that hill which has been read by some observers as the eroded memorial likeness of a Sinclair knight, complete with sword and shield, who died on that hill climb. To others, it resembles nothing more than glacial markings, perhaps improved by some practical joker to suggest a human likeness. The opposing factions will never agree – and, most likely, that is the case also with the entire chron-

icle of the brothers Zeno and Prince Henry Sinclair.

Shadows also remain around other travelling men who still haunt the serrated shore of Nova Scotia. Their names are mentioned, vaguely and fleetingly, in the great spurt of discovery encouraged by Henry the Navigator in the fifteenth century. Each man has his small circle of ardent champions who never cease demanding the world's recognition of their knight banneret.

Dr. Sofus Larsen, once chief librarian at the University of Copenhagen, took up in the 1920's the cause of the first of the Corte-Reals: the father João (John). In a paper entitled *The Discovery of North America Twenty Years Before Columbus*, Larsen gave details of a Danish expedition to America in 1472, undertaken at the request of Portugal. It was just another of the many attempts to find a sea route to the Orient and the Scandinavians were, of course, the experts at northern sea travel. Two German captains, Didrik Pining and Hans Pothorst – sometime pirates, now in the service of Denmark – were the sailing masters and João vaz Corte-Real was probably the over-all commander representing King Alphonso v of Portugal.

It is another fascinating paper-chase through the fragmentary pages of the archives of a past age. An accepted document, a letter written by a Danish city official in the sixteenth century, commented, among other things, on the Pining-Pothorst voyage of eighty years earlier to "the new islands and the continents in the north." The elder Corte-Real had long ago been rewarded by his royal master with the governorship of the island of Terceira in the Azores for his discovery of Stockfish Land – *Terra de Bacalhao*, commonly believed to be Newfoundland, which today includes Baccalieu Island off the Avalon Peninsula. Labrador (the "farmer" or "squire"), Fundy (from *fundo*: "deep"), Bonavista, Conception, and Cape Race (*Cabo Razo*) are other Portuguese place names on the eastern Canadian map resulting from this or other Portuguese voyages.

The resemblance to Nova Scotia, Newfoundland, and the Gulf of St. Lawrence of the lands depicted as lying west of Iceland on Martin Behaim's famed globe of 1492 is often remarked. Was cartographer Behaim, a scientist of high repute, simply guessing? Or did he have knowledge of the Corte-Real or some other unrecorded discovery? It is hard fact, anyway, that Behaim was married in 1486 to a relative of Corte-Real and that he lived for four years on Terceira during the Corte-Real governorship. It's fact, too, that two of João's sons – Gaspar and Miguel – were later lost at sea while attempting to confirm Portuguese ownership of the lands that had been discovered by their father. There had been a desperate urgency about the voyages of the younger Corte-Reals, because by that time all of Europe was ringing to the news of the discoveries of Christopher Columbus and John Cabot, and the imperialists were staking their claims.

Dela tierra de
os ue a tabla

anita

tutionaer.
estadas.
saagade
golelna

delespoñias.

rio de s. antonio
monjugnas.
rio de buenamadre
haya de manadre

baya

baya des:
tiago.

descubierta
qualle
nando

rio as gme
rio as bajo
rio del s. ancino
bel spiritu
chiba.
delas arenas
baya de s. mar.
c. de s. juan.

rio del spiritu santo.

marpequgna.
eubāa.
mantas del salvador.
rio de flores.

agustin.
rio dnieues.
arenal.
playa.
baya de arenas.
baya de miraclo aqui.
de sanbarco pansso denarinas.

ancon baya.
baya fonda.
yralland
rio detuampome

rio de jordan.
rio de s. negno.
amon.

baya.
c. baxo.
delacena.
c. de s. elena.
c. de s. roman.

s. cruaco.

OC

Genoa in the fifteenth century. Birthplace of John Cabot.

CHAPTER FOUR

The Temptation of Cathay

THERE are no more fascinating stories nor more teasing mysteries in the annals of discovery than those which still surround the man who found Canada, the mainland of North America, at the close of the fifteenth century. We are speaking here of John Cabot, citizen of Venice in the service of England, who raised the flag of King Henry VII on Cape Breton, Nova Scotia, on June 24, 1497.

A trader, map-maker, and navigator with a knowledge and philosophy beyond most minds of his age, Cabot was certain that Christopher Columbus, another Italian in foreign service, had not found the long-sought Asia of silks and spices on his lauded voyage of 1492, but only some primitive islands somewhere en route—probably the Antilla, already drawn from hearsay into the vague maps of the time. The fabulously rich Cathay and Cipango, described so temptingly by that other Venetian traveller, Marco Polo, two hundred years earlier, obviously lay further westward. Cabot's logic insisted that he would find them if he took the northern course to Iceland, to Greenland, then persisted beyond, following southwesterly the coast of the mainland which he expected to rise through the sea mists. Cipango lay, he reckoned, in the latitude of Lisbon.

It's ironic that Columbus not only failed to reach Cathay but that he never even set foot on the North America which so honours him today. In 1498, on his third voyage, he landed briefly on a beach at the mouth of the Orinoco in Venezuela, and in 1502 he coasted along the Central American isthmus, believing that he was nearing the mouth of India's Ganges. All knowledge of the Norsemen's Vinland, of stony Helluland and forested Markland, had, of course, been lost to the European record and no man knew that a great continent—a whole New World, in fact—stood in the western sea to bar the way from Europe to Asia. This was the tremendous discovery of John Cabot. He brought back to England the irrefutable report of "the newe founde launde."

The puzzle goes back to Cabot's very beginnings. Neither the date nor the place of his birth are known with certainty. He left no portrait to give us a likeness. The spelling of his name varies through the records—from Cabato to Chaboto to Gabota to Cabotto to the accepted Anglicization, Cabot. His given name also varies—from Giovanni to Zoane to Joanes to Johannes to John. He left no scrap of his handwriting. He had at least three sons; but of two of them we know nothing more than their names. The other, Sebastian, merely compounded the mystery with his strange or venal reports and reminiscences. The arrival of the father in England is obscure, and his death, or disappearance, in 1498 is merely deduced. He enjoyed only the briefest celebrity, and then fell even more swiftly from sight, his charts and journal lost or suppressed, lacking a biographer to spread word of his exploits.

Cabot was rescued from obscurity only in recent times by the devotion of a small group of international academic sleuths (they are called "Cabotians") and by some lucky breaks, mainly in the past half-century, that supplied significant cross references to John Cabot's voyages in documents of accepted authenticity. The most recent of these turned up in the Spanish national archives in 1956—a letter written by an Englishman, one John Day, to Columbus describing Cabot's 1497 discovery. The Cabot bibliography, including the ranking studies by Henry Harisse, Henry P. Biggar, and James A. Williamson, is still growing. From these and other works, it is now possible to sketch a picture of Cabot the man, and his achievement, with reasonable accuracy.

Genoa is accepted as his birthplace; the year was very close to 1450. He was thus growing up in that bustling Ligurian port with the weaver's son, Cristoforo Colombo, who was born at nearby Terra Rossa, probably in 1446. Genoa had already been a major trading centre for centuries, fought over by a long line of conquerors from Mago, brother of Hannibal, to the Goths and Carolingians. In its proud status as a separate republic it ruled Corsica and Sardinia. Its

Ferdinand v, King of Spain, sponsored voyages of exploration.

traders had established colonial outposts from Spain to the Black Sea, and only the equally aggressive men of Venice could match the Genoese for riches and power.

The battles between the two city states swayed one way, then the other. When the Venetians were defeated at Curzola in 1299, Marco Polo (then captain of a fighting galley) was captured. It was while he was imprisoned in Genoa that he dictated to a fellow captive his *Book of the Marvels and Wonders of the Kingdoms of the East*, describing his travels in China, the land of the Great Khan. In 1379, at Chioggia, in the Venetian lagoon, the Genoese fleet was decisively beaten by Admiral Zeno and his ship-borne cannons, and Genoa then fell under the domination of Milan in the fifteenth century.

Cabot's father, Guilio, a trader, may have moved his family to the triumphant Serene Republic of Venice sometime around 1460. The date and circumstances are uncertain, but John was granted citizenship of Venice before July 1473, and the regulations for this status required that an alien applicant had to first reside in the city for fifteen years. Cabot married a Venetian girl, Mathye, and when he was in his thirties, he appeared in the records again as being involved in some complicated law suits over property. His brother Piero was mentioned in these deals. By 1484, he had two sons, Ludovici and Sebastian, and another, Sancio, within the following twelve years.

In this period, Venice was described as "the fairest and noblest and most pleasant city of this day and age, and the most beautiful and the wealthiest in the world, for indeed merchandise gushes through it as does water in a fountain." It was governed by the leading merchants, the *nobili*, under the proposition that what was good for business was good for Venice. For generations in the Middle Ages, when most of the traffic and contact with Asia went through this entrepôt on the Adriatic, the proposition held good. In Cabot's time, the writer Aretino enthused: "I never look out of my window that I do not see a thousand merchants in as many gondolas." The doge sailed, on state occasions, in a gondola sheathed in gold. The merchants bankrolled caravans that went into the eastern hinterland on journeys lasting for years, returning with delicate porcelain vessels, with silks for the dresses of noble ladies, with the spices much in demand in Europe to season the monotonous fare of the time, and with the perfumes that masked the odours of the unwashed. The Venetian galleys plied regularly to Alexandria and Beirut, transhipment ports for the sacks of peppers, nutmeg, cloves, ginger, cinnamon, and other aromatics. They brought back ornate carpets from Persia and pebble diamonds from India. They ran a regular freight service to Antwerp, London, Southampton, and other north European ports. The spices changed hands many times on their way from the East Indies and the Malayan archipelago, and the Mediterranean merchants had only the vaguest knowledge of the places where they were grown and prepared.

This situation changed dramatically – and the decline of Venice began – when Portugal's Vasco da Gama sailed his expedition of four ships around the Cape of Good Hope, across the Arabian Sea and rattled his anchors down into the busy harbour of Calicut (now Kozhikode) on the Malabar coast of India on May 20, 1498. Da Gama had forged a new link between Europe and the East, but was still a long way from the Spice Islands.

Zuan Caboto – to give him the Venetian style of this period of his career – knew as much as any man about the spice trade. Employed by one of the princely merchant families who built the imposing *palazzi* which still grace the canals of Venice today, he travelled as far as Jeddah, near Mecca on the Red Sea, on trading journeys. There, and in other places, he questioned the men of the camel caravans, learning about the Far Eastern origin of the valuable trade stuffs. He must have studied industriously, having read and evaluated the earliest printed editions of Marco Polo's chronicles as told to Rusticiano of Pisa – a rare accomplishment for a working citizen in the fifteenth century.

With his grasp of navigation and astronomy, Cabot scoffed at the lingering beliefs of the flat-earth fraternity and began to dream of making his own attempt to reach Cathay–not by the tortuous overland trails to the east, or the long and still uncertain routes around Africa, but by the short voyage that seemed to be required across the western ocean from Europe. He had probably read the conclusions of Paolo dal Pozzo Toscanelli, the amateur cosmographer, one of the wealthy financiers who made Florence another important trading power. Toscanelli drew a map of the known world in 1474, but in wildly exaggerating the size of the eastward lands in their spread across the globe, he equally reduced the estimated width of the western ocean which separated Europe from the "end of Asia." It was an extension of the basic error of the Egyptian scientist, Ptolemy, giving all the fifteenth-century travellers a concept of a world with a circumference of only about 18,000 miles.

Like Columbus in those same years–but, of course, independently–Cabot took his plan in his pocket and went looking for a sponsor. Like Columbus, he went first to Iberia, where Spain and Portugal were competing hotly for trading power and overseas possessions.

The reports sent back to Spain by Pedro de Ayala, an envoy of King Ferdinand and Queen Isabella in England, are among the key documents in the verification of the Cabot story. In one of his dispatches, Ayala mentioned, among other things, that Cabot had "been in Seville and at Lisbon seeking to obtain persons to aid him in this discovery." He was, presumably, unsuccessful. Some papers found in the archives at Valencia in 1943 indicate that a certain Venetian named John Cabot Montecalunya was living in Valencia in the early 1490's and twice had audiences with King Ferdinand to explain a scheme he had for improvements to the port. Dr. Williamson, vice-president of the Hakluyt Society, acknowledged as the dean of Cabotians, says it is "very probable" that this man was *our* John Cabot, although no one has an explanation for the word "Montecalunya." Williamson points out that assuming it *was* John Cabot, he would then almost certainly be in Valencia when Columbus passed through in April 1493, on his triumphal way to Barcelona to report to his royal sponsor, Isabella, that he had crossed from the Canary Islands to "the land of the Great Khan from which the spices come" in thirty-four days' sailing.

Convinced by his reading and scientific study that Columbus had certainly not reached Cathay or Cipango, Cabot must have watched with mixed feelings the procession of naked bewildered captives from Hispañola, the parrots, and the paltry few crude gold ornaments, led by the grand admiral himself in rich cloths. Columbus had accepted from biblical references that only about fifteen percent of the earth's surface was water (instead of the actual 71 percent) and he jumbled medieval research until he figured that the coast of Asia could not be more than 2,500 miles to the west. (It is really over 8,000 from Europe.)

Queen Isabella, wife of Ferdinand, was the real ruler of Spain.

He wrote later to Queen Isabella that "in the carrying out of this enterprise of the Indies, neither reason nor mathematics nor maps were of any use to me; fully accomplished were the words of Isaiah."

The deluded but exultant Spaniards were in no mood to listen to a critic, and the Portuguese were determined to pursue their own sea routes eastwards in the Indian Ocean. (Bartholomew Diaz had already rounded the Cape of Good Hope.) At Tordesillas the following year, the two maritime powers agreed to divide the non-Christian world among themselves. Cabot packed his family and goods and took ship for his next best hope: England.

Some writers place him first in London, in the area still known as Blackfriars. The metropolis already had a long-established resident Italian group of brokers, insurers, and bankers' agents, known as the Lombards –although they did not all come from Lombardy. Several English kings had pledged their jewels and other property to the Lombards for money to pay for their wars. Indeed, Lombard Street in today's London is still an important banking centre. A man of travel and some learning like Cabot would get a welcome and would be able to arrange interviews within the English Court.

The centre of interest in Atlantic voyages was, however, the ancient port of Bristol, in southwestern

England, a protected harbour (then known as Bristowe) familiar since the earliest days of sail. Rich with exports of tin and iron, corn, and strong woollen cloths, Bristol's Society of Merchant Adventurers were the capitalists of the time, adding "Baywyndowes" to their houses on the stone-paved streets. Cabot is known to have been in Bristol by 1495, but he may have arrived as early as 1491. The source, again, is Ambassador Ayala. In a dispatch dated July 25, 1498, Ayala reported that "for the last seven years, the people of Bristowe have equipped two, three, and four caravels to go in search of the Island of Brasil and the Seven Cities in accordance with the idea of this Genoese [Cabot]."

The "Seven Cities of Cibola," in Spanish mythology, were set up by seven bishops who fled across the ocean when the Moors overran Spain. Legend held that the "cities" were encrusted with gold and spilling with jewels. Like "Brasil," the "Seven Cities" were merged into the image of the Fortunate Isles of the old fables. The Bristol skippers knew that there was some land mass in the far west, but to those brave enough to dare those foggy waters, it was merely an excellent fishing ground, better than the disputed waters around Iceland (where the King of Denmark had forbidden foreign vessels). Vilhjalmur Stefansson has noted that "Brasil" was sometimes synonymous with "wooded" and thus the name might arise from folk-memory of the Vikings' Markland (today's Labrador). Before the advent of Cabot, there is nothing in the written record to suggest that the British thought of the North Atlantic as a possible route to the riches of Cathay.

It is known that Cabot was drawing maps for sale in Bristol. Did others from that port put ideas of a route to Cipango to the test, unsuccessfully, before Cabot gained sufficient stature to win royal approval for his own voyage of discovery? Was it in Bristol, and not in Valencia, that Cabot first studied the details of the epochal first voyage of Columbus? It is just one more of the Cabot conundrums.

Columbus himself had called at Bristol about 1476 during a voyage in which he reached Iceland, according to some authorities. He was a friend of the sons of João vaz Corte-Real in the Azores and no doubt learned as much as possible from them of João's western voyage to Stockfish Land. The famous history of the Indies by Bartholomew de Las Casas included the following (believed to be part of a letter from Columbus to his son, Diego): "In February, 1477, I sailed about 100 miles beyond Thule . . . To this island, which is as large as Britain, the English sail with their goods, especially from Bristol. When I was there, the sea was not covered with ice." Modern historian Samuel Eliot Morison accepts that Columbus did go to Iceland to take the measure of the northern seas for himself, although it seems likely that the month of his visit is in error.

John Cabot's presence in Bristol is attested to by another item from the Spanish archives–a letter sent to Gonsalez de Puebla, the Ambassador in London, from the royal court–in which reference is made to "the arrival there [in England, before January 1496] of one like Columbus for the purpose of inducing the King of England to enter upon another undertaking like that of the Indies, without prejudice to Spain or to Portugal." Incidentally, the Spaniards would not by then be all that angry about Cabot's plans, because, to quote Williamson: "We should remember that the Columbian discoveries, after the first triumph in 1493, became very unpopular in Spain itself and were in some danger of being abandoned. Englishmen in Seville witnessed the glorious return in the spring of 1493 and the enthusiasm of the second sailing in the autumn. Thereafter, they saw only ruined men straggling back from the Indies with maledictions on the hell to which Columbus had lured them." Columbus himself was deposed as governor of his island discoveries and sent back to Spain in chains.

We know that Cabot and his family rented a house in St. Nicholas Street in Bristol from Philip Grene for forty shillings a year. The Welsh king, Henry VII, was in Bristol on August 12, 1496, but it was already six months since he had issued letters patent to "John Cabotto, Citezen of Venice, Lewes, Sebastyan and Soncio, his sonnys" for a voyage of discovery to all parts of "the eastern, western and northern sea"–to quote a quaint translation of the Cabot application. Obviously, Cabot must have had audience with the thrusting, canny Henry, the first of the Tudors, some time in 1495, as the issuance of letters patent–the formal royal granting of rights or privileges–was in those days a time-consuming matter in which the few legal experts available agonized for just the right phrase and nuance. Even the man who warmed the wax for the seal–he was the *chafewax*–had to be considered and paid his due fee.

There is some evidence that Cabot put a true Venetian push to things and got underway with a first attempt that same year. The formal histories seldom credit a 1496 venture, but the letter written by the Englishman, John Day, to Admiral Columbus from Andalusia in 1497-98 says: "Since your Lordship wants information relating to the first voyage, here is what happened: he [John Cabot] went with one ship, his crew confused him [threatened to mutiny?], he was short of food and ran into bad weather, and he decided to turn back." One of the later Icelandic sagas can be interpreted as reporting a visit by Cabot to the island in 1496, at which time he gathered every scrap of information available about the lands further westward. This visitor returned the following year with a small ship and a small crew and hired an Icelandic pilot to take him to Labrador. They sailed to the west and never returned.

Other men had turned back in failure from the exploration of the furthest reaches of the western sea.

The lateen sail on the Arab dhow above was adapted for use on Portuguese caravels. Without this sail Columbus would not have been able to make his voyages.

The earliest recorded attempt from Bristol is dated 1480 – the voyage sent out by the trader John Jay. The library of Corpus Christi College, Cambridge, holds a Latin manuscript written by Bishop William Worcestre which describes the voyage of a ship of eighty tons that left Bristol on July 15, 1480, "to look for the Island of Brasil." The skipper was John Lloyd, often described in contemporary journals as "the master mariner of England." After nine weeks of very rough treatment in northern seas, they were driven back to an Irish port. There is a document extant, dated June 18, 1480, which grants rights to Thomas Croft, William de la Fount, and Robert Straunge to trade "to any parts" with two or three ships. Experts believe that this licence may refer to the Lloyd voyage, with Jay figuring as another partner in the investing syndicate. The northern seas can be as rough as any in the world – twenty-five ships from England were lost in a storm off Iceland early in the fifteenth century – but it must still be considered probable that a man of Lloyd's experience would have gone far to the west in sixty days' sailing.

The tubby little oaken ships of Cabot's day were built to take high seas and long voyages, but they still had to be small and light enough to be rowed or towed when necessary. They developed from the Genoan and Venetian carracks of the thirteenth and fourteenth centuries. The discovery ships were seldom of more than fifty tons burden and about seventy feet in length

– the *Pinta* and *Nina* of Columbus' 1492 expedition were fifty and forty tons respectively. Martin Frobisher crossed the North Atlantic in the 20-ton *Gabriel*. The triangular lateen sail, still seen on Arab dhows today, was adapted for use on a mizzenmast in company with the square mainsail inherited from the Viking ships.

The vessels *Trinity* and *George* set out from Bristol in the summer of 1481 on a quest similar to that initiated by John Jay, but their main purpose may have been to fish the cod banks off Newfoundland or Labrador – they carried eighty bushels of salt. These ocean fishing voyages were now quite routine and, in fact, this particular one was recorded only because it led to the prosecution of a customs officer.

Among the short and broken threads of the recorded history of this period none is more tantalizing than the reference which suggests that there was a widely known discovery of the Canadian mainland in the early 1490's, several years before Cabot's exploit. In his letter to Columbus, John Day added: "It is considered certain that the cape of the said land [that is, the land which Cabot had claimed for England] was found and discovered in the past by the men from Bristol who found Brasil, as Your Lordship well knows. It was called the Island of Brasil and it is assumed and believed to be the mainland that the men from Bristol found."

Day boasted in his letter that "I am sure that

everything has come to my knowledge," but the general vagueness of the comment, the reference to the chimera of "Brasil," plus the possibility that Day was seeking to flatter Columbus by minimizing the importance of Cabot's claims–all these weaken the case. Day was a trader in lead, dependent on Spanish goodwill. Nevertheless, he may have had some evidence of a specific discovery that is now lost to us. He may, on the other hand, have been referring to the general knowledge of the dimly perceived Stockfish Land–João Corte-Real's *Terra de Bacalhao*, or today's Newfoundland, also seen by some writers as "Brasil."

Some other early claims are even more difficult to unravel, and the case of Robert Thorne and Hugh Elliot will suffice as example. Both men were Bristol traders and may, indeed, have been among the ship's company in Cabot's *Mathew*. However, in 1527, Thorne's son, then living in Spain, wrote a paper for the English government in which he stated that his father and Elliot were "the discoverers of the Newfound Landes." He also stated that if their crew had been willing to probe further, "the Land of the Indians from whence all the Gold commeth had bene ours: for all is one Coast." By 1527, Hernando Cortez and the other *conquistadores* had pillaged Montezuma's cities and Mexico was probably "the Land of the Indians" in the younger Thorne's statement. Also by this time, of course, the Corte-Real sons, Verrazzano, Gomez, and others had explored the North American coastline to some extent.

A later and fuller version of Thorne's claims and statements was prepared for Henry VIII and titled *The Declaration of The Indies*. Richard Hakluyt published this in 1582 in his first anthology, *Divers Voyages*, and ensured it of world attention when he included it in his Elizabethan masterwork, *Principal Navigations, Etc.* Dr. John Dee, in 1578, advanced the Thorne-Elliot claim when he listed their discovery on the back of a map of the North Atlantic, dating their voyage "circa An. 1494." A Welsh visionary, Dee was trying to establish Queen Elizabeth's claim to North America, beginning with a voyage by King Arthur of Camelot. Anyone eager to play historical detective can now ponder on the probable level of accuracy of Dee's map-notes made fifty years after the younger Thorne's first letter written from Spain about an event which had occurred thirty-three years earlier still. And was Thorne junior, like so many before him and since, merely trying to cash in on the deeds of others? Hugh Elliot, in any case, was still voyaging west in 1502, as proved by British royal archives.

Although the printed book was one of the sensations of the time, few men outside royal, religious, or scholarly circles could read. William Caxton did not print his first book in England until 1477, and as the century closed with the tang of discovery salting every sea breeze, the best-sellers of the times were often the elaborate maps which showed the real, and often the imaginary, islands and continents reported in the Indian and Atlantic oceans. One of the most interesting of the printed Renaissance maps, dated 1544, lodged in the Bibliotheque Nationale in Paris, adds its measure of confusion and controversy to the Cabot story. The "Paris Map," as it is known (although it was found in Germany in 1843), offers a version of the world as known after Columbus, Cabot, and their many followers of the succeeding fifty years. Its outlines are in places recognizable today but better maps existed at the time–it depicts Ireland as being as large as England and Scotland. Several "legends"–descriptive notes, in Latin and Spanish–were separately printed and glued to the map. One of these, placed near today's Nova Scotia, reads:

This land was discovered by John Cabot the Venetian and Sebastian Cabot his son, in the year of the birth of our Saviour Jesus Christ 1494, on the 24th of June in the morning, to which they gave the name First Land Seen (Prima Terra Vista), *and to a large island which is near the said land they gave the name Saint John, because it had been discovered on the same day. The people of it are dressed in the skins of animals; they use in their wars bows and slings. It is a very sterile land. There are many white bears and very large stags like horses, and many other animals; likewise there is infinite fish, sturgeons, salmon, very large soles a yard long, and many other kinds of fish, and the greater number of them are called baccallaos [the cod]; and likewise there are in the same land hawks black like crows, eagles, partridges, linnets, and many other birds of different kinds.*

Every Canadian will accept this as a pretty fair description for the first half of the sixteenth century–even if a 36-inch sole takes some swallowing. But the year given on the Paris Map appears to be a simple error, placing the Cabot discovery three years too early. This could, the experts suggest, have occurred in the transcription of the old Roman numerals. Later editions of the map carry the accepted date, 1497.

Perhaps the most significant item on the Paris map is the printing of the label "*Prima Terra Vista*" in such a position as to identify modern Cape Breton. The inscription runs from the northern point of the peninsula–today's Cape North, on Cabot Strait–out into the Gulf of St. Lawrence. This would possibly make the "large island which is near the said land" the present Scatari Island, off Louisbourg, or even St. Paul Island, or one of the Magdalens–but they are hardly "large" enough to earn that description. How far is "near" in a reference written by others fifty years after the event? In a version in Hakluyt's *Voyages*, the description is given as the island "which lieth out before the land." Exactitude was not a fetish in Cabot's day–and the references (and even the map itself) are considered to originate with Sebastian, who would

A DISCOVERER
ANNOUNCES
A NEW WORLD

In 1493, when Christopher Columbus announced his discovery of the New World, he published a letter containing the two engravings at the left. The engraving at upper left shows Spanish seamen going ashore to offer gifts to the natives. The engraving below it shows Ferdinand V, the three ships of Columbus, and the naked inhabitants of the Caribbean Islands. Above is a portrait of Columbus himself.

Five years before John Cabot's discovery of the Canadian mainland, Columbus had reached Cuba and Haiti, after having tried to reach the East by sailing westward across the Atlantic. The principles of cosmography which Columbus used as the basis of his "enterprise of the Indies" were in large part sound – though he was, of course, totally unaware of the two continents that lay between Europe and Asia. Columbus' subsequent voyages revealed the outline of the Antilles and the northeastern coast of South America, while men such as Gomez, Verrazzano, Magellan, and Ayalas sketched in other portions of the New World.

63

have been only about fourteen at the time of the discovery.

Did the two discoveries actually take place on the same calendar day, or merely close to the feast of John the Baptist? Was the "large island" indeed Newfoundland, with its capital and safe harbour named for St. John? In any event, Newfoundlanders today honour Cabot as their discoverer and June 24 as their founding date. "Only a churlish pedantry," writes Dr. C. L. Bennet of Dalhousie University, "would dispute Newfoundland's legal and moral claim to be the first discovery in the New World."

In making an assessment of John Cabot's personality, Dr. Williamson writes of "a certain magnificence and magnetism which fired the ignorant public no less than it drew support from the wary circle around the King." That magnetism, his sense of utter conviction, was put to its supreme test when, early in 1497, Cabot won the support of the hard-headed Merchant Venturers of Bristol to finance his voyage in the *Mathew*. His effort the previous year had ended in failure, like those of his several predecessors. He must have argued brilliantly, marshalling all his evidence from Ptolemy to Polo. He managed to procure a ship, though it represented a big comedown from the five-ship squadron specified in the letters patent of the previous year.

Henry VII was still struggling to pay for the Wars of the Roses, which had confirmed the Lancastrian line. And although he was eager to have England share in the new lands being discovered by the Spaniards and Portuguese, he didn't put up a penny. On the other hand, he cut in the royal exchequer for a fifth of any profits that the Cabots might make on any voyages. What follows is the text of the letters patent, signed by the King at Westminster on March 5, 1496, written in Latin, first printed in 1582, here in the translation made for the archives at Ottawa. It is nothing less than the founding document of Canadian discovery:

GREETING: *Be it known and made manifest that we have given and granted as by these presents we give and grant, for us and our heirs, to our well-beloved John Cabot, citizen of Venice, and to Lewis, Sebastian, and Sancio, sons of the said John, and to the heirs and deputies of them, and of any one of them, full and free authority, faculty and power to sail to all parts, regions, and coasts of the eastern, western, and northern sea, under our banners, flags, and ensigns, with five ships or vessels of whatsoever burden and quality they may be, and with so many and with such mariners and men as they may wish to take with them in the said ships, at their own proper costs and charges, to find, discover, and investi-gate whatsoever islands, countries, regions, or provinces of heathens and infidels, in whatsoever part of the world placed, which before this time were unknown to all Christians. We have also granted to them and any one of them, and have given licence to set up our aforesaid banners and ensigns in any town, city, castle, island, or mainland whatsoever, newly found by them. And that the before-mentioned John and his sons or their heirs and deputies may conquer, occupy, and possess whatsoever such towns, castles, cities, and islands by them thus discovered that they may be able to conquer, occupy, and possess, as our vassals and governors, lieutenants, and deputies therein, acquiring for us the dominion, title, and jurisdiction of the same towns, castles, cities, islands, and mainlands so discovered; in such a way nevertheless that of all the fruits, profits, emoluments, commodities, gains, and revenues accruing from this voyage, the said John and sons and their heirs and deputies shall be bounden and under obligation for every their voyage, as often as they shall arrive at our port of Bristol, at which they are bound and holden only to arrive, all necessary charges and expenses incurred by them having been deducted, to pay to us, either in goods or money, the fifth part of the whole capital gained, we giving and granting to them and to their heirs and deputies, that they shall be free and exempt from all payment of customs on all and singular the goods and merchandise that they may bring back with them from those places thus newly discovered.*

And further we have given and granted to them and to their heirs and deputies, that all mainlands, islands, towns, cities, castles, and other places whatsoever discovered by them, however numerous they may happen to be, may not be frequented or visited by any other subjects of ours whatsoever without the licence of the aforesaid John and his sons and of their deputies, on pain of the loss as well of the ships or vessels daring to sail to these places discovered, as of all goods whatsoever. Willing and strictly commanding all singular our subjects as well by land as by sea, that they shall render good assistance to the aforesaid John and his sons and deputies, and that they shall give them all their favour and help as well in fitting out the ships or vessels as in buying stores and provisions with their money and in providing the other things which they must take with them on the said voyage.

With this grand document to flourish, Cabot, now nearing fifty, pulled his thin cloak about him against the cold, wet winds off the Bristol Channel, and, with purse swinging from his leather belt, stamped the quayside streets of the Kingsrode in the early months of 1497. He would be captain, no doubt of it. But where could you raise a crew for Cathay?

MAPS
OF DISCOVERY

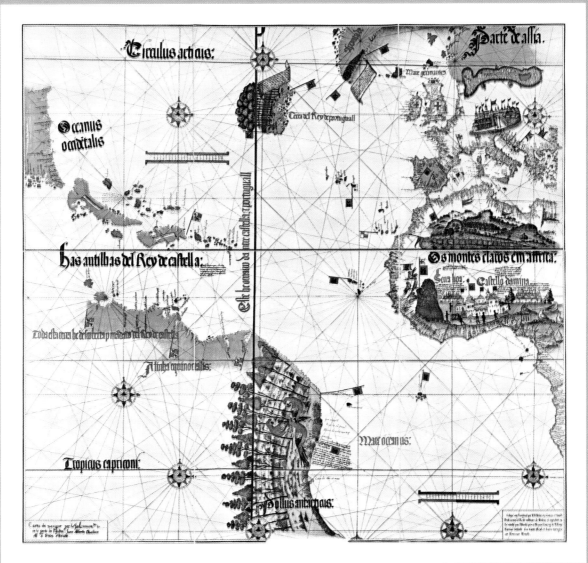

One of the earliest maps to depict the coast of the New World was the Cantino chart of 1502, a section of which is shown above. The flags at the top of the map represent landfalls made by the Corte-Reals in Greenland and Labrador. The fact that Labrador is shown as an island indicates that the explorers were quite unaware that an immense continent stood between them and the riches of Cathay.

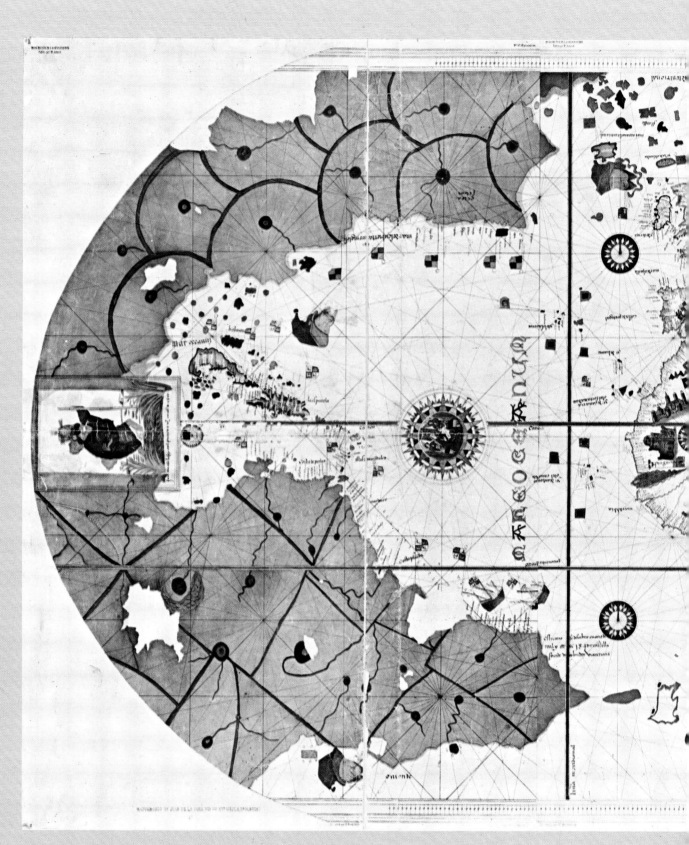

Juan de la Cosa, owner and captain of the *Santa Maria*, was a renowned cartographer and navigator. He sailed with Columbus on the voyage of 1493-94 and accompanied Vespucci during his exploration of the coast of South America. La Cosa's *mappemonde*, produced in 1500, embodies his far-ranging observations. On the left of the map, he has depicted the Antilles, the discovery of which was the initial result of Columbus' ventures. In the flags planted along the coast of the mainland to the northeast he has recorded the 1497 voyage of John Cabot. The inverted label lying along the same stretch of shoreline reads: *Mar descubierta por Inglese*, further testimony to the earliest of English discoveries.

In contrast to the Cantino map, which embodies the Portuguese
view of the world, the La Cosa map represents the Spanish viewpoint.
The bold vertical line which lies to the left of centre on both maps
defines the line of demarcation established by the Treaty of Tordesillas
in 1494. According to this treaty, all new lands discovered to the east
of the line were granted to Portugal, while all lands to the west went
to Spain. In the Cantino map, the islands representing Greenland and
Labrador have been shifted to the right so that they lie within the
Portuguese sphere of control. In the La Cosa map, on the other hand,
these same lands have been located west of the line of demarcation.

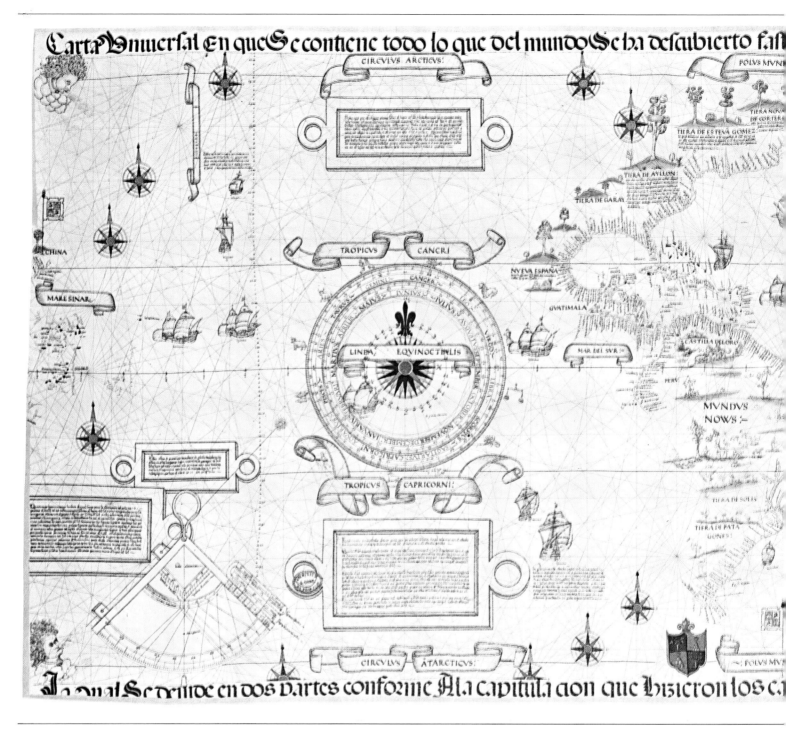

The above map, designed by Diego Ribero in 1529, is the earliest map to show a continuous eastern seaboard. The series of names along the northern part of this coast—*tiera del labrador*, *tiera nova de Cortereal*, and *tiera de Estevã Gomez*—indicate that the mapping of the New World was an enterprise which combined the efforts of many different explorers. Spain's endeavours in this direction were particularly well organized, and Ribero's map is evidence of this fact. For Ribero's detailed *mappemonde* is believed to be a copy of the Spanish *padrón general*, a huge map of the world put together under the direction of the Casa de la Contratacion in Seville. In effect, a combined board of trade and hydrographic office, the Casa was intended to govern Spain's territories overseas. To this end, it instructed pilots and examined all navigational instruments, including sea charts. The *padron general*, or master chart, constituted a kind of inventory of all the discoveries reported by Spanish seafarers. As such, it was subject to constant revision and refinement as reports accumulated over the years.

On the following pages is a map of 1555 which focusses on the east coast of North America.
It is the work of Guillaume Le Testu—a pilot and hydrographer of Le Havre who made voyages
to both Africa and America—and is taken from his *Cosmographie Universelle*, a large manuscript
atlas containing more than fifty maps of this type. In designing his maps, Le Testu has obviously
paid greater attention to artistic embellishment than he has to scientific exactitude. Relying heavily
on inventive flourishes, he has made ample use of swirling pennants, turreted castles, and rampant
beasts of various kinds. By decorating his maps in this way, Le Testu was simply following a prevailing fashion. Many maps of the period were intended for sale to the general public, and the
map-maker gave his works greater sales appeal by relying on pictorial devices and a vivid imagination.
Among the place names inscribed on the Le Testu map, it is interesting to note that the location
of the word "Floride" suggests that in the year 1555 the distance between Montreal and Miami
was a good deal shorter than it is today.

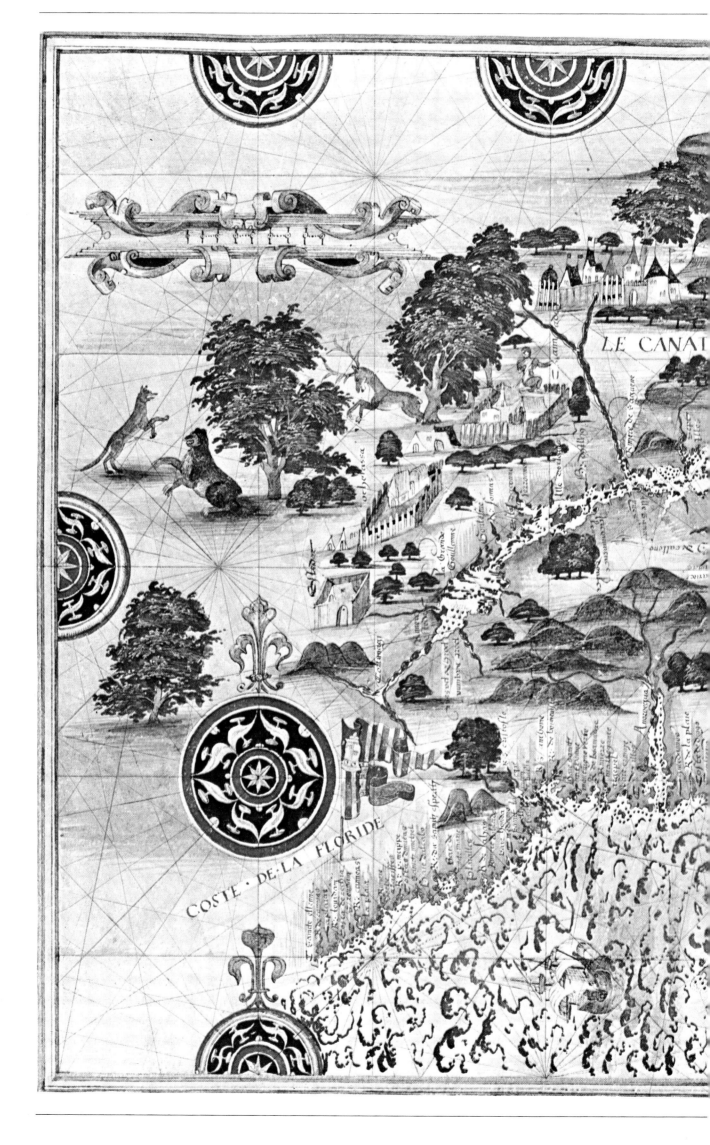

LE CANAI

COSTE · DE · LA · FLORIDE

TERRE DE LABORADOR

PARTIE DE LA MER

A
Colourful Close-up
of Cartier's River of Canada

In a Spanish atlas of 1547 is inscribed the name "Nicolas Vallard." This name is now used to identify the map below, though whether Vallard was the owner of the map or the maker is not known. The area depicted is by now a familiar one—the vast reaches of Jacques Cartier's *Rio do Canada*—and the Vallard map is but one of many to be

drawn from Cartier's map of 1535. If the reader has difficulty in recognizing this region, it is no doubt because the map is, from our point of view, upside down. Early maps were often oriented in this way, having north at the bottom rather than at the top. Another curious thing about the Vallard is that the place names are a mixture of French and Portuguese, thus indicating that the cartographer has enlarged on the information originally supplied by Cartier. The illustration at the bottom of the map is said to represent the building of Charlesbourg-Royal and the figure in the black cloak to be Cartier himself. Whatever the historical significance of this colourful scene, it is but one more reminder that maps of the sixteenth century were intended not so much to inform the navigator as to please the eye of a public which was fascinated by stories of discovery.

CHAPTER FIVE

In the Name
of King Henry

THE *Mathew* slipped down the stream of the Avon, between the sheer walls of the gorge that made Bristol impregnable, out into the channel that flows fast with the high tides running between Wales and Somerset. It was mid-morning on Tuesday, the second day of May, 1497. The fifty-ton bark, no bigger than a modern tugboat, was smaller than many of the merchant ships under sail off the Mouth of the Severn and it carried fewer hands than most—a total of eighteen, several of them traders, not seamen. John Cabot set his course to clear the Kerry coast of Ireland, then northing on the route for Iceland familiar to all experienced Bristol rovers.

Who were the adventurers that Cabot had enlisted for his journey into history? The ship may have been named for the captain's wife, Mathye, but the names of the ship's company are lost to us, likely forever. We can assume that some of them were merchants, willing to take the tall risks of the unknown for the chance to trade with the Great Khan in his treasure cities. It is possible—some think quite likely—that the teen-aged Sebastian Cabot was aboard. Most members of the crew were English, but there was one man from France and at least one Genoese. If the Icelandic story, *The Guest at Ingjaldsholl* is based on truth, then Cabot later took on an Icelandic pilot who had experience of the Greenland coasts. The Bristolians may well have included Robert Thorne and Hugh Elliot, but there is no direct evidence—and again we are confronted with another of the puzzles which cloud the Cabot voyages.

We can be reasonably certain that all of the men on the *Mathew* were volunteers, as there is no mention in the letters patent of impressing convicts for the lower deck, a common method of getting crew for dangerous missions. But the total company was small for such a voyage—other craft of the same general size often carried thirty—and this may have reflected the disillusionment spread by the men returned from the poor and primitive islands, including Cuba and Haiti, which Columbus still desperately insisted were part of golden Cathay.

The heroic age of British seafaring was not yet begun and most mariners were in coastal trade, with little taste for wide-ranging travels. At a time when the expectancy of life was thirty years, when the plague periodically cut swathes through the population, there were many ways for a man to die rather than sail in a scurvy-ridden, pestiferous ship at two pence farthing a day to shores where cannibals were known to reside. Even the ration of one gallon of beer per week was small inducement. No man had better than a fifty-fifty chance of surviving on the discovery voyages—and the expeditions from France and England that risked the cold and hostile shores of Canada suffered more than most.

Such an endeavour as Cabot's, under royal patronage, must have been noted at some length by the official scribes. For example, half a dozen later routine journeys by the *Mathew* in and out of Bristol are catalogued, including the names of the master and even of the merchants whose goods were in the hold. Voyages and deeds by others in Cabot's time, insignificant by comparison, are recorded in considerable detail. But in the strangely few papers in the Cabot archive, the shipping statistics are reduced to a paragraph from a Bristol chronicle written by one Maurice Toby, first published in 1565, lost in a fire in the nineteenth century, but preserved in a transcript copy. Toby was recording events of the Bristol year, the civic year, which ran from September 15, 1496, to September 14, 1497: "This year on St. John the Baptist's day the land of America was found by the Merchants of Bristowe in a shippe of Bristowe, called the *Mathew*; the which said ship departed from the port of Bristowe the second day of May and came home again the 6th of August next following." Even Toby's source must have been a copy: the term "America" to describe the new continent was not in use until after the German Martin Waldseemüller published his notable maps in 1507, based on the

Believing that Amerigo Vespucci was the first to discover the New World, a German map-maker labelled the western lands "America."

1500-02 voyages of Amerigo Vespucci (when the true Brazil was found at last).

Luckily, the Spanish and Portuguese ambassadors and private envoys in England were taking a close interest in all reports of voyages over the western ocean and were including in their dispatches any details concerning discoveries which were said to have been made in the zones already claimed by the Iberian powers. Some Italian envoys, too, noting wryly that the leading captains were mostly Italians in foreign service, were sending back to the ruling dukes well-written accounts gleaned from Westminster and, in some cases, from personal research. Several of these documents survive. From them, and from later English letters and muniments, the Cabot achievement has become firmly if sketchily known.

The consensus of the experts is that after clearing the stormy Irish coast, Cabot turned north and then westerly, keeping the bow of his lumpish little boat headed for the Orient, the Pole Star on his starboard side. "This can only mean," wrote Professor Oleson of the University of Manitoba, the Canadian authority on the early voyages, "that Cabot was threading islands–that is, sailing the old Vinland course of the Norsemen. He sailed from Ireland, to Iceland, then west to the east coast of Greenland, south along it to Cape Farewell...The categorical assertion that 'the sea is full of fish' concerns either the sea off Newfoundland or Labrador." Dr. Oleson continued that "the whole question of the course Cabot took to the New Found Land and his landfall there is bedevilled by the intriguing but exasperating question of the character of Sebastian Cabot and the veracity of his reports on his voyages and exploits. Sebastian Cabot is one of the most controversial and enigmatical characters in history"–and in this book, his story will be told in the next chapter.

It took the *Mathew* a protracted fifty-two days from the Irish coast to the shore of Nova Scotia, and part of this time was probably spent ashore in Iceland and Greenland. Cabot may have pushed as high as 67° north latitude up the west coast of the majestic ice-capped island where the Viking colony begun by Erik the Red had vanished a century earlier, and then struck across Davis Strait to Baffin Island, continuing on a southerly course down the coast until his landing place beckoned. Any man who peered at the Torngat Mountains or the bleak coasts of Baffin, Labrador, and Newfoundland in search of signs of the palaced cities of Cathay must have pushed quickly on.

Henry Biggar, in his book of documents on earliest European history of Canada, takes up narrative:

About five o'clock on Saturday morning, 24 June, they sighted what from the La Cosa* and Sebastian Cabot maps would appear to have been the western extremity of Cape Breton Island. With the royal banner unfurled, John Cabot set foot on land and in solemn form took possession of the country in the name of King Henry VII. *[He may also have planted the banner of St. Mark of Venice.] Finding the soil fertile and the climate temperate, Cabot was convinced that he had reached the northeastern extremity of Asia, whence came the silks and spices which had been displayed for barter at Mecca.*

The level-headed Cabot knew that his rocky beach was not the Cathay of Marco Polo, but he figured that he had at least reached Tartary and that Asia must stretch far to the north from the cities of pearls and gold. In describing Quinsay (modern Hangchow), Polo had spoken of "sailors of all nations" sauntering through the streets, of thousands of masts stretched skyward on the harbour, and of a population of about five million. Of another place he wrote: "You must know that the lord of this island has a very large palace, all covered with fine gold. Just as we roof our houses and churches with lead, so this palace is all roofed over with fine gold. All the other parts of the palace, namely the halls and the windows, are similarly adorned with gold." It didn't sound much like Cape Breton, then or now.

Cabot did find treasure—but not on land. There, all he could gather were some snares set for animals, a few bone needles, and further evidence of human occupation in axe-marks on trees near the waterline. He saw no inhabitants, but it is a fair assumption that he and his ship were carefully watched by cautious Indians. He seems to have had little desire to penetrate the country and set off immediately to trace the coastline. One can picture him scanning ceaselessly the myriad bays and headlands of that deceptive, serrated shore for that first glimpse of the jostling masts of Hangchow, hoping to catch a glimpse of the sun reflected from the golden roofs of Peking. One chronicle states that he coasted the mainland for three hundred leagues—about eight hundred miles—before turning to take his news to England. Considering that the *Mathew* was back in Bristol on August 6, this seems a likely exaggeration, unless it referred to his total journey following departure from Greenland's Cape Farewell. Assuming the Strait of Belle Isle to be just another deep bay, Cabot would see Newfoundland as part of the mainland of the "newe founde launde."

---

* Juan de la Cosa, captain of the *Santa Maria* in the first expedition of Columbus, drew a map in 1500 which labelled the area off the North American coast right down to the Carolinas as "Sea discovered by the English."

Vespucci's skills as a publicist made his name a household word.

The treasure the Venetian *did* find was the cod. The market in that period was insatiable. Most of Europe observed the strictures of the Roman Church, which then demanded close observance of meatless days—not only on the traditional Fridays, but on many saint's days and other religious celebrations. As towns swelled into sprawling cities, labourers left the estates, farms, and small holdings to take steady wages in the craft shops which prospered under the awakening technology. There were already millions of people to feed who never put spade to the earth. Fish could be easily dried or salted, and kept for years if necessary—and it was cheap. The Devon and Cornish fishermen fished for cod, the bread of the sea, in the disputed waters around Iceland. Cabot brought back incredible tales of fish teeming around the southern coast of Newfoundland which could be caught in baskets lowered from the gunwale.

Cabot's reports, touched with Latin imagination, might not have been believed by the dour West-countrymen except for the fact that "his companions who are practically all English and from Bristol testified that he spoke the truth." An Englishmen's word was, apparently, already his bond. Earlier voyages had noted the good fishing, but the immense riches of the Grand Banks were now fully revealed, and the rush was on. By 1522, a man-of-war was detailed to protect the British fishing fleet. The cod thus shares with the beaver the right to be the discovery symbol of Canada. The great French discoverers followed in the wake of the cod fishermen of Brittany, and the proclamation of British sovereignty over Newfoundland by Sir Humphrey Gilbert—it was Britain's first overseas colony—developed from the yearly visits of the fishing fleets.

There can be no doubt that Cabot made an immediate and enthusiastic report to Henry VII on August 10 and that the King was delighted. It would make a pleasant change from the news of the rebellions flaring in Scotland and Cornwall. Cabot must have explained that the discovery of the mainland confirmed his theories and that he must now prepare a larger expedition to sail directly to the *Prima Terra Vista*, and then south and west to Cathay and Cipango. Any written report that Cabot may have made to the King is lost, along with his log and journals. But the sensation created by Cabot's triumphant return in the summer of 1497 can be savoured in the dispatches and letters sent home by the diplomats who kept a well-tuned ear at the court keyholes. The most remarkable of these men was Raimondo de Raimondi de Soncino, one of the London Lombards and a special envoy of the paramount Duke of Milan. The highly literate Soncino arrived at Dover on August 23; and on December 18, he wrote to the duke:

Perhaps amid the numerous occupations of your Excellency, it may not weary you to hear how his Majesty here has gained a part of Asia, without a stroke of the sword. There is in this Kingdom a man of the people, Messer Zoane Caboto by name, of kindly wit and a most expert mariner. Having observed that the sovereigns first of Portugal and then of Spain had occupied unknown islands, he decided to make a similar acquisition for his Majesty. After obtaining patents that the effective ownership of what he might find should be his, though reserving the rights of the Crown, he committed himself to fortune in a little ship, with eighteen persons. He started from Bristol, a port on the west of this kingdom ... After having wandered for some time he at length arrived at the mainland, where he hoisted the royal standard, and took possession for the King here; and after taking certain tokens he returned.

This Messer Zoane ... has the description of the world in a map, and also in a solid sphere, which he has made, and shows where he has been. In going towards the East, he passed far beyond the country of the Tanais.* They say that the land is excellent and temperate, and they believe that Brazil wood and silk are native there. They assert that the sea there is swarming with fish, which can be taken not only with the net, but in baskets let down with a stone, so that it sinks in the water. I have heard this Messer Zoane state so much.

These English, his companions, say that they could bring so many fish that this Kingdom would have no further need of Iceland, from which place there comes a very great quantity of the fish called stockfish. But Messer Zoane has his mind set upon even greater things, because he proposes to keep along the coast from the place at which he touched more and more towards the east, until he reaches an island which he calls Cipango, situated in the equinoctial region, where he believes that all the spices of the world have their origin, as well as the jewels.

He says that on previous occasions he has been to Mecca, whither spices are borne by caravans from distant countries. When he asked those who brought them what was the place of origin of the spices, they answered that they did not know, but that other caravans came with this merchandise to their homes from distant countries, and these again said that the goods had been brought to them from other remote regions. He therefore reasons that these things come from places far away from them, and so on from one to another. Always assuming that the earth is round, it follows as a matter of course that the last of all must take them in the north towards the west.

He tells all this in such a way, and makes everything so plain, that I also feel compelled to believe him. What is much more, his Majesty, who is wise and not prodigal, also gives him some credence, because he is giving him a fairly good provision, since his return, so Messer Zoane himself tells me. Before very long they say that his Majesty will equip some ships, and in addition he will give them all the malefactors, and they will go to that country and form a colony. By means of this, they hope to make London a more important mart for spices than Alexandria. The leading men in this enterprise are from Bristol, and great seamen, and now they know where to go, say that the voyage will not take more than a fortnight, if they have good fortune after leaving Ireland.

I have also spoken with a Burgundian, one of Messer Zoane's companions, who corroborates everything. He wants to go back, because the Admiral, which is the name they give to Messer Zoane, has given him an island. He has given another to his barber, a Genoese by birth, and both consider themselves counts, while my lord the Admiral esteems himself at least a prince. I also believe that some poor Italian friars will go on this voyage, who have the promise of bishoprics. As I have made friends with the Admiral, I might have an archbishopric if I chose to go there, but I have reflected that the benefices which your Excellency reserves for me are safer, and I therefore beg that possession may be given me of those which fall vacant in my absence, and the necessary steps taken so that they may not be taken away from me by others, who have the advantage of being on the spot.

Meanwhile, I stay on in this country, eating ten or twelve courses at each meal, and spending three hours at table twice every day, for the love of your Excellency, to whom I humbly commend myself.

---

* "East" is used in the sense of the Far East. The Tanais was the ancient name for the River Don, which was once believed to mark the boundaries of Europe and Asia.

Obviously, the whimsical and energetic Soncino had gone in search of this "man of the people" and had heard of the wonders from Cabot's own lips. He pokes a little fun at "my lord the Admiral," but Cabot's sincerity rings through and the worldly Soncino feels "compelled to believe him." It is the most satisfying of all the Cabot documents. It was not, though, the first account of the discovery to reach Italy.

Within two weeks after Cabot had reported to the King in London, the news of his safe return from the far ocean was on its way to Milan – where the document in question can still be seen. In this message, Cabot was not named, being referred to as "a Venetian, who is a very good mariner and has good skill in discovering new islands." It added that "two very large and fertile new islands" had been found and that the "Seven Cities," those fabulous tempters, had been discovered about twelve hundred miles from England. The writer was perhaps passing on some London street or tavern gossip in a letter devoted mostly to other topics.

Yet another report derives from the diplomat Lorenzo Pasqualigo. Writing to his brothers Francesco and Alvise in the Venetian Foreign Ministry in a letter dated August 23, 1497, Pasqualigo was not yet prepared to commit himself too firmly on the stories that were buzzing about London. It is the earliest account in any depth of Cabot's first voyage that is known to exist, and much of the Cabotian lore and controversy stems from its references. For example, Pasqualigo implies that Cabot – with royal encouragement – now planned a sizeable settlement in the New Found Land, using convicts as his settlers. Soncino also later mentioned this as hearsay. At least, the quoted distance of something over two thousand miles was nearer the true mark:

That Venetian of ours who went with a small ship from Bristol to find new islands has come back and says he has discovered mainland 700 leagues away, which is the country of the Grand Khan, and that he coasted it for 300 leagues and landed and did not see any person; but he has brought to the King certain snares which were spread to take game and a needle for making nets, and he found certain notched trees so that by this he judges that there are inhabitants. Being in doubt, he returned to his ship ... and on the way back he saw two islands, but was unwilling to land, in order not to lose time, as he was in want of provisions.

The King here is much pleased at this ... and has promised him for the spring ten armed ships and has given him all the prisoners to be sent away, that they may go with him, as he has requested; and has given him money that he may enjoy himself until then, and he is with his Venetian wife and his sons at Bristol.

His name is Zuam Talbot [yet another version of "Cabotto"] and he is called the Great Admiral and vast honour is paid to him and he goes dressed in silk, and these English run after him like mad, and indeed he can enlist

as many of them as he pleases, and a number of our rogues as well.

The discoverer of these things planted on the land which he has found a large cross with a banner of England and one of St. Mark, as he is a Venetian, so that our flag has been hoisted very far afield.

In his book, *The Dawn of Canadian History*, Professor Stephen Leacock – historian, mathematician, and sometime humourist – refers to Cabot as "the hero of the hour," and adds that "it is one of the ironies of history that on the first pages of its annals the beautiful new world is offered to the criminals of Europe." Historian Biggar was quoting Pasqualigo when he wrote, in *The Precursors of Jacques Cartier*, of Cabot dressed in "new silk doublet and hose ... lionized during the winter by the rich merchants of London."

It was noted everywhere that the *Mathew* had completed the return trip across the Atlantic in fifteen days, driven by the prevailing westerlies – much faster than the two homeward voyages made by Columbus up to that time. Cabot was obviously an expert sailor, wise to wind and current, well versed in the use of the simple navigational aids of his day. It was also noteworthy that the *Mathew* had sailed alone. It was normal for the ocean venturers of the fifteenth century – such as Da Gama heading for India and Columbus seeking the Indies – to put together expeditions of three and four ships. One would be a deep-draught 100-ton storeship used to revictual the others and to carry the heaviest goods for trading or for the building of shore establishments. Another would be the lightest and fastest available, consistent with open-sea safety. Its job would be to run for assistance if need be and to maintain rapid contact with home ports. The mini-

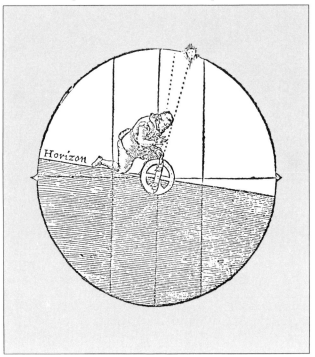

An astrolabe was used to measure the angle between sun and horizon.

The above painting is from a manuscript dealing with navigational instruments. In the foreground, a man uses an elaborate precursor of the sextant; while in the background, two ships make their way at sea. The ship on the left carries square sails,

fleet would carry pinnaces, longboats that could be lowered to explore shallow bays or river mouths.

The addition of a lateen sail to the square-rigged caravel made it possible to keep a tighter course against unfavourable winds – though in a storm, a captain still had little choice but to furl his sails and ride at the mercy of the gale. Even under normal sailing conditions, holding a true course as the caravels bucketed about in Atlantic troughs was almost impossible. The navigator held his astrolabe as steady as he could while he aligned its sights on the sun, then tried to read the circular scale of degrees. If he could fix the altitude of the sun above the horizon he could roughly determine his latitude – his position on the globe north or south of the equator – providing he was capable of the simple mathematics required.

which provide it with maximum speed when sailing before the wind. The ship on the right carries both square sails and lateen sails, a combination which gives it superior manoeuvrability and makes it possible for the navigator to tack into a headwind.

The earliest astrolabes were in use in Mediterranean waters before the birth of Christ and the basic technique is still embodied in the modern sextant (so-called because it uses a sixth of a circle), which was not developed until the early eighteenth century. Gross error with the astrolabe or the English quadrant was common at sea, and captains like John Lloyd and John Cabot would take many readings in the course of a day, then attempt to average them out. The magnetic compass, already a century old, was considered more reliable, although the variations from true north were only dimly understood, and guessed at. Close to familiar coasts, around western Europe and the Mediterranean, pilots' charts known as *portolans* had become increasingly common—but the navigator was strictly on his own in the open ocean.

In a bas-relief by Guido Casini, Henry VII grants letters patent to John Cabot empowering him to take possession of new lands. While John Cabot prepares to board the Mathew, *the Bishop of Bristol blesses the Cabot expedition before it sets sail.*

The main problem was to try to keep an accurate reckoning of the distance travelled east or west across the globe. Longitude was still a mystery to most, with the prime difficulty being the correct measurement of elapsed time. Since the earth spins through 360 degrees of longitude in every 24 hours, 15 degrees represents one elapsed hour. But before the development of the first chronometers, mariners had only the hourglass, with its trickling sand. They usually relied on "dead reckoning," each four-hour "watch" estimating the ship's speed at each half-hour, trying to allow for adverse winds, known current streams, and other factors. Sometimes, a chip of wood would be thrown off the bow and the time that it took to reach the stern would be chanted off. This led, after the days of Cabot and Cartier, to the development of the log-line, the attached cord being knotted at regular intervals. (Even today, a ship's speed is measured in "knots.")

The trouble that John Cabot had with his compass as he crossed on the northerly route to the Canadian mainland in 1497 was particularly noted in the long, detailed letter, written in Spanish and signed by the English trader, John Day. This letter was found–almost by chance–in the main Spanish archives in the castle at Simancas, in Valladolid, by the American researcher, Dr. A. L. Vigneras, in 1956. Dr. Williamson relates how Vigneras was tipped off by another scholar working in the archives who mentioned that he had seen, in passing, some document relating to English discovery of North America. Vigneras searched for some weeks before he found the letter within a folder which carried a title referring to an English voyage to Brasil.

The document is neither dated nor addressed. However, the penetrating deductions of the Cabotians have set the year at 1497-98 and the addressee as the Magnificent Lord Grand Admiral Christopher Columbus himself. As Day, in most humble fashion, told all that he had heard of the Cabot discovery, he included the comments–given in the preceding chapter–which are quoted by some as evidence of a mainland discovery sometime before John Cabot's first voyage. Leaving that issue aside, the Day letter added welcome confirmation of several key details of the Cabot story. An edited version follows:

. . . I am sending the other book of Marco Polo and a copy of the land which has been found. I do not send the map because I am not satisfied with it, for my many occupations forced me to make it in a hurry at the time of my departure [from England?]; but from the said copy your Lordship will learn what you wish to know, for in it are named the capes of the mainland and the islands, and thus you will see where land was first sighted, since most of the land was discovered after turning back. [This "copy of the land" was presumably a copy of John Cabot's own map, now lost.] Thus your Lordship will know that the cape nearest to Ireland is 1,800 miles west of Dursey Head, which is in

Ireland, and the southernmost part of the Island of the Seven Cities is west of Bordeaux River, and your Lordship will know that he [John Cabot] landed at the only one spot of the mainland, near the place where land was first sighted, and disembarked there with a crucifix and raised banners with the arms of the Holy Father and those of the King of England, my master; and they found tall trees of the kind masts are made, and other smaller trees, and the country is very rich in grass.

In that particular spot, as I told your Lordship, they found a trail that went inland, they saw a site where a fire had been made, they saw manure of animals which they thought to be farm animals, and they saw a stick half a yard long pierced at both ends, carved and painted with brazil, and by such signs they believe the land to be inhabited. Since he had only a few people, he did not dare advance inland beyond the range of a crossbow, and after taking in fresh water he returned to his ship.

All along the coast they found many fish like those which in Iceland are dried in the open and sold in England and other countries, and these fish are called in English "stockfish"; and thus following the shore they saw two forms running on land one after the other, but they could not tell if they were human beings or animals; and it seemed to them that there were fields where they thought might also be villages, and they saw a forest whose foliage looked beautiful.

They left England toward the end of May [it was actually May 2] and must have been on the way thirty-five days before sighting land; the wind was east-northeast and the sea calm going and coming back, except for one day when he ran into a storm two or three days before finding land; and going so far out, his compass needle failed to point north and marked two rhumbs below. They spent about one month discovering the coast and from the above mentioned cape of the mainland which is nearest to Ireland, they returned to the coast of Europe in fifteen days. They had the wind behind them, and he reached Brittany because the sailors confused him, saying that he was heading too far north. From there he came to Bristol, and he went to see the King to report to him all the above mentioned.

King Henry gave audience to Cabot on Thursday, August 10, 1497, and his Household Book–the Daybook of King's Payments–contains the neat record of the immediate reward he gave the Venetian: *Item, to hym that founde the new Isle, ten pounds.* H. P. Biggar estimated in his 1911 study that the gift was the equivalent of $600; it could represent as much as $1,500 today.

Just before Christmas, the King added an annual pension of twenty pounds for "our welbiloved John Calbot" to be paid out of the customs revenue of Bristol. They might be having trouble getting his name right, but they knew by now that their Italian had in truth staked out a portentous claim for England. With feverish impatience, they all awaited the next season's sailing weather when, surely, the way would be found to the glittering riches of Cipango.

An imaginary portrayal of Cabot approaching Labrador.

CHAPTER SIX

Journeys into Mystery

THE second and last voyage of John Cabot is, if anything, more mysterious than the first. It began in high excitement and anticipation of fame and wealth. It ended in death and disappointment, and in a dispute not settled even in our own times.

Now that the presence of the huge mainland was proved in the west (they knew nothing of the Pacific Ocean and never doubted they had found Asia), surely a thorough search of the coast towards the warmer latitudes would lead to the bustling ports and rich cities of the Great Khan. Raimondo de Soncino had reported that this was Cabot's plan for 1498: "He expects to go from that place already occupied, constantly hugging the shore, further towards the east until he is opposite an island called by him Cipango, where he thinks grow all the spices of the world and also the precious stones."

King Henry was now a firm believer. He had given Cabot an extra cash reward just after Christmas to tide him through the winter and, on February 3, 1498, had issued second letters patent—this time the Venetian was called John Kabotto—giving Cabot the right to take "at his pleasure" six English ships of up to 200 tons from any English port, paying rent for them at the rate the King himself would pay if he commandeered them for his own service. (That fee was three pennies per ton per week.)

The Daybook of King's Payments for the relevant period—Henry coined the word "sovereign" and bit every one before spending it—indicates that the King either paid for one ship himself or advanced some of the required funds. Other entries suggest that he also loaned money to some merchants who either sailed with Cabot or supplied goods for trading. A certain John Cair was given forty shillings for "going to the New Ile in rewarde," and a shipmaster named Launcelot Thirkill and a merchant, Thomas Bradley, may also have been in the company. Some Italian priests were reported to be planning to join the expedition in the hope of being appointed as bishops in the new

lands. One Giovanni de Carbonariis may also have gone—to leave his distinctive name on Carbonear, in Newfoundland's Conception Bay.

The five ships that finally made up the second expedition sailed in late April or early May. They put out into the Bristol Channel under a fine dress of flags—and then dropped below the horizon into deepest mystery. John Cabot was never seen again and his death is presumed that year. Where did the fleet go? What ships and which men, if any, returned to Bristol? Some authorities believe that all were lost.

For this drama of the early Renaissance, the stage is but dimly lit, the cast of players torn and lost, the plot devious and often incredible, and the critics' notices slight and sour. The script introduces the enigma of Sebastian Cabot, at one time the most famous individual in the age of discovery and now accused of perpetrating one of the greatest frauds in maritime history. It leaves a modern audience the task—intriguing but often baffling—of trying to put together an historical jigsaw puzzle, the pieces comprising a thin bundle of letters, diplomatic and other official papers, brief references, allusions and reports in sixteenth-century books, many of them at variance and some of them palpably false. The most patent difficulty is that created by the blatant—and for many years entirely successful—attempt by the son, Sebastian, to take credit for the achievements of his father. For in several areas, all the pertinent information that can be sifted is traceable to the son—who, indeed, may not have sailed on either voyage. Nevertheless, the infinitely patient Cabotians have knitted together an outline of the 1498 exploit, an amalgam of probabilities, that must suffice for the present.

The five ships began, routinely enough, to pass Ireland to their north and quickly ran into a storm in those restless waters. One vessel—it might have been Cabot's own ship—was damaged and turned for repairs into an Irish port. Historian Biggar, in his "working hypothesis," allows the rest of the fleet to proceed, soon being carried northwards. Greenland was sighted in early June and Cabot first followed this forbidding coast to the north (strangely contrary to his stated plan) until his crew would go no further among the numerous icebergs. Then he rounded Cape Farewell, and began to edge his way northwards again, up the western coast of Greenland – the old domain of Erik the Red and his son, Lief. Again, in the waters of Davis Strait, Cabot was turned back by icebergs. (Navigational errors in bad weather and a compass erratic in the relative proximity of true magnetic north may have played their parts in this baffling wandering.)

He now crossed westerly to sight the coast of Baffin Island and proceeded southwards along Labrador, past the lonely sands of Cape Porcupine, around the bulge of Newfoundland – again accepting the narrow Strait of Belle Isle as but another of the hundreds of bays – and thus through the marvellous fishing waters into the familiar territory of his voyage of the previous year.

Where were the glittering cities of the Grand Khan? Cabot now, at last, put his announced plan into effect and probed down the jagged seaboard of Nova Scotia, checking in vain the inlets known today as Chedabucto, St. Margaret's Bay, Mahone Bay, Pubnico, St. Mary's, and other bays to the south. He then crossed the Bay of Fundy, stepping maybe from Digby Neck to Grand Manan to Campobello, and running down the rockbound coast of Maine from Passamaquoddy Bay to Penobscot, and pushing as far south as the thirty-eighth parallel, near Chesapeake Bay. There – according to this admittedly conjectural reconstruction – with the summer gone, the remaining ships turned for England.

The cape at which they gave up the search for Cipango is, like almost every point related here, a subject of intense argument. For instance, what independent evidence is there that anyone of the 1498 company even saw the central coast of North America? First, there is the map, already mentioned, made in 1500 by the great Basque pilot, La Cosa, which marks the area off modern Virginia and the Carolinas as "the Sea discovered by the English" – La Cosa drew five small English flags on the adjacent waters. With the sharp diplomatic watch on western voyaging that was being maintained in London by Portugal and Spain, La Cosa's information seems likely to have derived from accounts circulated after the Cabot voyages. Second, there is another Spanish document which indicates that Cabot, the only "English" discoverer on the scene at the time, may have coasted the continent close to Florida and the Caribbean. In 1501, Alonso de Ojeda was granted letters patent by Isabella and Ferdinand of Spain for a voyage beginning on the coast of Colombia and swinging northwestward. He was ordered to go "towards the region where it has been learned that the English were making discoveries." Both of these references are taken by many to confirm that one or more of Cabot's ships *did* get back to

Bristol in the autumn of 1498. If Launcelot Thirkill sailed, then *he* returned at any rate – since he appears alive in records for 1501.

In any event, the survivors must have been a dejected lot. They had fully expected to bring home cargoes of luxurious silk stuffs, chinaware, sacks of spices, sandalwood, gold ornaments, pearls. Instead, they returned with their English trading goods – cloth, lace, ironwork, possibly supplies of the matchlock arquebus with which Henry VII had just armed half of his royal guard – and with only a handful of rough furs. It seems certain that Cabot put ashore at least once on this voyage: later explorers found a broken Italian sword and two silver Venetian ear-rings in the possession of Naskapi tribesmen. It was a sorry result, a sharp and salutary loss for the Bristol and London merchants – and no less for the King himself.

Scholars who have mulled over the Cabot voyages for most of a lifetime, aided by expert knowledge of the period, debate whether or not the lack of documentation of the second voyage can be ascribed simply to the apparent failure of the mission. In simplest terms, Cabot had doubtless found a huge and important land – a curious, empty, forbidding, primitive place it must have seemed to Europeans – but it was certainly not the Cathay of legendary wealth. Comparatively large sums of money had been lost in following the ideas of the Venetian, and the less said about it the better. Within this reasoning, John Cabot could have returned to Bristol and been snubbed and ignored, dying soon afterwards in obscurity – much like his contemporary, Columbus. Further support for this view is drawn from the fact that Cabot's pension granted by the King in December 1497, was paid in 1498 and 1499 (others believe the pension was paid to his widow, Mathye).

The opposite view – that John Cabot was never seen again after his departure from Bristol in the spring of 1498 – is supported by a manuscript reference by the Italian priest-historian, Polydore Vergil, in his *History of England*, written in 1512-13: "John Cabot . . . sailed first to Ireland. Then he set sail towards the west . . . He is believed to have found the new lands nowhere but on the very bottom of the ocean, to which he is thought to have descended together with his boat." Sebastian Cabot added to the confusion by stating, in one of his numerous accounts of his own supposed exploits, that his father had died in 1493, "at the time when news came that Signor Don Christophoro Colombo the Genoese had discovered the coast of the Indies."

To anyone who endeavours to follow the tangled threads of the Cabot research, the obscure figure of João Fernandez, the *llabrador* of the Azores, keeps appearing. Since his nickname denotes forever a large portion of Canada, he has a place in this narrative. It's a matter of official British record that Fernandez – along with five associates – was granted letters patent

EFFIGIES SEBASTIANI CABOTI ANGLI FILII IOHANIS CABOTI VENETI MILITIS AURATI PRIMI IN ET ORIS TERRÆ NOVÆ SVB HERICO VII AV

The enigmatic Sebastian Cabot made many journeys for several European powers, but his voyage to Canada is shrouded in mystery.

by King Henry in 1501 for a discovery voyage, and that earlier he had been given royal permission in Portugal by King Dom Manuel for a similar expedition. He is thought by some to have been on a Danish venture to Greenland between 1492 and 1494, with Pedro de Barcellos. Building on this, certain writers believe that Fernandez went with John Cabot on his 1498 voyage and that Cabot bestowed his pilot's nickname on Greenland – it was known as "the land of the Labrador" for sixty years before the term was appropriate for the Canadian territory of today.

Historian Biggar held that Cabot went to Lisbon in the winter of 1497-98 (after his first successful voyage in the *Mathew*) to meet Fernandez and was there persuaded to make that curious swing towards the Arctic during the expedition of 1498. Dr. Williamson of the Hakluyt Society, whose views are today's canon, says that there is no evidence at all of any meeting between Cabot and Fernandez and that, on the contrary, such an association would have been most unlikely. For one thing, Cabot would certainly have risked severe English displeasure had he made a rush trip to competing Portugal while supposedly busy mounting his own expedition under English auspices. For another, Cabot and the master mariners of Bristol late in the fifteenth century already had a reasonable knowledge of Greenland. Williamson further argues that the coasting-of-Greenland sequence in the account of John Cabot's voyage of 1498 arises from confusions between that journey and a later expedition by Sebastian Cabot in far northern waters – the two accounts melding in the process of being told and retold many times over. Williamson is not convinced, either, that João Fernandez actually made *any* trips to Greenland and suggests that the name "Labrador" was applied solely because the man from the Azores had energetically pushed a Greenland project after his arrival in Britain in 1500. Here, then, is yet another wrangle in the Cabotian riddle.

No element of the mystery, however, is more opaque than the character and actions of Sebastian Cabot. From the sixteenth to the nineteenth centuries, Sebastian was acclaimed – in British circles anyway – as the discoverer of North America, and his father's name, practically unknown, was seldom if ever mentioned. No individual, even the Elizabethan heroes Drake and Raleigh, was more revered than Sebastian Cabot, and his accepted adventures fired the imagination of generations of British youth. "Honour of England, brave Sebastian," runs a famous poem of 1596. When the tide turned, however, it ran out fast. Harold Lamb, in *New Found World*, states that Sebastian's fame was achieved by "consummate lies that have baffled historical geographers ever since ... Among the things he falsified was the voyage of 1498, which he claimed had been made by himself alone some ten years later." Henry Harisse wrote more soberly of Sebastian's "disregard of truth."

During his later life – he reached the ripe age of seventy-three – Sebastian gave many scribes varying accounts of his discoveries. Among them was the chronicler known as Peter Martyr, an Italian writing from Spain about 1515. Here follows an edited account of the Martyr version:

All men with one accord assert that the seas flow to the westward as rivers flow down from mountains ... Those who have tried the frozen coasts and afterwards have gone to the west say that those waters flow likewise to the west, not swiftly, however, but gently with a continual passage. A certain Sebastian Cabot has examined those [frozen coasts], a Venetian by birth but carried by his parents whilst yet a child into the island of Britain, they going thither as the habit is of Venetians, who in the pursuit of trade are the guests of all lands.

He equipped two ships at his own cost in Britain, and with three hundred men steered first for the north, until even in the month of July he found great icebergs floating in the sea and almost continuous daylight, yet with the land free by the melting of the ice. Wherefore he was obliged, as he says, to turn and make for the west. And he extended his course furthermore to the southward owing to the curve of the coastline, so that his latitude was almost that of the Straits of Gibraltar and he penetrated so far to the west that he had the island of Cuba on his left hand almost in the same longitude with himself. He, as he traversed those coasts, which he called the Bacallãos, says that he found the same flow of the waters to the west, although mild in force, as the Spaniards find in their passage to their southern possessions. Therefore it is not only probable but necessary to conclude that between these two lands hitherto unknown lie great straits which provide a passage for the waters flowing from east to west, which I judge to be drawn round by the attraction of the heavens in their rotation round the earth, but not to be blown out and sucked in again by the breathing of Demogorgon,* as some have supposed because they have been led to connect it with the flow and the ebb [of the tides].

Cabot himself called those lands the Bacallãos because in the adjacent sea he found so great a quantity of a certain kind of great fish like tunnies, called "bacallãos" by the inhabitants, that at times they even stayed the passage of his ships. He found also the men of those lands clothed in skins and not anywhere devoid of intelligence. He says there are great numbers of bears there, which eat fish. For the bears plunge into the midst of a shoal of those fish, and falling upon them with their claws grasping the scales, draw them to shore and eat them; on which account, he says, the bears are less dangerous to men. Many say that they have seen copper ore in places in the hands of the inhabitants.

I know Cabot as a familiar friend and sometimes as a guest in my house; for, having been summoned from Britain by our Catholic King after the death of the older Henry, King of England, he is one of our councillors, and is daily expecting shipping to be provided for him wherewith he may

---

* A fearsome mythological diety, said to dwell "in the deep abyss."

reveal this secret of Nature hitherto hidden. I believe he will depart on that quest in the month of March in the coming year 1516.

Spaniards are not lacking who deny that Cabot was the first finder of the Bacallãos and do not allow that he went so far westwards. Now I have said enough of the straits and of Cabot.

Martyr, in fact, had said enough to fuel argument among geographers and historians for centuries. With his "lower-class" father presumed lost at sea, and the trading missions a financial loss, could the 25-year-old Sebastian possibly have "equipped two ships at his own cost"? In that day, such ventures were for royal princes, ruling dukes, or consortiums of established merchants. And *three hundred* men! The three ships of Columbus' first expedition had, between them, a complement of only eighty-eight. It is interesting to note that Martyr closed his account by mentioning that some men were already doubting Sebastian's tales.

In another vague and rambling report published in Venice in 1550, Sebastian was quoted as saying that he had made his voyage to the northwest seeking "a shorter road to find the Indies" in 1496 – that is, a year *before* his father's first voyage – when he, Sebastian, by the best accounts, would have been either thirteen or fourteen years of age. In this version, he said that he had travelled at the expense of Henry VII, who "equipped for me two caravels with all things needful." Yet another Italian document relates that when Sebastian returned from his northern voyage, he found that King Henry had died during his absence. This would date the journey in 1508 or 1509.

Henry had granted Sebastian an annual pension of ten sovereigns a year in 1505 "in consideration of diligent service," but the specific service for which Sebastian was being rewarded is unknown. James Williamson surmises that it might have been for assistance in map-making and in the study of navigation. He is further persuaded that Sebastian *did* make his later northwestern voyage, in the course of which he was the first man to sail through Hudson Strait into Hudson Bay. In presenting his brief for the younger Cabot, Dr. Williamson adds: "The sceptic is invited to be vigilant."

Did the pendulum of criticism of Sebastian really swing too far? Henry VIII, coming to the British throne in 1509, cared "little for such an enterprise" – certainly, three years later Sebastian had moved to Spain, where, in 1515, he was appointed "Pilot to His Majesty." When Charles V ascended the Spanish throne, he raised Cabot to the rank of pilot-major, in succession to Amerigo Vespucci. R. A. Skelton, of the British Museum, writing in the *Dictionary of Canadian Biography*, supports the claims for Sebastian's northwestern voyage, "far north of the coasts traversed by his father in 1497." He adds that "it is an inescapable inference . . .

that Sebastian in 1508 sought a sea passage by the north of the continent and that he believed himself to have discovered such a passage." That is, he believed that in entering the inland sea of Hudson Bay he was sailing on what Ferdinand Magellan would soon name the Pacific. A globe made by the Flemish geographer Gemma Frisius in 1537 depicts just such an open-water lead across the top of Canada.

It must be added, however, that there is no shred of official document to support such a voyage by Cabot *fils*. The main backing comes from Peter Martyr who spoke with Sebastian personally, but not until about six or seven years after the event – by which time Gaspar Corte-Real and others had come back from the icy northwestern waters with reports of great rivers and inlets. Corte-Real's graphic Rio Nevado (River of Snow) could be Hudson Strait.

Professor Oleson was not convinced that Sebastian had made a northern voyage of any consequence. He pointed to the obvious confusion in Martyr's account between proximity to Cuba and the Bacallãos – here, Sebastian seemed to be claiming discovery of the Newfoundland reported by his father a dozen years earlier. There are no letters patent to indicate that Sebastian had permission to sail in 1508 into waters under dispute between the maritime powers, and it seems unlikely that he would still be working under the letters granted to John Cabot and his sons in 1496. (John himself had sought fresh permission by King Henry for his second voyage.)

As the experts spar, much is made of the fact that Sebastian apparently said nothing about his promising voyage into Hudson Bay until years after the event. The pro-Sebastians contend that after he left England because of the indifference of Henry VIII, Sebastian did not dare to report his attempt to go "by the north to Cathay" in case this should prejudice his position with his Spanish employers who were trying to bring the English to respect the Treaty of Tordesillas. There is also a typically tangled string of events which suggests that Sebastian, like some double agent in the novels of John le Carré, was trying to sell his secrets to Italy. The "antis" counter this by arguing that the reason Sebastian didn't report his success on returning to England from a voyage in 1508 was that it simply didn't happen at all. The wily Cabot dreamed it all up – possibly cribbing notes from his father's journals – when he later saw the chance to profit by the intense international competition to find a shorter and less costly route to the Spice Islands.

There is one damning contemporary comment which is difficult to brush aside. When Cardinal Wolsey was promoting an expedition "into the newfound Iland" in 1520, Sebastian Cabot was mentioned as the leader. When they learned this, the London merchant companies demurred. The drapers and the mercers discussed the situation and issued this cool opinion:

We thynk it were to sore aventour to joperd V shipps with men and goodes unto the said Iland uppon the singular trust of one man, callyd as we understand, Sebastyan, whiche Sebastyan, as we here say, was never in the land hym self, all if he makes reporte of many thinges as he hath hard his ffather and other men speke in tymes past.

In considering this opinion, we should disregard the oddities of sixteenth-century spelling and should bear in mind that the London livery companies were a level- and hard-headed lot, not likely to allow any fair chance of profit to slip through their fingers. In any event, Wolsey's project was abandoned.

There is cloud, too, over Sebastian Cabot's later ventures. For Spain, he led a three-year, four-ship, 200-man expedition to South America in 1526, spending five months of the following year exploring the *Rio de la Plata*, the great River Plate of the Argentine. He built forts, fought the Indians, searched vainly for gold up the Paraña, and returned to Seville with one ship, twenty-four of his original company, and fifty Indian slaves. He was promptly tried by the Council of the Indies on half a dozen charges–among them, the charge of disobeying instructions and causing the deaths of many of his officers–and sentenced to banishment for four years.

Cabot was back in English service in 1548, after ten years of lobbying for a position there. The advisors of the infant Edward VI granted him a fat salary and

Edward VI, King of England, ruled under the guidance of regents.

when Spain's Charles V demanded Cabot's return, the mariner refused to go and the British Privy Council supported him. Shortly afterwards, Cabot appeared once again to be playing tricky pool when he wrote to Emperor Charles pleading that poor health was preventing his return to Spain and that before he died he wanted "to disclose to Your Majesty the secret which I possess." The secret was probably news of a planned English expedition to Peru which Cabot was prepared to sell or trade for some preferment.

Sebastian finally became Governor of the Muscovy Company, organized in London to trade with the Russians via the White Sea passage, which, hopefully, would lead to a northeast route to Cathay. In 1556, he was reported at a sailing of one of the company's ships from Gravesend when he "entred into the dance himselfe amongst the rest of the young and lusty company." He is presumed to have died in the autumn of the next year. Those who puzzle over Sebastian's checkered career have one last clue to consider: he was bossed by a nagging wife.

Of silent John Cabot, Dr. Williamson offered this epitaph: "We may discover that he was a veritable leader of men, deprived of rounded historical greatness by premature death and lack of record." It can also be said that the two voyages of John Cabot established at last that the mythical Fortunate Isles of the western sea, the Island of Brasil, Atlantis, the Isles of Demons, Stockfish Land, and the folk memory of Vinland the Good all added up to a new continent which was not Asia but which held unplumbed treasures of its own. With its primitive inhabitants "clothed in beestes' skynnes," this huge mass of mountain, forest, ice, and naked rock barred the way to Cathay. This was "the intellectual discovery of America" which the savants allot to Cabot. It was to become the basis of the British claim to the Canadian shore, a claim which in time the British would have to fight to make good.

The Cabot revelation eventually set in motion the search for what became known as the Northwest Passage. In 1520, Magellan had found for Spain the stormy strait at the far southern tip of the New World leading into the Pacific. For England, intrepid men like Frobisher, Davis, Hudson, Bylot, Button, Baffin, Foxe, James, Parry, Back, and Franklin pursued for two hundred and fifty years dangerous voyages in the grinding, killing ice of Canada's Arctic apron, seeking a shorter route from Europe to the Orient. The quest cost dozens of fine ships and hundreds of brave men, and although it resulted in the charting of much of Canada's northern shores, it failed utterly in its prime purpose. The ice remained unconquered until 1906, when the Norwegian, Roald Amundsen, turned up in San Francisco, having slipped and slithered through the passage over three years in a 47-ton sloop. In 1969, it was still almost too tough a task for the 115,000-ton tanker, *Manhattan*, which could have carried Cabot's *Mathew* at the davits.

THE SCIENCE OF SEAFARING

The forceful outward thrust of European endeavours during the fifteenth and sixteenth centuries came as a result of several factors – religious, political, and economic. But the means by which the nations of Europe transmitted their influence to even the most distant of shores was the result of a revolution in technology. In the north, the decline of the Viking empire was also the death of Norse seamanship. And in the Mediterranean, the monopolies of the Italians preserved a naval tradition which reached back to the days of slave-driven galleys. But the nations of western Europe, willing to dare the unknown waters of the Atlantic, demanded new tools and new techniques. And the masterful mind of Renaissance man responded to that demand, producing an abundance of innovative devices which ushered in a golden age of discovery.

WATCHING THE SHIPS TAKE SHAPE

With the invention, early in the fourteenth century, of the mariner's compass, a rapid evolution in naval architecture and in the theory of ship-building took place. Since the mariner's compass made "coasting" more or less unnecessary, the introduction of a more efficient rig and other appliances became general and rapid. By 1400, the sailing ships of the maritime nations had attained considerable size. But they were heavy, broad in the beam, and generally clumsy in form. They also displayed a marked curve in the deckline, as seen in the picture at lower left. Henry v of England had several large vessels built—one of which was 165 feet long and 46 feet in beam. During the course of the fifteenth century, attention was paid to the idea of actually designing ships. The rule of thumb and the craftsman's eye, for so long the shipwright's only standard, were gradually replaced by the use of precise and preconceived standards.

Stradanus, a Renaissance artist, depicts Noah building his ark. He has set the scene in contemporary surroundings, showing shipwrights and carpenters at work with mallet, cross-cut, and adze.

19
VERAGVA PARS

At work at the drawing board, designers draft detailed plans before even the ship's keel is laid.

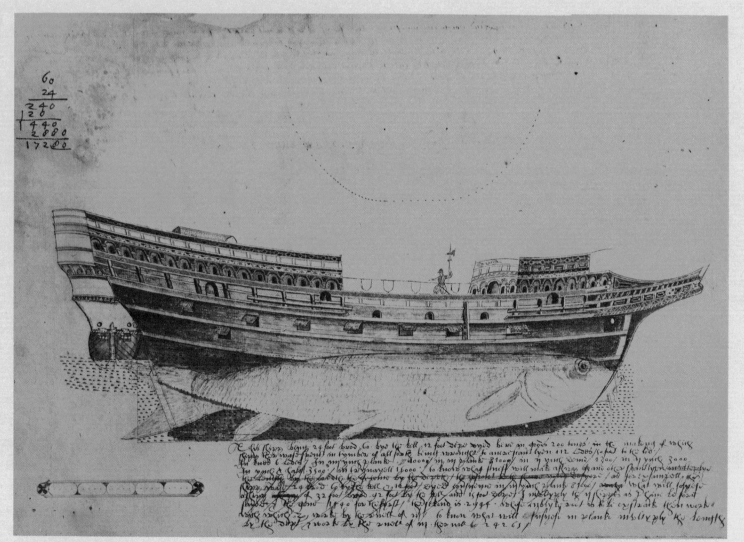

An admirer of aquatic forms conceived and executed this piscatorial ship's hull.

CARRACK AND CARAVEL

When the Portuguese captains began their reconnaissance of southern waters, they were not long in perceiving the marked superiority of Arab vessels. Of particular note was the *vela latina*–the lateen or triangular sail which made the ships of the Arabs so highly manoeuvrable. In adopting lateen sails, the Portuguese gave rise to the caravel, the earliest of the ships of discovery. It was in caravels–like the one shown below–that the sailors of Henry the Navigator made their tentative way along the west coast of Africa. But although it handled well and was therefore ideally suited to coastal exploration, the caravel was too limited in size to carry the amount of provisions needed on extended voyages. To offset this weakness, the explorers complemented their fleets with carracks, heavily built ships descended from the square-rigged merchantmen of the northern seas. The carrack on the right, with its forecastle and sterncastle standing high above its deck and its gunwales pierced by numerous guns, foreshadows the evolution of carrack into galleon.

Ioan Galle excud.

THE
TOOLS
OF THE
MARINER

The quadrant, a superior instrument for measuring the height of the sun, replaced the astrolabe on most ships.

Brightly coloured compass cards indicated the four cardinal winds and the thirty-two rhumbs of a course.

The nocturnal, as its name implies, was used at night. Its purpose: to enable pilots to tell time by the stars.

The ring dial made it possible to tell time by the sun regardless of the latitude at which the ship was sailing.

By the beginning of the 1400's, academic geographers had amassed an impressive body of knowledge—the only problem being that the theoretical insights of astronomers and cosmographers bore little relation to the practical experience of ordinary seamen. To the immense benefit of Europe's sea captains, nautical science was soon to combine the best of both worlds. Like many of the advances made during the Renaissance, the development of the science of navigation was often a matter of adopting old methods and putting them to new uses. As we have already seen, the lateen sail which the Arabs had used for centuries now became common on the Atlantic. Similarly, the compass—known as far back as the twelfth century—was now modified for use at sea. So too was the astrolabe, a device that enabled navigators to measure the angle of the sun and thus calculate the latitude at which they were sailing. Using these instruments, together with log-line, hour glass, and sea charts, the discoverers of Canada embarked on their remarkable voyages.

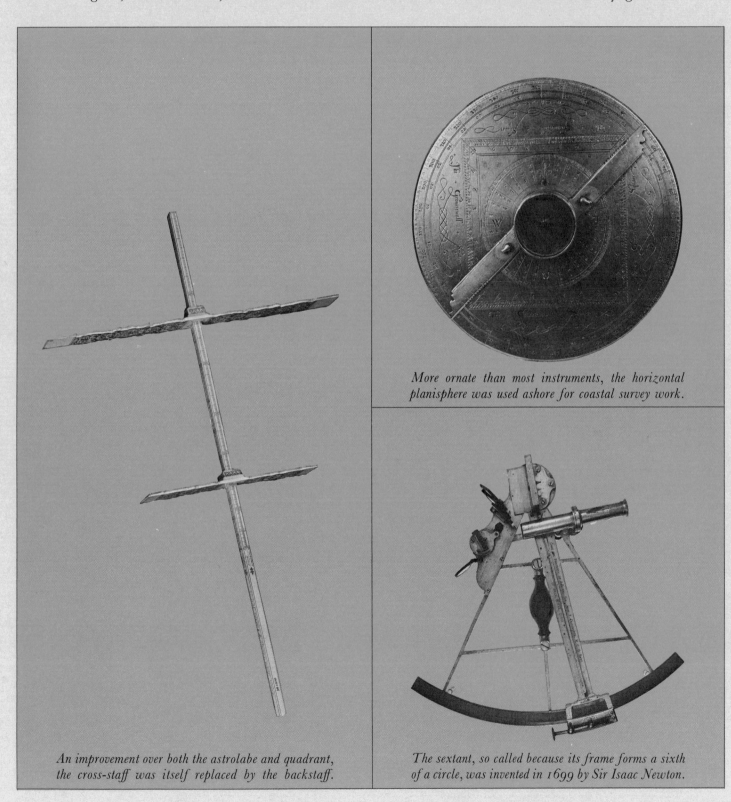

More ornate than most instruments, the horizontal planisphere was used ashore for coastal survey work.

An improvement over both the astrolabe and quadrant, the cross-staff was itself replaced by the backstaff.

The sextant, so called because its frame forms a sixth of a circle, was invented in 1699 by Sir Isaac Newton.

SCHOOL FOR NAVIGATORS

In 1410, Pierre d'Ailly produced the *Imago Mundi*, an extended work on geography that contained a vast store of quotations from Greek, Roman, and Arab authorities. Although a masterpiece of scholarship and erudition, the *Imago Mundi* was really no more than a mass of legends, Biblical references, and traveller's tales. As such, it was of little help to men concerned with the concrete problems of exploration. As the importance of nautical skills increased throughout the fifteenth and sixteenth centuries, books of a practical nature multiplied rapidly. Among these were *The Mariner's Mirror*, *A Sea Grammar*, and *The Light of Navigation*. The frontispiece of the later work is reproduced below; it depicts a group of scholars and seamen engaged in learned discussion. At left, a seaman instructs in the proper use of the astrolabe; at right, two men examine a cross-staff.

Part III
The Mariner
from St. Malo

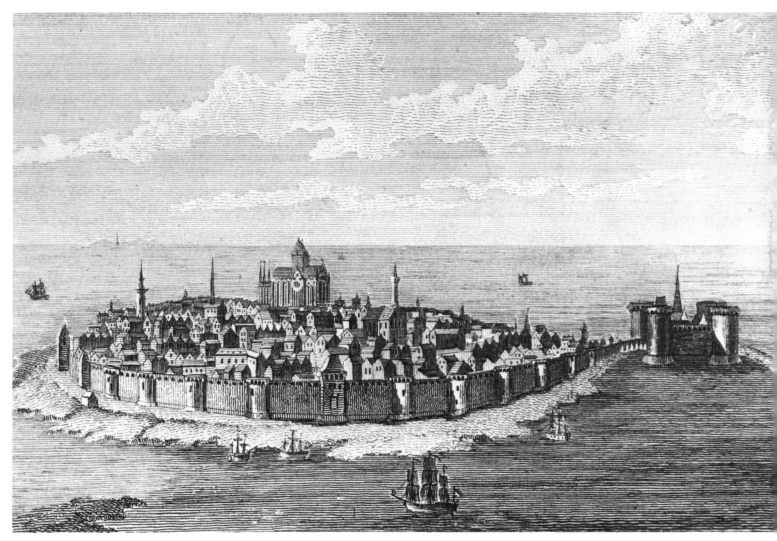

The island city of St. Malo.

CHAPTER SEVEN

The Cross
and
the Cannon

ACQUES CARTIER was just a lad of six clambering about the stone quays of St. Malo when John Cabot claimed the mainland that is now Canada for the British Crown. Then, half a lifetime later, on a headland across the Gulf of St. Lawrence from Cabot's landing place, Captain Cartier raised a wooden cross and shield bearing the inscription: "*Vive le Roy de France*." Thus, England and France, on their historic swing from sworn enemy to firm friend, each seeking a route to China, were first set in opposition in the New World. Cabot had only traced the Atlantic coastline, but Cartier penetrated and circumnavigated the Gulf of St. Lawrence, then discovered and explored the mighty "River of Canada," the vital artery into the heartland of the future nation.

With Cartier's epic voyages, Europeans stood on the sites of Quebec and Montreal and peered wonderingly at the great streams of the St. Lawrence and the Ottawa rushing down to their confluence from the unknown hinterland. They heard natives speak of vast sweet-water seas deep in the interior which no man living had seen, and of the far-off Kingdom of the Saguenay where one could find "immense quantities of gold, rubies, and other rich things." While sturdy fishermen of several races routinely crossed the ocean and reaped the harvest of the Continental Shelf and cared nothing for the looming land beyond, the small company of discoverers was drawn onwards past the brooding headlands by the siren's lure of the wealth of the Orient. They were destined to find only false diamonds and fool's gold. But as they probed for the strait that didn't exist, they began to reveal the shape and significance of a huge land which was as strange and as different to Renaissance Europeans as were any of the heavenly bodies that crossed the sky above their mastheads. Among this brave and select company, there was no more important figure than the grave and gritty mariner from St. Malo.

Cartier is another of the durable men of humble stock who put their unmistakable stamp on Canada.

Accepting the brilliant research of Sir Joseph Pope, we can place Cartier's birth between June 7 and December 23, 1491, making him three years older than is stated in some histories. No record of his baptism can be found at the twelfth-century Cathedral of St. Vincent within the walled town of St. Malo in Brittany. But in the baptismal entry for one of his brothers, the father's name is spelled "Quartier." The family, of fishermen and farmers, has been traced back to a grandfather, Jean, who married Guillemette Baudoin in 1457, and had four sons. The eldest of these, Jamet, was the father of Jacques; his mother was the former Geseline Jansart.

St. Malo was an exciting place for a boy to grow up in. Built on a rocky island connected to the rugged shore by a 650-foot causeway known as the Sillon, it was almost an integral part of the sea. The racing tides of the Rance, rising as high as forty feet, spume along the granite ramparts that enclose the old town and pour into the protected harbour. With a history as a religious sanctuary and then as a pirates' den, it was already prosperous and roughly handsome in Cartier's day, the Great Keep of the Castle having just been completed. It is a picturesque and even busier port today, the damage of the Second World War now repaired, the town's growth absorbing suburban Paramé and St. Servan.

Young Jacques watched the fishing fleets return from the codbanks of the New Found Land – before 1510 the merchants of St. Malo were selling their cured fish far inland. Today, the stoic fishermen are still making the same journey across the Atlantic each season, their boats blessed by the bishop on the Sunday before February 15. It was a town to inspire a young man to high endeavour. The ramparts were thrown up by a coterie of bishops who once held the town as a separate republic. The citizen's motto was "*Ni Français, ni Bretons, Malouins suis.*" St. Malo honours Jacques Cartier today as its most famous son, along with the politician and novelist, François-René de Chateaubriand.

Cartier carried his Malouin independence of thought and action like a badge, and it saved his skin in many a tight corner. Although there is no clear document to prove it, he probably went to the Grand Banks with the St. Malo fleet in his teens. In any case, when he was married in 1519 (at the age of twenty-eight) he was listed as "master-pilot." His rank, certainly awarded for major ocean navigation, probably helped in his wooing of a girl considerably above the Cartiers in social station. She was Marie Katherine Des Granches, daughter of the Chevalier Honoré Des Granches, High Constable of St. Malo. As a Chevalier of the Order of St. Louis, Cartier's father-in-law held a title which was equivalent to a British knighthood. From Cartier's fragmentary writings, we can assume it was at least a comfortable and pleasant union–Cartier was to name several new geographic features for his wife and the marriage lasted for thirty-eight years. Moreover, he took several of his in-laws with him on his expeditions.

In looks, Cartier has been described as being "of open countenance with kindly eyes and obstinate chin." In all likelihood, he adopted the trimmed beard of the master mariner of his period. Unfortunately, none of the portraits displayed today were painted from life. The portrait most often seen in Canadian texts–a pensive man with chin on hand–was not painted until 1839. In his book, *The White and the Gold*, Thomas B. Costain attempted a novelist's description: "A stocky man with a sharply etched profile and calm eyes under a high, wide brow; slightly hawk-billed as to mouth...The face of a man who finds philosophic calm in contemplation of the sea but can be roused easily to violent action...He was dressed in a thick brown cloak, belted in tightly at the waist. The tunic he wore under the cloak was open at the neck, where a white linen shirt showed. This was not the garb of a gentleman; it was intended for hard wear."

Cartier must have been fond of children, although he and Katherine had none of their own. He appears in the St. Malo church records as participating at baptisms no fewer than fifty-four times, and on twenty-eight occasions he was named godfather. At the first of these, on August 21, 1510, he stood for his nephew, Etienne, son of Jehanne Cartier, his sister, and Jehan Nouel.

There is a continuing debate about whether or not Cartier went, in his twenties or thirties, on discovery expeditions led by others to both South and North America. In the narrative of his own first voyage as commander, Cartier speaks several times of Brazil in such manner as to indicate that he was familiar with that country–for instance, he compared Indian grain which he found growing at Gaspé "like unto that which groweth in Brazil." Cartier spoke fluent Portuguese, and in 1528–when he would have been thirty-seven–his wife Katherine stood as godmother at the baptism of a girl listed only as "Catherine du Brezil."

An imaginative portrayal of Cartier and his young wife by Bécart de Granville.

The suggestion is that, like other far-roving mariners of the time, Cartier had brought back an Indian child as a souvenir of his venturing. The northeastern coasts of South America had become fairly well known in shipping circles by this time, following the voyages at the opening of the sixteenth century by Amerigo Vespucci.

Quebec historian Gustave Lanctot advances some evidence in support of Cartier's presence in the American expeditions of Giovanni da Verrazzano, the navigator from Florence, sailing out of Dieppe for Francis I, "the Valois," who had taken the throne of France in 1515. Francis, soon at war with the King of Spain and Emperor of the Holy Roman Empire, determined to share in the lands and loot of the New World. Referring to the Treaty of Tordesillas between Spain and Portugal, he declaimed: "The sun shines for me as for the others, and I should very much like to see the clause of Adam's will which shuts me off from my share of the world." As this remark indicates, Francis I was responsible for formulating the principle which states that effective occupation of a territory is essential to substantiating ownership.

Inheriting the "discovery mantle" from his fellow Italians–Columbus, Cabot, and Vespucci–the 44-year-old Verrazzano was chosen in 1523 to seek a route to Cathay and the Indies, north of the Spanish continental lands then becoming known as "Florida." With the single small bark, *La Dauphine*, Verrazzano made his landfall the following spring below Chesapeake Bay and coasted north, entering New York harbour and then Narrangansett Bay, before proceeding around Cape Cod to the coast of Maine. Beyond the Atlantic coast of Nova Scotia, Verrazzano wrote of islands that offered "many fair harbourages as do the islands in the Gulf of Venice and Dalmatia." He may here have been in the Gulf of St. Lawrence, known for many years simply as "Grande Baye." If so, he would still not have been the first. There is a chronicle of Dieppe which records a voyage by Thomas Aubert in 1508 that included some penetration of the St. Lawrence River. And an even earlier map of the gulf is credited to Jean Denys of Honfleur. Verrazzano's own charts indicate that he reached the vicinity of Cape Charles in southern Labrador.

Cartier appears to have been absent from France during the period of Verrazzano's voyages (on a second journey to the West Indies, the Florentine was eaten by the Caribs), and certainly before he left on his own discoveries, Cartier announced that he was sailing directly for the Strait of Belle Isle (then the Baie des Chateaux), obviously familiar territory. But as Professor Marcel Trudel of Laval University points out, Cartier never once alludes in his journals either to Verrazzano or to an earlier visit to the North American seaboard. Further, the Verrazzano expeditions were mounted in Dieppe, and it would be most unlikely at that time of religious strife and provincial jealousies that the Normans would include a Breton in their crews. In any event, the relevant voyage of Verrazzano, the whole frail structure, depends on a letter supposedly written by Verrazzano to Francis I in the summer of 1524–and there is no evidence that the King ever acknowledged either Verrazzano's discoveries or even his bare existence. The next year, as it happened, Francis was taken to Madrid as prisoner by his archenemy Charles V, after the French forces were routed at the battle of Pavia.

In an interval of peace, in 1532, Francis made a pilgrimage to the magnificent sea-girt abbey of Mont St. Michel, in the vicinity of St. Malo. The abbot of the time was Bishop Jean Le Veneur, Grand Almoner of France, and also Count of Lisieux in nearby Calvados. Bishop Le Veneur had a special interest in the discovery of new lands and he introduced Master-Pilot Jacques Cartier to his King. He proposed that his protégé be sent on a royally-sponsored voyage to take up the quest at the point at which the luckless Verrazzano had turned for home in 1524. Le Veneur backed up his suggestion by asserting that Cartier had already been to Brazil and to the New Found Land that had been discovered by the English.

The King decided to pursue his western ambitions once again and confirmed the choice of the now-mature Cartier to lead an expedition "to discover certain isles and countries where it is said there must be a great quantity of gold and other precious things to be found." Cartier's commission has been lost, but the King's order to his treasurer to equip two ships for the voyage at a cost of 6,000 *livres** still exists. Cartier

* The *livre* remained the basic monetary unit of France until the Revolution, when it became the *franc*.

The abbey of Mont St. Michel, where Cartier first met Francis I.

began to seek his crews in 1533. He had to enlist the help of the courts, because the fiercely independent ship-owners of St. Malo wanted to keep all of the experienced seamen to man their fishing fleet. They believed, also, that any exploration of the lands beyond the Grand Banks would only entice more ships to the lucrative fishing grounds and thus bring them unwanted competition.

Cartier had more powerful friends. The King had recently appointed Philippe Chabot, Baron d'Aspremont, the Sieur de Brionne, as High Admiral of France, and Chabot (another man of Calvados) supported the son-in-law of the Chevalier Des Granches and personally signed his commission. Cartier was later to repay this debt by naming the Ile Brion, one of the Magdalens, for his patron. Chabot sent his vice-admiral, Charles de Mouy, to supervise the preparations. Two fully-decked caravels of sixty tons each were provisioned for six months, and crews totalling sixty men selected. Flintlock muskets were carried and the ships were armed with four cannons each. These were light pieces, not much use in a stiff fight against, say, the guns of the ships being launched by Henry VIII of England, but quite noisy enough to awe the natives of the New World.

In mid-April 1534, the Chevalier de Mouy ordered the sailing masters of the two ships and all crew to the Cathedral of St. Vincent, where they were required to swear most solemnly that they would truly and faithfully serve *François, le Trés Chrétien Roi*, under their commander, Captain Cartier. The bishop's blessing, too, would help ward off the fiends of the Isles of Demons that some superstitious fishermen believed lurked in the far northern waters. André Thevet, the meretricious sixteenth-century historian, wrote: "True it is, and I myself have heard it, not from one but from a great number of the sailors and pilots with whom I have made many voyages, that when they passed this way, they heard in the air, on the tops and about the masts, a great clamour of voices, confused and inarticulate, such as you may hear from the crowd at a fair or marketplace." These airy demons, with other fabulous sea monsters and ogres, were often drawn on the margins and in the oceans of the early maps.

Finally, on April 20, as the Malouins lined the ramparts and the Sillon to cheer and pray, Cartier took his ships out into the Gulf of St. Malo, skirted the nearby islands of Jersey and Guernsey, and set his course for Newfoundland. Before brisk east winds, they scudded across the Atlantic to Bonavista Bay in twenty days, and it is obvious from the captain's terse log entries that he treated the trip as merely the routine first leg of his journey.

"The Captain" – except for one solitary reference, this is the only name given to Cartier in the accounts of his voyages, and the actual hand that wrote the narratives is still cloaked in mystery. The story of the first voyage was published in Italian and English before appearing in French in 1598. The second voyage, that of 1535-36, was covered in the best-known *Brief Récit*, which was published anonymously in Paris ten years after the event. Three manuscript copies of this account survive in museums, but biblio-philes argue that they are all copies of a lost original, possibly by Cartier himself. The final fragmentary journal of the last voyage was published by British anthologist Richard Hakluyt in his epic *Principal Navigations, Etc.* in 1600, from a French manuscript which he had found in Paris about fifteen years earlier and which is now lost. It is a baffling scene, even for the expert. Entire studies have been published in the attempt to trace the authorship of the narratives, and the interested reader can sample the plot in the erudite introduction to *The Voyages of Jacques Cartier*, by H. P. Biggar, publication No. XI of the Public Archives of Canada. It must be also kept in mind throughout that one of the major motives behind the journals was to spark and sustain the interest of the King – thus events were presented in a manner which was likely to win his approval and continued support.

The late Marius Barbeau, associated for most of his lifetime with the National Museum of Canada, suggested that the French satirical novelist, François Rabelais, had a hand in the making of books from Cartier's supposedly sparse seaman's logs. The third volume of the rollicking history of Gargantua and his son Pantagruel – thought to represent Francis I and his son Henry II – follows the lines of the Cartier voyages. Another theory holds that Jehan Poullet, a gentleman of Dol, in Brittany, who acted as purser, was the author of the *Brief Récit*, because of "the exaggerated importance given to him in that volume [his name is mentioned four times]." The most widely held view is that while Cartier kept scrupulous voyage notes – his *journaux de bord* – others developed publishable manuscripts from them, perhaps in some cases enlarging his comments and descriptions following personal discussions with the discoverer between his journeys or during his fifteen years of retirement. Nevertheless, the situation still remains as Marcel Trudel put it in 1965: "For the time being, the author of the accounts remains unknown and the problem persists in its entirety." The excerpts from the journals which appear in these chapters have been further edited and have often been put into more popular style by the present author.

The Breton ships could not get into Bonavista Bay in May 1534, because of late ice. They therefore slipped down the coast of Newfoundland, about ten miles, to today's Catalina – Cartier named it Ste. Katherine's Harbour, presumably after his wife. They remained there for ten days, repairing the ships and rigging, and then pushed north toward Belle Isle, on a course that touched the remarkable offshore rocks known now as the Funk Islands:

On May 21, we set out with a west wind and sailed north as far as the Isle of Birds, which was completely surrounded by drifting ice. In spite of this, our two long-boats were sent to get some of the birds, whose numbers are unbelievable unless one has seen them. In the air are a hundred times as many as on the island itself.

Some of these birds are as large as geese, black and white in colour, with a beak like a crow. They are always in the water as they cannot fly, their wings being only about the size of half a man's hand. They are so marvellously fat. We call them apponats *and our longboats were loaded with them in less than half an hour. Each of our ships salted four or five casks, not counting those we were able to eat fresh...*

There is another smaller kind of bird which roosts under the larger ones [the main island is only 800 yards long by 400 yards wide] and other white ones that keep apart from the rest – these are difficult to seize for they bite like dogs [gannets].

Even though the islands lie thirty miles from the mainland, bears swim out to it to feed on the birds. Our men found one bear as big as a calf and as white as a swan that sprang into the sea in front of them. The next day, as we continued our journey, we caught sight of this bear swimming towards the land as fast as we were sailing. We chased him in our longboats and captured him. His flesh was as good to eat as that of a two-year-old heifer.

Conservationists shudder at the thought of Cartier's men clubbing the clumsy *apponat*, which was, of course, the great auk. Cartier later made another trip to his "Isle of Birds" to replenish his meat barrels and this practice became so widespread that the French cod-fishermen were soon bringing only small stocks of meat with them from Europe. The Funk Islands still swarm with sea birds, but not with the great auk. It has been extinct since 1844.

The Strait of Belle Isle was still choked with ice when Cartier arrived at the ocean portal, and he again had to cool his heels. This time, he dropped anchor in Quirpon Harbour, just under Cape Bauld. He called the cape (the most northerly point of Newfoundland) Point Degrat, and the harbour he dubbed Carpunt.

Common enough in the days of Cartier, the great auk is now extinct.

(Near here, five hundred years earlier, some Viking wanderers had built sod huts and smelted the local bog iron.) After a wait of several days, Cartier moved into the narrow passage that separates Newfoundland from Labrador, and after bestowing his wife's name on an island, he worked his ships along the northern shore to the white sands of Blanc Sablon.

The territory was already quite well known – Englishman John Rut had wintered in St. John's Harbour in 1527 – and many of Newfoundland's capes and bays were already named. The prominent layered basaltic rock towering along the Labrador shore, giving the appearance of battlements, had suggested the earlier name, Baie des Chateaux, the Bay of Castles. It has been suggested also that this dramatic natural feature, seen from a lurching caravel standing out to sea, had been confused with the mythological towered Seven Cities of Cibola. Opposite Belle Isle, the prominent inlet is still known as Chateau Bay.

About three miles west of Blanc Sablon, the Bretons entered Bradore Bay, now on the Labrador-Quebec border, once the site of Fort Pontchartrain, a frontier stronghold of the seventeenth century. Close by was a site bearing a familiar name – Brest, already a rendezvous for the sturdy Breton and Basque whalers. Later in the sixteenth century, it was reported to have a summer population of about one thousand. This depot, too, required defence against hostile tribesmen and a stone fort armed with cannon was eventually raised. Here, on June 11, 1534, after picking up fresh water, Cartier's crews held church service in celebration of the feast of St. Barnabas – the first recorded Christian religious service in Canada.

The following excerpt from the Cartier narrative has three surprises for the average reader. First, it records a casual meeting with another French voyager from La Rochelle. Second, it mentions the raising of

the first cross in Canada – not at Gaspé, as every schoolchild is taught, but at Port St. Servan on the high northern shore of the gulf. And third, it demonstrates that the modest, sober Cartier was not lacking a fleck of vanity.

On the next day, June 12, we continued our way through these islands and at the end of the thickest portion of them we found St. Anthony's Harbour. Further on, we came to a small, very deep passage between high shores. It is a good harbour, and a cross was set up there. It was named St. Servan's Harbour [Servan was one of the founding saints of St. Malo].

Ten leagues farther on, there is another good opening somewhat larger and where there are many salmon. We named it St. James's River. While here, we saw a large ship from La Rochelle that in the night had run past the harbour of Brest [today's Old Fort Bay] where she wanted to fish. We went on board and brought her into another harbour, one league farther west than the River St. James. This harbour is in my opinion one of the best in the world. It was named Port Jacques Cartier.

The journal continues with one of the most famous phrases ever linked with Canada, an epithet which once discouraged immigration and which is still used by supercilious European pundits – most of whom know even less about Canada than did Cartier:

The land should not be called the New Land, being composed of stones and bare rock . . . Along the whole of the north shore I did not see one cart-load of earth, although I landed in many places. Except at Blanc Sablon, there is nothing but moss and stunted bushes. I am inclined to believe that this is the land God gave to Cain . . . .

For the first time, we have a detailed description of the Canadian aborigine – the original "red" Indian – probably Beothuks, who became extinct in Newfoundland in the early nineteenth century:

There are people on this coast whose bodies are fairly well formed but they are wild and savage folk.* They wear their hair tied up on top of their heads like a handful of twisted hay, with a nail or something of the kind passed through the middle, and into it they weave a few feathers. Both men and women wear furs, but the women are wrapped up more snugly and have a belt around their waists. They paint themselves with colours. They have canoes made of birchbark in which they move about and from which they catch many seals.

On the morning of Monday, June 15, Cartier came to a decision. The north shore was hopeless, offering neither possible openings towards the Pacific nor any land worth having. He could see high peaks rising above the waves on his port bow and he crossed the

---

* The early English chroniclers followed the Spanish lead in referring to the natives of the New World as "Indians." The French used the term *"les sauvages,"* which then meant "wild men" or "aborigines."

top of the gulf to the western shore of Newfoundland – it was not yet known as an island – making landfall about today's Hawke Bay. With another loving nod to his lady in the Rue de Buhen in St. Malo, the captain named the peaks the Monts des Granches. Persistent fog spoiled his charting of the coast for the long stretch down to St. Paul's Inlet and Cow Head. The weather continued stormy and the caravels were buffeted about until the course becomes difficult to follow. They raised Cape Anguille, on Newfoundland's southwestern tip, on June 24, promptly naming it Cape St. John in honour of the supreme baptist.

From this promontory, Cartier appears to have struck blindly westwards. But he may, in fact, have had some knowledge from other mariners who had been in the gulf. His next solid sighting was a genuine discovery – the island he named Brion for Admiral Chabot. It is four miles long by one mile wide, nestling at almost mid-gulf above the Magdalen Islands.

*This island is fringed with sandbanks and there is excellent anchorage all around with a depth of six and seven fathoms.** *This island is the best land we have seen, for one of its fields is worth more than the whole of the New Land. We found it to be covered with fine trees and meadows, fields of wild oats, and peas in flower, as thick as I ever saw in Brittany. There are many gooseberry bushes, strawberry vines, roses, parsley, and other useful herbs.*

Around this island, are many great beasts like large oxen which have two tusks in their jaw like elephant's tusks and swim about in the water. There was one asleep on shore near the water's edge and we set out in our longboat to try and catch him. But as soon as we drew near, he threw himself into the sea. We also saw bears and foxes. This island was named Ile de Brion.

In the neighbourhood of these islands the tides are strong and run southeast and northwest. I am inclined to think from what I have seen that there is a passage between Newfoundland and the Breton's land. If this were so, it would prove a great saving both in time and in distance.

From this excerpt, the rare thrill of discovery can perhaps touch the reader sated with television's tasteless hash. To be with Cartier, via his journal, as he sees his first walrus is sheer fun, and then note his inspired guess at the existence of Cabot Strait between Newfoundland and the Cape Breton mainland of Nova Scotia. In these lines, one can see Canada taking shape.

Cartier at first thought that the sandstone cliffs of the Magdalens formed the mainland of the south shore of the gulf, "as it is the beginning of the good land." From June 28 to 30, he ran by Wolf, Grindstone, and Amherst Islands. Continuing southwesterly, he noted the mainland again – "a prominent headland named by us Cap Orléans [after Prince Charles, Duc

A conjectural painting of Cartier, who never sat for his portrait.

d'Orléans, the third son of Francis I]" – but this time, he was in fact admiring Prince Edward Island's Cape Kildare. Canada's smallest province was not discovered to be an island until after 1600.

Admiration for the "Garden in the Gulf" was the order of the day. "All this coast is low and flat," the journal says, "but the finest land one can see, and full of fine trees and meadows...We went ashore in our longboats at several places, including at a shallow river where we saw some Indians in their canoes." When they saw a single native running on the beach near North Point, the Malouins landed and tried to encourage him to come near; but he proved too timid. They left a knife and a woollen scarf dangling from a branch for him. Turning the cape, they coasted the sandy western shore, landing on four beaches, noting the "beautiful and very fragrant" trees, among which they found elm, ash, cedar, yew, willow, and pine. There was a field of oats which gave the impression of having been sown and cultivated.

To the north, they could now see New Brunswick's Point Escuminac. Thus, they concluded that the waterway they were in (which we now know as Northumberland Strait) was merely a bay. They therefore crossed over to Miramichi Bay, and for the first time since leaving the Quebec north shore on June 15, they were back along the true mainland of Canada. As they rounded Miscou Island, they stared

---

* The French fathom was eight inches shorter than the English measure, but to count a fathom as six feet is fair enough.

in sudden hope at the 25-mile-wide penetrating bight of Chaleur Bay. At last, here was a possible passage to Cathay to supersede Magellan's strait in the far south!

The cape on the south shore we named Hope, for the hope we had of finding a strait. We coasted along the northern shore of the bay looking for a harbour and entered an inlet which we named St. Martin's Cove, it being St. Martin's Day [July 4]. We remained in this cove until July 12, examining the bay by longboat ... to see which way the coast ran.

When we were half a league from a point [Paspebiac Point], we caught sight of two fleets of Indian canoes that were crossing the bay – in total, about forty or fifty canoes. When one of the fleets reached this point, a large number of Indians sprang out on the beach and set up a great noise, waving to us to come ashore, and holding up furs on poles. But as we had only one boat we decided not to risk it, and rowed away.

They now launched two of their largest canoes to follow us, and these were joined by five more from the second fleet. All came after our longboat, showing signs of excitement and happiness, and of their wish to be friends with us. They shouted words we did not understand. We did not care to trust them, and waved them back. But they surrounded our longboat with their seven canoes.

Since they would not go back, we ordered two small cannon to be fired over their heads and this at first sent them paddling back toward the point. However, they proceeded to come on as before and we shot off two fire-lances which frightened them so much that they paddled away as fast as they could and did not follow us any more.

This may well have been the first gun fired in the Canadian wilderness and it suggests that contrary to the tradition of easy French coexistence with the Indian, Cartier, Champlain, and other leaders who followed them (like European discoverers in all lands) turned instantly to their firearms to win all arguments. There were only a few thousand Indians in all the northeastern lands and news travelled fast by the woods runners. From Cartier's day onward, when the white man spoke, the Indian heard the rumbling echoes of his awesome cannon. And later, when tribes such as the Mohawk or the Fox chose to oppose the might of the French, the order went out to exterminate them utterly.

Cartier's St. Martin's Cove was our Port Daniel, a name that remembers Captain Charles Daniel, a contemporary of Champlain. From here, Cartier's men explored the 75-mile length of Chaleur Bay – right to the mouth of the Restigouche – and knew that this was no way to the Indies, "whereat we were grieved and displeased." On the way back to the caravels, the French were offered cooked seal meat by the Indians, who were obviously still anxious to trade. Several sailors went ashore "with hatchets, knives, beads, and other things," and the delighted Algonquins crowded close, offering even the furs that they were wearing.

Some of the Indian women stood in the sea up to their knees and sang. Others came boldly to the visitors and caressed them.

The long, heroic, and vain attempt to win the Canadian savage for Christ probably began with the line in Cartier's journal which ran: "*Nous congneumes que se sont gens qui seroint fassilles a convertir.*" Cartier's own sincere conviction comes through clearly in the narratives and he often acted kindly and respectfully with the Indians – though his religion did not prevent him from kidnapping and deceit, when such means suited his purpose.

As soon as he was sure that there was no outlet from Chaleur – which he decided was "as temperate as Spain and the finest it is possible to see" – Cartier coasted northeast to the rock of Percé, and when the seas made up rough, he took shelter in Gaspé Bay. One of the ships lost an anchor and they moved for safety about twenty miles further into the basin, where they

An Iroquois wearing a strange headdress made of beavers' tails.

remained for ten days. Here, the French encountered Indians "not at all of the same race or language as the first we met" and the chronicle gives us the following graphic description. These people were probably Iroquois, then holding all the territory of the St. Lawrence:

The savages numbered more than three hundred—men, women, and children—in forty canoes. They came to the sides of our ships and we gave them combs, beads, knives, and other gewgaws, at which they showed signs of joy, lifting up their hands to heaven and singing and dancing in the canoes.

These people may well be called savage for they are the sorriest folk there can be in the world, and the whole lot of them had nothing above the value of five sous, their canoes and fishing nets excepted. They go quite naked, except for a small skin with which they cover their genitals, and for a few old furs which they throw over their shoulders.

They have their heads shaved all around, except for a tuft on the top which they leave long like a horse's tail. They have no other dwelling but their canoes, which they turn upside down and sleep on the ground underneath. They eat their meat and fish almost raw, only warming it a little on the embers... They never eat anything that has a taste of salt in it. They are clever thieves and steal everything they can carry off.

There was, Cartier must have decided glumly, nothing here to give even a hint of the riches of the Indies, and he made ready to push on. First, however, he performed, on July 24, the ritual act known to every Canadian—the raising of the 30-foot cross on Penouille Point at the entrance to the bay with its *fleur-de-lis* and its inscription: "Long live the King of France." The journal does not specifically state that this was intended as a formal claim of ownership. In fact, Cartier told the Indians in sign language that it was meant to serve as a landmark for ships that would follow his expedition to the bay. The Indian chief at the fishing camp came out in his canoe "with three of his sons and his brother" and delivered a long harangue obviously angry at the French for having erected a permanent structure on his domain without his permission.

The blunt Breton captain was in no mood to mince matters. In his interpretation, Gustave Lanctot writes: "After Cartier had tricked them into coming nearer he had them seized and carried aboard his ship. There he gave them food and drink but forced the chief to agree to two of his sons travelling to France, with the promise to return the youths within a short time." Some writers claim that the chief was Donnacona of Stadacona, others that the old man in the black bearskin was perhaps Donnacona's brother. He might have been some other territorial potentate—Cartier doesn't tell us, and throughout the rest of the first voyage the captives are referred to as "the two savages from Canada." The following year, when the two were brought back to Canada and welcomed by the Indians at Stadacona, the journals name them as "Taignoagny" and "Domagaya."

In any case, the angry chief was sent off mollified with presents of axes and knives and the two captives were soon strutting the deck in French shirts and ribbons, wearing red caps. Later that day, canoes put out from the shore to bring fish to the two Indian youths, and, from sign language, the French got the impression that the natives would not pull down the cross. Cartier didn't wait to check, sailing the next morning around the curve of Cape Gaspé.

While he stood on an east-northeast course, he sighted the shore of Anticosti Island and immediately jumped to the conclusion that it was part of the mainland and that he was in another of those wide, infuriating bays. A half-day's sail would have shown him the mouth of the St. Lawrence River. This day his destiny beckoned, but he was looking the other way. He crossed to Anticosti at about the present Southwest Point, then circled that large, low-lying island to the eastwards, rounded Heath Point and pushed against now-contrary winds into the narrowing *fleuve* between the island and the Quebec mainland. In the vicinity of the Mingan Islands, where the travellers could easily keep both coasts in view, Cartier tried to establish if he was in yet another of the ocean inlets that led only to frustration.

The winds and tides set strongly against the ships, but Cartier made one last determined attempt, putting a longboat crew ashore on Anticosti with orders to go on foot to the most westward point and determine the lay of the land beyond. At Cap de Rabast, they appeared to learn only that the coast began there to swing to the southwest. Back on the ships, the captain is reported to have called a meeting of all hands.

When they had stated one after the other that, considering the heavy east winds that were setting in, and how the tides ran so strong that the vessels only lost way, it was not possible then to go farther. Also, as the storms usually began at that season in Newfoundland and we were still a long way off and did not know the dangers that lay between these two places, it was time to return home or else remain here for the winter. When these opinions had been heard, we decided by a large majority to return home.

It seems a jarring, unreal note, perhaps added by a later amanuensis. Would the master-pilot of St. Malo, the King's choice of commander of the expedition to the New World, hold a town meeting to decide his course? Every leader knows that if he asks his troops if it is to be "forward" or "back," the majority answer will come to venture no further. If Columbus had listened to his crew in the *Santa Maria* he would have turned back three days short of that first sight of America.

Nevertheless, it is true that Cartier *did* turn about on August 1, 1534, and by September 5 his ships were safely back at St. Malo.

CHAPTER EIGHT

The River of Destiny

THE handsome Francis, King of France before his twenty-first birthday, liked wine, women, and war, and became also an inspired patron of the arts. He fought his cousin Charles v of Spain no fewer than four times, revelled in a court life "notable for its licentiousness" at Fountainebleau, and took pains to support men of genius like Leonardo da Vinci, Benvenuto Cellini, and Andrea del Sarto. It is a further mark of his versatility and depth that he also never ceased to encourage Jacques Cartier, the *homme honête* of St. Malo, who brought back only promises to match the treasure from the New World which was pouring into the coffers of Spain.

When Cartier reported the meagre results of his voyage of 1534, hopefully introducing his Indian captives, the King summoned patient enthusiasm, promoted his navigator to the rank of pilot-general, and approved a second expedition for the following spring. Cartier had certainly shown that the Grande Baye was in reality a major inland sea and that great areas of fertile land lay waiting for the plough along the southern shores. But others had been trading and fishing there before him – without aid from the royal purse. Richard Hakluyt wrote in 1600 that Cartier's "principall intention was to seeke out the passage which he presumed might have beene found out into the East Indian Sea, otherwise called the passage to Cathaya," but his discoveries were summed up as being, "as it were, on the backeside of Newfoundland."

The King's hopes probably fastened on the final pages of Cartier's report, which disclosed the strong tides of the sea passage trending westwards between Anticosti – still thought to be part of the mainland – and the Quebec north shore. Cartier had named it St. Peter's Strait, but we now know it as Jacques Cartier Passage. During the winter of 1534-35, as the kidnapped Indian youths were understood to speak, in halting French, of gold and other precious metals in the "Kingdom of Saguenay" beyond their own territory of Canada, the keenest minds of France no doubt asked the prime question – how far did the Strait of St. Peter run? The New World was narrow enough at the Isthmus of Darien where Vasco Balboa first saw the Pacific in 1513. But how broad was it across the northern latitudes? Cartier's new *detroit* was about the same width as the English Channel between Calais and Dover – plenty of seaway for French caravels to reach the Spice Islands! It was an opportunity that had to be taken.

High Admiral Chabot had sent Cartier his fresh commission promptly and the captain busied himself selecting his ships, his sailing masters, and crews, and in ordering provisions for fifteen months. It was thus anticipated that the second expedition would winter somewhere on the route to the Saguenay. Cartier now had the widest powers as commander and he selected three ships of St. Malo: *la Grande Hermine*, of 120 tons; *le Courlieu*, of sixty tons (immediately renamed *la Petite Hermine*); and the handy bark, *l'Emerillon*, of forty tons for shallow-draught work.

Cartier decided to sail the *Grande Hermine* himself, with Thomas Fromont as mate. Macé Jalobert, Cartier's brother-in-law, was appointed captain of the *Petite Hermine*, with Guillaume le Marie as mate. The *Emerillon* was in the hands of Guillaume le Breton Bastille, son of a small landowner near Limoilou, who had another Cartier in-law, Jacques Maingart, as his second-in-command. A brightly plumed bunch of gentlemen-adventurers joined the company, sailing with Cartier himself. These included – significantly – Claude de Pontbriant, son of the Sieur de Montréal,* one of the king's most famous soldiers. There was also Charles de La Pommeraye, a relative of the Canon of St. Malo, Jean de Goyon, Jehan Poullet of Dol, and a few others. The St. Malo archives contain a portion of the crew list for this voyage; it gives seventy-four names, including several seamen bearing the patronyms of Cartier's wide family circle. The total number

---

* The title of *"Sieur"* (from the Latin *"Senior"*) is the origin of the English "Sir," and was the near equivalent of English knighthood.

of men on all three ships–including the returning Indians, Taignoagny and Domagaya–is believed to be one hundred and twelve.

By Sunday, May 15, 1535, all was at last in readiness and the pilot-general commanded all hands to attend Mass in St. Vincent's Cathedral. They received a special blessing from Bishop François Bohier. Three hundred and fifty years later, Honoré Mercier, the Quebec politician and orator, set a plaque in the floor of the cathedral to commemorate the event. Farewells were said, and the ships then had to wait for three days until a favourable wind took them out to sea. For nearly a quarter of them, it was the last time they would see the ramparts of St. Malo.

They were almost a full month behind the departure date of the previous year and they were further delayed by atrocious weather. In mid-Atlantic on June 25, the ships lost sight of each other and the larger flagship arrived alone at the Funk Islands on July 7. Cartier stocked up again with two boatloads of the easy-meat auks, then pushed on through the Strait of Belle Isle to Blanc Sablon–where, according to the sailing plan, all ships were supposed to rendezvous by July 15. It was another eleven days before the two smaller ships arrived together. The *Brief Récit* makes light of the buffeting fifty-day crossing: "Here we refitted, took on wood, fresh water, and other necessaries."

With a dawn start on July 29, Cartier now pressed directly onwards to St. Peter's Strait, eager to put to the test all of the theorizing of the past winter. He closed on the shore of Anticosti, but as in the previous summer, he ran into strong tides and contrary winds. Returning to the Quebec side in the area of the Mingan Islands, he sheltered in "a very fine bay, full of islands and with good entrances and anchorage for any weather. This bay may be known by a large island which stretches out beyond the others like a headland, and on the mainland, some two leagues away, stands a mountain that looks like a shock of wheat. We named this bay St. Lawrence's Bay." In this way, the name of Lawrence–once deacon of Rome, protector of the poor, martyred by fire, revered in Brittany– came to Canadian waters. It was soon to be applied to both the gulf and the great river that drains into it. Cartier himself referred to the river as "the River of Hochelaga," but on Gerhardus Mercator's map of 1569, the saint's name was applied. By Champlain's day, it was affixed for all time.

Pinning down the exact bay in which Cartier took shelter is a geographer's delight. In that district of a hundred coves, it is conceded to be the present Pillage Bay, with the actual anchorage being Ste. Geneviève Harbour. The "large island which stretches out beyond the others" is Ste. Geneviève Island, the most easterly of the Mingan group. The mountain "like a shock of wheat" is the isolated 300-foot limestone hill that is known locally as Mont Ste. Geneviève.

Shortly afterwards, possibly as they began to recognize landmarks which they had once seen from canoes, Domagaya and Taignoagny informed Cartier that the land to the south (Anticosti) was an island, and that beyond it, further south again, lay the route from Honguedo (the Gaspé), where they had been taken captive, to the territory of Canada. It was a river, they indicated, narrowing as it bit deeper and deeper into the land, and no men had been known to reach its source.

It will help us to keep things straight if we remember that in this period, on an upstream journey on the St. Lawrence, the traveller passed through, in order, the tribal hunting grounds, or "countries," of Saguenay, Canada (from Ile aux Coudres to Trois-Rivières), and Hochelaga (centred on the junction of the St. Lawrence and the Ottawa). It is also necessary that we keep in mind that the Iroquois gave the French the impression that the fabulous "Kingdom of Saguenay" was above the Ottawa, and not solely the river and territory of that name today. There is a strong possibility, too, that on top of language confusions, the Indians were simply telling the god-like creatures from the "floating islands" what they urgently wanted to believe.

The excitement must have quickened among the gentlemen in the *Grande Hermine*–the mysterious Saguenay, with its copper mines and hoards of gold, lay straight ahead, only two days' journey through St. Peter's Strait! But Cartier coolly kept his main purpose in mind. He was looking for an ocean passage to the *north*west, and this wide inlet beyond trended to the *south*west. Furthermore, the Indians said that their river turned sweet "at Canada" and only small boats could proceed further. It therefore held scant promise of connecting with the Pacific. After crossing the 60-mile-wide mouth of the river to the Gaspé shore, viewing Mont Louis and the "marvellously high" Notre Dame Mountains, Cartier returned to the north shore of the river. He noted that the water was over six hundred feet deep.

Cartier was determined not to miss a single likely opening along the rugged coast. It should be noted that it was already August 18, more than a fortnight later than the turnabout date of the previous year.

The captain ordered the ships to return and to steer in the opposite direction, and we coasted the north shore, which runs northeast and southwest in the form of a semicircle. On the following day, we came to seven steep islands, which we named the Round Islands. They lie some forty leagues from the south shore, and stretch out into the gulf to a distance of three or four leagues. We coasted in our longboats . . . very dangerous sandbars which become bare at low water.

At the end of this low shore is a river which enters the gulf with such force that the water three miles from shore is still fresh. We entered this river [the Moisie, beyond Sept Iles, Quebec] with our longboats . . . Up this river were several

This fragmentary drawing, though done in the seventeenth century, is believed to represent Cartier's flagship, la Grande Hermine.

fish in appearance like horses which go on land at night but in the day remain in the water, as our Indians informed us. We saw a great number of these fish.

We made our way along the shore until we had examined all the omitted portion and had arrived at Assumption Island [the name Cartier had now given to Anticosti]. When we had made certain that we had examined the whole coast and that no strait existed, we returned to our ships which we had left at the seven islands.

This dogged fruitless loop back to the vicinity of St. Lawrence's Bay must have deeply disappointed Cartier and he probably decided there and then that the Grande Baye would never offer France a fairway to the Indies. But the *Brief Récit* reveals no sign of languishing spirits. The pilot-general turned his bows without comment into the yawning mouth of the river where he was to find his great and lasting fame. That day, Tuesday, August 24, 1535, his destiny beckoned again–and this time he went gladly.

The survey had given a name to Seven Islands, now the outlet for the ore wealth of Knob Lake–richer than

a dozen dreams of Saguenay gems. Cartier, however, had miscounted; there are actually only six of his "Round Islands," the seventh being the peninsula that protects the fine harbour (it looks like an island from a distance). Cartier's generally excellent charting was soon incorporated in maps like Pierre Descelier's six-foot sheepskin world map, drawn at Arques, near Dieppe, in 1550. This map places the Seven Islands accurately enough at 50° north latitude. On the southern shore a later cartographer was to inscribe Cartier's own name on the peak that rises above the Shickshock Mountains in Gaspé National Park–Mont Jacques Cartier, at 4,160 feet the highest mountain in eastern Canada.

The excerpt above also appears to indicate that more than one hand wrote the journals. The "fish in appearance like horses" in the Moisie were walruses (quoting H. P. Biggar), but they are here described by someone who is obviously seeing them for the first time. Cartier had seen and described walruses "like large oxen" at Brion Island in the gulf the previous year. No man could forget what a walrus looked like.

An artist, working three centuries after the fact, has attempted to re-create the drama of Cartier's arrival at Stadacona.

Another clue was spotlighted by Professor Stephen Leacock. Simple sailing directions are presented in muddled fashion in the narratives, not as they would come naturally to a most experienced navigator.

Pressing into that river, one of the world's major waterways, until that day unknown to the European record, the discoverers were awed and excited as the outline of first one shore and then the other rose above the racing tides. For five days, the three ships moved upstream, clinging first to the north shore, around Pointe des Monts and on to the Manicouagan, then across to the wooded Ile du Bic, and into Bic Harbour, a few miles below Rimouski. Word of their coming raced ahead along the forest trails. After a two-day halt, they swung on a long tack to the opposite shore to examine the dark, dramatic cleft of the Saguenay exit. Strangely, there is no talk of gold or gems – the narrative merely comments that this was "the river and route to the Kingdom of Saguenay, as we were informed by our two *hommes du pays de Canada*." They entered the mouth of the river, where Cartier on September 1 described the site of Tadoussac – in the Indian tongue it means "breasts" – where Pierre Chauvin was to build the first permanent house in Canada and the *Récollet* father, Jean Dolbeau, was to set up the first mission to *les sauvages*.

At the mouth of the river, we found four canoes from Canada that had come to fish for seals and other fish. When we had anchored, two of the canoes came towards us, but in such fear and trembling that one of them finally went back. The other approached near enough to hear one of our Indians who gave his name and told who he was and encouraged them come alongside...

We made sail and got under way...and discovered a species of fish which none of us had known before. It was as large as a porpoise but has no fins. It is very similar to a greyhound about the body and head and is as white as snow, without a spot on it. There are a very large number in this river, living between the salt and the fresh water. The people call them "adhothuys" and say they are very savoury and good to eat.

The Frenchmen were marvelling at the beluga, or

white whale. They caught hares on the Ile aux Liè-vres, and further upstream, at the gateway to the Kingdom of Canada, they picked bushels of hazel nuts on the Ile aux Coudres – bigger and better filberts than were to be found anywhere in France. The 6-mile-long island was fringed with reefs and the diarist noted the stakes of nets set by the Indians to catch the small whales. The nut island was the scene of what is generally said to be the first Mass said in Canada, on Tuesday, September 7, 1535 – perhaps forgetting the reported service at Brest, high up the gulf the previous year. Actually, it is a hotly argued question as to whether or not Cartier ever brought any priests to Canada. There is no concrete evidence. A granite cross today marks the spot where he is believed to have come ashore on the island.

The river was closing in, a dozen or more islands loomed ahead, and Cartier chose to anchor between the largest island and the north shore. Noting the profusion of wild grapevines, the French called the place the Isle of Bacchus – though Cartier also referred to it by the name that stuck: "Ile d'Orléans." Only five miles beyond lay another place with a name that would be remembered – "Kebec," the place where the river narrows.

We came upon several natives who would not come near until our two Indians had spoken to them. When they had made their acquaintance, they began to welcome them, dancing and going through many ceremonies. Some of the headmen came to our longboats, bringing eels and other fish [including sturgeon] and some Indian corn and large pumpkins. During that day, many canoes came to see and speak with Domagaya and Taignoagny. The captain received them all hospitably, giving them some small presents.

The next morning, September 8, le seigneur de Canada, Donnacona, came to our ships with a large party of men in twelve canoes. Ten canoes waited back while the chief with two canoes first went close to the Emerillon. *He began to make a speech, jerking his body about as is their custom when showing joy. Then he came to where "Grande Her-mine" was anchored and he spoke to Taignoagny and Domagaya. They told him what they had seen in France and of the good treatment they had received. The chief was very pleased and asked the captain to stretch out his arms to him that he might hug and kiss him, which is the way they welcome one.*

The captain stepped down into the canoe of this agou-hanna *[chieftain] and ordered food and drink to be brought for the Indians. When this had been done they were much pleased . . . and the parties took leave of each other.*

It is a curiously touching scene, this "state welcome" by Donnacona to Cartier. The episode obviously made a deep impression on the chronicler. There was a certain dignity and pride, conveying the sense of an important meeting of equals, and none of the kowtowing or grovelling that the "white gods" from Europe

often found on arrival in other new lands. The convoy of twelve canoes immediately brings to mind any modern president with his flanking limousines and motorcycle squads.

In many of the books that have been inspired by Cartier's voyages, there are often a few pages devoted to the question of the exact tribal affiliation of the two Indians who were kidnapped by Cartier at Gaspé in 1534. It is the kind of dusty debate that academics delight in. Were the captives truly "recognized" at Ile d'Orléans as men of Canada, and of Stadacona particularly? Or just as Indians with a marvellous tale to tell? There are several references in the two relevant narratives which support the view that Taignoagny and Domagaya were either sons or nephews of Donnacona. But the European scribe is here, of course, imposing a European concept of family relationships on the tribal nature of Indian society. Also, would it not be unusually high coincidence if the names of two Indian youths who were picked up at the Gaspé were recognized by natives four hundred miles away more than a year afterwards? Modern knowledge of tribal movements and communications counsels that it *would* be unusual.

Some analysts question if "Taignoagny" and "Domagaya" were, in fact, the proper names of the captives. No names were allotted to them in the journal of the 1534 voyage and it is suggested that these names were spontaneously given to them by the welcoming Indians at Stadacona in 1535 – the words being in some way descriptive of the incredible adventures they reported having had in France. To make things more puzzling, throughout the *Brief Récit*, "Domagaya" is written *"dom Agaya,"* and it is accepted that in this period the prefix "Dom" denoted priestly status. During his winter in Brittany, was that member of the Canadian pair introduced to the Church and given, just in informal affection, a priestly title. In any event, it was Domagaya who remained the staunchest friend of the French – even to being the kindly agent in saving the lives of at least half the company.

It is another absorbing study to pinpoint and then explore the river bank where Pilot-General Cartier ordered his ships to tie up and where, as he spent and suffered the severe winter of 1535-36, so many "firsts" were set into Canadian history. Here is how Cartier saw it all:

The Captain ordered out our longboats to go upstream with the tide and find a harbour and safe spot in which to tie up the ships. We came to a forking of the waters, an exceedingly pleasant spot, where there is a small river and a harbour with a bar, on which at high tide there is a depth of from two to three fathoms. We thought this river [the narrator is referring to the St. Charles, a small tributary from the north joining the St. Lawrence at Quebec] a suitable place and we named it Ste. Croix.

Near this place lives a tribe of which this Donnacona is

chief, and he himself resides there. The village is called Stadacona. This region is as good land as it is possible to find anywhere, being fertile and covered with the same kinds of trees as in France—oak, elm, walnut, yew, cedar, hawthorn, and others.

After visiting the river, the Captain was returning to the ship when he saw one of the headmen of the Stadacona Indians coming to meet us, with several men, women, and children. He began to make a speech, expressing joy and contentment "a la facon du pays," while "les femmes" danced and sang, being in the water up to their knees. The Captain ordered the longboat to go toward them and gave them some knives and beads. When we were three miles away, we could still hear them singing and rejoicing.

The next day, the first small dark cloud drifted over this Canadian Eden. Cartier ordered his ships to move from the anchorage off Ile d'Orléans into the St. Charles, leaving the *Emerillon* just offshore but taking the others over the bar upstream to where the Lairet creek debouched. Here, they were grounded for the winter. The Lairet was only a dozen feet wide at low tide, but since the tide there rises fifteen feet, Cartier's *Grande Hermine* could get up at high water. Today, the Quebec docks face the site. Twenty-five canoes came to welcome the Frenchmen, but Taignoagny and Domagaya, "who were completely changed in their attitude and goodwill," refused to come aboard. Cartier asked the two former captives if they would still guide him upstream to Hochelaga, "the place where the river is obstructed." They replied that they would do so, but at this time the French "began somewhat to distrust them."

The early historians, often whitewashing their heroes, express puzzlement as to why Domagaya and Taignoagny should turn sour. Yet they had, for one thing, just escaped from what can only be termed a year's captivity. Few white men could believe that an Indian would, if he had the choice, prefer the forest and the longhouse to the European city and the delights of modern society. For another, they had seen the harbours of Brittany choked with sail, blacksmiths at their forges, the tables groaning with food, the burghers in Sunday velvets and crisp linen, the spiralling cathedrals with their gold plate, ornamented statues, and silver chalices—and they compared all this with the paltry tin rings, glass beads, and cheap knives with which Cartier sought to buy tribal goodwill. Finally, the two travellers had in all likelihood come under Donnacona's orders to try to prevent the white men with their metal and cloth goods from extending their largesse to the next competing tribal group. In this, the chief's intentions are clear—to a people who lived half the year on the fringe of starvation, the material wealth of the white man was a prize of immeasurable value and one not willingly relinquished.

The exact position of Stadacona—a fortified Iroquois village of large communal huts—is difficult to fix. But historians have painstakingly set it down on what is now St. Geneviève Hill in modern Quebec City. It lay under the north brow of the rearing rock that Cartier was to name Cap aux Diamants. (Some writers claim that it was a Montagnais village, temporarily occupied by the Iroquois.)

Cartier, in a summary of his findings, spoke of the settlement at Quebec: "Here the river becomes narrow, swift, and deep, and only a quarter of a league in width." He spoke also of other adjacent Indian villages completely lost to our records. He called them Ajoaste, Starnatum, Sitadin, and Tailla. The last-named was said to be "on a mountain" and the others were on the string of islands threaded by the river below Quebec Basin. Above the narrows lay Tequenonday and Achelacy (at today's Portneuf), with Hochelaga (the Montreal-to-be) in the far distance.

Cartier also reported the presence of much game, stags and bears—including a mysterious "beast with only two legs whose tracks we followed over sand and mud for a long way." He noted wild cats, squirrels, muskrats, foxes, otters, beavers, martens, and wild geese, ducks, and pigeons. After his keen interest in the white whales of the lower river, he listed mackerel, mullet, salmon, lampreys, pike, trout, carp, bream, and "as good smelts as in the Seine."

The Indians, he noted wryly, were not men "of great labour," but they did painstakingly fell trees with fire and stone axes to clear land which the women tilled. Corn was hoed with a wooden stick "about half a sword in length," and melons, pumpkins, cucumbers, peas, and beans were grown. The women worked much harder than the men at fishing, gathering firewood, and manufacturing clothing from skins. A certain curious custom of the tribesmen fascinated Cartier, and it was he—not Sir Walter Raleigh—who first brought tobacco to the notice of Europe. Here, in an old English translation—to match the original old French—is the relevant excerpt:

There groweth also a certaine kind of herbe whereof in Sommer they make great provision for all the yeere, making great account of it, and onely men use of it, and first they cause it to be dried in the sunne, then weare it about their necks wrapped in a little beast skinne made like a little bagge, with a hollow peece of stone or wood like a pipe: then when they please they make powder of it, and then put in one of the ends of the said Cornet or pipe, and laying a cole or fire upon it, at the other ende sucke so long, that they fill their bodies with smoke, till that it commeth out of their mouth and nostrils, even as out of the Tonnell of a chimneh. They say that this doth keepe them warm and in health: they never goe without some of it about them. We our selves have tryed the same smoke, and having put it in our mouthes, it seemeth almost as hot as Pepper.

Relations continued to be troubled at Stadacona as Cartier's skippers set out buoys in the river and began other preparations for the wintering settlement. On September 15, a large group of Indians came from the village to watch, their awe dwindling rapidly. Chief Donnacona, the two Indian interpreters, and a group of headmen stayed aloof at a distance on the point across the St. Charles. Cartier decided to prick the bubble and marched up to the group with a squad of armed men. Taignoagny seemed to be ringleader in the discontent and he now informed the French commander that his chief was offended that Cartier's men always carried so many weapons while the Indians carried none. Cartier replied calmly that it was the custom in France to carry weapons and that his men would continue to do so in Canada. His suspicion of Indian intentions was already so sharp that he would never have fallen for such a transparent ruse. Even at full strength, the French at Stadacona that autumn were outnumbered five to one.

The next day, Donnacona brought a dozen of his headmen to the *Grande Hermine*, where Cartier fed them and gave them presents. Taignoagny then told Cartier that the chief was angry because the Captain still intended to go further upriver to Hochelaga, not accepting the chief's word that the trip would be worthless. The interpreters had been forbidden to go.

Cartier continued to deal his cards face up. He had been commanded by King Francis "to complete the discovery of the western lands" and he intended to carry out his orders–come what may. It was both threat and warning. But he would be handicapped without the interpreters who had been trained so laboriously in France and he tried to tempt Taignoagny "with a present that would please him." Both the Indians, however, refused. According to the narrative, Cartier now decided that Taignoagny was worthless and malicious and that he was not truly representing the views of Donnacona. From this long distance, and considering the research now available in analysis of Indian behavioural patterns, it appears more likely that the chief was closely directing the whole affair.

If the withdrawal of the guides and interpreters wouldn't work, would bribery succeed? Bringing eels and other freshly caught fish as gifts, Donnacona arrived at Cartier's chosen ground, where the two larger ships were already beached, on the morning of Friday, September 17. The crowding villagers began to sing and dance. Then the chief ordered all his people to stand to one side, and he drew a large circle in the sand with a stick. He invited Cartier's party to stand inside the ring. Donnacona now began one of his celebrated long harangues, the meaning of which did not get through to the Frenchmen. Perhaps that was just as well, as the chief was holding a girl of about twelve by the hand, and he now presented her to Cartier as a gift. All the Indians shouted three times: "Ho! Ho! Ho!" (The narrator says that these were "cries in sign of joy and alliance.") Next, Donnacona led two small boys into the ring and gave them to the Captain.

Taignoagny stepped forward and the French understood him to say that the girl was one of Donnacona's nieces and that one of the boys was Taignoagny's brother. One of the earliest translators, John Florio, who produced an English version in 1580 of Giovanni Battista Ramusio's Italian account from the monumental *Navigationi e viaggi*, complicated the situation with a translation error which had Donnacona stating that one of the lads was *his* brother. The combination of this erroneous relationship with the one claimed between the interpreter and the boy has led to endless confusion, particularly in assessing the blood relationship, if any, between Taignoagny and Donnacona. In any event, Cartier grasped clearly that the human presents were offered on the condition that he promise not to proceed with the expedition to Hochelaga. He immediately refused them, adding that nothing would induce him to cancel his plans.

The narrative runs that the more sympathetic figure, Domagaya, interjected–*after* Cartier's indignant refusal–that Donnacona had meant Cartier to have the girl and the boys "out of affection and in sign of alliance." Then Domagaya and Taignoagny held what seemed to be a public argument, which apparently convinced Cartier of the chief's intentions because he had the "gifts" sent aboard his ship.

The Captain decided to show himself equally generous and sent servants to fetch two swords and two brass basins as presents for Donnacona.

It was the next act in the tight little melodrama which brought the blast of cannon fire to the river. The *agouhanna* asked Cartier to fire his guns, about which he had heard from the interpreters. For his own good reasons no doubt, Cartier decided to fire a broadside of twelve cannon "with their shot into the woods that stood opposite to the ships and the Indians." (If the narrator reports the number of guns correctly, it would be a difficult manoeuvre, as the *Grande Hermine* probably had at the most only six guns per side and the *Petite Hermine* two per side. Using ball, it's hard to see how a dozen guns could be fired simultaneously "into the woods that stood opposite.") In any event, the noise and flame of the explosion, the press of the blast, were enough to set the Indians "to howl and shriek, that one would have thought hell had emptied itself there." Another translator hit a more popular line: "It seemed hell had broken loose."

As if on cue, Taignoagny now claimed that two tribesmen had been killed by the guns of the *Emerillon*. At this news, "all scurried off in such haste that one would have thought we had wished to destroy them." In Hakluyt's *Voyages*, Taignoagny is described as a "craftie knave," but this time he outsmarted himself. The *Emerillon* had not joined in the barrage.

Donnacona had one last convincer to stage. It was his masterwork. It involved Christ and the Devil, the Virgin Mary, perfect timing, fiery monologues, the Canadian climate, sorcerers, messages of doom–all within a script that would put most television playwrights to shame.

THE FIRST CANADIANS

More than five centuries passed between the brief Viking efforts to establish a Vinland colony and Champlain's attempts to reach the "Western Sea." In those five hundred years, the face of Europe was transformed dramatically – while the natives of Canada remained steadfast in their ways. Admirably adapted to their environment, the Indians subsisted as hunters, farmers, and traders, preserving a mode of life which was already ancient when the Pyramids were built.

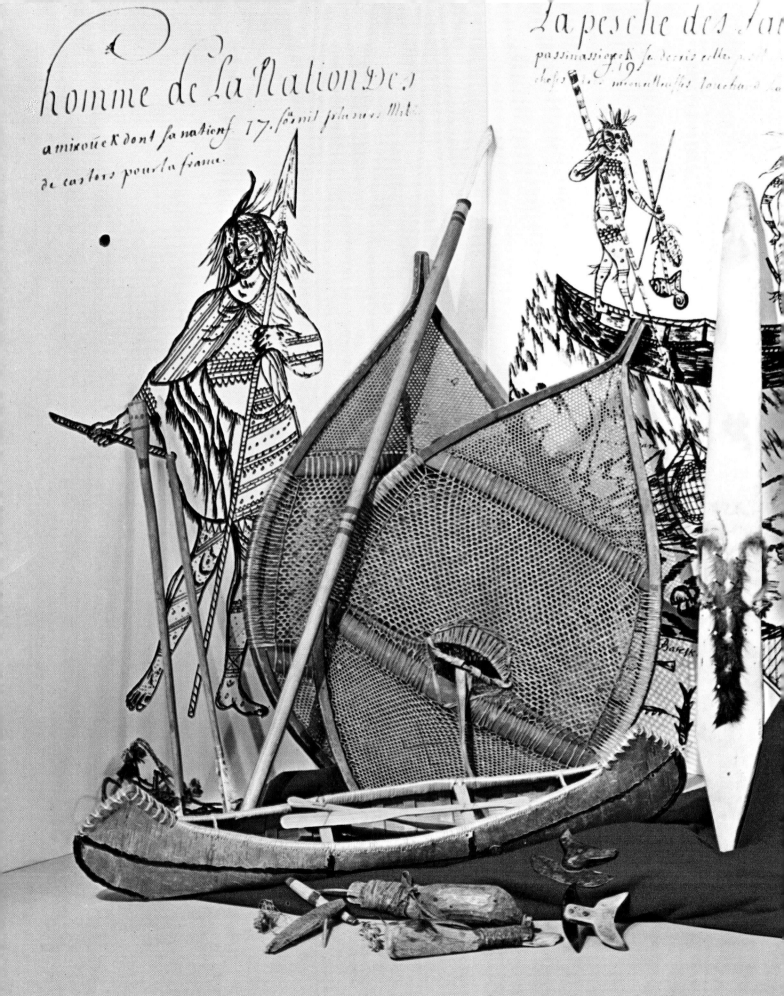

NOMADS OF FOREST AND ROCKLAND

In all likelihood, among the tribes that the early Viking expeditions met were Algonkian Indians, members of the vast family of tribes that ranged from the Beothuks of Newfoundland to the Cree and Blackfoot of the central plains. In the eastern half of this broad area lived Micmacs and Malecites, Naskapi and Montagnais, Algonquins and Ojibway—nomadic tribes who hunted, fished, and trapped through more than a thousand miles of rugged Laurentian woodland. Though most of the objects displayed here are products of the Naskapi, they permit us to visualize, in broad

outline, the life of the Algonkians generally. Thus, the snowshoes and model canoe represent the primary means of transportation. The decorated bear skull, a ceremonial object, was used in rituals designed to foster good hunting. Other items, more utilitarian in nature, include a spear, arrows, wooden fish-hooks, fleshers, and semilunar knives. On the right, a beaver skin is stretched on a wooden frame; to the left of centre, a mink pelt. With the coming of the white man, furs such as these became the object of a thriving trade and the basis of a new way of life.

THE PEOPLE OF THE LONGHOUSE

When Cartier reached Hochelaga in the fall of 1535, he discovered a large, palisaded village surrounded by fields of corn. This encampment, containing about fifty longhouses and several hundred people, was the typical form of Iroquois habitation. The Iroquois—a confederacy of five tribes, including Mohawks, Oneidas, Onondagas, Cayugas, and Senecas—were centred in the area that is today New York and Vermont. Having made the crucial transition from hunting to agriculture, they were able to support large, semipermanent communities. For this reason, they are often described as *sedentary* tribes—as opposed to the *migratory* Algonkians to the north.

Arrayed here is a selection of goods from both cultures—Algonkian and Iroquoian. The mortar and pestle, used to grind kernels, emphasizes the importance of corn as a staple item in the diet of the Iroquois. The strip of wampum (at the base of the mortar) was also used by the Iroquois—for the purpose of recording treaties and conveying messages, as well as a form of currency. The maple-sap bucket, birch-bark box, and long-stemmed pipe are Algonkian in origin. The latter object reminds us that to the Europeans of Cartier's time, the smoking of tobacco was a complete novelty—and a pleasure to which few responded favourably on first acquaintance.

WARRIOR
AND
MYSTIC

Of the artifacts shown above, the awesome weapons and colourful prisoner cord reflect the war-like nature of the Iroquois. Proud and dauntless warriors, they were greatly feared by their enemies. They have been characterized by some writers as "the kinsmen of the wolves" and "the Prussian Junkers of the Indians." The burnished war clubs and steel-headed tomahawk indicate the marked change in intertribal warfare which accompanied the spread of European trade goods. What had been traditionally an intermittent testing of territorial boundaries became, in the seventeenth century, a desperate and ruinous struggle for control of the growing trade in furs.

Quite apart from their renowned abilities as warriors, the Iroquois were also much concerned with matters of religion. The grotesque masks shown here were the accoutrements of the False Face societies, witch-doctor groups whose ceremonies were intended to combat adverse influences, both spiritual and physical. The several types of rattle—also used in False Face rituals— were made from a variety of materials: gourds, turtle shells, deer hooves, and bison horns. The white pouch attached to the rattle on the left contains a small quantity of tobacco, a substance considered sacred by the Iroquois and used as an offering on all important occasions.

CANADA'S FIRST FEMINISTS

In all the tribes of the northeastern woodlands, women played an important role. Among the Iroquois–unlike our own patterns of kinship and descent–the "head of the family" was a woman, and property and possessions passed from mother to daughter–rather than from father to son. Under a different moral code, a woman might bear children to different fathers, but her blood would run in all her offspring. Women owned the longhouses, and the headwoman in certain clans selected chieftains. Thus the feared Iroquois offered an early example of a matriarchal society.

CHAPTER NINE

The View from Mount Royal

IN his search for a gateway to the Orient, the dimly known land of Hochelaga was Cartier's last fading hope. He was already 850 miles from the open Atlantic and he had learned that it was only about 150 more miles to where the great river became impassable. But then there was talk of a lake just beyond a roaring *sault*, with the river bearing on always west-by-south, with more rapids, more lakes, beyond where man had ever travelled. Furthermore, there was this *other* big river, the one that came into Hochelaga directly from the west, the one that seemed to be the main route to the riches of the Saguenay. It also led to some great fresh-water sea, known only by hearsay to the Iroquois of the St. Lawrence. But if there was any gold or other precious metal, surely Donnacona would mount some display. Yet the Indians were incomparably poorer in material goods than the lowliest peasant in Brittany. Moreover, there could be no road here to the Spice Islands either – these people did not even flavour their food with salt!

Another less-dutiful commander might have decided that, considering his main purpose, further river exploration was not only a waste of effort, but decidedly dangerous. True, the Indians had nowhere offered any violence to the French, but Cartier was disturbed by the latest manifestations. To push on to Hochelaga would require a sizeable body of armed men – and the force at Stadacona, already greatly outnumbered, would be left that much weaker.

There is no indication that Cartier ever considered halting in the face of the opposition of the Indians at Stadacona, and this time there was no "town meeting" called to seek other opinion. He selected the party for Hochelaga – himself, Macé Jalobert, Guillaume le Breton, the gentlemen-adventurers, and fifty armed sailors (roughly half his total strength) – and quietly ordered those remaining to begin fortifying the wintering depot on the St. Charles. He planned to leave in the *Emerillon* on Sunday, September 19, 1535. On the Saturday, Donnacona staged his miracle play, designed to shake the French in their determination.

The curtain rose on the usual mass approach to the ships by the villagers of Stadacona to observe the activities of their endlessly fascinating visitors. But on this morning, they did not emerge from the woods on the point opposite the St. Charles – instead, they waited there for about two hours, to the puzzlement of the French. Then, as if on signal, they moved onto the beach in front of the ships, still keeping a greater distance than usual. The tide had now turned and was running strongly.

All heads suddenly turned to midstream where a canoe appeared carrying some unearthly beings. Wearing horns "as long as one's arm," dressed in black and white dogskin, their faces coloured black, three Indians floated down close to the moored ships. The weird figure in the middle of the canoe made "a wonderful harangue," but the craft slipped by on the tide without the "devils" once turning their faces to the French – who were both astonished and amused. The canoe was then run ashore, where it was seized by a group led by Donnacona himself. The medicine men now played dead and both canoe and occupants were carried into the forest, a stone's throw from the *Grande Hermine*. For about thirty minutes, only the sounds of loud voices emerged, but then Domagaya and Taignoagny appeared, holding hands, their caps under their arms.

"Jesus! Jesus! Jesus!" intoned Taignoagny, raising his eyes to heaven. Domagaya chimed in with, "Jesus! Maria! Jacques Cartier!" When Cartier inquired solicitously what had happened, the pair told him there was bad news. The men in the canoe had been emissaries from the god Cudouagny, who had made a pronouncement at Hochelaga saying that if the white men tried to travel that way there would be so much ice and snow that all would be frozen to death.

The French could not restrain their laughter and told the Indians that Jesus would keep them safe from the cold. Taignoagny shrewdly asked Cartier if he had spoken to Jesus and the Captain countered by saying that his priests had. (He was perhaps founding this on the blessing the expedition had received before sailing from St. Malo.) The interpreters went back to the forest after this exchange and all the Indians then "at once came forth pretending to be pleased at what the Captain had said."

A little later, Taignoagny and Domagaya made one final, and obscure, bid to alter Cartier's plan. They said that Donnacona would not permit them to accompany the French unless Cartier left a hostage with the chief. The *Brief Récit* says that Cartier refused this offer out of hand, saying that if the Indians were not prepared to go willingly, he would rather go without them. Since he fully intended to return from Hochelaga in plenty of time to beat the arrival of winter, and since the fate of those left in garrison would be sealed anyway if he did not return with the captains, it is hard to see why the pragmatic Cartier didn't at least investigate that offer. He was to be severely handicapped without his interpreters, and our knowledge of the first men on Montreal Island is the poorer.

Right on schedule, Le Breton, the master of the *Emerillon*, ordered her anchors raised and moved off on the Sunday morning tide. Now begins one of the great idylls of Canadian history. Through the 3,000-foot gap where the Laurentian Shield thrusts to the river bank, the forty-ton bark moved upstream, towing two long-boats ready for any shallows. Beyond the point where the Quebec Bridge was to be thrown across in a later era, the river broadened to two miles and the land smoothed out into alluvial plains, which the narrator described lyrically.

Along both shores we saw and discovered the finest and most beautiful land it is possible to see, being as level as a pond and covered with the most magnificent trees in the world. On the banks were so many vines loaded with grapes that it seemed they must have been planted by farmers. But because they are never cultivated, the grapes are not so sweet nor so large as French grapes . . . The sailors came on board with arms full of them.

We saw oaks, elms, walnuts, pines, cedars, spruce, ash, boxwood, and willows. There are likewise many cranes, geese, swans, bustards, partridges, pheasant, thrushes, turtledoves, larks, blackbirds, goldfinches, canaries, linnets, nightingales,* sparrows, and other birds.

We noticed a large number of huts along the banks, and these Indians catch great quantities of the many good varieties of fish in the river. These people came towards our boats in as friendly and as familiar manner as if we had been natives of the country, bringing us fish or whatever else they possessed in order to trade, stretching their hands towards heaven and making many gestures of joy.

One of these Indians took the captain in his arms and

Though it does not portray Hochelaga in a realistic manner, this drawing does show the longhouses and palisades that were typical of

MONTE REAL

---

* North America has no nightingales. Cartier's men probably heard the song sparrow or thrush. His turtledoves were no doubt passenger pigeons, and his cranes were the great blue heron.

carried him on shore as easily as if he had been a six-year-old child, so strong and big was that Indian. We discovered that they caught many muskrats which live in the water and are as large as rabbits and very good to eat.

Of the ecstatic welcome, there could be no doubt. Thirty miles upstream, at the foot of the Richelieu rapids, there was the village which the French termed "Achelacy" (and sometimes "Hochelay"). Here, the *agouhanna* came out with several canoes and gave Cartier due warning of the dangers of the *sault* that extended intermittently for ten miles over hidden boulders and shoals. He also tried to give Cartier two of his children, a girl and a boy. The Captain accepted the girl "of about eight or nine years," but refused the boy as being too young. Cartier gave "a small present" in return, and continued his odyssey.

After nine days, during which time the Captain kept them moving "without losing a day or an hour," the French passed the several mouths of the St. Maurice at Trois-Rivières, and shortly, when the river widened to eight miles, they thought they were at the beginning of a great lake. To honour their sovereign's family, they called it Lac d'Angoulesme—the King had been Francis of Angoulême before he succeeded his cousin, King Louis XII. (When Champlain reached the spot on St. Peter's day sixty-eight years later, he renamed the lake for the saint.) Guillaume le Breton was worried about the keel of his ship all the way up the lake's twenty miles—nowhere could he find more than twelve feet of water. He noted that here the ocean and river met as equals and the tidal influence went no higher.

When the lake narrowed again, at the islands between present-day Sorel and Berthierville, Cartier sent out the longboats to try to find the best channel leading to Hochelaga. As is normal in the fall, the water was at its lowest level and the travellers could see by the high-water mark that in the spring there would be another dozen feet of water over the shoals and sandbars. When a deep enough channel could not be found, Cartier decided he would have to split his party again. The Indians had told him that it was only three days' journey to Hochelaga, so he now armed and provisioned the longboats and embarked in them, taking his skippers, Jalobert and Le Breton, Claude du Pontbriant, Jehan Poullet, Charles de La Pommeraye, Jean de Goyon, and twenty-six mariners. The rest of the company remained in the *Emerillon*, which was anchored near the mouth of the Richelieu River.

Over the final forty-five miles, the strong arms of the Breton sailors pulled the boats to Hochelaga against the current, arriving at their destination, a thousand miles from the Atlantic, on the afternoon of Saturday, October 2.

No Doge of Venice in his golden gondola ever received a more tumultuous welcome. This was the scene as described by an eyewitness, when Cartier's boat touched the hill-crowned island, at the down-

Iroquois villages. The picture appeared in Delle Navigationi aet Viaggi, *a book written by Gian Battista Ramusio in 1606.*

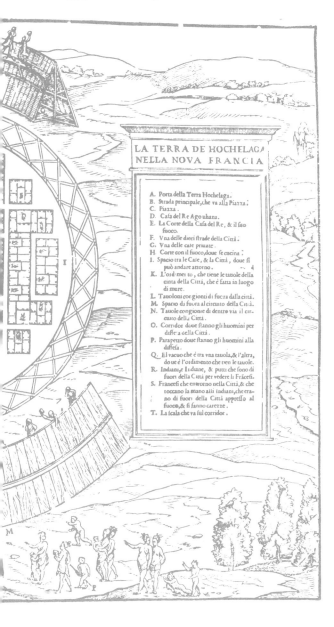

stream end of the riffle called St. Mary's current, where the Montreal docks stand today:

There came to meet us more than a thousand persons, men, women, and children, making great signs of pleasure. The men danced in one ring, the women in another, and the children also apart by themselves. They then brought us fish and corn bread, throwing so much of it into our boats that it seemed to be raining bread. The Captain and several of his men now went ashore and the Indians crowded about them, the women bringing their babies for us to touch. The welcome lasted for half an hour.

The Captain placed all the women sitting in a row and gave them some beads. To some of the men he gave knives. He then returned to the boats to have his supper and sleep. The Indians stayed on the shore, keeping a string of fires burning and shouting excitedly.

At daybreak, the Captain put on his armour, left a corporal's guard over the boats, and marched twenty men to pay a formal call to the home of these people, and to visit the mountain which he could see nearby. Three Indians conducted us along a well-trodden path, amid many oak trees, the ground being covered with acorns.

It must have been a chilly day (as October can easily provide in Montreal), because the Indians had thoughtfully provided a fire at a halfway point and suggested that the French rest there awhile. Men in the breastplates of the day probably welcomed the halt. The chief (curiously, he is never named) made a speech at this point, just as the mayors of our time are likely to do when anyone sits down. Cartier needed no prompting and loaded the chief down with two hatchets, two knives, and a crucifix. He held the cross to the Indian's lips to be kissed, then hung it around his neck.

The path now cut through cultivated fields of ripe maize. This area may have contained several hundred acres, with family plots marked off in some manner. Cartier called it "the corn of the country" and his repeated interest in it was well merited – the domestication of maize by the Indians ranks as one of the major feats of horticulture. Primitive varieties were being grown in Mexico more than 3,500 years ago, and the seed corn came north up the chain of tribes on the eastern seaboard of the continent. The Iroquois – now idolizing the French, later to be their bitterest enemy – may themselves have had their tribal beginnings in the far south. It is a story lost in the mists, and the written history of the Canadian Indian begins substantially with Jacques Cartier.

In the middle of the fields was the fortified town of Hochelaga, now considered to have stood in the area of the modern City of Montreal, south of Sherbrooke Street, below McGill University. Skeletons and old fireplaces have been found there. The narrator of this voyage left us the only description extant of the place (it had vanished by Champlain's time):

The town is circular, enclosed by a palisade of poles lashed together in three tiers like a pyramid, the whole structure being about sixteen feet high. There is only one entrance, a barred gate. Over the gateway and around the walls are galleries with ladders where stones are piled ready to drop on the heads of attackers. There are about fifty houses in the village, fifty paces long and between ten and fifteen paces in width, built of sticks and covered in with large pieces of bark. Inside are many rooms, and in the middle a large space where they light their fires and live in common.

Similar Iroquois villages would later be found elsewhere, with longhouses measuring as much as one hundred feet.

Cartier's party was led into the open square in the middle of the town and immediately mobbed by the women. They touched or rubbed the Frenchmen's faces, arms, and chests, and indicated that they wanted the visitors to put their hands on their babies. The women were weeping for joy. The menfolk now took over and seated themselves in a circle around the French "as if we were about to perform a play." Some women brought in woven mats which were placed in the middle of the square and invited the French to sit on them. Then the *agouhanna* was carried in on a stag-skin throne by ten tribesmen.

The chieftain was crippled – "full of the palsy" – probably with acute rheumatism, and he pointed to his arms and legs, inviting Cartier to touch them. The humble Breton, devoutly religious, was no doubt deeply affected and embarrassed by this trusting faith in his powers. Nevertheless, he made a show of rubbing the chief's limbs and the Indian then took off the band of red skin he was wearing in lieu of a crown and handed it to Cartier. Other sick and crippled villagers now crowded in so that the Captain could lay hands on them and, the journal continues, "one would have thought Jesus Christ had come down to earth to heal them."

Cartier was probably appalled at the situation, but he acted with judgement that would have graced an emperor born. He read the Gospel according to St. John – "In the beginning was the Word, and the Word was with God, and the Word was God ... All things were made by Him" – and made the sign of the cross over the sick, praying that God would bring them to baptism and life everlasting. The Indians listened to the strange, meaningless words, copying any gestures they noted among the French. Cartier then distributed more presents, letting the children scramble for trinkets. As a finale, he ordered a flourish of trumpets, "whereat the Indians were much delighted."

Cartier was determined to climb the hill that rose eight hundred feet behind the village and from its summit take a searching look into the hinterland. Could this possibly be the Tartary of Marco Polo, "the extremity of Asia"? Would the reported sweet-water seas beyond give birth to rivers other than the

It is evident from this engraving of Cartier's ascent of the St. Lawrence that the artist never set foot on Canadian soil.

one he knew, rivers that would flow west and north, carrying small boats at least to the other ocean of Magellan? Cartier loyally named the long-extinct volcano "Mont-Royal"–and, as millions of sightseers have done since, he described the sweeping impressive sight.

On reaching the summit, we had a view of the land for more than thirty leagues [ninety miles] around. Towards the north, there is a range of mountains running east and west [we call them the Laurentians], and another range to the south [the Adirondacks]. Between, lies the finest land it is possible to see, level and arable. In the middle of this flat territory is the river [St. Lawrence], extending beyond the spot where we left our longboats to a most violent rapids [Lachine]. As far as the eye can reach, one sees that river, large, wide, and broad, which came from the southwest and flowed near three fine conical mountains [mounts Rouge-mont, St. Bruno, and St. Hilaire, near Beloeil] which we estimated to be some fifteen leagues away.

It was made clear by signs by our Indian guides that there were three more such rapids in that river, and after passing them one could navigate along that river for more than three moons. And they showed us that along the mountains to the north there is a large river [the Ottawa] . . . We thought this river must be the one that flows past the Kingdom of the Saguenay.

Without asking any questions or making any sign, they seized the chain of the Captain's whistle, which was made of

silver, and a dagger-handle of yellow copper-gilt like gold and gave us to understand that these metals came from up that river, where lived the agojuda, *which means hostile people, who were well armed, using an armour made of wood laced with cords. They also seemed to say that these people waged war continually, one tribe against the other, but through not understanding their language, we could not make out what the distance was to that country.*

It had been a long and exciting day, one of the most significant in our national story. Cartier's men were growing tired as they clambered back down the slopes of Mount Royal and the Indians picked them up effortlessly and carried them down "as on horseback." There is no whisper of apprehension in the journals to this point, but as soon as they reached the longboats, Cartier insisted on an immediate departure "for fear of any misadventure." The Indians, on the other hand, showed "great regret" at the departure of their guests and followed them by canoe for some distance.

On Monday, October 4, the longboat crews enjoying the downstream current reached the *Emerillon*, tied up in the vicinity of today's Sorel. We can easily imagine the eager questions asked by the party that had remained as guard for the ship and Cartier replying stiffly, perhaps, that, no, he had found no gold, nothing of material worth to a king whose treasury had been emptied by European wars, just another primitive Indian town perched on the side of a mountain on the doorstep of a vast empty forested land, beribboned with great streams. Some writers have suggested that the "evidence" about the precious metals in the Saguenay country might have been merely an Indian attempt to illustrate the difference in colour between the silvery St. Lawrence and the yellowish, muddy Ottawa. The lure of the Saguenay–like the tale of the jewelled Seven Cities of Cibola–was to die a lingering death; and the Ottawa, striking deep into the west, was to remain the focus of French effort in Canada for generations.

The next day, the expedition slipped downstream under sail for Stadacona, breaking the journey where the St. Maurice tumbles into the St. Lawrence. Cartier erected "a fine large cross" on Ile St. Quentin and sent a longboat past the site of today's Trois-Rivières and Cap de la Madeleine for a short inspection of the river. The *Emerillon* was back in the St. Charles on October 11, where Cartier found to his satisfaction that the garrison had built a fort, completely enclosed with large logs, with guns pointing every way, on the shore beside the moored ships. In a land that was to be tamed and colonized from forts,* this was the very first.

It soon became apparent that the breach with Donnacona had not healed in his absence, so Cartier had the defences strengthened with wide, deep ditches, over which a drawbridge led into the stockade. He mounted a night guard in four watches, and had a trumpet sounded at each change of watch. The French had been warned by the *Agouhanna* of Achelacy, who had visited his daughter in Cartier's care, that Donnacona, Taignoagny, and Domagaya were plotting against them.

Cartier had made a thorough effort on his return from Hochelaga to mend his fences with the Indians of Stadacona, marching fifty men to the village for a formal visit during which he gave away more presents. He noted disapprovingly that girls at puberty were "placed in a brothel open to everyone" until they were chosen as wives. Donnacona showed Cartier the scalps of five enemies whom he called "Toudamans."† This tribe attacked them constantly, he said, and had ambushed two hundred on an island near the mouth of the Saguenay River. The French grasped that Donnacona's people were seeking blood vengeance.

The French now came to grips with the real Canadian enemy–cold. In their fort on the same latitude as Fountainbleau, they were not prepared for the ferocity of the Laurentian winter–and that year it was apparently a bad one. Few Europeans at that time had made winter penetration of any northern land mass. As evidence of the common ignorance, Richard Hakluyt in 1600 explained the cold of Canada in these terms: "The land is not tilled, nor full of people, and is all full of woods, which is the cause of cold because there is not store of fire nor cattle." From the middle of November, Cartier's men watched the ice in the St. Lawrence thicken to more than twelve feet and the snow drift higher than the rails of their ships. Cider froze in the casks and below decks there was four inches of ice on the timbers.

Cordial relations would be renewed with Donnacona for certain periods. The French could hardly believe their eyes when Indians–men, women, and children–came across the ice to the ships on the coldest days, "the majority of them almost naked." Donnacona elaborated fancifully on his reports of the Kingdom of Saguenay, saying that the people there were white-skinned and wore woollen clothes like the French, and that there were many towns with a great store of gold, rubies, and copper. He had also visited territories where "the people, possessing no anus, never eat or digest," and where men walked on one leg. Donnacona confirmed that the best route to the Saguenay was via the Ottawa River, possibly taking the tributary that we know as the Gatineau, which rises in the north close to Lake St. John.

Scurvy struck the fort about Christmas–although neither Cartier nor any of his educated gentlemen seemed to recognize the disease which had taken, for instance, half of Vasco da Gama's crew nearly forty years earlier. A diet of salted meat or fish and hard tack biscuits provided no Vitamin C, resulting in a breakdown in the blood vessels with hemorrhaging into the tissues. Cartier described the symptoms with horrified fascination:

Some lost all their strength, their legs became swollen and inflamed, while the sinews contracted and turned black as coal. In other cases, the legs were found blotched with purple-coloured blood. Then the disease would mount to the hips, thighs, shoulders, arms, and neck. And all had their mouths so affected that the gums rotted away down to the roots of the teeth which nearly all fell out. The disease spread to such an extent among the three ships that by mid-February, of the 110 men forming our company, there were not ten in good health so that one could help the other–which was a grievous sight considering the place where we were. Eight men were already dead and more than fifty seemed in hopeless condition.

The Captain seems to have remained among the fit–at one time, the healthy had been reduced to three–and his main preoccupation was in attempting to hide the weakened state of the garrison from the Indians. The journal says: "We were in great dread of the people of the country." But Donnacona's people were also suffering from "the pestilence," and a reported fifty of them had died. Cartier ordered his own dead to be hidden in the snow inside the fort–twenty-five succumbed in all–and he kept the sick hammering on the inside of the hulls to conceal his vulnerability. All

---

* See the author's *Forts of Canada*, McClelland and Stewart Limited, 1969.

† Probably the Seneca.

Having felled a white cedar, Cartier's men are taking it back to their ship, where they will boil the bark as a cure for scurvy.

who could walk were marshalled to Sunday service at a statue of the Virgin Mary that had been placed in a tree about fifty yards from the fort. It was the pagan Domagaya, however, who saved the lives of most of the remaining garrison.

The interpreter, who had been suffering from scurvy himself, told Cartier that he had been cured by the juice of the leaves of an evergreen. Cartier inquired as casually as he could manage, *which tree?* The Indian sent two women to point out the *annedda* tree – probably the white cedar – and to help Cartier gather branches. They also demonstrated how to strip the bark and leaves, to macerate them, and then boil them. When the vegetable material had settled in the kettle, the "tea" was drunk every two days and the lees spread on the legs or other affected spots. The effect of the drink on the sick was incredible and modern doctors are frankly sceptical. The journal says

the result "must clearly be ascribed to miraculous causes." After only two or three drinks, some men were fully restored to health and in eight days a whole cedar was stripped and consumed. Even some sailors who had contracted venereal disease several years earlier were pronounced cured.

Towards the end, of the long winter, the French intelligence service learned that Donnacona had departed on a hunt for venison, but Cartier believed that the chief was secretly raising a large force to attack him. When Donnacona returned on April 22, after the ice had broken up, and many new faces of "fine-looking powerful Indians" were noticed, Cartier became obsessed with the fear that an assault on his fort was planned – unless, of course, he was merely setting the stage for the treachery which marred the last days of his expedition.

The narrative of the final three weeks is a confused

127

accounting of visits back and forth between the ships and Stadacona, with Cartier sending emissaries to enquire after Donnacona's health (actually, to spy on the supposed enemy), with Taignoagny suggesting that Cartier kidnap a certain Chief Agona and take him to France, and with the French plotting to seize Donnacona and his headmen. With the previous experience of Taignoagny and Domagaya to guide them, the Indians were justly suspicious of the intentions of the French. Because of his losses, Cartier was short of crew for three ships and he decided to scrap the *Petite Hermine*. He gave the hulk to the Indians of Sitadin so that they might extract the nails.

Donnacona would now not risk crossing the St. Charles, but Taignoagny came and pressed Cartier to take the unwanted Agona with him to France. The Captain refused, informing the interpreter that King Francis had forbidden him to take any man or woman away on this voyage. The journal continues blithely: "The Captain spoke thus in order to calm their fears and to induce Chief Donnacona, who still kept on the other side of the river, to cross over." On the following day, May 3, Cartier had a cross thirty-five feet high erected within his stockade. It carried the arms of France and the slogan: "Long live Francis 1, by God's grace, King of France."

Donnacona, Taignoagny, Domagaya, and several other tribal leaders crossed the river in the afternoon and were invited by Cartier to a feast aboard the ships. Taignoagny warned his *agouhanna* not to enter the ships under any circumstances, and it looked as though the French stratagem might fail. Cartier then plunged ahead and ordered an armed party to seize

The traditional picture of Cartier claiming Canada for France.

Donnacona, three other headmen, Domagaya, and Taignoagny. The six men were hustled into captivity, while "the Canadians, beholding this, began to flee like sheep before wolves, some across the river, some into the woods, each seeking his own safety." The metaphor was well chosen.

That night, the stricken villagers lined the river bank and "howling like wolves" called out imploringly: "*Agouhanna! Agouhanna!*" Cartier would not show his captive until noon the next day, when the largest crowd of Indians the French had yet seen appeared to be preparing a rescue attempt. He told the chief that he was taking him to meet the King of France so that he could relate personally what he had seen in the Kingdom of Saguenay and that he would be returned to Canada within a year with a fine present. Donnacona then appeared on deck to his people and made several speeches which the narrator could not understand. (Taignoagny and Domagaya, the interpreters, were most likely still in chains below.) Cartier had given the chief some presents, including two brass kettles, and these Donnacona sent ashore to his family.

Some headmen now paddled out to the ships—which had been moved into the roadstead—and presented Cartier with twenty-four strings of wampum, their most valued possession. Many texts see this as a "gift" to Cartier, but it was surely a despairing effort to buy the chief's freedom, an idea perhaps suggested by Donnacona in his speeches. Then, as the ships made obvious preparations to depart, Indian women were sent out with fresh meat and fish and corn bread for the captives. They communicated by signs, that Cartier would be well rewarded when he gave back their beloved *agouhanna*.

On Saturday, May 6, 1536, the *Grande Hermine* and the *Emerillon* raised their anchors and slipped down the river, with the entire population of Stadacona standing heartbroken on the bank of the St. Charles to bid farewell to Donnacona. There were perhaps ten Indians aboard—all Iroquois—as Cartier had retained the children given him earlier as gifts. Of these, only one (the girl given to him at Achelacy), would ever see the St. Lawrence again. Donnacona and the others died in Brittany under circumstances that are lost to us.

During his long and tedious voyage home, Cartier further sketched in the map of Canada by discovering that the Magdalens were islands, not mainland, and that his guess about the existence of a strait between Newfoundland and Cape Breton was indeed accurate. Unfavourable winds caused him to make stops at Port aux Basques (which he called the Harbour of the Holy Ghost) and the islands of St. Pierre and Miquelon (which remain French to this day). His ships picked up fresh water in Trepassey Bay, near Cape Race, on June 19, and were back under the ramparts of St. Malo twenty-seven days later.

MYTHS AND MONSTERS

An allegorical figure sets sail in a symbol-laden ship, straight out into the hazards of unknown seas. Equipped with a wealth of practical aids — helmet and breastplate, naval gunnery, and globe and compasses — he must nevertheless contend with fearsome adversaries. But whether he stands in greater fear of real hazards or of the uncertainties and projections of his own mind is a question which the seaman does not think to ask. For him, concrete events and traditional myths are of the same order of reality — and it will take two centuries of exploration and discovery to separate the two.

AN ABUNDANCE OF BEASTS

"A beast is born in the Indies called a Manticora. It has a threefold row of teeth meeting alternately; the face of a man, with gleaming, blood-red eyes; a lion's body; a tail like the sting of a scorpion; and a shrill voice which is so sibilant that it resembles the notes of flutes. It hankers after human flesh most ravenously. It is so strong of foot, so powerful with its leaps, that not the most extensive space nor the most lofty obstacle can contain it." In this way, a Latin bestiary of the twelfth century describes one of the strange composite creatures that prowled through the mind of medieval man. The bestiary, or book of beasts, was a serious work of natural history, though it is evident that the author's view of the world was shaped as much by legend and hearsay as by actual observation. Thus, along with reasonably accurate accounts of animals as common as the cat, mouse, or dog, the bestiary also offers fantastic descriptions of satyrs, gorgons, griffins, and unicorns.

Heirs to the compendious knowledge of the bestiaries were naturalists such as Konrad Gesner and Edward Topsell and historians such as Olaus Magnus. On the left, the woodcuts of Magnus show how a lively imagination and an acceptance of far-fetched tales can greatly distort a man's concept of the world around him. Magnus was a Swedish ecclesiastic living in Italy, and though his *History of the Northern Peoples* was highly regarded by his contemporaries, his artwork suggests that his acquaintance with creatures of the sea was not first-hand. In the same way, the Swiss naturalist Konrad Gesner was unable to fully divorce fiction and reality—though he collected specimens from life as well as from library shelves. Gesner's massive, four-volume *Historia Animalium* is considered the starting point of modern zoology, yet it is still very much a repository of medieval misconceptions. So too is *A History of Four-Footed Beasts*, by Edward Topsell, a work that is illustrated at right.

THE FABULOUS CREATURES OF CHARLES

An artist of unusual ability, De Granville had little time in which to demonstrate his talents. Born at Quebec in 1675, he had just turned twenty-eight when he died of smallpox in the epidemic which ravaged New France i the early 1700's. The drawings that appear on these two pages, taken from *Les raretés des Indes*, reveal that even during his short lifetime, De Granville developed a highly distinctive style. It is interesting to note that his work embodie two tendencies. In the seahorse on the left, we see evidence of the artist's willingness to create images solely on the basis of second-hand reports. On the other hand, the "mountain rat" at lower left and the giant turtle on the right reflect a closer look at real animals, although the are described in terms that are clearly exaggerated. The *rat des montagnes* would seem to be a muskrat, but it is said to be as big as a spaniel. Similarly, the giant turtle is reported as being so big that its shell would serve as a large carriage–a possibility that is not likely to arise anywhere outside of the Galapagos Islands

THE MONSTER AT CLOSE QUARTERS

Between 1534 and 1778–the first voyage of Jacques Cartier and the last voyage of Captain Cook–the wildlife of the New World ceased to inspire misconceptions and became instead a subject of accurate observation. In this period of almost 250 years, the Canadian landmass had been coasted and penetrated by numerous explorers. As far back as 1576, Frobisher had sailed north along the coast of Baffin Island, while Champlain's trek of 1615 had confirmed the presence of the Great Lakes. At about the time of Champlain's discovery of the "sweetwater seas" the daring voyages of men such as Hudson, Baffin, and Munck made evident the forbidding nature of Canada's northland. With Cook's close scrutiny of the west coast and the overland explorations of La Vérendrye, Kelsey, and Hearne, the face of an immense land was slowly becoming known. In a sense, this growth of geographical knowledge is reflected in the art of the period. The fabulous monsters of an earlier day have given way to monsters of a more substantial nature–the latter being frightening enough in their own right, as the drawing on the right makes clear. But by and large, the creatures which inhabit the pages of both sketch pad and printed book resemble closely the animals which actually populated the land. Admittedly, the artist's occasional distortion of reality produces amusing results. But as the pictures at left demonstrate, the aim of the naturalist is no longer to stir the imagination but to record faithfully what he has seen.

DEATH OF THE MONSTER

Just as the images of the roc, the dragon, and the mermaid are expressions of the medieval mind, so too this seventeenth-century engraving of a beached whale manifests the changed attitude of man toward nature. Gone are the grotesque sea creatures of Olaus Magnus and in their place is simply the large but inert carcass of a commonly-known species. Thus, the triumph of the whaler signifies the death of the monster in more ways than one. For not only have these seafaring hunters defeated a true leviathan, but in so doing they have shown their freedom from archaic fears and medieval restraints.

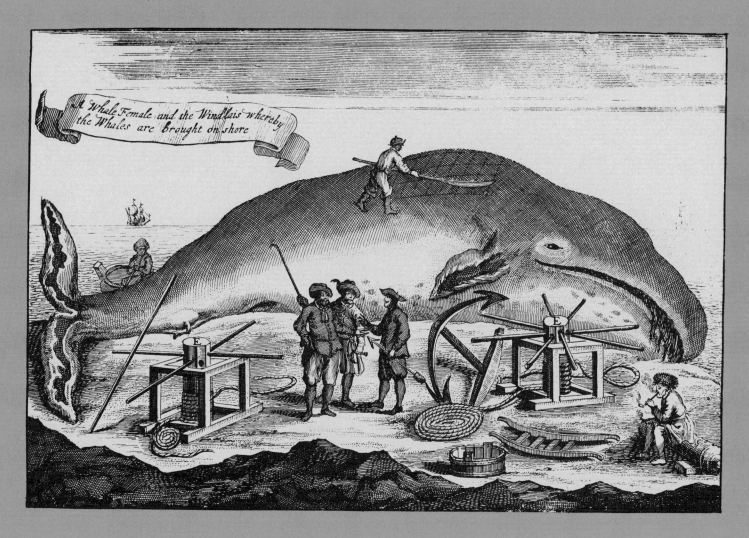

A Whale Female and the Windlais whereby the Whales are brought on shore

CHAPTER TEN

Capital at Cap Rouge

A FORGOTTEN man of the discovery saga is Jean-François de La Roque, Sieur de Roberval, the luckless Protestant chosen by the Most Christian King, Francis I, in 1540 to establish the first organized settlement in Canada. By far the most nobly born of all the adventurers of our early centuries, he was a soldier, courtier, landowner, a sometime corsair, and, perhaps, an engineer. He brought three ships and two hundred people safely to Canada, made a river trip to the Lachine Rapids, probed the mysterious Saguenay, spent a winter on the St. Lawrence, then returned to France with his colonists in the face of Indian opposition, surviving for another twenty years, until, with a group of other Huguenots, he was killed by a Catholic mob in Paris.

Roberval is obscure mostly because his story is usually hidden in the account of the third voyage to Canada of Jacques Cartier. Yet the truth is that the famous pilot-general of St. Malo was retained only as the guide and shipmaster of the expedition and was placed under Roberval's command. So much of the documentation of the expedition is lost that it is impossible to draw a detailed picture of the relationship between the two men – the educated courtier and the dedicated mariner. There is only one reported instance of friction between them – and in that instance, Cartier refused to obey an order from his commander and left him and his inexperienced settlers in the lurch in the New World. A lesser man would have paid with his life for such a mutinous act.

Most of the early chroniclers (many of them priests) and some later historians have championed Cartier in this strange aberration in a notable career, perhaps disturbed at the possibility that a major hero could be seen to have feet of clay. They have given Roberval a "bad press" by tagging him with stories of flogging and hanging his settlers – reports which were wildly expanded by André Thevet, a sixteenth-century Franciscan who was never in North America and who put into his well-known work, *Cosmographie Universelle*, some of the silliest bilge ever written. The only recognized record of the Roberval expedition says that one man, Michael Gallion, was hanged for theft, another man put in irons, and several others whipped – severe punishment, certainly, but routine in that period. Two facts need to be added: a fair number of the settlers were convicts, including murderers; and Thevet was a personal friend of Cartier. It might also be mentioned in this context that one of Samuel Champlain's first acts at Quebec was to behead one of his company. It was everywhere a violent age.

It is true, by all counts, that the Cartier-Roberval venture of 1541-43, although only sketchily known, is one of the strangest and most fascinating episodes in our history. It is documented in two short accounts which were first published by the English chronicler Hakluyt in the final volume of his *Voyages*, neither of them complete and each of them posing as many questions as it answers. In each case, the original manuscript is lost, perhaps still mouldering in a forgotten niche in some stone castle along the Seine. Over the four centuries that have elapsed, some other snippets of information – sidelights, casual but relevant references unearthed in other European archives, historical deductions that have withstood the tests of time and argument – have added a few threads and colours to the story.

When Cartier returned in midsummer of 1536 from his second voyage, France was under invasion by Spain and the King had little time to spare. He did grant audience to his pilot-general, and met, with obvious interest, Chief Donnacona and the other Indians whom Cartier had brought home with him. He ordered Cartier to see to the religious instruction of the savages (three of whom, at least, were later baptized), and he made the navigator a present of the *Grande Hermine*, complete with all gear and rigging. There was obviously a huge land there for the taking along the "River of Canada" but there was no gold, no silver, no profitable trade – nothing to match the Inca treasure that Pizarro was shipping back to Spain.

Roberval, leader of the ill-fated colony at Charlesbourg-Royal.

And the Canadian winters! How could modern man prosper where even the land itself froze for almost six months of a year?

As the months lengthened with no sight of a new commission, Cartier probably at first concentrated on the education and questioning of his Indian captives. He had been ordered by the King to make a written report with special emphasis on Donnacona's tales of the Kingdom of Saguenay, and the *agouhanna* had given his soaring imagination full play. Apart from repeating his accounts of gold and silver, he spoke of men with wings like bats who lived in trees. A considerable French-Indian vocabulary was compiled. As the years turned, Cartier must have moved to other pursuits, putting aside his promise to the Indians to return to Canada "within ten or twelve moons." All the Iroquois men appear to have died by the end of 1539 – we have no clear record of their tragic captivity. Taignoagny's worst assessment of the white man had come true, and he and Domagaya tasted the extra bitterness of being two-time losers. Other Europeans, particularly the Spanish *conquistadores*, treated the American native more viciously than did the French in Canada – but in such matters it is little comfort to argue degrees of inhumanity.

It is suggested that Cartier may have sailed to Ireland to bring the rebel Gerald Fitzgerald, Earl of Desmond, to safety in Brittany – but the story rests on dubious grounds. As a ship-owner, Cartier was now a man of some means and he was probably devoting time to the development of his modest farm at Limoi-lou, a few miles outside of St. Malo.

When Francis agreed, by the Treaty of Nice, to a ten-year truce in his wars with the Emperor Charles, he turned again to thoughts of a North American empire with which to balance Spain's possessions in the south. He refused to acknowledge the claims of the Iberian powers to total shared-ownership of the Americas. With a diplomatic eye on papal support, he announced that the main object of his colony in Canada would be the propagation of the Christian religion among the pagans of the New World. But, since he chose a well-known Protestant as his viceroy, since no priests are mentioned in the journals, and since the bulk of the settlers were drafted from the jails of France, it can be safely assumed that he was still hoping that he could tap the fabled riches of the Saguenay. He once boasted that Cartier had brought back some nuggets of gold from Canada, but he may have been trying simply to impress a foreign visitor. Cartier's journals make no mention of such a find.

Many writers have speculated on Jacques Cartier's feelings when he learned that the aristocratic Roberval had been appointed Viceroy and Lieutenant-General in Canada, Hochelaga, Saguenay, Newfoundland, Belle Isle, Carpunt, Labrador, Grande Baye, and Baccalaos. His own role in the forthcoming expedition was to be merely navigator – captain-general of the ships. In effect, as Professor Trudel put it recently: "Cartier became in truth Roberval's subaltern." Recalling that Cartier had been in full command of all aspects of the previous expedition, some writers detect a snub and build on this to explain Cartier's later actions. It seems more likely, considering the unchallenged social order of sixteenth-century France, that Cartier accepted Roberval's appointment as entirely routine. In fact, he was probably delighted that the King was showing such a degree of involvement in the Canadian discovery. The granting of vice-regal status for a foreign post was then unique in the kingdom.

Roberval is a village near Senlis, by the Oise, north of Paris. The La Roque chateau, later owned by the Prince de Soubise, Marshal of France, has been entirely rebuilt since the days of Cartier, but Roberval's few papers are still preserved there. The La Roques (often spelled "La Rocque") belonged to the southern branch of a very old family, Jean-François being born in many-towered Carcassone in 1500. He was a son of Isabeau de Poitiers and his father, the Sieur de Chatelrein, Governor of Carcassone, was also an ambassador and Gentleman of the King's Household. Jean-François' maternal grandmother was the formidable Alix de Popincourt, the Dame de Roberval in Picardy. The young man lived at the court of Prince Francis at Angouleme before "The Valois" took the throne of France and, as an early Protestant convert, was protected by the King. He proceeded to distinguish himself as an officer in the campaigns of Marshal de La Marck. His portrait by Clouet *fils* is in the collection at Chantilly of portraits of members of the French court.

Young officers around the hard-fighting, high-living King gambled for high stakes and kept coteries of pretty mistresses, and this perhaps led Roberval into financial troubles. In any case, by his late thirties, he was seriously in debt to his aristocrat cousins in Armagnac, Languedoc, and Picardy—and his own lands in the Ile de France were in jeopardy. The idea took hold that in Canada he would rebuild his fortune with one bold stroke, and there must have been long study of the English and Breton discoveries before the King finally signed his commission in January 1541, allowing him a tremendous subsidy for the day of 45,000 *livres*. Roberval was also dubbed Lord of Norumbega—the earliest name for the Atlantic lands now known as New Brunswick, Nova Scotia, and the State of Maine.

Cartier was ten years older than his general and also the most experienced captain and navigator in France. Hakluyt records that the two men "agreed together" to rig out and man their five ships at St. Malo and "the said Monsieur Roberval sent Cartier thither for the same purpose." No doubt Roberval, who (judging by his management of his estate) was an indifferent administrator, was only too pleased to give Cartier a free hand in that department. He signed over to Cartier 30,000 *livres* of the money that he had received from the royal treasury (and later gave him another 1,300). Cartier had now also been given the trusty little *Emerillon* as a further mark of the King's gratitude. The King had reserved for himself a third of any profits won in the New World.

Roberval set about trying to recruit his settlers, and although he was able to raise a small company of gentlemen-adventurers, younger sons from the minor aristocracy (one of them, Robert de Longueval, being a Gentleman of the King's Bedchamber), it was a difficult task—then, later, and even today—to tempt Frenchmen away from their blessed homeland. On February 7, 1541, he received further letters patent permitting him to sift the jails of Paris, Bordeaux, Rouen, Dijon, and Toulouse, taking any man (or woman) he wanted who was under sentence of death—excepting those convicted of counterfeiting, high treason, or heresy. In Brittany, Cartier was also having his recruiting problems and he was likewise authorized to take prisoners to make up his crews. He was expressly ordered by the King to sail by April 15.

The mounting of a five-ship expedition to the New World could not be done secretly and the kings of Spain and Portugal soon heard alarming news from their spies at Fountainebleau and St. Malo. The Emperor Charles had already protested—in mild terms—about a proclamation which Francis had issued the previous August giving his subjects permis-

sion to go to the "New Lands" in America. He now issued an order to his fleets to attack any of Cartier's ships which they might find in the disputed waters and "to throw all men aboard into the sea without sparing a single person." In fact, though, neither Spain nor Portugal, from their own research, considered the northern stretches of the continent to be worth a barrel of powder. There is a hoary legend that the very name of Canada derived from the Spanish "*aca nada*"—"nothing there."

The King's deadline for departure apparently could not be met, but Cartier had the ships fully provisioned for two years and swinging at their chains in the St. Malo roadstead by the middle of May. Still to arrive, however, were the essential guns, powder, and shot to arm the forts to be built in the New World. Also, it seems that some merchants' accounts had not been settled for goods supplied. Roberval was still having money troubles—he was selling some property and borrowing more funds—and rather than displease the King by delaying the sailing still further, he reviewed all the "gentlemen, soldiers, and mariners" chosen by Cartier and gave his captain full authority to depart and "to govern all things as if he [Roberval] had been there in person." The viceroy himself returned to Rouen to round up the missing equipment and "other things necessary," saying that he would follow in two more ships from the port of Honfleur, at the mouth of the Seine. As it turned out, Roberval did not manage to get away that year. When he did get his problems ironed out, he set sail in great style with two hundred persons in three ships, from La Rochelle, the Protestant stronghold on the Bay of Biscay, on April 16, 1542. He acted like a man who had just come into money.

During the interval of eleven months, he had not been idle. One method of raising money quickly which was considered acceptable even in the best of circles was to turn pirate and seize the ships of other nations. In association with the corsair, Bidoux de Lartigue, Roberval preyed on Channel traffic until the English Ambassador complained loudly. King Francis liked to call Roberval "*le petit roi de Vimeu*" and he promised to punish him. But since he was at odds with England's Henry VIII (and would be at war with him within two years), he probably looked the other way with a grin. Francis would likely have seconded the description of Roberval given by the dean of Quebec's historians, Gustave Lanctot: "Adventurous, hard-hitting, strenuously active, and striking in mien and bearing."

Returning to Cartier, Hakluyt reports that he cleared St. Malo on May 23, 1541, and suffered his worst passage yet to Newfoundland—three full months of weary sailing without "ever having in all that time thirty hours of good wind to keep us on our right course." They ran out of water for their cattle, pigs, and goats and had to broach cider casks for them. Still apparently expecting Viceroy Roberval to catch up from Honfleur, they waited for a time at Carpunt (Quirpon Harbour), Newfoundland, then continued across the gulf and down the St. Lawrence, reaching the mouth of the St. Charles on August 23.

It must surely have been a tense moment for Cartier, returning after five years to the scene of the miserable wintering of 1535-36, to face the tribe to whom he had made firm promises that he would return their leader and headmen. When the canoes of welcoming tribesmen put out from Stadacona, they were calling for the old *agouhanna*, Donnacona. Cartier informed them solemnly that Donnacona had died in France. Then, apprehensive of the effect which the whole truth might have on his questioners, he added the flat lie that all the other kidnapped Indians were alive but had married in France, were living there like lords, and refused to return to Canada. It was a sorry moment.

However, the new *agouhanna*, Agona, was delighted because the news left him in undisputed command of the village. He gave wampum presents to Cartier, hugging him around the neck, and the Captain responded with presents for Agona and for his wives.

Then he treated his Indian visitors to a feast in the *Grande Hermine*. Some analysts have deduced that Cartier had deliberately plotted to bring about this result, after it had been made plain to him in the spring of 1536 that Agona was challenging for the band leadership. Donnacona and his henchmen had, by this theory, been removed by Cartier at least partly because they were showing clear signs of obstructing French intentions in Canada.

Cartier immediately showed that in the interim he had not lost his distrust of the Indian. He turned his shoulder to Stadacona and took his ships nine miles upstream to the cove where the Cap Rouge River joins the St. Lawrence. Here, a high cliff offered a prime site for a fort that would command the landing beach and mooring places below. A priority job the next day was the removal of cannon from three of the ships into positions of defence on the shore. These vessels–the *Grande Hermine*, the *Emerillon*, and one other–were moved over the bar at high tide into semi-permanent moorings, while the other two–the *Georges* and the *St. Brieuc*–were left at anchor in the stream.

When all the settlement's stores were ashore, Cartier exercised his *locum tenens* authority by ordering the *St. Brieuc* and the *Georges* to return to France forthwith with letters for the King describing the situation of the new settlement, grandly named Charlesbourg-Royal, and reporting that Roberval had not yet arrived. Assuming that his commander had sailed later in the same season from Honfleur, he suggested that since the weather had been so bad on the Atlantic, the second half of the expedition may have been driven back to the European coast. The returning ships, captained by Mace Jalobert, Cartier's brother-in-law, and Etienne Nouel, his nephew, were back at St. Malo by October 3.

The fragmentary narrative of the third voyage describes the forts that Cartier built that autumn–one at the lower level by the narrow river mouth, the other perched on the promontory of reddish limestone above. A set of steps were cut from one post to the other. Palisade logs, building timbers, and firewood were easily cut from the plentiful oak, maple, cedar, and beech. From the top, the French guns could command "the nether fort and the ships and all things that might pass as well by the great as well as by this small river." There was also a spring close to the top of the cliff, ensuring a supply of fresh water even under siege.

The most thrilling incident, however, was the discovery on the cliff of "a good store of stones which we esteemed to be *diamants*," and at the foot "a goodly myne of the best iron in the world." Not only this–by the river bank "we found certain leaves of fine gold as thick as a man's nayle." Diamonds, iron, and gold! When the sun shone on the *diamants*, the journal states, "they glister as it were sparkes of fire." Several barrels were filled with the precious metals and closely guarded. When reading these passages today, one must recall the blissful ignorance of the sixteenth century and note that even two hundred years later, Dr. Johnson and his learned circle were still discussing means of producing gold from base metals by alchemy.

We do not know the number of men and women who disembarked at Cap Rouge, but it was probably considerably more than two hundred. It will be remembered that Cartier had 112 from three ships when he began his sojourn on the St. Charles in 1535. Some estimates of the total complement run as high as 450. A few of those at Cap Rouge are known to us by name. The Vicomte de Beaupré, a son of the old Chevalier Des Granches, was there, as was the Breton, Martine de Paimpoint. Thomas Fromont, described as Cartier's right-hand man, former mate of the *Grande Hermine*, appears to have died on the long voyage out.

Once the hammers were ringing on the new buildings, Cartier selected two longboat crews and set off to pay a return visit to Hochelaga. His main purpose was to examine the three rapids which barred the route to the Kingdom of Saguenay–in the jumbled directions he had pieced together from the late Donnacona's orations. He planned to spend the winter "making all things needful" to pass the rapids the following spring. He left Beaupré in charge at Charlesbourg.

The narrative of this river trip is one of the most puzzling portions of the Cartier travels. The mariner of St. Malo must have been in charge. Yet, if he was, he could not have either written or even read over the only record extant. From the time the longboats left Cap Rouge, there is no mention of Hochelaga and its Mont-Royal, and the *saults* of St. Mary's current and Lachine are described as though being seen for the first time. A village called Tutonaguy seems to be roughly in the position that Hochelaga occupied six years earlier. True, even substantial agricultural villages like Hochelaga could be moved swiftly when the crop yields in the unfertilized ground began to diminish. But it would be remarkable indeed for a returning explorer not to pass at least some comment. On the other hand, the record does list a call on the *Agouhanna* of Achelay, near today's Portneuf, the chieftain who had given Cartier a young girl in 1535 (the only survivor among the Iroquois taken back to France and possibly Cartier's sole interpreter on the third voyage). Two French boys were now deposited with the chief in the hope that they would learn the Iroquoian tongue, and Cartier distributed especially fine presents – including a cloak of Paris red with tin buttons of yellow and white and small bells.

On September 11, the French double-manned one of the boats to pull it past St. Mary's current beside today's Montreal Island, but came to a horrified stop at the foaming, rock-strewn Lachine Rapids. They walked westward along a well-beaten path around the *sault*, where there was another Indian village at which they were obviously expected. Four braves escorted them to the end of the Lachine Rapids, and explained the navigational obstacles ahead, using sticks of varying lengths to indicate distances. Cartier doesn't seem to have had a clear picture of how the Ottawa – the river flowing seven hundred miles from the west and the supposed route to Donnacona's Saguenay – joined the St. Lawrence through three main channels, one of them running south of Montreal Island into Lake St. Louis, the others to the north. It is, in fact, still confusing to today's young students of geography.

Four hundred Indians were waiting patiently for the French to return to their longboats and Cartier dutifully handed out "certaine small trifles, as combs, brooches of tynne and copper, and other small toyes, and unto the chief men every one his little hatchet and hooke, whereat they made certain cries and ceremonies of joy." But in case anyone should think that the Captain had gone soft, the narrative continues: "But a man must not trust them for all their faire ceremonies and signes of joy, for if they had thought they had bene too strong for us, then would they have done their best to have killed us, as we understood afterwards."

This last remark, full of darkness, was never explained. The narrative was broken off when the longboats returned to Charlesbourg and recorded only that some of the French had been to Stadacona and that when they reported to Cartier that they had found the tribes ominously gathering there, he "caused all things in our fortresse to be set in good order." These are the last words of the works known as the Cartier journals.

There is, fortunately – also thanks to the indefatigable Richard Hakluyt – the short narrative of Roberval's travels to confirm that Cartier *did* have serious trouble with the Indians that winter. When Roberval's three ships – the *Valentine, Anne*, and *Lechefraye* – reached St. John's, Newfoundland, on June 7, 1542, he took a few days' respite to rest his seasick settlers and

Cartier's summer residence in Limoilou, near St. Malo, France.

"gentlemen of qualitie" after a notably stormy crossing. The Viceroy was no doubt astonished to witness soon afterwards the arrival there of Cartier's three ships, the Captain having abandoned Charlesbourg-Royal without orders. Cartier reported to his commander that he had discovered diamonds and gold ore, and there and then some of the ore "was tryed in a furnace and found to be good."

Cartier also reported that "he could not with his small company withstand the Savages which went about dayly to annoy him." This is all we have to confirm that the Indians drove Cartier out. The Franciscan, André Thevet, published a story (possibly told later at St. Malo by Cartier) that the Indians threw two Frenchmen over the cliff at Cap Rouge. Another tale of thirty-five Frenchmen being killed was carried home from Newfoundland by Basque fishermen.

Roberval had two hundred "souldiers, mariners, and common people" with him, and as a veteran of European campaigns, he was unlikely to be deterred by a few hundred Indians, however hostile they may have appeared. He ordered Cartier to prepare to turn about and guide the augmented fleet back to the St. Lawrence. Cartier's response was to set sail the following night – but directly back to France. The Roberval narrative says scathingly that Cartier and his company "moved as it seemeth with ambition, because they would have all the glory of the discoverie of those partes themselves, stole privily away the next night from us, and without taking their leaves." And, of course, they had those barrels of gold and *diamants*.

Roberval's stay at St. John's was lengthened by the need to settle a dispute between some Frenchmen and Portuguese – there were seventeen fishing vessels in the harbour at one point. This was probably the first official act in his new domain by the Viceroy and Lieutenant-General – in effect, the first expressed authority of the French Crown in the new realm.

With Pilot Jean Alfonse at the wheel of the flagship, the Roberval expedition moved into the gulf, taking a month to reach Cap Rouge. The leaders included Paul d'Aussillon, the Sieur de Sauveterre, captain of the *Anne*, who was Roberval's second-in-command,

and others bearing the names Longueval, Lespinay, Guinecourt, Le Vasseur, Norefountaine, Lamont, Frotté, La Brosse, De Mire, and Royeze. There was also another gentleman carrying a name that would later resound in the Canadian story: La Salle. The narrative, strangely, makes no clear mention of taking over the forts presumably left only a couple of months earlier by Cartier. (Had the Indians removed them stick by stick in that interval?)

As befitted the courtier, Roberval renamed the place "France-Roy" and called the St. Lawrence the "France-Prime." He built an impressive structure on the heights, with a lookout tower, kitchens, and separate quarters for the gentlemen and for those described in Hakluyt as "all the meaner sort." On September 14, he sent two ships back to France under the command of the Sieur de Sauveterre and Captain Guinecourt. They were ordered to inform King Francis of the situation—no doubt including the defection of Cartier—and to return the following year with food and other stores. Roberval was particularly interested in receiving expert opinion on the diamonds which Cartier had taken back. Before Sauveterre sailed, Roberval wrote him a pardon for the killing of a "refractory sailor." This paper, dated September 9, 1542, still exists and is considered to be the oldest official Canadian document.

Roberval's administrative weakness seems indicated again by the fact that the supplies of food for the winter were soon found to be barely sufficient—although the time lost because of the three-month voyage from La Rochelle might have aggravated the situation. A rationing system was quickly set up, and salt beef and pork and beans were eked out with "the great store" of shad and other fish brought to the forts by the Indians. The lack of fruit and vegetables brought on scurvy, and it would seem that Cartier had not passed on the vital information about the *annedda* tree, whose juices had restored his men on the St. Charles. About fifty of the colonists at Cap Rouge died that winter. There is no record of an Indian attack, or even threat.

The following June, Roberval led a longboat expedition upstream "toward the said province of Saguenay" and the Descelier map indicates that he reached Lachine, or beyond. He began with seventy men in eight boats, and at some intermediate stage—perhaps at Lachine—he left a staging camp containing thirty men with two boats. The Franciscan Thevet is the only source for a note that a fort was begun "on the bank of a river called in the language of the barbarians the Land of Sinagua [Saguenay]." If that bit of hearsay held any truth, it would mean that Roberval had launched into the Ottawa via Lake St. Louis. He informed the stay-behind group that he expected to reach the Saguenay and return within three weeks. We do not know how far he penetrated, nor when he returned to his settlement at France-Roy. If he was trying to get up the Ottawa rowing five heavy longboats, it is unlikely that he passed the Long Sault, below today's Hawkesbury.

The postscript was written in France. Cartier's diamonds were, of course, merely pieces of quartz and the gold, iron pyrites — and the phrase, "as false as a Canadian diamond," became a popular expression of scorn. Roberval obviously found only disillusionment, and his colonists were returned to France in 1543. (There is still argument about whether or not Cartier was sent with ships to carry them home.) There is controversy, in truth, about nearly every element of the Roberval-Cartier association. Samuel Champlain, for instance, believed that the two men wintered together at Quebec. It is fact, though, that the two leaders appeared before a tribunal the following year, 1544, when the accounts of the expedition were examined. Roberval was ruined financially, and his chateau was mortgaged and then sold—though he remained a favourite at court. When Henri II succeeded his father, Francis I, he granted Roberval the exclusive rights to operate the mines of France. Yet Roberval was still deeply in debt at the time of his death.

French literature, on the other hand, was in debt to Roberval, since it was his personality and verve that made the deepest impression. Queen Margaret of Navarre included in her *Heptameron* the legendary story of how he was supposed to have marooned his niece, Marguerite, with her lover on one of the Mecatina Islands in the Gulf of St. Lawrence. François Rabelais wrote of Roberval in the character Robert Valbringue, and court poets Marot and D'Amboise dedicated works to him. An epic poem in Latin, *Robervalensis Epitaphium*, mourns his murder at the hands of religious bigots.

Jacques Cartier dropped into comfortable *bourgeois* obscurity at his country place at Limoilou—where his simple stone house, its courtyard walls, and gateways are now preserved as an historic shrine. France was again rent by invasion and split by bitter civil wars of religion, and the inspiration of a New France along the "River of Canada" swiftly faded. There was no Peru there for French fortune hunters or spendthrift kings, and no ship passage offering a short cut to the Spice Islands and the silks and gems of the Orient. Montaigne was to sum up the prevailing French attitude to America: "We grasp at everything, but we catch nothing but air."

Cartier was taken by the plague on Wednesday, September 1, 1557. By then, Canada was already slipping back into solitude, and it was soon again a shadowy place, the stories of its strange redmen walking naked in the snow, its fearsome rapids and dark endless forests, swiftly dissolving into the stuff of folklore. Unipeds and pygmies, fish the size of oxen that walked on the land, griffins, ostriches, and unicorns—these wondrous creatures peopled the blank spaces on the maps beyond the wide river of St. Lawrence the Martyr.

Part IV
The Champlain
Crusade

In an allegorical scene entitled The Arrival of the French in North America, *Champlain directs the colonization of Canada, incorporating under his command all aspects of the enterprise – religious, military, and commercial.*

No authentic portrait of Samuel Champlain exists, but many artists have been inspired by the story of his discoveries. Above is R. Harris' imaginative portrayal of Champlain.

CHAPTER ELEVEN

Tabagie at Tadoussac

THE way it began, Samuel Champlain did not choose Canada—but Canada *did* choose him, curtly demanding the core of his love and the rest of his life, giving him little but wounds of body and spirit, then, only in the long reaches of time, allotting him his fitting reward as the true Father of Canada. By birth, a humble man, son of a seaman, ranking only as a sergeant in his mid-thirties, he ate rotting fish and slept with verminous savages—then rose to argue in silken hose for his colony at the sophisticated court of Henri IV, to cross verbal swords with the genius Richelieu, and, in his age, to sit in the governor's chair at Quebec with a simple dignity and dedication that few born to the purple could emulate. He was cartographer and geographer, writer and fighter, trader and colonizer—and, in the exercise of those self-taught talents, he also brought more of Canada into modern knowledge than any other man. His path led from the Atlantic coast to Lake Huron, from Lake Nipissing in the north to Lake Ontario in the south; he was the first to shed light on a huge territory larger than western Europe, touching five provinces of the modern Confederation.

Until the spring of 1603, the idea of crossing to the silent wilderness described by Jacques Cartier apparently did not cross Champlain's mind. In the sixty years since Viceroy Roberval had abandoned his capital at Cap Rouge, the homeland had been torn by foreign and civil wars, both political and religious, and there had been no serious thought of fresh ventures abroad. "Blazing hamlets, sacked cities, fields steaming with slaughter, profaned altars and ravished maidens" was the way in which historian Francis Parkman described the condition of France up until the time that the Protestant prince of the Pyrenees, Henri of Navarre, crushed the Catholic League. After his victories at Arques and Ivry, Henri negotiated peace with Spain in 1598 under the Treaty of Vervins and, in the same year, proclaimed the Edict of Nantes, guaranteeing (for the time being) the religious rights of the Huguenots. In order to unite France, he then embraced Catholicism—with the cynical aside that "Paris is worth a mass."

Champlain was probably also raised a Protestant, as his Christian name would suggest—Catholic parents almost always gave their sons the names of saints. Brouage, the port on the Bay of Biscay where he was born in 1567, was in the very heart of Huguenot territory and was twice attacked and taken by the Catholic League during his boyhood. He was an avowed Catholic by his thirties, however, and in his later years, conspicuously devout.

But until some incontrovertible documentation is discovered, a haze will remain over Champlain's antecedents and over his early years. What history knows about him in the first third of his life is only what he himself chose to put on the record in his maturity—and many a modern self-made man would quietly enjoy such an opportunity to add a bar or two to his escutcheon. Even the journal in which Champlain does offer us some information about his pre-Canadian years is itself under question. Some Canadian and French scholars say flatly that the book (not published until more than two hundred years after his death) is a deliberate fraud; some think that Champlain may have written it late in life when his memory was slipping; while others hold that he didn't write it at all. This book, known familiarly as the *Brief Discours*, of which an illustrated manscript lies in the library at Brown University in Providence, Rhode Island, describes how Samuel Champlain of Brouage made a voyage to the Spanish Main in 1599, in order "to make a true report to his Majesty [King Henri]."

Champlain sets his own stage. The journal tells us that he had been a quartermaster-sergeant in the King's army fighting the Holy League in Brittany "for some years," and that when the war was over in 1598, he was out of a job. The last Spanish invaders had been penned up in Blavet—now Port Louis, opposite Lorient on the south coast of Brittany. French ships were chartered under the peace treaty to repatriate the Span-

*From any angle, Cardinal Richelieu, who outlined
the economic policies of New France, was a formidable man.*

iards, and Champlain (so the story runs) there "found an uncle of mine named Captain Provençal" who had command of the fleet. Champlain sailed with the troops to Cadiz and apparently sweet-talked his way into a soft berth as a non-paying passenger with a large convoy heading for New Spain—a considerable achievement for a very recent enemy.

The *Brief Discours* takes Champlain to Guadeloupe, to the Virgin Islands, by a virtually impossible route to Puerto Rico (where he describes an English raid on San Juan that actually took place the previous year), through a running battle with thirteen pirate ships, and on past Cuba to Mexico (on a time scale that would have allowed only twenty hours for 400 miles of ocean). He was later at Panama, Cartagena, and Havana. From Vera Cruz, he went inland to visit Mexico City, reporting that "a more beautiful country could not be seen or desired." He described the fauna and flora at great length, including cochineal, "which comes from a fruit the size of a walnut which is full of seeds." (The dye is actually made from the crushed bodies of a cactus insect.) The journal's sixty-two coloured illustrations include a drawing of a cochineal plant. He also described and drew "dragons with a head like an eagle, wings like a bat, a body like a lizard, two large feet and a scaly tail." He was properly fascinated by the iguana, the llama, and turtles so big that three men could go to sea in their empty shells. The Indians, he noted, "are of a very melancholy disposition," possibly because they were handed "thirty or forty blows with a stick" for not attending mass on Sundays. Somewhat earlier, they were burned at the stake—sometimes in bunches.

The *Brief Discours* records Champlain's return to Seville after an absence of two years and two months—making it then March 1601. An independent document places him in Cadiz the following summer. The West Indian journal is an important and totally fascinating document. But it must be pointed out that

it could all have been written and illustrated by an industrious and well-read man who had never left Spain—a man, that is, in whom ambition to claim renown could at times overcome scruple. It must be just as plainly pointed out that Champlain, if he *did* write the journal, certainly did not send it to any printer. Professor Morris Bishop, author of the ranking biography, says flatly that Champlain wrote and illustrated the *Brief Discours* in order to reinforce his claim for a pension—or in order to justify it—and gave it to Henri IV, who, in turn, handed it to his treasured ally, the Governor of Dieppe, Aymar De Chastes, a man concerned with long sea voyages. A convent library in Dieppe held the manuscript in the nineteenth century, when it was bought by the John Carter Brown Library in the United States. It was first published in English in 1859, and then in its original French in 1870.

There is one other source that offers some early Champlain background: an edition of the *Biographie Saintongeoise*, published in 1852. Champlain's birthplace, Brouage, twenty miles south of La Rochelle, was in the old province of Saintonge, now the *departement* of Charente-Maritime. This provincial "who's who," prepared close to the crumbled walls of the town that once was regarded as the second port in all of France, gives the date of birth of its most famous native son as 1567, his parents as Antoine Champlain and Marguerite Le Roy, and the family trade as fishing. The compiler also stated that Champlain was at one time working on the provisioning of ships at Dieppe. If accurate, this record would serve handily to fill the silence between Champlain's return from Spain and his invitation to join the De Chastes' expedition from Honfleur to Canada in 1603. When in his sixties, Champlain wrote that he had gone to see De Chastes "from time to time."

Almost as soon as he could turn from his victorious wars, the hawk-faced King Henri looked to the expansion of his domain. He once announced his creed: "I make war, I make love, and I build." (He was, incidentally, capably handling the second task. Historians have traced more than sixty of his love affairs, and in his lifetime, he acknowledged eleven illegitimate children.) Across the western ocean, England had claimed sovereignty in Newfoundland twenty years earlier "two hundred leagues everyway from St. John's," and Francis Drake had proclaimed New Albion on the northern Pacific coast of America during his circumnavigation of the globe. Martin Frobisher's three northern voyages had marked what we now know as Hudson Strait (and had proved that there was fool's gold in the Arctic as well), and John Davis of Devon was publishing his accounts of his vain search for the Northwest Passage.

In the meantime, France's fishermen and traders had not been waiting for any royal say-so to exploit the entry to the Gulf of St. Lawrence given them by

Cartier and others. In fact, cod boats from Dieppe, Honfleur, St. Malo, and La Rochelle had been fishing the Grand Banks and other American waters for as long as memory then ran. One old Breton admitted in 1607 that he had been to the banks for forty-two successive years. One hundred and fifty French ships were engaged in the cod trade by the turn of the seventeenth century. The English had almost as many, the Spanish a hundred, and the Portuguese about fifty.

Returning fishermen brought back beaver pelts which they had bartered from the Indians, and the fur was prized for the ultra-fashionable high-crowned gentlemen's hats. The beaver, once common in Europe, had been extinct since the Middle Ages and freelance traders soon set out for Canadian waters in their small, blunt square-riggers. Some of these ocean-going vessels were so small that crewmen could reach over the gunwale at times and wash their hands in the sea.

Undaunted by the record of failure in French colonies – not only in Canada, but in Florida and Brazil as well – an impoverished Breton nobleman, the Marquis de la Roche, decided on a fresh attempt in America. He had no trouble getting from the Crown all the resounding (and empty) titles and appointments that had once been showered on the Sieur de Roberval, plus a monopoly of the fur trade. The Lieutenant-General of Canada, Hochelaga, Etc., also had permission to sift the prisons for his "colonists" and he herded them into a ship and set sail in 1598. The first land he saw was Sable Island, that treeless, ship-graveyard 180 miles off the Nova Scotian coast. Here he disembarked fifty of his convicts and pressed on to seek a more promising site for his capital city. Offshore storms drove him back into the open Atlantic and he returned to France, where he was promptly imprisoned for debt. Eventually, he told his story to the humane Henry, who dispatched a fishing boat to look for survivors in 1603. Eleven bearded men were found, dressed in sealskins. They had existed partly on the wild descendants of domestic cattle, presumably left behind by an even earlier optimist.

An infinitely more resourceful man now came on stage, one of the true heroes of the Canadian chronicle – François Gravé, Sieur du Pont, a man as flinty as the stone in the ramparts of his beloved St. Malo. Usually called Pontgravé, skilled as a navigator and as a hearty captain of men, he teamed with Protestant Dieppois Pierre Chauvin, the Sieur de Tonnetuit, who was now trying to exercise a new ten-year monopoly of the fur trade. Pontgravé had been up the St. Lawrence as far as the site of Trois-Rivières before 1599. Chauvin, a naval captain like his friend Aymar De Chastes, was a close wartime comrade of the King.

Chauvin and Pontgravé took four small ships to the Saguenay in 1600 and built a *habitation* under the frowning 600-foot cliffs that guard that river fiord. With them was another associate who was due to play

King Henri IV was the chief sponsor of Champlain's voyages.

a major role in the Champlain saga: Pierre du Gua, Sieur de Monts, a nobleman who also had the ear of the King. At Tadoussac, already established as the main summer trading point with the Indians, they left sixteen men to spend the winter (under the terms of his monopoly, Chauvin had to begin the colonization of New France). The settlers quarrelled and starved in the long bitter cold, and only the charity of *les sauvages* kept a handful of them alive until Chauvin's return the following year. The free-lance traders, then as later, bitterly contested any trade monopoly. The new Lieutenant-General, Etc., took the remnant of his settlers back to Dieppe, where he died while planning a third voyage.

The titles and the monopoly were now assumed by the aging Catholic, Governor De Chastes, who, despite the continued bad news from the River of Canada, was prepared to try once more. When the Indians would exchange a thick beaver pelt for two biscuits or a knife (any scrap of sharpened metal was considered a knife), there was a great fortune to be won by anyone who could establish a permanent *dépôt* staffed by traders. The exclusive territory was extended to include all of present-day New Brunswick and Nova Scotia – with scant recognition of England's claims to the seaboard since Cabot's time a century earlier.

De Chastes, son of a baron and marshal of the Order of St. John of Jerusalem, had fought in the wars of religion. It is therefore possible that he had known earlier of the steady Samuel Champlain of Brouage, whose final task in the army appears to have been in the arranging of billets for the troops. Assuming that De Chastes had seen Champlain's manuscript describing the voyage to New Spain, the Governor may well have decided that here was the perfect geographer—experienced abroad and possessed of a fine writing and drawing hand—to bring him back a full and up-to-date description of the upper reaches of his new fief. Professor Marcel Trudel writes that there is no solid backing for the oft-repeated statement that Champlain held the appointment of Royal Geographer. This title was dreamed up by Marc Lescarbot for a laudatory sonnet written a few years later.

What we do know for certain is that Champlain sailed from Honfleur in the 120-ton *Bonne Renommée* under the command of Pontgravé, on March 15, 1603. There were two other ships in the convoy, one each from Rouen and St. Malo. Champlain was then about thirty-six, and respectful of the grey hairs of the fiftyish Pontgravé. The two men hit it off immediately and Champlain later wrote: "I was his friend, and his years would make me respect him as my father." But Champlain also much later accused Pontgravé of trying to keep all the beaver for himself. Whatever other chores Champlain may have had on board, he immediately bent to his task as journalist, beginning the chronicle which would be published in Paris later that year under the title, *Des Sauvages*. It bore a dedication to Lord Charles de Montmorency, Admiral of France (later a duke), whose name the writer immortalized by giving it to the picturesque waterfall seven miles below Quebec.

This book, a best-seller written in the heat of Champlain's first experience of Canada, marked the beginning of his crusade, his lifelong devotion to the land and its people. It carried the conviction—which Champlain never lost—that the Canadian waterways must inevitably lead to China and the East Indies. It is infinitely touching in this era of planetary travel to consider the sober-minded Champlain, tramping through the woods, slipping silently down some rock-rimmed stream that spills from the Laurentian Shield, his eyes always hopefully straining to the spires of Peking, his ears reaching for the tinkle of a temple bell. His matter-of-fact style seldom permitted such purple prose and only part of his information was strictly new to the expert. His books, however, were remarkably influential in bringing the story of an awakening Canada to the literate population. They were the most important Canadian documents to that time.

In all—leaving aside the West Indies journal—Champlain published four books: *Des Sauvages*, with which we are concerned in the present chapter; *Les Voyages*, published in 1613; *Voyages et Découvertes*, of 1619; and a two-volume work dedicated to Cardinal Richelieu, *Les Voyages de la Nouvelle France dicte Canada* (1632), a somewhat choppy, edited version containing the essentials of his earlier Canadian books plus a history of previous French voyages in the region, as well as Champlain's comments on colonial policy, Indian affairs, and notes on the art of navigation. *Des Sauvages* was available in English as early as 1625, when it was included in a famous anthology of travel chronicles published by the English parson, Samuel Purchas. *Les Voyages* and *Voyages et Découvertes* were translated in Boston and published between 1878 and 1882, and have since been re-edited and re-issued several times. The discovery sections of the final work (the 1632 rewrite) were presented in English in 1906 in the *American Explorers* series. Champlain's total *oeuvre* was then collected and published—with illuminating notes and with both French and English texts—for the Champlain Society of Toronto in 1922 by a group of six Canadian scholars working under the general editorship of H. P. Biggar, then chief archivist for the Canadian government. The excerpts from Champlain's works included in the following pages have, in many cases, been drastically shortened, and words and expressions that have dropped out of fashion are usually given in currently popular style.

There is nothing of note in Champlain's first Canadian journal until Pontgravé rattled down his anchors off Tadoussac on May 24. It was by now a routine trip, and they had taken longer than most. Dutifully, Champlain had recorded the passing of Cape Ray on Newfoundland's southwestern tip and Cape St. Lawrence on the Cape Breton headland, correctly estimating the distance across Cabot Strait (he called it "the Gulf of Canada") at about sixty miles. He logged Anticosti, the Gaspé, and Bic; then crossed the "River of Canada" to the Saguenay. A few days later, he accompanied Pontgravé to an Indian *tabagie* (feast) and made his first acquaintance with the endlessly fascinating natives.

Two Indians who had been in France with Pontgravé were now returned to their tribe and they gave the customary detailed reports of their good treatment. Professor Leacock, historian and humourist, maintained that the Indian harangue was the direct ancestor of the modern luncheon-club speech. The Indians said that the French king wanted to make peace with their enemies or send force to crush them. The enemies were named as the Iroquois, the first clear confirmation of the shift in tribal groupings, loyalties, and hunting grounds since Cartier's reports of the previous century.

It must be noted here—and kept in mind throughout the Champlain story—that in reporting Indian orations or conversations, Champlain was seriously handicapped by his language block. It may well have led to certain confusions concerning the existence of salt seas in the west. Biographer Bishop writes: "Champlain was no linguist; in thirty years' association with the Algonquins, he did not learn to speak their language." It should also be noted in passing that Champlain, from what we know of him, was something of a prig—not a rare condition in 40-year-old bachelors.

When Chief Anadabijou [he was smoking tobacco and passed his pipe to Pontgravé and Champlain] had ended his speech, they began to hold their tabagie, *eating the meat of moose, bear, seal, and beaver, with great quantities of wildfowl. They had eight or ten kettles full of meat, each on its own fire. The Indian men sat on both sides of the lodge, each with his birch-bark bowl. They feed very dirtily, for when their hands are greasy they rub them in their hair, or else in the hair of their dogs, of which they have many for hunting. Before the meat was cooked, one of the headmen grabbed a dog and went leaping about between the kettles. When he was in front of Anadabijou, he threw the dog violently on the ground and all present cried: "Ho! Ho! Ho!" This ceremony was continued by other men until the food was ready.*

After the feast they began to dance, taking the scalps of their enemies in their hands. Some sang; others beat their hands in time on their knees. They cried "Ho! Ho! Ho!" and panted as though out of breath. Then they danced again, celebrating a victory over the Iroquois. One thousand warriors of three nations had been allied in the war, Etchemins [Malecites], Algonquins, and Montagnais. They are much in dread of the Iroquois, but on this occasion they had surprised them at the mouth of the River of the Iroquois [the Richelieu] and had killed one hundred.

In this fashion Champlain was made aware, even on his arrival, of what would immediately become the cruel and classic problem of New France–the bitter enmity established between the northern tribes, particularly the nomad Algonquins, and the inordinately fierce and proud Iroquois, who by that time were living mostly in the lands south of Lake Champlain and east and south of Lake Ontario. It appears that appeals had already been made for official French support and sides had already been chosen. It is quite possible that the French decision to join the foes of the Iroquois cost them the mastery of the whole continent. Professor Trudel, from the Chair of History at Laval University, says that the French-Iroquois enmity really had its beginnings in the policy and behaviour of Jacques Cartier.

While Pontgravé led the trading, Champlain scribbled notes about everything–the length and weight of a canoe, the construction of a lodge, the local trees, the nature of the soil, the Indian concept of the Creation ("After God made all things, He took a number of arrows and stuck them into the ground; and from them He created men and women"), about the herb called *tabac*, of the power of witch doctors. He recorded burial customs, cannibalism, and the clever snowshoe. He seems to have been shocked by Indian nudity.

On June 9, the savages all began to make merry together . . . They arranged all their women and girls side by side and themselves stood behind. Suddenly, all the women and girls proceeded to strip themselves stark naked, showing "their privities" . . . When the songs were over, they all cried

All Europeans were fascinated by the Huron Feast of the Dead.

"Ho! Ho! Ho!" and the women covered themselves with their mantles and had a short rest. When they suddenly resumed singing, they dropped their clothing again. They do not move around when they dance, but make certain gestures and motions of the body, first lifting up one foot and then the other, stamping on the ground . . .

All these people are well built, without any deformity. They are agile and the women have good figures, plump and rounded, of a swarthy colour because of the pigment with which they rub themselves . . . They have a form of marriage–a girl of fourteen or fifteen may have several suitors and keep company with as many as she likes. After five or six years, she will take the one who pleases most as her husband.

Champlain was a true scion of the Renaissance–he was interested in everything, and his need to find out for himself brought rich dividends to his books. Many travellers had already written of the dark cleft and great depth of the Saguenay River, but Champlain took a boat and went up the river–it is more like a sound in its lower reaches–for about forty miles to see for himself. Here is the discoverer in action. He

Champlain's map of the area where Montreal was later built.

A. *Small open space which I had cleared.* B. *Small pond.* C. *Small Island on which I had a stone wall built.* D. *Small stream in which the boats are kept.* E. *Meadows where the savages encamp when they come to these parts.*

F. *Mountains which are seen in the distance.* G. *Small pond.* H. *Mount Royal.* I. *Small stream.* L. *The rapid.* M. *The spot where the savages portage their canoes along the North shore.* N. *The spot where one of our our men and an Indian were drowned.* O. *Small rocky islet.* P. *Another islet where the birds build their nests.* Q. *Heron island.* R. *Another island in the rapids.* S. *Small islet.* T. *Small round islet.* V. *Another*

islet half covered with water. X. *Another islet on which are many river fowl.* Y. *Meadows.* Z. *Small river.* 2. *Fairly large and beautiful islands.* 3. *Places which appear above water when the water is low and where there are great ripples as in the said rapid.* 4. *Meadows covered with water.* 5. *Places where the water is low and shallow.* 6. *Another little islet.* 7. *Small rocks.* 8. *St. Helen's Island.* 9. *Small islet bare of trees.*

reached Ha Ha Bay and pressed close to the falls around Chicoutimi, since harnessed to provide hydro-electric power for the aluminum smelters of Arvida and other heavy industry (a greater wealth than had ever glowed in the wilder dreams of Chief Donnacona).

Champlain was repelled by the stark country – "a most unpleasant land" – but he learned from the Indians of the river's source in Lac St. Jean, 112 miles from the St. Lawrence, of the network of rivers rushing down from the Mistassini country, and of the existence of other tribes in the northwest.* These people were said to be within sight of a salt sea – and there, in 1603, seven years before Henry Hudson's discovery, Champlain decided without any fuss that this sea must be an inland gulf of the Atlantic "which overflows in the north into the midst of the continent." His inspired acceptance of Hudson Bay is regarded as remarkable by all researchers. Here is the geographer in action.

On June 18, in a twelve-ton longboat that had been carried on the deck of the *Bonne Renomée*, Champlain continued his journey up the St. Lawrence, with François Pontgravé in command. The purpose was simply stated as being *"pour aller au sault."* They were carrying out De Chastes' orders to examine the higher reaches. The *sault*, of course, was the rapids that barred the river beside Cartier's Mont-Royal. On the way, Champlain mentioned most of the islands in the river, using the names bestowed by Cartier and already incorporated in the early maps. He was suitably impressed by the falls which he named for Montmorency just prior to halting at Quebec. The man who was to fight so stubbornly and excellently to plant a nation at this spot gave its dramatic rock only brief notice at first look.

We came to anchor at Quebec, which is a narrow part of the River of Canada . . . At these narrows, on the northern side, is a very high mountain which slopes down on both sides. All the rest is a level and beautiful country where there is good land covered with oaks, cypresses, birches, firs, and aspens, also fruit trees and vines. In my opinion, if this soil were tilled it would be as good as ours. Along the shore of Quebec are diamonds in the slate rocks which are better than those of Alençon.

Champlain made no reference whatever to Stadacona, the fortified Indian village that had been the hub of Cartier's Canada – presumably, it had disappeared during the Iroquoian retreat from the St. Lawrence. He was soon announcing that he had reached the river thirty miles above Quebec (today's Jacques Cartier River) which, he said, marked the furthest extent of Cartier's journeys. It is an indication of Champlain's early lack of interest in Canada – or perhaps to his lack of literary appetite – that he was not familiar with the *Brief Récit*, which had been pub-

* Presumably, the Mistassini Cree, who at that time bartered with the Montagnais for a share of the French trade goods gained at Tadoussac.

lished in Paris in 1545. Champlain apparently had no knowledge at this time of Cartier's ascent as far as Montreal, and he makes no reference to the village of Hochelaga, where his embarrassed fellow countryman once "touched" the natives afflicted with diseases. He did introduce the name Trois-Rivières for the delta of the St. Maurice and added: "In my judgement this would be a place suitable for settlement that could be quickly fortified." Here is the colonizer in action.

Pontgravé had been to the St. Maurice before, but from that point on, where the river broadens seven miles into the lake which Cartier called "Angoulême," the country was new to all the party. No doubt ignorant that the lake already bore the family name of a French king, Champlain called it Lac St. Pierre. At the head of the lake, they cruised into the River of the Iroquois (the Richelieu), where the Algonquins and their allies were established in a fort close to the site of modern Sorel, preparing to attack their enemies. They were equally prepared for flight – Champlain tells us that the fort, sheathed in oak bark, was strong enough only to give the war party time to escape by canoe.

In their thorough examination of the country, Pontgravé and Champlain went up the Richelieu about fifteen miles, at which point they were halted by rapids. Through some quite remarkable but uncredited interpreter, Champlain learned that the river mounted by a series of rapids into a lake (Lake Champlain), then through a *sault* into another lake (Lake George), and that closeby was another river (the Hudson River) which led to Florida. Champlain would return to this waterway six years later to stage the most controversial act of his life.

Returning to the St. Lawrence, the boat party reached Montreal on July 2 – the actual landing spot is given as the foot of the present-day Rue St. Joseph. Where a thousand villagers met Cartier, Champlain does not mention any welcoming party – or, for that matter, any inhabitants at all. He does describe, in colourless fashion, the cluster of islands that stretch for thirty miles across the mouth of the Ottawa River, and the eminence of Mount Royal. He was, though, stirred by the foaming rapids that he had come so far to see.

I assure you I never saw any torrent of water with such force... It descends step by step, and whenever it falls it boils up astonishingly owing to the force and speed of the water. There are many rocks out in the stream... and it is so dangerous that it is beyond the power of man to pass with any boat, however small it may be. We went by land through the woods to see the end of the rapids... He who would pass them must provide himself with the canoes of the savages which a man can easily carry... Then one may travel freely and quickly throughout the country, up the little streams as well as the big rivers. By taking the help of the Indians and their canoes, a man may see all that is to be seen within the space of a year or two.

Champlain had instinctively read the requirement of Canada. To fight the environment, to insist on European attitudes in the northern wilderness of white water and green forest, was to invite defeat. He was to learn that lesson so well that he would soon ride down even the fearsome *chute* of the Lachine in a canoe, and the broad application of his policy was to enable a mere handful of Frenchmen to mark out a fabulous realm. The Indian guides pointed out the river route to empire. They told Champlain about the Ottawa waterway into the Algonquin country, and of the other rapids to be negotiated in the upper St. Lawrence on the way to a great lake (Lake Ontario). They made mention of Niagara Falls, yet another lake (which has to be Lake Erie), the Detroit River, and the huge Lake Huron beyond.

The Indians knew of no man who had actually been in these farthest territories, but they were certain that the water of the second great lake was salt. At least, that's the way Champlain read it. He seized this remark, and by flavouring it with other items from some fevered reasoning of his own, convinced himself that the lake in question must be the Pacific Ocean. Somewhere on its unseen shore would surely rise the golden roofs of Cathay! But always in Champlain's character, the pragmatist fought the romantic – and usually won. So he added a word of caution, just in case he turned out to be wrong. In any case, the prospect provided a zesty dash of spice to the report which he took back to France.

THE EUROPE
THEY LEFT BEHIND

The Marco Polo expedition leaving Venice's Grand Canal and lagoons for golden Cathay (1271).

It was from such rich and glittering cities as Venice that the first discoverers set out for China and the Indies. Later, the Europe of the discoverers centred on the Atlantic coast: the Genoese Columbus would leave Spain to discover America; and Cabot, a naturalized Venetian, would leave England to discover Canada. Instead of sophisticated China, the world they found was inhabited mainly by societies of Stone-Age culture. It is little wonder the early chroniclers found primitive Canada difficult to understand. The following pages give a glimpse of the cultural gap that yawned wider than the Atlantic itself.

CABOT'S ENGLAND

The England of Cabot's day—at once traditional and turbulent—was changing slowly. Trading vessels still went mainly to northern Europe and the Mediterranean. But Cabot's voyages were an initial strike across the Atlantic, mightily enlarging the cod fishery. Social values, customs, and ideals were soon to be challenged by the upheavals of the Reformation, the Industrial Revolution, and all that followed.

Henry VII, *first Tudor king and first English monarch to sponsor a voyage to America.*

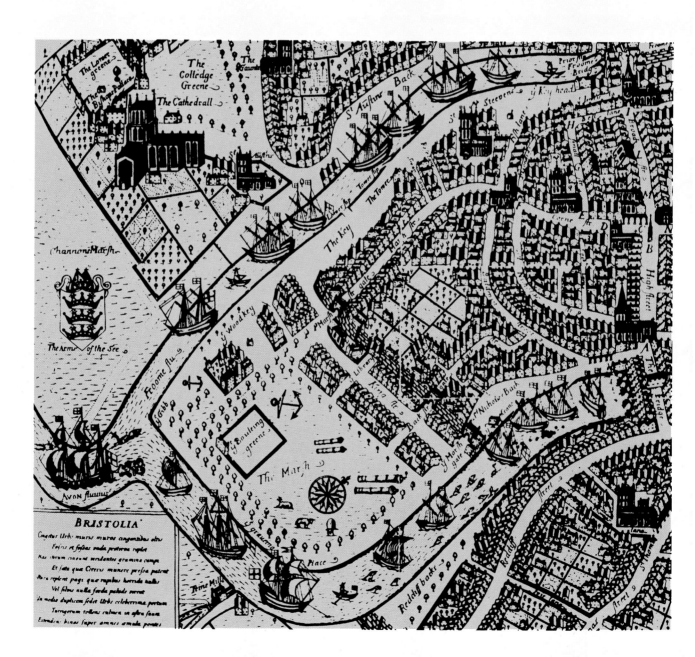

A stained-glass portrayal of working the fields in October.

Tapestries lined walls for decoration and warmth. Many were imported from France.

Tudor England boasted two great ports, Bristol and London. Bristol became the gateway to America. From London, ships sailed to all the countries of Europe. At the far left is the England Cabot knew, the Bristol of the seafarers. Far in the west of England, Bristol and its men looked to voyages of trade and exploration across the broad Atlantic as much as to familiar European commerce. At the near left, the London of the era is seen; but, in the late medieval style, the tapestry deals with the world of dukes and knights, battles and towers, rather than the world of trade and business, discovery and exploration.

CARTIER'S FRANCE

Renaissance France was the largest, most populous united country in Europe. Contemporaries considered it to be at the very centre of western civilization. Largely recovered from the Hundred Years' War, it now enjoyed national unity under a nearly absolute monarch; the power of the feudal nobility had been greatly reduced. Its soil was rich; its resources were varied. Life could be pleasant and agreeable as in few other parts of Europe. Under its young King Francis I, there was a striving for achievement in architecture, painting, music, and the arts and learning generally. But Francis also yearned for military glory and was soon engaged in costly dynastic struggles with the Hapsburgs, led by the Emperor Charles V. Much of the wealth of the French people was consumed in this endless fighting, and worse was still to come in the religious wars of the next generation.

Francis I, king from 1515 to 1547, was charming, cruel, frivolous, learned, irresponsible, a patron of the arts and of Jacques Cartier's voyages. The portrait shows the long, sharp nose, the bold sly eyes, and suggests the athletic body.

The Field of the Cloth of Gold near Calais, June 1520. In a spectacular but unsuccessful effort to gain the alliance of Henry VIII, Francis entertained the English monarch in almost unbelievable magnificence.

The peasant's life was hard, but it was never a lonely one. On feasts of patron saints and other occasions the cheerful sound of the pipes would set the dancing going.

A scene of sixteenth-century town life. Along the street are tailors, an apothecary, a barber, and furriers.

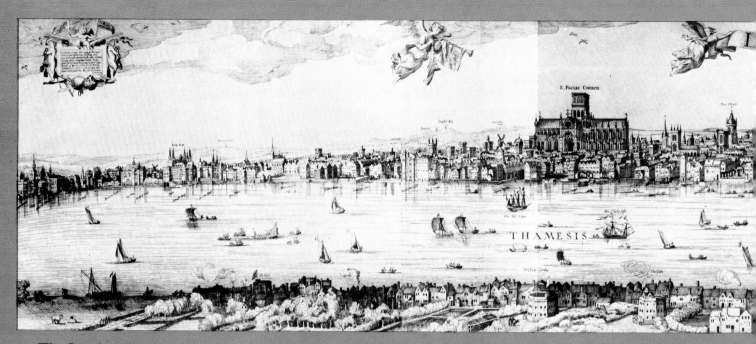

The London that knew Shakespeare was the great centre of trade, entertainment, and government, controlled by the rising middle class, not by the declining nobility. In Elizabeth's time the heart of the growing Puritan movement, it was later the core of Cromwell's Roundhead strength. The 1616 engraving shows the

In the forty-five-year reign of Elizabeth I, the English people laid the foundation of the vast empire won and lost in later centuries. Foreign commerce was energetically pursued by the Muscovy Company, the Levant Company, the East India Company, and others. The companies' capital and business skill were important in English expansion. Explorers, notably Frobisher and Davis, struggled to find a northwest passage, and greatly enlarged geographical knowledge. Other sailors, above all the "sea dogs" Sir John Hawkins and Sir Francis Drake, combined discovery with daring attacks on Spanish treasure ships coming from the New World. Philip II, the King of Spain, decided he must conquer England or lose the wealth of his empire. In the summer of 1588 the vast armada of high galleons entered the Channel. They were no match for the smaller, more manoeuvrable and better gunned English ships. A great storm, blown up by a "Protestant wind," then finished off the Armada. England was not only Protestant but increasingly Puritan. The Puritans were troublesome subjects, but their zeal and energy changed England at home and added to its greatness abroad.

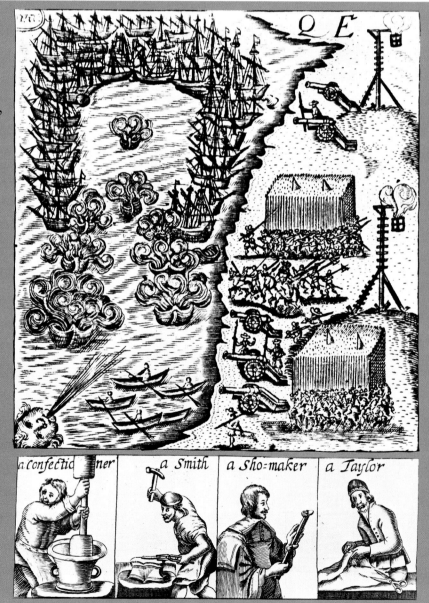

Top, the English prepare against invasion as the Armada approaches (1588). Below, four London tradesmen. Many of them were Puritans and lay preachers.

River Thames as the main thoroughfare in a city still closely surrounded by farm lands. St. Paul's Church dominates the north bank of the river. The severed heads of criminals make a grisly decoration on the southern gate of the famous Bridge, while the Southwark shore is the site of the Bear Garden and the Globe Theatre.

Charles I opening Parliament in the first year of his reign, 1625. Their later quarrel brought on the Civil War and in 1649 the execution of the King.

The first two Stuart kings, James I and Charles I, ruled over a restless, difficult people – a people who were now ready to form permanent settlements overseas. With little or no help from the government, they set up colonies in Virginia and Maryland and in New England. On the other side of the world the East India Company was establishing footholds on the Indian subcontinent. At home Parliament jealously guarded (and tried to expand) its rights and privileges, and closely questioned the King's acts and policies. The clash was severe enough when James was on the throne, but became far worse under his son. In fact, Charles tried to get along without Parliament during eleven years of "personal rule" (1629-40). Financial embarrassment forced him to recall Parliament, which met in a mood of bitterness because of the King's arbitrary taxation. His persecution of the Puritans also made him unpopular: one author who attacked bishops was fined, imprisoned, and had his ears cut off. The Long Parliament, beginning in 1640, put to death leading advisers of the King, rammed through constitutional reforms, and called for more radical changes. The country was torn between Parliament and the King's supporters.

THE
TWO FACES
OF FRANCE

When Champlain set sail in 1603, France was still the foremost country of Europe. Indeed, in the coming years under Louis XIV, *le roi soleil*, it was to strengthen its leadership in many aspects of the arts and sciences. In its great palaces and *châteaux* it revealed wealth, taste, and power that no country could begin to match. But France also went through terrible times in this era. There had just been over thirty years

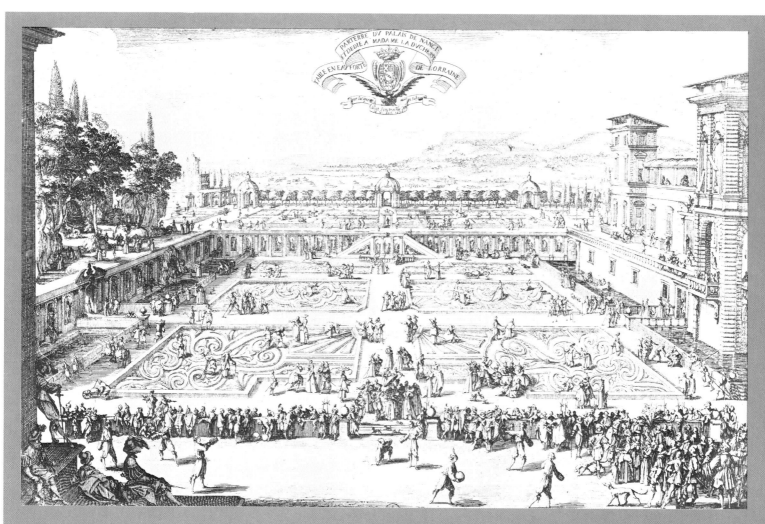

Above, the formal gardens of the ducal palace at Nancy in eastern France, an etching by the famous engraver Jacques Callot in 1624. Below, a view of the Louvre from across the Seine. Begun as a fortified royal palace in the thirteenth century; a museum since the Revolution.

of religious wars that nearly tore the country apart. Under Henri IV (1589-1610), with whom Champlain had campaigned, there was a period of rebuilding: a reviving France supported Champlain's founding of Quebec. After Henri's murder the great nobles tried to reassert themselves. Cardinal Richelieu then restored the power of the central government, but only at the expense of more warfare and bitter misery for the masses.

Ces pauures gueux pleins de bonaduetures
Ne portent rien que des Choses futures.

Callot pictured the miseries as well as the splendours of France. Richelieu's invasion of Lorraine showed the artist the grim features of war. Peasants were often dispossessed and forced to wander about the countryside (top left), looking for food, sometimes begging and sometimes terrorizing those who still had homes. In retaliation the authorities (upper middle) used ruthless methods to stamp out peasant revolts or even to punish minor thefts. Public executions were common in France (and elsewhere) until well into the nineteenth century. One cause of peasant unrest was the wretched state of the armies of the period. Without regular pay, and even without adequate food and clothing, soldiers (lower middle) were sometimes forced to pillage and to steal. But (bottom left) the peasants often turned on their oppressors in savage and desperate fury.

EVERYDAY ENGLAND

The land Captain Cook left behind is often called "Dr. Johnson's England." It was a period of relative calm and stability when Englishmen complacently felt theirs was by far the best country to live in. It was an age of elegance and taste, of great art, music, and literature, when the philosophers were in full spate and the great merchant fortunes were begun. At the same time it was a vulgar age, of incredibly heavy eating and drinking and gambling. An aristocratic age, it was also a rather free-and-easy time.

The caricaturist Thomas Rowlandson showed the coarse sides of life, even exaggerated them. Right, a street peddler hawking his wares, rat and mouse-traps. Below, "polite conversation" after dinner and too much port wine.

Left, Rowlandson draws a merchant examining a ledger book. It was a time of greatly expanding wealth and increasing trade. Better roads and more travel brought the inns into their own. The interior of one is seen to the right. Below, "Last Dying Speech and Confession" reminds us that hanging for petty offences was still common. Note the pickpocket in the background.

12 Months in London

GETTING READY TO SAIL

In the age of sail every great port had a life and character of its own. London was the port of the trade to India; Liverpool was the great embarking point for North America; Portsmouth was above all the port of the Royal Navy. It was here in 1755 that James Cook began his career in the navy as an ordinary seaman. Just before sailing could be a time of tearful parting as families said goodbye. But Rowlandson shows it as noisy, hilarious, usually drunken. A sailor and his money were soon parted.

CHAPTER TWELVE

The Map-maker of the Maritimes

SAMUEL CHAMPLAIN once gave his own list of the necessary virtues of "a good captain," and as he ran up his tally of thirteen voyages to Canada, he came close to reaching his own ideal. Such a man, he decided, had to be "hardy and active, possess good sea legs, and prove himself untiring at his work, so that whatever happens he may be able to appear on deck and in a loud voice issue orders to his crew. Occasionally he should lend a hand himself." Champlain went on in still greater detail:

He should see that the storerooms are dry and that there are plenty of provisions of good quality, with too much rather than too little, since the length of the voyage depends entirely on the weather. Prayers should be said night and morning, and the routine of the day carried out in an orderly manner. In conversation, a captain should be quietly spoken and affable, but peremptory in his orders, and on not-too-familiar terms with his ship's company, except for the officers. Disobedience he should punish severely, but he should encourage good behaviour, both with affection and with the granting of favours.

He should keep a compass of his own and should consult it frequently to see that the ship is on the right course. He must make certain that every man on watch is doing his duty. He must lie down in his clothes – ready, in case of an accident, to appear on deck quickly. Should an accident happen, the captain must give proof of his courage, even in the face of death, issuing his orders in a calm voice.

With the kind of infinite caution that Champlain himself sometimes displayed, the Canadian people have, over a span of more than three hundred years, taken him to heart as their principal national hero. A nation that is now a melting-pot of races can find inspiring universal virtues in "the good captain." His biographer, Bishop, says that following Champlain's first visit, "thenceforth his life was given to Canada . . . He first, and almost alone in his time, foresaw the future greatness of Canada. The principles he laid down for his colony enabled Canada to live, a strong, self-sufficient, permanent community. His adventures are blood-stirring to read, heart-stirring to reflect upon. He had the capacity to conceive great ideas and the force and vigour to put them into execution, despite every opposition of nature and of man. When others turned back, he went forward."

Certainly, on his return to France in September 1603, with his long and detailed report ready for his patron (and for the printer), it must have seemed that the jinx which had been riding Canadian events still prevailed. At Le Havre, he learned that Governor De Chastes had died shortly after he had dispatched the Pontgravé mission, and now the Baron de Rosny (later the Duc de Sully), the King's chief minister and the second most powerful man in France, was confirmed in his belief that the Crown should not invest in colonies in northern regions.

Utterly devoted to the demanding Henri, Rosny was trying desperately to restore the financial position of king and country. New France had no precious metals, it seemed, and its offshore fishing could not be held for France alone. The fur trade was certainly lucrative – profits of forty percent on a voyage were common. But since the Indians would trade with anyone at any point of contact along lengthy shores, it would be exceedingly difficult to maintain a monopoly. Moreover, Rosny did not believe that a sufficient number of Frenchmen would prove willing to rough it in the wilderness in the hope of later success. His policy was to make colonies pay for themselves by tying conditions of colonization to every fur monopoly. It must have looked like solid common sense at the time – but its soundness may be gauged by the fact that at the time of Champlain's death, thirty years later, there were still not one hundred Frenchmen residing in New France.

Champlain had an amusing bauble for his King – an Indian boy named "Canada," a present for the 3-year-old Dauphin – and he travelled to Fontainebleau to deliver his gift in person. He also gave the King a map that he had prepared of New France. The human gift did not long survive and neither did the map. Champlain was cheered somewhat to learn that De Chastes' place was to be filled by a man from his own province of Saintonge, the Sieur de Monts, Governor of Pons, a Protestant companion-at-arms of the King. De Monts had already made one voyage to Canada as an observer, travelling as far as the Saguenay. The nobleman was given all the fancy titles that had already been through several hands (he was also created vice-admiral) and a monopoly of the fur trade for ten years between the fortieth and forty-sixth degrees of latitude – that is, from Cape Breton to Delaware Bay.

For Champlain, there was a commission as a captain in the navy and an appointment as geographer and map-maker with the new expedition that De Monts was preparing for the following spring. Although Canada was to bring him little but hardship and financial loss, De Monts also fell victim to the curious lure of the northwoods. Indeed, without the steadfast support of De Monts over the next decade, all of Champlain's dreams would surely have crumbled to dust.

That winter, De Monts set up a new company with a capital of 90,000 *livres* to hold the monopoly, bringing in subscribers from St. Malo, La Rochelle, and other trading ports. In all, five ships were gathered. For his own units, De Monts chartered Captain Pontgravé's reliable *Bonne Renommée*, and a 150-tonner from Le Havre under Captain Timothée. Without resorting to the use of prisoners, he gathered together 120 workmen and soldiers, a Catholic priest and a Protestant parson, and a few noblemen who were seeking new seats for their families. The leading gentleman was Jean de Biencourt, Baron de St. Just, Sieur de Poutrincourt, another of the old Huguenot soldiers who had supported Henri on his rise to the throne. Others were the Sieurs d'Orville, Sourin, Beaumont, Boullé, Fougeray, De Genestou, and La Motte.

De Monts' ship sailed from the mouth of the Seine on March 7, 1604.* Having set a rendezvous for Canso, the narrow strait which leads past the foot of Cape Breton Island into the bottom of the Gulf of St. Lawrence, he left Pontgravé and his veteran pilot, Guillaume Duglas, to follow a few days later. It is not clear why De Monts settled on the little-known territory of Acadia (today's Nova Scotia and New Brunswick) for his settlement – in preference to some point on the St. Lawrence. Of course, the craggy seacoast had been known since the earliest voyages to the New World, but neither De Monts nor Champlain – nor any other member of the expedition, as far as we know – had ever set foot there. The fur-trading on that coast was scant when compared with that of the St. Lawrence valley. And of course, Champlain had been pushing hard for a colony on the river to provide a base for his exploration of the "salt sea" which he

* Champlain gave the sailing date as April 7. He was as fallible as the rest of us.

dreamed would carry him to the waving palms of the Moluccas. He may have set back his own cause with the chapter of sheer hearsay, which he included in *Des Sauvages*, about the silver, copper, and other mines supposedly found in *Acadie*, a country he described as being very beautiful and flat. On the other hand, De Monts, who had been no farther south than Tadoussac, may have simply decided that it was just too damned cold up there.

On May 8, the flagship entered the sheltered bay at La Have on the Canadian mainland, just below the Lunenburg of today. From this day on, as Champlain immediately set about his given task with compass, protractor, pencil, and chart paper, the coastline of the Maritimes and of New England begins to take clear shape. Before this day, the coasts were known only through the usually vague narratives of the earlier voyagers – Gomez, Strong, Pring, and Gosnold – and by the always obscure maps which bore only the faintest relation to the regions which they professed to describe. In his three years in the Maritimes, Champlain was to draw three brilliant maps of that immensely complicated shoreline, plus another baker's dozen of special charts of important harbours. These maps (which seem crude enough to modern eyes) represent, in fact, the most advanced cartographic achievement of their time.

Dr. W. F. Ganong, the great botanist and cartographer of Saint John, New Brunswick, once explained the daunting problems which faced Champlain in his charting forays along the coast, mostly in a bobbing open boat:

It is well-nigh impossible for anyone who has not himself mapped new country to realize the difficulty of transferring topography to paper accurately. The impression made by a complicated topography on the eye at its own level is so different from that given by the inspection of a modern map that the two hardly belong to the same psychological order... It is surprising how deceptive an appearance the actual country can present, how limited at times is the range of human vision, how opaque the hills, how like to islands the peninsulas the connections of which are hidden, how deep may seem a bight and how shallow a bay, and how completely telescoped to a uniform line a varied coast may become when seen in the haze of distance. All these difficulties, which the modern charts abolish for us, Champlain had to face, and to make his maps in the teeth of them.

For their main purpose – to guide the mariners who would follow – Champlain's maps quickly became the standard references, and, in general terms, they are still surprisingly accurate today.

Professor William L. Morton, in *The Kingdom of Canada*, says that Champlain's "eagerness to explore combined the intellectual curiosity of the scholar with the intuitive eye of the scientist." Dr. E. G. Bourne, former professor of history at Yale, adds an American

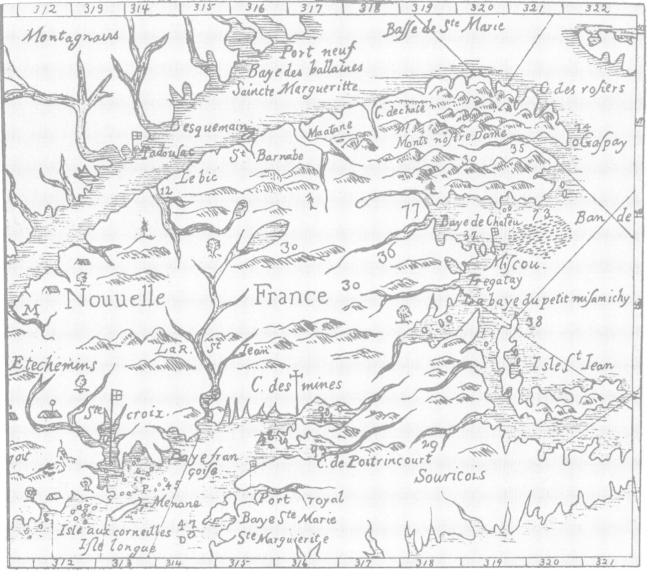

Champlain's map of the Maritimes shows a large number of place names that have survived to the present day.

accolade: "In addition to all this, he [Champlain] stands forth as perhaps the ablest of the earlier makers of America, a leader of indefatigable energy and sterling character... His fame is impregnably established and grows with the lapse of time."

From La Have, Captain Timothée took De Monts and his company into several harbours, including Medway and Liverpool Bay, before settling down for a month in Port Mouton—a name which they bestowed after a sheep bolted overboard, was drowned, recovered, and eaten. They had already seized the ship and cargo of a free-lance trader which had been carrying on business in ignorance of (or in defiance of) De Monts' sweeping monopoly. A longboat was sent up the coast to bring the *Bonne Renommée* to Port Mouton, and it found that the spirited Pontgravé had also seized some fur-traders at Canso. Champlain was sent in the opposite direction in another boat—twelve men in an eight-ton craft—to examine the southerly coast

and begin the search for a settlement site. He may have had a Micmac guide.

They jinked along to a summer breeze, and Champlain, sharply conscious of his discovery role, began to bestow names on bay and headland. Cape Negro got its name from a prominent black rock in the harbour; at Cormorant Island they took a barrel full of eggs; Cape Fourchu was indeed forked. Rounding sandy Cape Sable, they "found the shore completely covered with seals, whereof we took as many as we wished." The budding zoologist in Champlain had him scribbling down the first known list of birds of the Canadian Maritimes: ducks of three kinds, cormorants, snow geese, murres, wild geese, puffins, snipe, fish hawks, sea gulls, plover, herons, curlews, divers, loons, eiders, ravens, cranes, and others. He took his boat up into the narrow sleeve of St. Mary's Bay, after noticing the *petit passage* giving access into the Bay of Fundy which they soon called *la grande baye Francaise*.

On a small bay that we know today as Mink Cove, Champlain showed that he had not forgotten the tales of silver mines. He recorded (quoting a miner, *Maistre* Simon, who was in his crew) that "in this place there is a very good silver mine." (When others checked it out later, it was found to be lead ore–galena–of no commercial value.) On the eastern shore of St. Mary's Bay, he examined the harbour of today's Weymouth, at the mouth of the Sissiboo River. On the return journey to Port Mouton, the "good captain" had one of the many opportunities that would occur to display his cool leadership. His small boat was caught off the reefs of Cape Sable by a gale and he swiftly chose a sandy cove and ran ashore without any damage worth mentioning.

Pontgravé had delivered the stores from the *Bonne Renommée* and had departed to trade at Tadoussac. Champlain now led the two remaining ships–De Monts' own plus the prize that he had seized–into St. Mary's Bay. The low tidal flats, however, did not appeal to the soldier in De Monts, and after a short reconnaissance, he ordered further search up the Fundy shore.

Before they departed, there was a great to-do when it was realized that Father Nicolas Aubry, a priest from Paris, was missing. He had, as it happens, lost his way on Long Island, and although De Monts ordered cannons fired and sent out search parties, Aubry could not be found. In his version of this story, Marc Lescarbot, the lawyer-turned-writer who came out to Acadia in 1606, said that a Protestant minister with whom Aubry had often argued about religion was suspected of murder. Much later, Champlain was to write: "I have seen the minister and our *curé* come to blows in a religious quarrel. I do not know which was the more courageous, but I know very well that the minister complained sometimes to Sieur de Monts of

having been beaten ... I will leave you to judge if it was a pleasant sight. The savages were sometimes on one side, sometimes on the other, and the French mixed in according to their respective beliefs ... These insults were really a means to the infidel of making him still more hardened in his infidelity." In any case, the parson had been most maligned because Aubry was, by the sheerest chance, found by a fishing party on that long wilderness shore seventeen days later. He had kept himself alive with berries.

Champlain does not seem to have been unsettled by his chief's negative reaction to his discovery of St. Mary's Bay, and he cheerfully set off with him into the Bay of Fundy via the *petit passage*. They quickly came to the beckoning entry of Digby Gut, the narrow gateway into the beautiful land-locked Annapolis Basin. Champlain describes it ecstatically as "one of the finest harbours I had seen ... where two thousand ships could lie in safety. This place was the most suitable and pleasant for a settlement that we had seen." Champlain says that he named it Port Royal; Lescarbot credits De Monts with choosing the name; the nineteenth-century historian Parkman says that it was the Sieur de Poutrincourt who chose it. Whoever *did* name it, it was Poutrincourt who *received* it, as De Monts with his viceregal authority made him a gift of the place–an act that was later confirmed by the King.

But even the smiling tree-lined shores of this salt-water lake, its 750-foot entrance easily guarded by cannon, did not satisfy De Monts. He appears to have been drawn irresistibly by the hope of wealth from the mines which had been reported the previous year. The party crossed the easterly arm of Fundy, apparently missing the entrance to Minas Basin, where the world's highest tides toss as high as seventy feet. The mines, however, were never found–though the French label of "Bay of Mines" stuck, eventually being corrupted

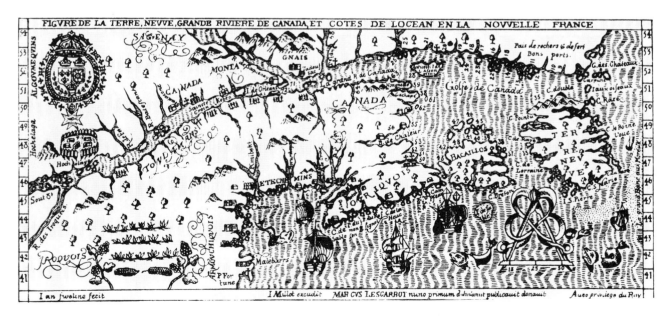

This map appeared in Lescarbot's Histoire de la Nouvelle France, *a book that was immensely popular in England as well as in France.*

into the present form. All along the towering cliffs of Advocate Harbour and Cape Chignecto, they searched until the end of June, at which time De Monts decided that they had better find a settlement site while good building weather yet remained.

Leaving the westerly arm of Chignecto for later exploration, they cut across the bay, and, on June 24, 1604–St. John's Day–they first saw and named the St. John River, at the site of the future metropolis of New Brunswick. On a gravel point, they erected a cross–a site now buried under Saint John's wharves and waterfront buildings. Perhaps the tidal phenomenon of the Reversing Falls which Champlain drew carefully into his chart of the harbour, appeared too great an obstacle to inland travel and De Monts ordered the search to continue.

When the Governor finally *did* select the site of the future capital of New France, he chose disastrously. The longboat had probed into the next major inlet below the St. John and, threading the many islands, entered the River of Etchemins–our St. Croix, the international boundary between Maine and New Brunswick. A steep five-acre island in midstream, close to today's St. Stephen, was agreed by all to be the perfect spot. We know it today as Dochet Island and it *was* perfect for one thing only–defence. Champlain, the old campaigner in the battles of Brittany, wrote:

The island is covered with firs, birches, maples, and oaks. It is naturally very well placed, with only one low area, which can easily be fortified. The shores of the mainland are about nine hundred to a thousand paces on either side and any ships using the river would be at the mercy of our cannons. This place we considered the best we had seen . . . considering we should be in the midst of "les sauvages." In time, we hope to pacify them and to put an end to the wars they wage against each other, in order that they might work for us and be converted to Christianity . . . We began to erect a barricade on a small islet, and this served as a platform for mounting our cannon.

Since all the Canadians whom Champlain or De Monts had seen up to this time had been absorbed by tribal warfare–it seemed almost to be the national sport–and proud of their merciless behaviour on the field and afterwards around the victory fires, it was natural that the French should allow defence to dominate their actions. As it was, though, the Micmacs and Malecites of the Maritimes never raised a hatchet to the white man–unless they were incited to do so by another white.

But even under the spell of a sunny July, De Monts should have remembered the main enemy–the Canadian climate. Dochet Island is about fifty feet above the tide on its eastern side but is sloped to the water on the west and north. Thus, although the commander ordered an outer ring of cedars to be left as a windbreak, his elaborate encampment was open to the pitiless nor'westers of winter. When the snow came, drifts lay four feet deep, there was not enough wood left on the island for firewood, and the 25-foot tides in the river jostled huge cakes of ice back and forth, often making foraging trips to the mainland quite impossible.

Summer was already over when the main buildings of the *habitation* were up, in the style of a fortified Normandy manor house. Poutrincourt now left for France, taking the two larger ships with him, and Champlain set out in one of the longboats rigged for sail, with a dozen sailors, to continue his coastal discovery. The Baron was eager to get men and materials together to take up his seigniory of Port Royal. Champlain, on the other hand, was just as eager to investigate the old stories of the Norumbega, as the Penobscot River was then known. André Thevet had published hearsay reports that there had been a small French fort about thirty miles upstream, at which point salt water met fresh water.

As Champlain doubled the capes and plumbed the inlets of Maine, he saw an arresting island jutting from the foaming sea. "It is very high," he wrote, "and cleft in places, giving it the appearance from the sea of seven or eight mountains, one alongside the other. The tops of most of them are bare of trees . . . I named it Mount Desert Island." His name has been retained (accented on the last syllable) by this famed New England summer resort where the palaces of the nineteenth-century multimillionaires clustered around Bar Harbour. Rather earlier, in 1613, the Jesuits attempted to establish here their first mission in America.

Champlain's two Indian guides made contact with local natives who led the party through the channel separating Deer Island from the mainland and into the wide mouth of the Penobscot. On this first venture into the legendary Norumbega, Champlain quoted its Indian name as "Pemetegoit," which was later rendered as "Pentagouet," the name seen on the old French maps of the region. In his revised works of 1632, Champlain mentioned a legend that the hub of the Norumbega country was "a large city, well populated with Indians, who are skilful and expert, making use of cotton thread." Then he added: "I am confident that most of those who mention them did not see them, and speak from what they heard from those who knew no more about them than they did." Champlain himself, seeking a meeting with the paramount chief of the region, Bessabez, pushed upstream sixty miles, as far as the site of today's Bangor, Maine, where rocks barred further progress by longboat. He went by canoe about two miles further, to the point at which a low waterfall creamed over a rocky ledge–known today as Treats Falls. In all this distance, he saw not a single village, only "one or two cabins of the savages with no one in them."

When Chief Bessabez arrived–in the company of a

minor chieftain, Cabahis, and about fifty followers – on September 16, Champlain himself delivered a harangue – first making certain that his men had their muskets ready "to do their duty in case they saw any movement of these people against us."

The Sieur de Monts had sent me to see them, and also their country; that he wished to remain friends with them, and reconcile them with their enemies, the Souriquois* and Canadians. He wanted to settle in their country and show them how to cultivate it, so that they might no longer lead so miserable an existence . . .

I made them presents of hatchets, rosaries, caps, knives, and other things; then we separated. The rest of this day and the following night they did nothing but dance, sing, and make merry, awaiting the dawn when we bartered a certain number of beaver skins. Afterwards, each returned – Bessabez with his companions in their direction and we in ours, well pleased to make acquaintance with these people.

Champlain learned that from the headwaters of the river across a portage over the height of land, the Indians could get into the Chaudière River, and thus into the St. Lawrence not far from present-day Lévis. He came back down the Penobscot to the Atlantic, past the site at Castine where, only nine years later, Claude de La Tour would build Fort Pentagoet. With one eye on the deteriorating weather, he pushed along the coast, trying to reach the next major waterway (called "*Kennebec*" by the Indians), but was forced to turn back by head winds. He had his mini-expedition back at the St. Croix on October 2.

Four days later, snow fell on the only Europeans known to be living on the continent north of Spanish-held Florida. The one small spring on the island froze completely, and by December, the ice in the estuary made it hazardous to cross to the mainland. The story of that awful winter – apparently much worse than average in the region – is a staple item in Canadian texts. Of seventy-nine men at St. Croix, thirty-five died and another twenty were close to death when the spring of 1605 came tardily.

Scurvy undoubtedly caused most of the deaths, and the disease was a dark mystery to the expedition's surgeons. They performed post-mortems with the same results that Cartier had noted at Quebec sixty-nine years earlier. Champlain noted that "we ate only salt meat and vegetables during the winter which produced poor blood; such in my opinion was in part the cause." It should be remembered that these thoughts of his were not published until 1613, by which time he had heard about scurvy from "learned men" and had obviously had Cartier's report of the healing *annedda* tree brought to his attention. It was, however, not until 1753 that the naval surgeon James Lind proved that limes and lemons, not to mention cabbages and

potatoes, cured this vitamin deficiency, bequeathing to his nation's sailors – and eventually to all Englishmen – the nickname "Limey."

Baron de Monts was understandably dismayed – he had, after all, lost half his settlers – and when his ships had not returned from France by early June, he was ready to give up and head for the St. Lawrence in the longboats, seeking rescue by the fishing fleets. It was the old reliable, the grizzled, earthy Pontgravé, who turned the tables, arriving on June 15 by longboat with the news that his loaded ship was anchored a few miles away and that a second ship, the *St. Etienne* of St. Malo, was on the way with more supplies. In his *Histoire de la Nouvelle France*, Lescarbot (who wasn't there himself) wrote: "You may imagine the great joy of all, how the cannons roared a welcome, how the trumpets sounded." Champlain contented himself with: "He was welcomed to the joy of all."

There now developed a renewed spirit of determination. De Monts immediately ordered a deeper examination of the southwestern coast which had been traced by Champlain the previous fall, seeking a more favourable site for his capital. He personally led a party of about twenty-five in the largest longboat, or pinnace, leaving only three days after the arrival of Pontgravé. This journey soon developed into the discovery voyage of New England, as Champlain's map-drawing hand never ceased to record the fiord-like river estuaries, the sandy bays, and the long fingers of rock that claw into the restless ocean.

After an exhaustive probing of the Kennebec and its tributaries, the Frenchmen crossed Casco Bay (which they called Baie des Sept-Iles), then proceeded purposefully down the southern strip (reading from the modern map) of Old Orchard Beach, Biddeford, Kennebunkport, Wells, Kittery, Hampton, Newburyport on the Merrimack, and around Cape Ann into the wide sweep of Massachusetts Bay. Champlain's notebooks recorded a profusion of items: the peaks of New Hampshire's White Mountains; the wild grapes on Richmond's Island, which earned it the name "the Isle of Bacchus"; the hair styles of the savages, similar to today's "hippie" cultists; the well-weeded patches of corn and beans at the populous villages; the flight of the red-winged blackbird; the point at which dugout canoes took over from the superior birch-bark craft of the north; the "horse-foot crab."

With the Indians of Cape Ann, Champlain demonstrated one of his ways of hurdling language barriers. Using a piece of charcoal, he drew a rough map of the cape and the immediate locality. He then showed this to the admiring natives and offered the charcoal to an Indian with a gesture to the southwards. The man took the hint and drew a larger bay (Massachusetts Bay), and by placing stones along the bayline, indicated that each stone represented the locale of a tribal band.

The odyssey continued into Boston Harbour, where Champlain christened the river emptying into the bay,

---

* The Micmacs of Acadia. French friendship with the Indians of the Maritimes is traditionally believed to have begun with this speech.

la riviere du Gua, commemorating the family name of his boss, De Monts. (The river is called the St. Charles today.) If the same De Monts had thought the site entirely suitable, he could have established his capital on the lands of the future Boston–a fascinating speculation in the 1970's. It was, after all, the ruin of his fortified settlement on the St. Croix that was accepted in 1797 as marking the border between the United States and Canada.

At Plymouth, fifteen years before the arrival of the *Mayflower*, Champlain went ashore to chart the harbour. He was welcomed by many Indians, some of whom had been line-fishing with bone hooks from canoes in the bay. They were obviously quite familiar with the white men from across the great lake and offered gifts of small squash, which, Champlain wrote, "we ate as a salad like cucumbers and they were very good." He noted that now the natives were wearing breechclouts of grass and hemp, indicating a shortage of animal skins. He called the place Port St. Louis. When the pilot realized that Cape Cod Bay was encircled by the long spit of Hyannisport and Chatham, he set a course to round the tip of the cape where Provincetown would later rise, and coasted along the eastern ocean beach into Nauset Bay. Here occurred the incident which was to dominate the entire summer's experience and which was to help shape French policy in America forever.

De Monts took his craft over the sand bars at the harbour entrance in order to inspect the busy Indian village around the beach. It must have been the forerunner of our suburbs, since "all around it [there were] little houses, about which each owner had as much land as was necessary for his support." Men and women, practically naked, their faces painted red, black, and yellow, danced a welcome. On July 21, De Monts, always the prudent old soldier, took ten armed men (including Champlain) ashore with him, leaving the rest to guard the longboat. They walked about two and a half miles along the shore, through flowering corn five feet high, noting beans, squash, and tobacco. Communication was extremely difficult, as the French had no interpreter who could understand the regional tongue.

The Indians coveted the large iron kettles which the Europeans were using to carry water from a spring in the sandhills, and on July 23 they snatched one from an unarmed sailor. A confused mêlée occurred in which the French seized an Indian who was visiting their boat, and the Indians on shore loosed their arrows at the man who had been robbed of his kettle. He was transfixed, and the Indians then stabbed him to death. The French fired muskets from their boat (Champlain's exploded in his hands and almost killed him) and then raced ashore. The natives scattered at the fusillade and the dead man, a carpenter from St. Malo, was collected and properly buried.

A number of the French wished to seek revenge, but De Monts chose to free the Indian prisoner, believing that it would be wrong to make the innocent suffer for the guilty. Champlain adds: "We were unwilling to do them harm, although it was in our power to avenge ourselves." The sentiments were admirably Christian and did honour to the French–but they were probably read as signs of weakness by the Indians.

As soon as the weather permitted, De Monts set off on the 400-mile return journey to the St. Croix, deciding that none of the places he had visited were suitable for his settlement. The murder of July 23 undoubtedly clinched matters for him. The lower coasts were heavily populated with Indians and some of them, at least, would kill for a kettle. This was a dangerous region in which to risk wintering with a mere handful of men, however well armed. (The British colonists who were shortly to follow the French to these New England shores had yet to learn this bitter lesson.) When the French returned to Acadia, switching their settlement site from St. Croix to Port Royal, on the opposite shore of the Bay of Fundy, one of their first acts was to site their four brass cannon.

Champlain and Pontgravé slowly scanned the shores of the Annapolis Basin and picked a small rise on the northern side of the head of the basin, protected by hills from the nor'wester, close to fresh water, with a good landing place. All the imported joinery and furniture was shipped over from St. Croix, and trees were felled on the spot to make a range of buildings compactly set around a central courtyard. The rear walls were loopholed for muskets, and the front was palisaded, with the cannons mounted on a projecting platform.

Here at last, of all the frail settlements so far raised in the northern latitudes of America was the first that would prevail. Port Royal would be several times attacked and razed, temporarily abandoned, but always revived. And on its site today–at Lower Granville, Nova Scotia–there stands a trim replica of the original in a national historic park. In 1904, Annapolis Royal, close by on its river, happily acknowledged its French beginnings with a monument to the half-forgotten De Monts.

Only three of the survivors of the St. Croix winter volunteered to take their chances at Port Royal: Champlain, the Sieur de Fougeray, and the pilot, Pierre Champdoré. They were joined by the forty newcomers who had arrived from France that June with Pontgravé, and the old Huguenot trader was given command of the settlement when De Monts sailed. Champlain showed no rancour at being passed over. Within the tightly classified society of France of the seventeenth century, he was to spend the greater part of his life as someone else's deputy. After planting his garden, Champlain made a brief foray by longboat, revisiting the St. John River, where he persuaded a chieftain to help him search once again for those elusive copper mines at the head of the Bay of Fundy.

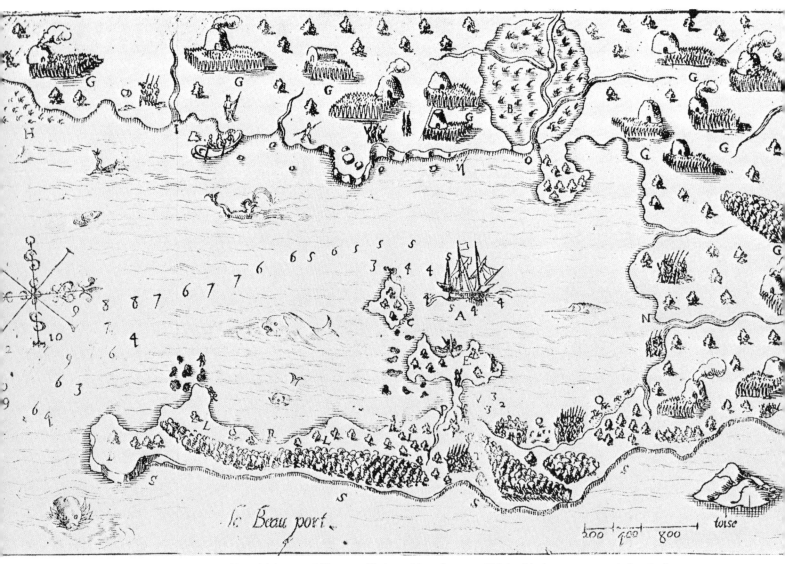

Champlain's map of Gloucester Harbour, Massachusetts, which he visited seventeen years before the first English settlement there. It also illustrates an incident that occurred when a group of Indians, who intended to surprise some men washing their linen (P), were in turn surprised by Champlain (V) and Sieur de Poutrincourt (T) and began to dance, pretending they meant no harm. The remaining letters indicate topographical features and Indian dwellings.

It was a happier winter at Port Royal–it didn't snow until December 20–but the story of how the colonists lived, quarrelled and hunted, made acquaintance with Chief Membertou and his friendly Micmacs (particularly the obliging Indian girls) is told in many other volumes. Champlain wrote up the notes of his discoveries, drew fair copies of his maps and charts, and waited impatiently for spring so that he could renew journeying beyond his previous limit at White Cape (Cape Cod).

On March 16, 1606, Champlain and Pontgravé set out in the larger longboat "on a voyage of discovery along the coast of Florida." They were pushing their luck so early in the season and were driven ashore on an islet off Grand Manan Island by a storm, being extremely lucky to escape with only a slightly damaged boat. But Pontgravé, who apparently had a heart problem, became ill and the expedition returned to Port Royal. They tried again a month later, but this time were wrecked in a fog while trying to negotiate the channel of Digby Gut. They now had no craft suitable for long journeys, and the plan languished.

When the Sieur de Monts had not arrived from France by the middle of July, despair seemed to hang over the courtyard of Port Royal, and Pontgravé decided to take his settlers in small boats around to the Gulf of St. Lawrence in order to seek rescue from the fishermen of Brittany. They left two volunteers at the fort–not including Champlain this time–and set off on July 17. A week later, slowly rounding Cape Sable, they spotted De Monts' associate, Ralleau, heading for Port Royal by longboat. He bore the heart-lifting news that the Sieur de Poutrincourt was on his way with more settlers and supplies in the *Jonas*, a ship of 120 tons. Dolour vanished and the Port Royalites turned about with a cheer.

By the time they got back to their base at the head of the Annapolis Basin, the *Jonas* was already there, having been welcomed by cannon by the two volunteers, Miquelet and La Taille (who surely deserve their own bronze plaque on the wall of the *habitation* at Port Royal). Poutrincourt had had his troubles in France trying to recruit settlers for his baronial seigniory, but now he had with him Jean, his 15-year-old son; Robert, the son of Pontgravé; and two men whose pages in the Canadian story would soon outshine his own–Louis Hébert, a Paris druggist with a yen to farm, and the previously mentioned Marc Lescarbot. With Champlain later at Quebec, Hébert would win recognition as Canada's first farmer and founder of a *habitant* dynasty. And after a single season in Acadia, during which he wrote Canada's first poem and first play, Lescarbot went home to compose his massive *Histoire de la Nouvelle France*.

Turning down a chance to return to France with the elder Pontgravé, Champlain now led his third Acadian commander, Poutrincourt, on a voyage down the southern coasts, still looking for a settlement site in a warmer climate. This venture added practically nothing to the discoveries of 1605 because Poutrincourt would not take Champlain's advice to sail directly to Cape Cod and begin looking from there. Instead, he strangely insisted on seeing the territory that De Monts, the "little king of Canada," had already rejected. There was nothing of the season left when they passed down the eastern shore of Cape Cod and entered the bay known as Stage Harbour.

As the French made preparations to leave their Indian hosts after a fortnight's stay, the tragedy of Nauset Harbour was virtually re-enacted. Five men were slow to obey Poutrincourt's order to return to the boat and four of them paid for their tardiness with their lives. Champlain tells the grim tale:

The next morning, the 15th of October, the Indians came as expected to check on our men, whom they found asleep, except one who was tending the fire. Seeing them in this condition, the Indians, to the number of 400, came quietly over a little hill and shot a salvo of arrows at them as to give them no chance of escape. Fleeing as fast as they could

towards our longboat and crying out, "Help, they are killing us!" some of them fell dead in the water, while the rest were all pierced with arrows. One more of the sailors died a short time afterwards.

When a rescue party–including Champlain, Hébert, Daniel Hay, and the surgeon–got ashore, the Indians fled out of musket range and watched while the dead were buried and a cross raised. As soon as the white men returned to their boat, the natives dug up the corpses and pulled down the cross. The French fired their small cannon, probably a *perrier*, but the Indians had obviously had previous experience of European weaponry and flung themselves to the sand at every report, allowing the shot to whistle harmlessly over their heads. Lescarbot reported the final indignity: "They turned their backs to the longboat and made mock at us by taking sand in their two hands and throwing it between their buttocks."

The French sailed away in anger and frustration. Young Robert Pontgravé had lost three fingers when his musket exploded in his hand. Champlain said: "There was little chance of taking vengeance . . . That we must postpone until it should please God." Attitudes had hardened since the incident at Nauset Harbour two years earlier. A short time later, they duped a group of Indians into coming to the boat, and half a dozen of them were callously "hacked and hewed in pieces." Champlain comments: "We did not depart without the satisfaction of feeling that God had not left unpunished the misdeeds of these barbarians." (At this point, one may be forgiven for asking *who* were the barbarians.)

After a brief run along the south coast of the cape, during which they sighted the island that millions of visitors have since enjoyed as Martha's Vineyard, the French were turned back by head winds. This was to be the southern limit of Champlain's voyaging and he wrote his signature to the map by giving his own name to an insignificant river flowing into Nantucket Sound at Wood's Hole. It lost the name over the centuries, but it can still be seen on his masterwork, the *Carte de la Nouvelle France*, of 1632. It was the modest gesture of an unassuming man.

CHAPTER THIRTEEN

The Fateful Volley

THE truly remarkable thing about the discoveries and achievements of Samuel Champlain is that they happened at all. At nearly every turn, he was a pawn in a game played by others. His career often hung on distant events which he could not influence and, frequently, of which he was in total ignorance. He was merely lieutenant to half a dozen of the leaders of his time (some of them poor stuff indeed); he was always struggling against impossible odds; he was forgotten, slighted, unrewarded, and eventually sacked (without his even knowing it). Yet, inspired and sustained by a unique blend of realism and mysticism, and by an unpretentious courage, he kept to his chosen course and founded Canada. He was the first to understand this country and to accept its peculiar challenges, and anyone seeking to take the measure of modern Canada can do much worse than reflect upon his life.

When the Duc de Sully in 1607 cancelled the ten-year fur-trade monopoly of the Sieur de Monts, causing the temporary break-up of the colony in Acadia, Champlain, now past forty, is immediately seen back in France pressuring De Monts for a fresh establishment in the interior, on the St. Lawrence River. De Monts refused to accept defeat at the hands of his enemies at court. Francis Parkman says that "the passion for discovery and the noble ambition of founding colonies" had taken possession of De Monts, and we have Champlain's own word that De Monts "decided to continue such a noble and worthy enterprise, not counting the difficulties and labours it had cost him in the past."

Champlain argued that the Atlantic coast was poor in furs and that his long journeys had shown there was no strait in those latitudes leading to the countries of the Orient. At Quebec, however – he recalled from his 1603 voyage how the mighty "River of Canada" narrowed there – a comparative handful of men in a strong fort could deny the waterway to both illegal traders and the raiding Iroquois. They could make quick trading journeys up to the rapids of St. Louis – to Cartier's Mont-Royal – and gather the furs into safety at their *dépôt* by the great rock that reared three hundred and fifty feet above the narrows. And there was always the prospect of the "salt sea" which had been described by the Indians as being about 1,200 miles away in the western hinterland. What could it be but the Pacific of Magellan and Drake?

Henri IV listened sympathetically to his old comrade-at-arms, and early in 1608 he countermanded his own council's decision. De Monts could have his trading monopoly in New France renewed, but only for one year – and he must establish a settlement. The King knew that the English, under James I, were now taking a foothold in Virginia. The Dutch East India Company had taken a rich haul of furs out of the St. Lawrence in 1606, helping it to pay a dividend of seventy-five percent. Spain, England, and France were now all claiming the northern continent.

Thus, it is quite conceivable that Henri assisted the hard-pressed De Monts to raise the sizeable sum which he needed to charter, equip, and provision three ships. One ship, skippered by the experienced Pierre Champdoré, would return to Acadia; François Pontgravé would take the second, the *Lévrier* (under Captain Nicholas Marion), to trade in the St. Lawrence for the summer; while the third, the *Don de Dieu* (captained by Henri Couillard), would take Champlain and a band of settlers to Quebec. Champlain was now officially appointed as De Monts' lieutenant and he sailed from Honfleur on April 13, 1608.

In the dog-eared school readers and the buckram histories alike, this is the founding voyage of Canada, followed league by league down the great river from the pages of Champlain's *Voyages*. Within that prosaic diary, one can feel a faint pulse begin to beat, and when the book closes (in 1612) there is the waif of the wilderness nearing five years of age. Few infants have needed greater luck to survive.

In the first place, both Pontgravé and Champlain could easily have been dead before the summer and the whole project stillborn. The old trader had sailed a week ahead; and when he reached Tadoussac, he got a rough answer as he tried to enforce the new monopoly on a Basque party which was already bartering for furs with the Montagnais. Historically beset by the aggressive princes of France and Spain, the Basques would not honour the writ of Henri of Navarre and they turned their cannon on the *Lévrier*, possibly without warning, wounding Pontgravé and three of his crew with the first blast. They then boarded and disarmed the French vessel, allowing that they would return the guns when they were ready to sail for home. Pontgravé had been seriously wounded, and one of his men had succumbed.

This was the situation that greeted Champlain, who reached the Saguenay on June 3. The Basque captain, Darache, sent out a small boat to parley with the newcomer, apparently contrite but determined to continue trading. Champlain left the *Don de Dieu* in the roadstead and went in to see his associate. Apparently, Pontgravé was on the mend and they talked over the difficult situation. "We concluded," Champlain wrote, "that only by force could I enter the harbour, and to avoid the loss of the settlement for the year, we thought it best (so that a good cause should not become a poor one and thus all be ruined) to reassure them that we should take no action against them . . . and that they should undertake nothing against the King's interest. All differences would be settled in France. All this was agreed to and signed by each of us." Champlain then went aboard the Basque ship, where he was entertained hospitably. He was already exhibiting that flair for pragmatic compromise which is at the core of most Canadian progress.

Cartier and Roberval had taken their big ships right up to Quebec. Champlain, however, chose to leave the *Don de Dieu* anchored at Tadoussac and he set his carpenters to fitting out the roomy longboat which had been carried across the ocean as deck cargo. While they worked, he made another probe up the tantalizing Saguenay. "I have often desired to explore it but have been unable to do so without the natives, who have been unwilling that I or any of our people go with them." The Montagnais, of course, were not about to ruin their middleman trade by allowing the Europeans to make direct contact with the tribes in the northern hinterland who "were in sight of the salt sea." It is interesting, though, to speculate that if Champlain had insisted, he might well have put his name on the inland sea that Henry Hudson would not reach for another two years. As for the fabled Saguenay country, Champlain still thought that it wasn't worth a *sou*.

On the now-familiar excursion upstream past the islands of the *lievres* and the *coudres*, Champlain affixed names to Salmon River, Cap a l'Aigle (Eagle Cape), Whirlpool River, La Malbaie (Murray Bay), and Cap Tourmente (where, he noted, the water began to turn fresh). He repeated a lot of topographical detail which he had given in his *Des Sauvages* five years earlier, remarking this time that the cataract of Montmorency was 150 feet high. (Just about everyone still underestimates its height; it is actually 265 feet high.) "The fine, good country of the great river" began at the Island of Orleans, and immediately beyond was Quebec, Champlain's undoubted goal. He says that when he arrived there with his company of thirty-two on July 3, he "looked for a place suitable for our settlement" – but he certainly didn't look anywhere *else*. When he came to revise and edit his journals in 1632, he remained content with these impressions:

I could not find any place more suitable or better situated than the point of Quebec, so called by the natives, which was covered with nut trees. I at once employed a group of our workmen in cutting down trees to clear a site, another group in sawing planks, another in digging the cellar and making ditches, and another in going to Tadoussac in the longboat to bring more supplies. The first thing we made was the storehouse to put our supplies under cover, and it was finished quickly through the hard work of everyone . . .

Our quarters were in three main buildings of two stories. Each one was 18 feet long and 15 feet wide. The storehouse was 36 feet long and 18 feet wide, with a fine cellar six feet deep. All the way round our buildings I had a gallery made, outside the second story, which was very convenient.

There were also ditches 15 feet wide and 6 feet deep. Outside these I made several salients which enclosed a part of the buildings, and there we put our cannon. In front of the building, there is an open space about 24 feet wide and 30 or 40 feet long which reaches the river bank. Round about the buildings are very good gardens, and an open place on the north side of 100 or 120 yards long and 50 or 60 yards wide.

Not exactly epic prose – but that was the capital of Canada in the summer of 1608. You can look down on the spot today from the boardwalk of the Dufferin Terrace, alongside the Chateau Frontenac which has sat in turreted splendour on the rock of Quebec since 1893. The moat ditches of the *habitation* run deep under the church of Notre Dame des Victoires and beneath the adjacent market square in the present Lower Town.

While the artisans and workmen toiled, slapping blackflies and mosquitoes, Champlain crossed the mouth of the St. Charles and searched for the site of Cartier's fort, which had been abandoned seventy-two years earlier. About two miles up the St. Charles, he found "the remains as of a chimney . . . what seem to have been ditches . . . large, squared, worm-eaten pieces of timber . . . three or four cannonballs." Somewhat enigmatically, he adds: "All these things show clearly that this was a settlement founded by Christians."

Champlain the cartographer

A. *The site where the settlement is built.* B. *Cleared land where wheat and other grains are sown.* C. *The gardens.* D. *Small stream flowing from among the swamps.* E. *River where wintered Jacques Cartier, who then named it St. Croix, which was transferred 15 leagues above Quebec.* F. *Stream from the marshes.* G. *The place where hay was collected for the live stock that had been brought hither.* H. *The great Montmorency Falls which descend from a height of more than 25 fathoms into the river.* I. *End of the island of Orleans.* L. *Very sharp point on the shore to* the east of Quebec. M. *Boisterous river leading to the Etchmins.* N. *The great river St. Lawrence.* O. *Lake of the boisterous river.* P. *Mountains in the distance: Bay which I named New Biscay.* Q. *Lake of the great Montmorency Falls.* R. *Bear River.* S. *Son-in-law river.* T. *Flats which are covered at every tide.* V. *Du Gas Mountain very on the bank of the river.* X. *Flowing stream suitable to work every kind of mill.* Y. *Gravel bank where one finds quantities of diamonds slightly better than those of Alencon.* Z. *Diamond Point.* 9. *Places where the Indians frequently encamp.*

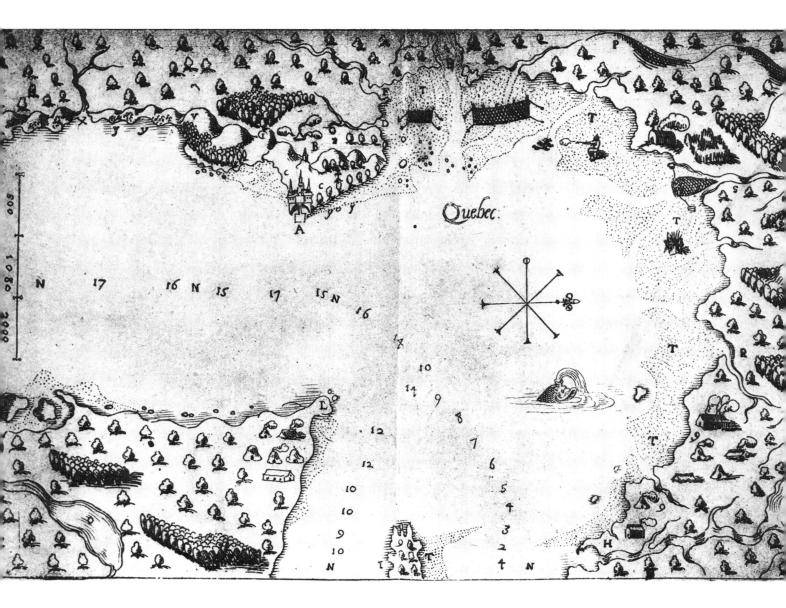

Champlain deliberately distorted the scale of this map of Quebec and the surrounding area in order to include features of particular interest.

A. *The Warehouse.* B. *Pigeon-loft.* C. *Detached building where is the smithy and where the workmen are lodged.* G. *Galleries all around the lodgings.* H. *The Sieur de Champlain's lodgings.* I. *The door of the settlement with a drawbridge.* L. *Promenade around the settlement with ten feet in width to the edge of the moat.* M. *Moat the whole way around the settlement.* O. *The Sieur de Champlain's Garden.* P. *The Kitchen.* Q. *Space in front of the settlement on the shore of the river.* R. *The great river St. Lawrence.*

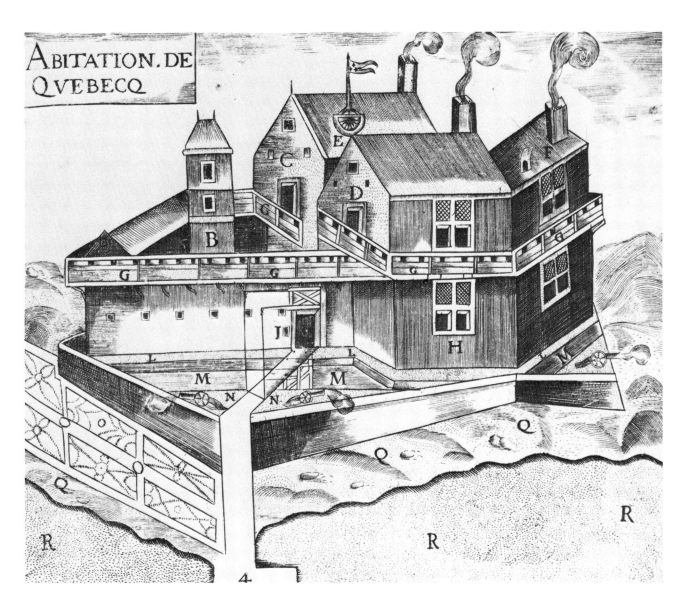

Champlain's drawing of the Habitation built at Quebec in the summer of 1608.

The incident at Cape Cod where the mutinous Duval was nearly killed.

began working on the cupidity of the remainder. We have Champlain's own word that "so successful were they in their plotting that they would have attracted all to their side, even my servant, making them many promises which they would not have met."

Le Testu returned before the trap was sprung and one of the conspirators, Antoine Natel, quailing at mutiny at the last minute, blabbed the whole story. Natel was afraid of his fellow plotters, as they had "all promised mutually" that the first to speak out would be stabbed to death. Le Testu promised him sanctuary, and took him to where Champlain waited alone in the woods. As soon as he had the facts, Champlain hatched a counterplot. He gave two litres of wine to a trusted man and told him to share it with the four remaining conspirators. The cover-story was that the wine was a present from the ships at Tadoussac. At 10:00 P.M., by which time the two bottles were drained and the men tipsy, Champlain strode in and ordered them arrested.

"Then were my gentry properly astonished" – Champlain allowed himself this wisp of wry humour. He now awakened the whole settlement and demanded the truth from the shamed and quaking crowd. They all blamed Duval and his cronies. As always, Champlain allowed common sense to conquer any anger and he forgave all but the key plotters, who were taken under guard to Tadoussac. All concerned made and signed statements, and the urgent work of securing the buildings against the coming winter was pushed ahead with a new energy.

When Pontgravé – who was soon to sail for France with a rich haul of pelts – brought the prisoners back to Quebec, a criminal trial was held. It was the first recorded in Canada.

The decision to turn the other cheek to the Basques at Tadoussac now threatened to cost Champlain his life. The most famous plot in the entire Canadian drama begins to unfold on that narrow stage. When the French crew went ashore at the Saguenay, the Basque skipper, although outwardly amicable, probably fed a few malcontents (every ocean-going ship of the day had some) the idea of murdering their leader once they reached Quebec and handing over all the trading goods, stores, provisions, and guns – in return for a substantial reward. The free-lance traders would then be able to pass up the river and trade without hindrance. The details of the plan suggest a more subtle mind than that of the unlettered locksmith, Jean Duval, who was the putative ringleader. Someone would raise a false alarm of Indian attack at night, and when Champlain ran out, he was to be shot. In the darkness and confusion, it would be difficult for anyone loyal to Champlain to be sure just what had happened, and the cabal would seize control.

It seems that the loyalists were pretty thin on the ground, anyway. Champlain had sent five of the most trustworthy to Tadoussac on another supply trip under the orders of the pilot Guillaume le Testu, and Duval "corrupted four of the worst characters" and

After Pontgrave and I, along with the captain of the ship, the surgeon, master, mate, and other seamen had heard their depositions and cross-examinations, we decided it would be sufficient to execute Duval as the ringleader, and to serve as an example to those who remained to conduct themselves properly in future, and in order that the Spaniards and Basques who were numerous in the region might not rejoice over the affair. We decided the three others should be condemned to be hanged but meanwhile should be taken back to France and handed over to the Sieur de Monts to receive fuller justice, according as he might decide . . . Duval was hanged and strangled at Quebec and his head placed on the end of a pike and set up in the highest place in our fort.

It is another, austere face that Champlain turns toward us here. Jean Duval, an old comrade, had been in Acadia with the Sieur de Poutrincourt and had been a member of the 1606 expedition down the Atlantic shore. During the Indian treachery at Cape Cod, he was the only one of the five Frenchmen attacked who lived, though wounded by an arrow. What *les sauvages*, those barbarians who insisted on hanging the scalps of their enemies on poles, thought about the Christian head grinning on its stick over Quebec is nowhere recorded.

With his prisoners in chains, Pontgravé sailed on September 18, leaving Champlain with twenty-eight men amid the brief scarlet and gold of autumnal colour. Anyone who was not working on the buildings was out clearing ground for gardens and crops. While the leaves were falling on October 15, Champlain was sowing rye. Even later, he planted some native vines for wine, which–believe it or not–"prospered extremely well."

An Indian band had camped around the *habitation* while they trapped eels in the river and Champlain had his first chance to study them at leisure. "When they have food," he wrote, "they save nothing for another day. They eat their fill day and night–and then starve." They would come running for shelter to his gate when someone had a nightmare which foretold harm. He tried to reassure them that "they should not take dreams as truth" and that if they feared attack by the Iroquois they should set out sentries at night, each man taking his turn. But, he adds, "this advice was of small avail." Champlain would allow the Indian women and girls into his courtyard during these scares, but he shut the warriors out on security grounds. He blamed the eels for a wave of dysentery that brought the first French deaths–the informer Natel and a sailor. As the winter deepened, the hungry Indians ate even stinking carcasses that the French had hung in the trees as bait for martens.

None of Champlain's preparations could ward off the scurvy, and although it didn't strike in full force until February, it was soon scything through the thin company. The surgeon, Bonnerme, was one of the first to go of "the inward corruption" and by spring only eight remained–of whom four were ill. It was a much worse casualty rate than that at St. Croix in the winter of 1604-05. The *annedda* tree that saved Cartier's men had slipped back into myth. In exasperation, Champlain noted: "As far as I have seen, this sickness attacks quite as much the man who takes great care of himself as it does the man who lives wretchedly." He was convinced that salted meat was a prime cause, but he also blamed "certain vapours" that exuded from earth when it was dug for the first time.

As sure as the seasons, Pontgravé was back at anchor at Tadoussac on May 28, 1609, sending his son-in-law, Claude Godet, the Sieur de Marais, by longboat to check on the state of Quebec. The laconic Champlain records only: "This gave me much satisfaction." Godet held the fort while Champlain went downstream to hear the news from home and to confer with his colleague. Pontgravé handed over a letter from the Sieur de Monts, whose monopoly had now expired, ordering Champlain to return to France in the autumn to report on his activities and his explorations. It was now the travelling season, and Champlain was eager to sketch his way into those great voids on the straggling maps of New France. His fate was in the hands of others and he could not be sure that he would ever return to the St. Lawrence.

He had made promises to the Montagnais and the Hurons that he would help them make war on their inveterate enemies, the Iroquois. It was already obvious to him that unless the Algonquins could travel freely on the western rivers, no furs would reach Quebec–and without profits, the colony must quickly wither. Thus, he ensured that the French-Iroquois enmity, born in Cartier's time, was rekindled to flame for the next century. For the present, though, the warpath was also the road to discovery.

With twenty men, Champlain set out from Quebec on June 18, meeting at Batiscan, about seventy miles upriver, a large war party of Hurons and Algonquins who were on *their* way to Quebec to meet their French ally. Most of these braves had never seen a European before and they crowded around Champlain, touching his steel breastplate and clothes in wonderment. They were of two tribes, under the chiefs Iroquet and Ochateguin. After abundant speech-making, the chiefs asked Champlain to fire some muskets, possibly as a convincer to some of the warriors. "They uttered loud cries of amazement," Champlain noted, "especially those who had never heard or seen the like." The Indians then wanted to go to Quebec to see the French buildings, objects of awe to men with Stone Age implements. With tireless good humour, Champlain agreed to retrace his steps.

After a few days' sightseeing and feasting at Quebec–during which Pontgravé arrived in response to an urgent note from Champlain–the combined party set off for Lake St. Peter, where the "River of the Iroquois" emptied into the St. Lawrence. After two days, probably by prior arrangement between them, Pontgravé turned back to attend to his trading and Champlain continued with a group totalling twelve Frenchmen. It included Claude Godet and the pilot La Routte. Somewhere about the site of modern Sorel, where the Richelieu ends its eighty-mile run, about two-thirds of the Indians changed their minds about crossing the doorstep of the feared Iroquois. The remainder, in twenty-four canoes, escorted the French longboat up to the first big rapids, until the oarsmen gave up the struggle. At Chambly, Champlain went ashore with five men to see if there was any chance of getting the boat through. It was hopeless.

The Indians had told him of a "very large lake filled with beautiful islands" up ahead and he was determined to add it to his new map. "No Christians but ourselves had ever penetrated to this place," he noted. He called for volunteers to go on with him in the canoes, which the Indians easily portaged around the rapids. Only two men stepped forward. The other faint-hearts he ordered to return to Tadoussac with the longboat. From twenty, the French stiffening had shrunk to three; and from three hundred, the Indians were down to sixty—though not a single arrow had yet been loosed. Champlain seemed serenely confident, and as he buckled on his steel breastplate, he told the departing sailors that, by God's grace, he would see them shortly.

On St. Theresa Island, he again tried to persuade the Indians to set out sentries at night, but they told him they worked too hard during daylight to stay awake at night. They sent a reconnoitering squad ahead a few miles and otherwise took their chances in the dark. As they neared the Iroquois, they began to sleep all day and travel all night, eating a ration of previously baked meal to avoid lighting cooking fires. They relied on their witch doctors, who would writhe about naked while in converse with the spirit world, to inform them of the chance of battle.

On July 13, Champlain ascended into the lake that was later to carry his name. In the dawn of the next day, the shining water in the verdant valley stretched to the southern horizon, hemmed in by the Green Mountains to the east and by the hazy blue Adirondacks to the west. The islands at the foot of the lake— Grande, La Motte, Valcour—were uninhabited, no-man's land in the internecine struggles between the Algonquins and the Five Nations of the Iroquois Confederacy. In clearings and river meadows, bears ambled unconcerned and stags lifted their great racks to watch the canoes pass.

Travelling by night, the war party consumed a fortnight in passing up the strategic waterway, which, in the long years ahead, would become the traditional invasion route from Canada to the United States—and vice versa. At 10:00 P.M. on July 29, paddling quietly, expecting ambush now, the lead canoes spotted a flotilla of the heavy elm bark canoes of the Mohawk off the promontory known today as Crown Point. With a courtesy as refined as their cruelty, the combatants agreed to fight on the nearby shore "as soon as the sun should rise." Champlain and his two fellow Frenchmen, whose names were not recorded, were armed with "light weapons"—perhaps pistol and dagger— and each took an arquebus, a short-barrelled, muzzle-loading musket with a range of about fifty yards. Champlain loaded his with four steel balls. The French were kept hidden from the enemy until the action began.

The Iroquois called themselves the *"ongue honwe,"* the "superior men," and on this occasion they certainly had the superiority of numbers—about two hundred to sixty. But they were about to meet men from a different and more dangerous world, armed by a culture which was thousands of years more advanced than their own. When the blast of Champlain's musket had ceased curving from the tree trunks at the lake edge, the three Mohawk chieftains lay shot, dead and dying. When another musket roared, more men dropped, and the Iroquois broke and fled. Champlain reloaded and pursued "and killed still more of them."

The delighted Algonquins and Hurons seized a dozen prisoners for the torture stakes. Champlain described the grim scene:

Our Indians lit a fire and each took a brand and burned this poor wretch a little at a time to make him suffer the greatest torment. To revive him, they would throw water on his back. They tore out his nails and applied fire to the ends of his fingers and to his penis. Afterwards, they scalped him and dripped molten gum on the crown of his head. Then they pierced his arms near the wrists and pulled out his sinews with sticks...

They begged me to join them, but I pointed out that we did not commit such cruelties but that we killed people outright... When they saw I was not pleased, they told me to shoot the man with my arquebus... When he was dead, they cut off his head, arms, and legs... They cut the heart into several pieces and gave it to his brother and other prisoners to eat.

It's possible that the shock wave of the French firearms —the first that any of the Indians of the interior had known—would have opened the way for Champlain to extend his discovery even further south. The braves who fled from Ticonderoga (a memorial tablet today marks the approximate site of the encounter) would make certain that the story did not lose in the telling. The lesson was repeated at Sorel the following year, when Champlain was wounded in the ear and neck by arrows. And from that time forward, the frontal attack was dropped from Indian tactics and the silent, swift raid was perfected.

Champlain knew that he had reached the rapids connecting his lake to another. The singing water reminded the French of bells and they later named the place "Carillon." The Indians informed him—presumably, mostly by sign language—that at the head of this second lake (Lake George) a path extended to a river that led to the coast of Norumbega, adjoining Florida. This was, of course, the Hudson River, which could have taken the three Frenchmen to Manhattan seventeen years before the Dutch established New Amsterdam. The elated victors, however, were eager to return to their villages with their gruesome harvest of scalps, and with prisoners for their women and children to torment. Champlain was the first to record this chilling aspect: "They [the women] greatly surpass the men in cruelty, for by their cunning they invent more cruel torments, and take delight in them."

The canoes covered about twenty-five miles that same day, and running with the current, the Montagnais had the Europeans back at Quebec in three days. Champlain went on with his allies to Tadoussac, where he was entertained by the spectacle of all the women stripping naked and running out to welcome the canoes. They hung the Iroquois scalps "around their necks as if they had been precious chains." They gave a scalp to Champlain too, and he solemnly promised to present it to his King.

The Father of New France

*Like all portraits of Champlain, this one by Hamel is
imaginary. We can only assume he was short and slight.*

Samuel Champlain, seaman and soldier, explorer
and map-maker, colonizer and writer—the list
of achievements is both long and impressive,
and the man credited with these achievements
is one of the most remarkable figures in the
history of Canada. His origins may be obscure,
but the details of his later life comprise a
story of steadfast courage, resourcefulness, and
truly indomitable persistence. At various points
in his active career, he charted the coast of
New England, defeated the Iroquois at Lake
Champlain, and journeyed inland as far as
Lake Huron. Yet most important of all, he was
responsible for securing French holdings in
Canada and for building, in the face of much
opposition, a "New France" in the New World.

A Man at his Trade

Champlain's journeys into the interior of Canada were, in a sense, the holidays of his life, for at no other time was he so free to follow the true bent of his genius. As a geographer on the eastern coasts of America, he had been subject to the whims and directives of De Monts and Poutrincourt. And at the courts of Fontainebleau, he waited for weeks and months in the antechambers of prelates and nobles. But in the vast wilderness of Canada, Champlain was the unquestioned leader of Frenchman and Indian alike. Here, in the uncharted reaches of forest and lakeland, he reaped some of the richest rewards of his long career. Champlain was indeed the historian of St. Croix, Port Royal, and Quebec–but only secondarily. Both by temper and by inclination, he was the discoverer–a decisive man of action whose inland quests along the rivers of eastern Canada are among the most remarkable achievements of our early history.

The artist De Rinzy's conception of how Champlain travelled in the wilderness.

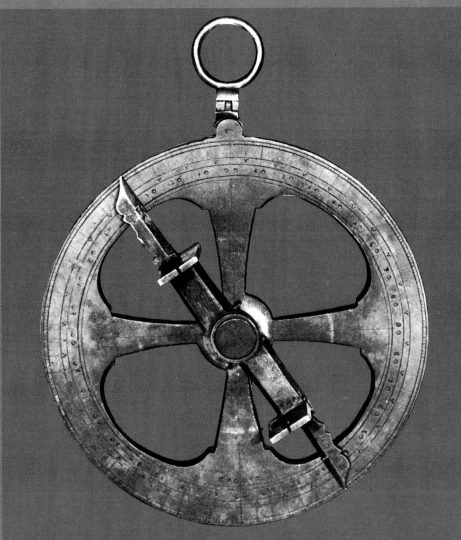

Above is an astrolabe bearing the date 1603. It was found at Green Lake, north of the village of Haley's Station, Ontario. Some authorities are certain that it was lost there by Champlain when he was on his way north to visit the Algonquin Indians of Allumette Lake in 1613. It is known from his account of the journey that he had such an instrument with him to take the latitude, for he was always the geographer, even when on political missions.

Against The Iroquois

Champlain was following French policy when he made his first expedition against the Iroquois in 1609. As early as 1603 the French had agreed to support the Hurons in their efforts to subdue the Iroquois and keep the valuable role of middleman in the fur trade for themselves. In this and succeeding forays, Champlain was accompanied by Huron or Algonquin war parties. The last one, in 1615, was an attack on a stockaded Iroquois fort in present day New York. Champlain wished to use classic siege tactics, but the impatience of his allies caused his plans to go awry. As a result, he himself was wounded, and the whole party had to retreat back across Lake Ontario. The Iroquois, though no more advanced culturally than their Huron cousins, were to be the ultimate victors in the tribal warfare. Their confederacy gave them superiority in numbers, and they were very soon receiving guns and ammunition from the Dutch and British in exchange for furs. The man at the lower right is wearing an elaborate coat of European cut, probably given to him by a white ally. By 1650, the Huron nation had been shattered, and for the next hundred years the Iroquois threatened the lower Great Lakes and St. Lawrence region. As a result, the French moved west to contact other tribes.

Above, a tattooed Iroquois brave; below, an important chief, both painted by Grasset St. Sauveur.

In the rather romantic battle scene above, Champlain heads his allies in attacking an Iroquois stockade on Lake Champlain in 1609. Below, he assaults an Iroquois fort the next year at the mouth of the Richelieu. Both engagements were successful.

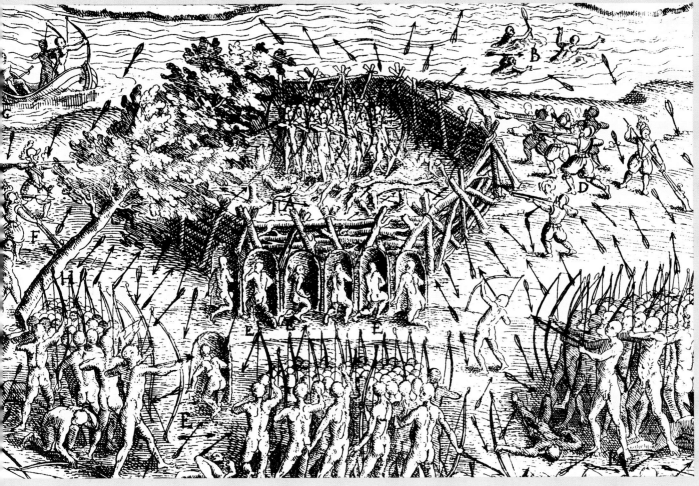

A tragic beginning...

When the expedition of the Sieur de Monts sailed out of Le Havre on March 7, 1604, France was embarking on a new phase in the colonization of Canada. Following Cartier's discovery of the St Lawrence in 1535, the French had done little to exploit the resources of their new-found possession. The Roberval settlement of Charlesbourg-Royal had lasted only one winter, and the few later attempts at settlement were even less successful. But with the arrivals of De Monts and Champlain in Acadia, the history of New France was given a new permanence and continuity – though its beginnings were hardly auspicious. When De Monts decided to winter on Dochet Island at the mouth of New Brunswick's St. Croix River, he was unaware of what awaited him in the course of a long, severe winter. Snow fell as early as October 6, and by December 3, ice was forming around the edges of the little island. By midwinter, the settlers were reduced to drinking melted snow, and their restricted diet brought on the dreaded scurvy. By spring, 1605, two-fifths of the settlers had died.

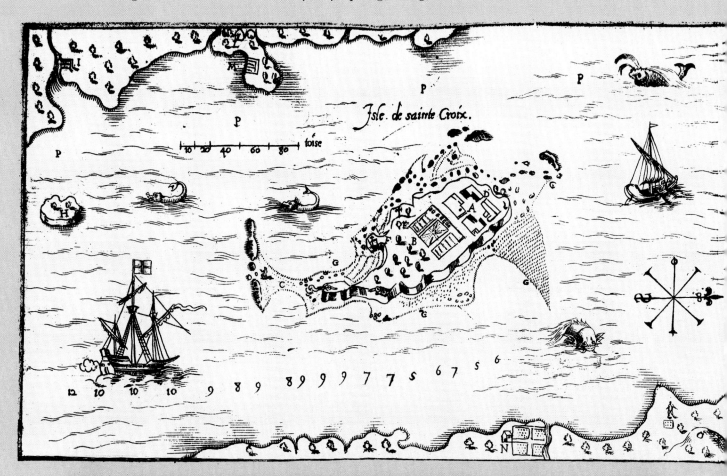

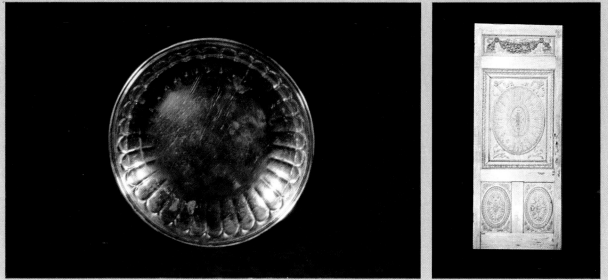

...and hope reborn

It was not until the early summer of 1605 that the survivors on Dochet Island were freed completely from their distress. For it was not until June 15 that Pontgravé arrived from France with fresh stores and supplies. Now, with renewed hope and ambition, Champlain and De Monts set out to explore the New England coast. They proceeded as far as Cape Cod (where they lost one man in a clash with the Indians) and then turned to the task of selecting a new site for their settlement. Because the coast of New England did not seem well suited to the fur trade, and because the Indians of that area had proved hostile, the French returned to Acadia. Here, they transferred their goods—buildings and all—from the St. Croix River to Annapolis Basin, setting up, on this natural harbour, the settlement of Port Royal. The fortunes of the colonists improved and this time their endeavours were rewarded. Sustained by its own crops and helped through winter months by Champlain's *Ordre de Bon Temps*, Port Royal became the first permanent settlement in Canada.

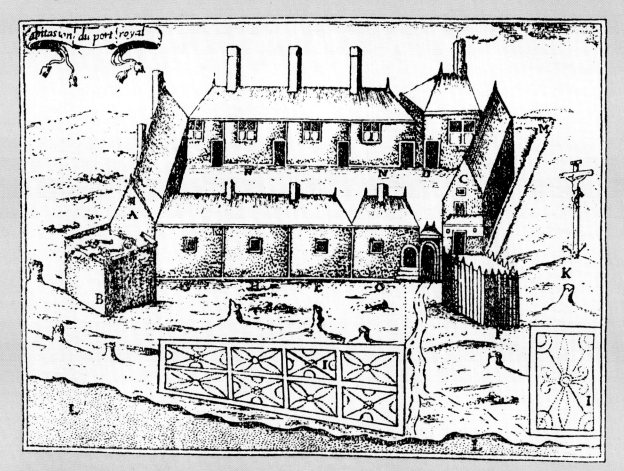

The artistry of New France: *far left, an ornamented tray or bowl of solid silver, made by Jacques Page of Quebec; left, a wooden panel from the Jesuit chapel in Quebec, probably carved by Denis Mallet; centre, weathercock of laminated iron from an old church near Terrebonne; right, votive painting in the church of Notre Dame de la Victoire, Quebec, by Paul Beaucourt.*

Quebec:
the Settlement
that Survived

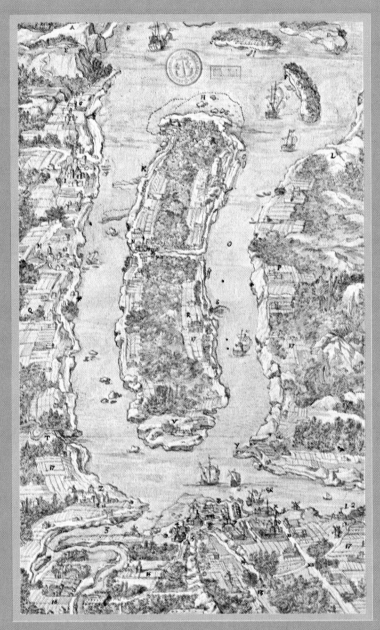

The St. Lawrence River and the City of Quebec in Canada [drawn between 1670 and 1693]. The numbered and lettered places are identified as follows: A. Cap St. Paul. B. channel [La Traverse]. C. Isle of Geese. D. Ile aux Dames. E. Cap Tourmente. F. Ile au Roi. G. farms. H. sands. I. Ste Anne. K. Ile d'Orleans. L. South Hill. M. Chateau Richer. N. Ste-Famille. O. regular channel. P. farmhouse. Q. L'Angegardien. R. St-Francois. S. St. Patrice Cove. T. falls of Montmorency. V. tip of Ile d'Orleans. Y. Cape Lévi. Z. Beauport. ⦵. the port. 1. Sillery. 2. Cap Rouge. 3. St. Charles River. 4. the Hospitalers. 5. the brewery. 6. episcopal palace. 7. the Jesuits. 8. lower town. 9. the Ursulines. x. the chateau. xi. upper town. xii. Grande Allée. 13. Notre Dame de Foy. 14. St. Jean highway. 15. the Recollets. 16. Les Islets. 17. ploughed lands. Size, 12 leagues by 6 leagues.

CHAPTER FOURTEEN

The Lure
of the
"Salt Sea"

No man of prominence managed to keep his private life more his own than did Samuel Champlain. He had an endless curiosity about the lives of others, detailing in his journals the eating, sleeping, fighting, playing, sexual, and marriage customs of the Indians. But of his own life, he tells us virtually nothing. Nowhere in his several books does he indicate his own height or weight, the colour of his eyes or the cast of his features–and none of his contemporaries seems to have thought it worth recording a personal description. All the supposed portraits of him are fakes. The one most commonly seen, showing a plump Champlain with pointed beard and moustache, was painted in the nineteenth century by an artist who, born without arms, painted with the brush between his teeth. Even at that, the painting is a copy of an earlier portrait of one of Louis XIV's court officials–a man named Particelli. It may be unsettling for a country to have a national hero of completely unknown looks–but that's the way it is.

Champlain's secretiveness can, perhaps, be best measured by the fact that he never once mentioned his wife or his marriage in anything he wrote. He gives the impression of being the kind of man who can live a reserved but satisfying life without women. "In spirit," wrote Professor George Wrong, "he was half monk and half crusader." In journals written with an eye to royal and church approval, Champlain was, of course, most unlikely to include any hints of dalliance with the freely offered girls of the Indian villages–and his morality in this and most other fields seems beyond reproach. It was not an age, though of sexual repression, and it would be a man of especial character who would spend an entire winter without female companionship within a tribal society where such abstinence was more likely to cause offence than to create esteem.

When Champlain did finally marry–in Paris, on December 30, 1610–he made a choice that has never ceased to attract comment. At the age of forty-three,

he took "in lawful wedlock" in the church of St. Germain-l'Auxerrois a girl of twelve. Certainly, the contract expressly stipulated that the marriage "shall not be effected until two years elapse," but this clause had the rider that the consummation could be brought forward to an earlier date if it "be decided between them, their relatives and friends." Even at a time when Henry IV had been ready to go to war over a girl of sixteen and the Duc de Richelieu would be cooled out in the Bastille for attempting to deflower the 13-year-old Duchesse de Burgundy, it was an unusual alliance.

The girl was Hélène Boullé, daughter of Nicolas Boullé, Secretary of the King's Chamber, and his wife, Marguerite Alix. They were a Protestant family, but Hélène was probably accepted as a convert at the time of her marriage. Monsieur Boullé paid 4,500 *livres* of the dowry of 6,000 before the ceremony: a sizeable sum indeed, and proof of the desirability of Champlain–described in the contract as "Captain-in-Ordinary in the Navy"–as a son-in-law. Champlain added only 1,800 *livres* to the marriage portion. His old patron and friend, the Sieur de Monts, signed the contract as witness. Also present on that day were De Mont's secretary, Ralleau, who had been at least twice to Port Royal, and Lucas Legendre, Hercule Rouer, and Marcel Chesnu, all merchants who were involved in the financing of the Quebec expeditions.

From what we know of it, the marriage must be considered something less than a success. The following spring Champlain resumed his almost yearly voyages to Canada and not until 1620 did he take his wife to Quebec. She had a rough crossing, and was perhaps appalled at the leaky collection of huts which made up the capital of Canada. There was at least one other familiar face–her younger brother, Eustache, had emigrated two years earlier. Her husband built Fort St. Louis on the brow of the cliff and had a new and more comfortable *habitation* under construction when they sailed for France in 1624. But Madame Champlain never returned to Canada, taking up residence in Paris in the Rue de la Marche (now the

Arriving at Quebec in 1620, Champlain's wife was to spend the next four years in Canada – though once she left, she never returned.

Rue de Saintonge). They had no children, and on her husband's death, she entered a convent.

Did Champlain marry for love or for money? Or was his child-bride a surrogate for the family he could have had? His biographer, Bishop, considers that Champlain, the campaigner and mariner, was *gauche*, timid with women. "He dreamed of women's kindness and love, but he had no strong physical need for their caresses... He recoiled from the lush and bouncing daughters of his friends. Champlain had his pleasure merely in taking his child-bride by the hand to see the sights of Paris, to watch the pomp of Notre Dame, a caroussel in the Louvre, the free shows of the tooth-drawers on the Pont-Neuf." It is a pretty if fanciful picture.

In any event, his wife's *dot* must have been welcome and timely to Champlain, because his colony was suddenly in dire jeopardy. When Pontgravé and Champlain reached Honfleur in the autumn of 1610, the news was confirmed that a religious maniac had stabbed Henri IV to death and that the 10-year-old Louis XIII was on the throne, with the royal widow, Marie de' Medici, acting as regent. De Monts, Champlain, and the rest of the old comrades from civil-war days could no longer expect any favours. The fur trade had deteriorated too. With the monopoly rescinded, the St. Lawrence was full of free-lance traders who had bid up the price of a beaver pelt from two knives to twenty. The Indians sensibly went from ship to ship with their furs, seeking the best bargain. Speaking of the 1610 season, Champlain wrote that the trading

was so poor for the number of ships involved "that many will long remember the loss they sustained that year." However, while he looked for a new champion at court, Champlain was somehow able to persuade De Monts and his partners to finance the Quebec settlement for yet another year.

There was always the shining hope that further exploration of the rivers of Canada would one day open a commercial route to the Pacific. When news of Henry Hudson's discovery of the inland sea to the north filtered back to Europe, French hopes were spurred afresh. It was not yet known that Hudson Bay was almost landlocked, as only the eastern shores had been charted. The discovery of the western coasts had to await the voyages of Foxe and James. Thus, as far as Champlain knew, the sea might extend clear across the top of the continent at 53° north latitude, then sweep south into the Pacific. He tried to persuade the Montagnais to lead him into the northwest via the St. Maurice, but they did not want the French to be in direct contact with the northern tribes and they gave him evasive answers.

On May 28, 1611, Champlain was down at Montreal Island, where he had arranged a meeting with his allies of previous years. He had left a boy–probably Etienne Brulé*–with the Algonquins for the winter, to learn their language and, incidentally, to keep his eyes and ears open for clues about that "salt sea" in the west. He had taken to France, in exchange, a

---

* Quebec historian N. E. Dionne says that it was Nicolas Marsolet.

Huron lad whom the French knew as "Savignon." These youngsters were now to return to their respective peoples, and (so Champlain and his associates hoped) a wide new fur-rich area was to be tapped. It was a poorly kept secret. The independent traders, several of whom had battled heavy ice in the gulf in order to beat Champlain to the traditional trading spots, were ready with longboats to follow his every move. Nevertheless, he had slipped away undetected.

While he waited for his Algonquin allies, Champlain chose the site on the island where the largest city in Canada would rise. Thirty-one years before the Sieur de Maisonneuve was to arrive with his settlers, Champlain laid out his Place Royale, where several small streams met in a riverside meadow. It was no quick or light decision.

Having examined both shores, in the woods as well as along the river banks, to find a suitable place for a settlement, I went about twenty miles by land, skirting le grand sault... *I examined the country very carefully, but after looking everywhere found no spot more suitable than a little place to which small boats could ascend with a strong wind, or by going a roundabout way because of the strong current. Near this Place Royale, there are more than sixty arpents of land which have been cleared, where one might sow grain and plant gardens.*

Formerly, Indians cultivated these lands, but they have abandoned them on account of the frequent wars*... There are many other fine meadows which would feed as many cattle as one could wish. There are all the varieties of wood which we have in France, with many vines, butternuts, plums, cherries, strawberries, and other kinds of fruit. Game birds are abundant and animals numerous, such as stags, fallow deer, roebucks, caribou, rabbits, lynxes, bears, beavers, and many small animals.

I ordered the trees of Place Royale to be cut and cleared to level the ground and make it ready for building... A short distance away lies a small islet about one hundred yards long and twelve feet high where a good strong habitation might be built. There I built a wall [of clay] four feet thick, three or four feet high, and ten yards long, to see how it would last during the winter when the waters came down.

In the middle of the river is an island which we named St. Helen's Island† where there is room to build a good strong town.

The reader who is eager to identify the early acres of Canada can, with imagination and patience, find Champlain's Place Royale under the towers and sprawl of modern Montreal. He left us a fine map of the island and its guardian rapids. His small streams ran down from Mount Royal towards the docks, and they still do – only now they flow through concrete

sewers. The little river St. Pierre provided the bed for the Lachine Canal. Place Royale itself occupied the site of the Custom House Square of today. C. H. Laverdière, in his massive *Oeuvres de Champlain* (1870), suggested that St. Helen's Island was named for Champlain's child-bride of six months, and Biggar and other authorities have since gone along with this pleasant thought. The saints of that name stretch back, however, into the first Christian century. There are those who also suggest that Lake St. Louis – the broadening of the St. Lawrence just above Montreal – was named for a servant of De Monts who was drowned when a canoe tipped in the torrent. It is perhaps more likely that the discoverers had in mind the saintly Crusader-King Louis IX.

Champlain remained about the rapids from May 28 until July 18 that year of 1611. The French youth – let's say it *was* Brulé – was brought back on schedule by Chief Iroquet of the Algonquins. Champlain writes: "He was well pleased with the treatment he had received, and he explained to me all that he had seen during the winter and what he had learned." The information couldn't have been very exciting, however, as Champlain doesn't give us any of it. The trading was disappointing, too, and most of the independent merchants who had tracked Champlain upstream had trouble covering their expenses. Their aggressive methods unsettled the Indians, with the result that the Indians called Champlain to a secret conference, above the rapids, probably at the Lake of Two Mountains. They gave him a present of fifty beaver pelts and four wampum belts (to be shared with "his brother," Pontgravé) and asked him to come alone the next year. They feared that the bickering hucksters in the other boats would kill them – perhaps they were in league with the Iroquois, who were stepping up their fur raids into Algonquin and Huron territories.

Champlain never missed a chance to turn the conversation to the lands to the west, still totally unexposed to European eyes. His journal now records: "Four of them assured me that they had seen a sea, far from their country, but that the way to it was difficult – both on account of enemies and on account of the difficult terrain to be crossed." They were probably speaking of Lake Superior, but any such reports were like a spark to the tinder of Champlain's imagination. Any "sea" to the west could be the one that also washed the steamy coasts of China. Champlain rashly promised that he would ask the French king for forty or fifty armed men to help the Algonquins in their wars.

On the way back to Montreal Island, Champlain stripped to his shirt and shot *le grand sault*, the Lachine Rapids, in one of a flotilla of eight canoes. It was a game performance for a man of forty-four who was an admitted non-swimmer. The Indians told him that if his canoe went over, he was to hang on to the wooden

---

*This is as close as Champlain ever comes to mentioning the vanished Indian settlement of Hochelaga, where Jacques Cartier was welcomed by 1,000 dancing Indians.

†In the original, the name is given as *"l'isle de saincte Elaine."*

struts and they would rescue him. Among Europeans, only the tough and agile Brulé had shot the rapids before. Champlain wrote: "I assure you that even the bravest who have not seen nor passed this place in small boats such as theirs could not do so without great apprehension."

The success of the experiment with Brulé led to the Algonkian. There is later evidence that Brulé, then winter—this one from a free-lance trader named Bouvier. From Champlain's party, another *jeune homme* went off with the Hurons, with Chief Tregouaroti, the brother of the well-travelled Savignon. Unfortunately, we never learn the names of these young men. Some authorities think that it was Brulé who now went with the Hurons to add their tongue to his knowledge of Algonkian. There is later evidence that Brulé, then aged twenty, thoroughly enjoyed the freedom and privileges of the Indian male—although he was to suffer torture by the Iroquois and, in 1633, death under mysterious circumstances.

It was, however, another adventurous young man who was to lead Champlain into his next journey of discovery. A second contingent of Algonquins, living on the upper Ottawa by modern Pembroke, arrived late at the Montreal rendezvous, since most of them had been on the warpath. Their chief was Tessouat, whom Champlain had met at Tadoussac eight years earlier. They too made a secret present of skins to Champlain and asked for a French wintering guest, promising to "treat him like one of their own children." The chosen *hivernant* was Nicolas du Vignau.

Champlain returned to France in early September, 1611, and went immediately—not to his wife in Paris—but to Pons, where the Sieur de Monts was still governor. There was no rosy report to give of trading profits while the scramble for pelts continued on the St. Lawrence and De Monts' partners were now fed up with the whole venture. The governor's faith in New France was never more severely tested, but he listened again to Champlain's siren song of new evidence of a way to the western sea, dug deeply into his pocket, and bought out his partners. Perhaps a trade monopoly could be restored by setting up a combine of the warring traders. In the meantime, De Monts arranged for Pontgravé to go to Canada, as usual, in the spring.

De Monts and Champlain arranged to meet at Fontainebleau and to present their plan at court, but Champlain was seriously hurt when his horse fell on him. We don't know where this occurred, but since Pons is not far from Brouage, it's possible that Champlain was able to convalesce in his hometown. He records that "this fall delayed me a long time." In fact, he was not to return to the *habitation de Québec* for eighteen months. As it happened, important unexpected business had prevented De Monts from pressing his arguments to the advisors of Queen Marie, and when Champlain was fit to travel, he took over the negotiations personally.

The role of the courtier, demanding skills which are not acquired on a pitching caravel or at an Indian *tabagie*, must have sat uncomfortably on the fisherman's son. Henri IV, in his 21-year reign, had made Fountainebleau the most brilliant court in Europe. But he had always found time to relax with the hearty men of action who had fought with him in his rise to the throne. Now, since his assassination, the glorious Renaissance palace in its huge forest on the upper Seine seethed with plot and intrigue in the true Medici style. No doubt advised by De Monts, or by some of the several noblemen with whom he had rubbed shoulders in the freer atmosphere of the New World, Champlain first gained an interview with Pierre Jeannin, an influential administrator and diplomat, then in his seventies. Jeannin thought the combine idea might work, and Champlain then sought to "place myself under the protection of some great man."

Through the good offices of the Sieur de Beaulieu, Chaplain to the King, he was received in the autumn of 1612 by Charles de Bourbon, Comte de Soissons, the Governor of Normandy. Prince Charles saw some hope of profit in the scheme, had it approved, and had himself appointed Viceroy of New France. In turn, on October 15, he had Champlain commissioned as his lieutenant. The new monopoly was good only west of the St. Lawrence, and Champlain was ordered to look for gold and silver mines—and, of course, for an easy route to China and the Indies. Within a month, however, his new patron was dead from the smallpox and Champlain had to put on his most confident smile and look elsewhere.

The next to assume the mantle of viceroy—first created by Francis I for the Sieur de Roberval in 1541—was another Bourbon, Soissons' nephew, the young Prince de Condé. One of the perks was the annual gift of a horse worth 1,000 *écus*. He confirmed Champlain's position, and dug in his royal heels when the merchants of Rouen, St. Malo, and elsewhere kicked up a fuss about the monopoly. Champlain had put his case succinctly: "It is unreasonable when one has caught the sheep for another to have the fleece." Preparations were begun for a fleet of ships to go to the St. Lawrence the following spring. Although always acutely aware of the need for trading profits to nourish his colony, Champlain in his middle age was hewing closer to his central motive. He wrote in his journal of his desire to make "new discoveries in New France for the welfare, advantage, and glory of the French name, as well as of bringing these poor peoples to the knowledge of God."

Pontgravé now arrived back at Honfleur from Tadoussac, reporting another season of scrabbling for pelts with a swarm of quarreling traders. A horde of Indians had arrived at Montreal Island looking for Champlain, expecting to see his "forty or fifty armed men" who would help them on the warpath. They

Champlain's map of 1613 shows the "Sea of the North," the goal that he pursued on his expedition with young Nicolas du Vignau.

were deeply disappointed, and then worried when some of the other traders, seeking the inside track for themselves, whispered that Champlain was dead. Presumably, Pontgravé also brought back Nicolas du Vignau.

During the winter of 1612-13, Vignau gave Champlain an electrifying report of his stay with the Algonquins on the Ottawa. He said he had travelled with his hosts to the source of the Ottawa, which was a lake that also emptied into *la mer du Nord*. He had personally seen this ocean, just then becoming known following Hudson's last tragic voyage. In fact, he had seen the wreckage of an English ship from which eighty men had escaped only to be killed by the Indians. Vignau claimed that he had seen the scalps of these Englishmen and that his Algonquin friends were holding a young English boy as a present for Champlain. The entire journey from the great rapids at Mont-Royal to the sea and back could be made in seventeen days.

Champlain accepted this story–it fitted reasonably well into what he already knew, or wanted to believe–and he was burning with impatience to get back to the mouth of the "River of the Algonquins" (as he

called the Ottawa) to check the route for himself. Nearly sixty years before the Hudson's Bay Company was chartered, Champlain foresaw the economic danger of permitting the English to tap the fur riches from the shores of the northern sea. He obtained for Vignau a passage to Quebec with a seafaring merchant from La Rochelle, and he himself sailed from Honfleur with the Sieur de l'Ange in Pontgravé's ship on March 6, 1613. It was Champlain's eleventh crossing of the North Atlantic.

After his long absence, he was relieved to find that the garrison at Quebec had wintered without illness under the highly competent Sieur du Parc. Champlain paused there only six days before taking a longboat for Montreal, arriving at the rapids on May 21. Here, he learned from a party of Indians that the tribesmen considered they had been badly treated the previous summer and that twelve hundred men were going on the warpath instead of coming down to the trading grounds. Now Champlain had an extra reason to push into the Ottawa country: the new monopoly would be worth nothing unless he could persuade the Algonquins and Hurons to come out of the west. He bought two canoes, and quickly made up a party of six—himself, an Indian guide, four Frenchmen, including Vignau and probably the interpreter Thomas Godefroy. The departure was from St. Helen's Island on a rainy Monday, May 27.

As far as the written record is concerned, the Ottawa now comes into modern knowledge. For the next two centuries, it would remain the main trade route to the Canadian West. Champlain had packed a good supply of arms, food, nets, and snares, as well as presents for the upriver Indians he wanted to meet. The French soon learned the weight of all this when they began portaging around the rapids. "It is no small labour," Champlain wrote, "for those who are not used to it." Especially, one might add, for a man of forty-six who had recently been crushed by a horse. From Lake St. Louis, they forked into the Ottawa, on their guard against prowling Iroquois. (From a train or a car today, speeding over the bridges into Montreal, it is exciting to consider Champlain and his handful of men fighting the swift current with their paddles more than three hundred and fifty years ago.) Beyond the Lake of Two Mountains, they dragged their canoes up the Carillon rapids with ropes from the shore, nearly losing one of them at the Chute à Blondeau.

Near today's Hawkesbury, above the Long Sault, they met an Indian party. Champlain cajoled them into providing a second man for his team and sent the weakest member of his French group back to the St. Lawrence. The Algonquins tried to dissuade Champlain from probing further upstream towards the Nebicerini.* The way was very difficult, they advised—and they weren't kidding on that score. At one tow path, the rope with which Champlain was pulling his canoe tautened suddenly, almost severing his hand. The weary French, admittedly leaning on their Indian guides, toiled to the maze of waterways where, on the southern shore, the City of Ottawa would eventually rise.

On the 4th of June, we passed near another river which comes from the north [the Gatineau]... This river is not wide but has a large number of rapids which are difficult to pass. Near its mouth, there is another river coming from the south [the Rideau] and at its mouth there is a marvellous waterfall [une chute d'eau admirable]. It falls with such force that it forms an archway nearly four hundred yards wide. For the sheer fun of it, the Indians pass underneath it without getting wet, except for the spray.

The surrounding country is filled with all sorts of game so that the Indians like to make a halt here. The Iroquois also come here sometimes and surprise them as they pass.

We passed a rapid which is about a mile wide and has a fall of about forty feet. Here there are several small islands of steep rocks. At one place, the water falls with such force upon the rock that with the passing of time it has hollowed

out a wide, deep basin. The water whirls around here in such a way that the Indians call it Asticou, which means "chaudière."

Through the shoals where the Champlain Bridge would one day leap from islet to islet, joining Ontario and Quebec, they passed into Lake Deschênes. At the long rapids of Des Chats, the tiring French jettisoned all non-essential food and gear to lighten their loads, and then rested on an island in Lac des Chats, close to modern Arnprior. Champlain had a rough cross fashioned out of red cedar and erected it, calling the island St. Croix.

Near Portage du Fort, the Indians ruled that the party must leave the main river and strike inland over a long portage to run up the string of small lakes and ponds that lie to the south. The Ottawa ahead was an obstacle course of rapids—and in any case, it made a long swing to the north before turning south again to flow around Allumette Island. Champlain was surprised when Vignau argued lustily against this course, and he ruled in favour of the Indians.

With his copper astrolabe he took the latitude of the spot where they left the mainstream—identified as Gould's Landing—and the men were soon cursing the rough going and the clouds of mosquitoes. After about seven miles, they were dead beat. They had eaten only a few morsels of fish in twenty-four hours, and with fallen pine trees blocking the portage trail, the party alternately climbed over or under the trunks. Champlain was toting three muskets, three paddles, and other gear, and at one of the obstacles near Green Lake, he dropped his astrolabe. It was found right there 254 years later by a boy out for a ramble.

A local chieftain named Nibachis came from his village at Muskrat Lake to marvel at the Europeans in their fine clothes stumbling, fly-bitten and starving, through his bush. He offered tobacco, fresh fish, and probably corn held over from the previous season—the new season's crop could be seen growing in the fields. Here was the surprise of a semi-agricultural tribe in the deeper forest. Champlain promised French help in future wars and Nibachis supplied canoes and men to take the party to the headquarters of the paramount regional chief, Tessouat. This was situated on Morrison Island, in Allumette Lake, near the present-day town of Pembroke.

The one-eyed Tessouat was astonished to see Champlain in the wilderness and he called immediately for a tabagie of welcome. He also recognized Vignau, who had spent the winter of 1610-11 with his family. Champlain put on his diplomat's hat and told the chief that the reason for his failure to keep his promise the previous summer was that King Louis had ordered him to fight in European wars. He was now ready to again help the Algonquins against the Iroquois—but first, he wanted to push on to the west in order to pay a courtesy call on the Nebicerini. He asked for four canoes

---

*"Nebicerini" was the name which the French gave to the hinterland tribes living as far west as Lake Nipissing.

Henry de Bourbon Prince de Conde Duc danquien et chateroux, premier Prince du Sang &. et premier Patr de France.

The Prince de Condé was appointed Viceroy of New France in 1612.

When Louis XIII *became King in 1610, he was but nine years old.*

and eight Indian braves for the journey. He didn't mention that his true purpose was to get to the northern sea which Vignau had reported. They should, incidentally, have been nearing that goal, considering Vignau's round-trip time of seventeen days; they had already been two weeks on the outward leg.

Every tribal chief that Champlain met had tried to block him from penetrating to the next tribe's hunting ground—and Tessouat was no exception. The people of Lake Nipissing were sorcerers who could kill by magic, they were men of little courage and no use as allies, the portages were appalling, etc., etc. Champlain, however, persisted, remarking that the difficulties could not be so great because, after all, Vignau—he pointed to the young Frenchman—had already been there. Sensation! When the Indians understood what had been said, they shouted that Vignau was a liar and rushed on him "as if [Champlain wrote] they would have eaten him or torn him asunder." The good captain then credited Tessouat with a speech of denunciation which would have earned applause in the *Parlement de Rouen*. The burden of the speech was that Vignau was a barefaced liar. "Every night you slept alongside of me and my children and rose every morning at that place. If you visited those people, it was in your sleep."

The naive streak that ran in Champlain made him, at first, defend Vignau (a Frenchman's word against

that of a savage?) and thus he had to suffer a further humiliation when Vignau finally confessed on his knees that he had never been any further west than Tessouat's village. All the rest—the eighty English scalps, the wreckage of the ship, the rough map of the route—was sheer fabrication, made up in France during the previous winter in the hope of reward and as assurance that he would get back to Canada. He had figured that if any later travellers tried to check his story, the difficulties of the Ottawa route or the opposition of the Indians at Allumette would make them turn back. Vignau had heard something of the Hudson discovery and had built on that.

For once, the sober and steady Champlain blew his top. "In a transport of rage," he later wrote, "I had him removed, being no longer able to endure his presence." The Indians, always ready for some blood-sport, asked for the wretched Vignau. "They were all howling to get at him, and their children still more loudly." But Champlain composed himself and decided to take the culprit back with him. The French had lost face before the Indians, and Champlain tried to recoup by promising to return the following year ready to go on the warpath. He set up a cedar cross bearing the fleur-de-lis and told the Indians that if they allowed it to stand, it would protect them from their enemies. He seems to have been quite distracted.

Champlain had pushed to the farthest limit of overland discovery in North America, marking well the site of the future capital of Canada on the way. Nevertheless, he felt that his journey had been a failure. True, the Algonquins did accept his invitation to make a late trip to Montreal Island, where the company traders were glumly waiting with their chests of hatchets, knives, pots, beads, and bolts of cloth. A total of eighty canoes went downstream, and bartering was brisk. But Champlain had to prepare to return to France to inform the arrogant and acquisitive Prince de Condé that he had chased a will-o'-the-wisp. Canada had taunted him again—but his love for this realm of rock and river was proof against all rebuff.

CHAPTER FIFTEEN

Expedition through Ontario

WHEN Champlain's *Les Voyages*, a handsome illustrated book on fine paper, came out in Paris in 1613, the author's name had gained a flattering flourish – it was given as the Sieur de Champlain. It carried a main dedication to Louis XIII, the boy King, another to Marie, the Queen Regent, and yet another to the Prince de Condé. The bluff geographer from Brouage was moving in exalted circles and some of the purple seemed to have rubbed off.

Historians and biographers in these egalitarian times have been probing quietly but relentlessly to pin down the source of Champlain's apparent rise into the minor aristocracy. His "*Sieur*" would entitle him to the equivalent of the British "Sir." Some of the writers hint broadly that Champlain simply allowed the style to be adopted, much as a wartime colonel does not chide those who continue in peacetime to give him his rank. In royal France, nobility was conferred only by direct noble descent or by letters of nobility. "In the absence of the latter," says Professor Trudel in the *Dictionary of Canadian Biography*, "whether they did not exist or have been lost, one must accept with considerable caution the titles that Champlain assumed or allowed himself to be given."

The trend is first noticed in the marriage contract, one of the few Champlain documents which have survived. Up until that time (he was then forty-three) he had signed himself plain "S. Champlain." Now he was listed as "nobleman Samuel de Champlain, Lord of the said place, Captain-in-Ordinary in the Navy, residing in the town of Brouage, province of Saintonge, son of the late Athoine de Complain, in his lifetime Captain in the Navy, and of Dame Margueritte Le Roy." Professor Bishop, in his sympathetic biography, comments: "Henceforth he will always insert the *de*, which conveys a hint of honourable rank, a hint at least of land ownership. Perhaps Champlain inherited land in Brouage at his father's death; or perhaps the *de* was adopted merely for the gratification of Hélène

and his new family. The appellation '*noble homme*' means as little. The notaries so called almost any respectable person." There is also the possibility that the mature son-in-law was a mite tired of being just plain "mister" when his authority in New France – however dependent on the whims of courtiers – brought him in constant contact with lesser men who carried handles on their names.

The new book caught right up with Champlain's journeys and discoveries – his torturous 200-mile ascent of the Ottawa in 1613 – and by the time it was in the bookshops, he was steadily occupied with further facets of his plans for Canada. He had a truly indomitable nature, the ability to bounce back from any reverse or embarrassment. His progress was never dramatic, but always measurable – one is reminded of the ceaseless drop of water that wears the stone. The imposter Vignau was put out of mind, the loss of face before the tribes accepted (until the Almighty offered the opportunity for redress), and the wretched weariness of the long portages forgotten. Champlain now set about forming, with royal approval, the *Compagnie des Marchands de Rouen et Saint-Malo* in order to get the Canadian trading monopoly onto a firmer base. The Prince de Condé, as viceroy, obtained an extension of the company's monopoly until 1624, and the staunch Sieur de Monts took shares, relinquishing his sole ownership of the settlement at Quebec. Champlain insisted that the shareholders guarantee to send out six families of colonists each year, and he gratefully received his first regular salary (a mere 600 *livres*).

He now turned to his other long-term desire – to take the message of Christian salvation to *les sauvages*. "To attain this end," he writes, "I exerted myself to find some good priests whom I might persuade to come with me to this country to try to plant the faith." Four years earlier, he had tried to persuade the Jesuits to send a mission to Quebec, but they had turned him down. He found his missionaries right in his hometown of Brouage, four sturdy *Récollet* priests who had taken vows to live in absolute poverty and seek nothing except the glory of God, for others rather than for themselves. They were strict followers of St. Francis of Assisi, their name deriving from "*recollectio*" – meaning "meditation." Champlain accepted them gladly. But, as he confessed, he personally could not pay their way, and "moreover, no persons offered to contribute to it."

As it happened, however, the Estates-General was due to meet in Paris – that ancient French conclave of the three "estates": church, nobility, and bourgeoisie. Champlain, the Sieur Houel of Brouage (who had suggested the *Récollets*), and leaders of the order all buttonholed the delegates and squeezed out a meagre contribution of 1,500 *livres*. Still, it was enough for food and vestments for the four priests. In this way, Canada got its first permanent churchmen: Fathers Denis Jamet, Joseph le Caron, Jean d'Olbeau, and the lay brother, Pacifique du Plessis.

With these important affairs under way, Champlain decided to remain in France for the year of 1614. He seems to have been mostly in Paris, or at Fontainebleau, and we can presume that he now gave some substance to his marriage. Hélène was in her fifteenth year and the two-year wait imposed by contract had long since expired. However, while telling us, for instance, that Louis Houel was the boss of the salt works at Brouage, Champlain continues to exclude his wife from any mention in his works. That fall, the company ships returned from Canada, reporting excellent business.

The *St. Etienne*, a big ship of 350 tons, owned by the company and under the command of Pontgravé, took Champlain and his priests to Canada in the spring of 1615. There is no word of any settlers, the shareholding partners simply ignoring that part of the deal. They had no wish to set up a colony, as they believed that any Europeans established in Canada would eventually come between their trading shipmasters and the Indians at the summer fairs. The *St. Etienne* made Tadoussac by May 25 – a brisk 34 days' sail.

Champlain would now remain in Canada for fifteen months and in this time make the last and longest discovery journey of his career. Into his fiftieth year, he would carve a great circle across the present provinces of Quebec and Ontario, entering two of the great lakes, and pushing into the territory of what is now New York State. He would mount and lead his most ambitious campaign against the Iroquois, introducing European battle techniques to the interior, being again wounded by arrows. He would then suffer a "Gehenna of pain," spend the long winter amid fleas and filth in a Huron village in southern Ontario, produce the world's first detailed report of North American Indian manners and mores, and, finally, return to France to learn that his princely patron was in jail and that his own commission had been rescinded. One is reminded, inescapably, of Sisyphus and his stone.

The story begins in some confusion of dates and journeys. Champlain was notoriously inaccurate with calendar and other data, at times getting the days, months, and even years mixed up. When the *St. Etienne* anchored at the Saguenay, Le Caron, the junior among the priests, insisted on dashing directly to *le grand sault*. Burning with ardour to come to grips with the unsuspecting pagans, he would not pause at Quebec while Champlain checked up on his garrison and heard the news of the winter. Champlain, of course, should have ordered him to cool it, but the good captain was never at his best in a battle of wills. "Seeing him impelled by so holy a zeal," Champlain says mildly, "I would no longer seek to turn him from it."

The end result of this permissiveness was that Le Caron eventually plunged into the interior from Montreal Island in Champlain's absence, taking with him a dozen of the Frenchmen who had been laboriously husbanded for service on the warpath. This put in jeopardy Champlain's entire plan to penetrate the Huron country and redeem his several promises made over the past five years to help crush the Iroquois. But into his journal he inscribed only: "This news troubled me a little, because if I had been there I should have ordered many things for the journey which I was not now able to do, both in respect to the small number of men and also because there were not more than four or five among them who knew how to handle firearms." As far as Champlain knew, the Iroquois might already have some muskets of their own, as the Dutch had established Fort Orange on the Hudson River (now Albany, New York) two years earlier and were paying especially well for the thick furs brought out of the north.

Champlain made immediate plans to leave on Le Caron's heels, but he was lucky to catch rides for himself, Etienne Brulé, and "my own man" (the servant and interpreter Thomas Godefroy) with ten Indians in two canoes. In such overcrowding, all provisions – arms, ammunition, and extra clothing – had to be reduced to the bare minimum, since every ounce had to be carried over those back-breaking Ottawa portages. By July 9, they were skimming across the Lake of Two Mountains, their pace dictated by the Hurons' ever-present fear of Iroquois ambush.

The journey to the Allumette Lake territory of Chief Tessouat has been described in the previous chapter, and this second time around it was certainly no less arduous. Priests making their first trips to the Huron missions later wrote of the murderous insects, and the dirty food served by Indian cooks in birchbark bowls that had been used as urinals in the canoes. Along the twenty-mile canyon of the Deep River stretch of the Ottawa – where Canada's first atomic reactors would one day be built – Champlain was repelled by glacial gouges on the 700-foot granite walls and the general desolation of the Precambrian Shield. "This frightful and abandoned region," he described it. But he enjoyed the blueberries which the Indians gathered there.

Where the Ottawa swings north towards Lake Timiskaming, Champlain's canoes continued west via the Mattawa River. Here, they were three hundred miles from the St. Lawrence and forty miles from the wide expanse of Lake Nipissing. They entered the lake by the site of today's bustling city of North Bay. At last, Champlain was among the Nebicerini, the Algonkian tribe of sorcerers. The French found them kindly and hospitable, and the Nebicerini assumed that their country must be more favoured than France – why else were the white men coming to *them?* As Champlain's Indian crewmen sped down the French River – the waters now running fast to the west – he remarked sourly that he "did not see in the whole length of it ten *arpents* of arable land."

Even in circumstances that would have tested a saint, Champlain seldom allowed himself to complain. On this trip, the danger of starvation was always near at hand, averted only by the blueberries and raspberries gathered along the way. He wrote of the "bad management" of the Indians "who ate so heartily at the start that towards the end very little remained, although we had only one meal a day." When Champlain met the *cheveux relevés*, the "high hairs" (later known as the Ottawas) he remarked on their elaborate *coiffures* and their total nakedness. But when he included a sketch of them in his next book, he priggishly added skirts to both the men and the women.

Now, after eighty years of rumours and vague reports, Champlain looked upon *la mer douce*, the "freshwater sea," and brought Lake Huron into the ken of civilized man. Brulé probably saw it in 1611 and Father le Caron and his companions were somewhere ahead – you can never be entirely certain in the Champlain chronology – but none of these men were concerned with discovery. It is easy to imagine Champlain eagerly tasting the water, seeking any trace of salt. He was, of course, in Georgian Bay with its countless islands (95,000 *have* been counted) and he may not have seen the main breadth of the lake, beyond Manitoulin and the Bruce Peninsula. The view from today's Tobermory or Southampton would have surely brought him renewed visions of a western waterway to the Orient.

Scenting their home fires, the Indians increased their pace down the bewildering islet-studded eastern coast of the bay, past the entry to Parry Sound, past Go Home Bay, and into Matchedash Bay. On its western side, about modern Penetanguishene, the canoes ran up on a white sand beach before a village which Champlain called Otouacha (later known as Toanché). It was August 1, 1615. They had paddled seven hundred miles, half of it upstream, reeling off an average of thirty-two miles a day.

Champlain's spirits lifted at the sight of this smiling land. Huronia occupied the present Simcoe County, between lower Georgian Bay and Lake Simcoe, one of the finest stretches of land in Canada. Thirty thousand

Hurons at work and play – a typically misinformed interpretation.

Hurons lived there in four bands – the Bear, Cord, Rock, and Deer – housed in portable villages practically impossible to trace with certainty today. The French named these tall, well-built people for their wild appearance, but the Hurons shared the intelligence and habits of the Iroquois, to whom they were related by blood and by language. They called themselves the *Wendat*, from which the alternative Wyandot was derived. When Champlain chose them as the chief ally and instrument of the French in Canada, he brought them some brief days of delight with European tools and arms, but he also ensured their almost total destruction by the Confederacy of the Five Nations within the next thirty years.

The Indians of the Bear band at Nottawasaga gave Champlain a hearty welcome – including, innocently, all of the comforts of home.

They received us very kindly, making a feast with their bread, squash, and fish. The chief begged me to stay there, which I could not grant him ... On the second night, a shameless girl came boldly up to me, offering to keep me company, which I declined with thanks, sending her away with gentle remonstrances, and I passed the night with some of the savages.

He had eye enough to note later "the women and

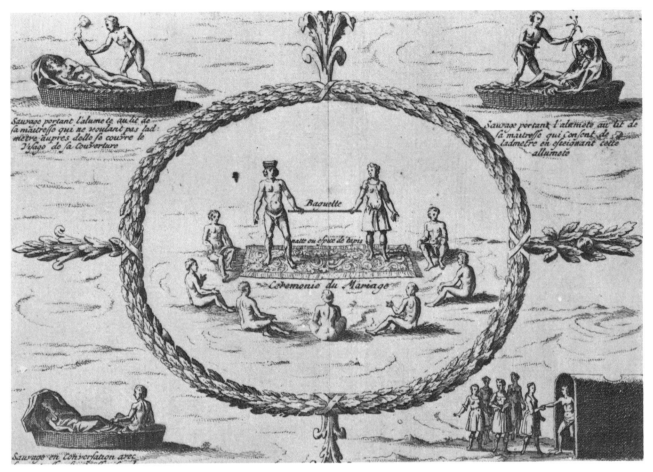

Many scenes of courtship, including a wedding ceremony in the middle, are shown on this old engraving describing Indian customs.

girls, a good number of whom are pleasing and pretty both in figure, complexion, and feature, all in harmony. Their breasts hang down very little, except when they are old." He went into considerable detail in describing their courtship patterns:

When a girl is eleven, twelve, thirteen, fourteen, or fifteen years of age, she will have suitors, many of whom will sleep with her for some time... The lover, or suitor, will give the girl a present of wampum necklaces, chains, and bracelets. After perhaps two weeks, if they are not compatible, she will leave the man who will thus lose his gifts. [Champlain found one girl wearing necklaces weighing about twelve pounds.] He will seek out another girl, and she another suitor. In this way, some girls have more than twenty husbands and these are not the only ones who enjoy the creature, however much married they may be. For after nightfall, the young women run about from one lodge to another, as do the young men, who possess them whenever and wherever it seems good to them, leaving all to the wishes of the woman.

After a few days, Champlain learned that Father le Caron and the rest of the Frenchmen were at the village of Carhagouha, on the eastern shore of Nottawasaga Bay, and he arranged for a guide to take him there. Reporting his meeting with the priest, Champlain says only: "We were very glad to see him in good health,

and he was likewise delighted to see us." Le Caron reported that his compatriots were, in his view, behaving badly with the "utterly shameless" Indian girls. The worthy priests in early Canada were always struggling to prevent other Europeans from "debasing" the natives, although in the sexual realm—as Champlain and others make clear—it was the European who was the tyro.

The word sped down the bush telegraph that the great French warrior, the victor of Ticonderoga, was in Huronia. And while Champlain fumed in impatience at the waste of the best campaigning weather, the preparations for war went on. The interminable dancing and feasting often seemed to the whites the main purpose of the campaign. But in their ignorance of the complicated culture of the Indian, they were applying sophisticated European philosophies and standards to mystically inspired primitive peoples.

A quarrel between Champlain and the Algonquin chief, Iroquet, provides an interesting sidelight. When a small group of Iroquois, mostly women and children, were captured, Iroquet took out his knife and cut a finger off one of the women. Champlain remonstrated with his old friend, saying that to be cruel to women was not the act of a warrior, since women had "no defence but their tears." The chief argued heatedly that he was merely doing what the enemy would do to the Algonquin women. When Champlain threatened to retract his promise to help them in the fight ahead, Iroquet said, all right, he wouldn't torture the women—only the men.

The warriors were to assemble at the Huron capital of Cahiagué—close to Lake Simcoe, near Warminster—and Champlain headed there on August 14, stopping on the way to call at five other palisaded villages in the closely settled countryside. He records that "we set out with ten of my companions." Thus, if the "we" included himself, Brulé, and Godefroy, there would be thirteen Frenchmen in the party—considerably less than the "forty or fifty armed men" which Champlain had originally suggested he could raise. When Brulé went off with a patrol of a dozen Hurons to seek the help of the Andastes, a friendly tribe living below the Iroquois in modern Pennsylvania, the French group was reduced to twelve. At the same time, the Indians, who had spoken of 2,500 men taking up the hatchet, could finally field only five hundred.

At Cahiagué, a sizeable town of two hundred lodges, Champlain renewed his friendship with Chief Ochateguin, with whom he had fought on the Richelieu in 1609. He also met Chief Darontal, who was to become perhaps his closest Indian friend. On September 8, the expedition had proceeded only as far as the narrows between Lake Couchiching and Lake Simcoe, where more *tabagies* were held. Shortly afterwards, the army glided into movement, the fleets of canoes slipping down the eastern shore of Lake Simcoe to a portage entry leading to the lakes which we now call the Kawarthas.

To follow Champlain's discovery route to Lake Ontario after three and a half centuries, the reader should trace the present line of the Trent Canal as it snakes its way through river and lake for 240 miles. From Balsam Lake, the waterways descend 600 feet to the Bay of Quinte, through lakes Cameron, Sturgeon, Pigeon, Buckhorn, Stony, and Clear, the Otonabee River (through today's prosperous Peterborough) on to Rice Lake and the final sixty miles of the Trent River. On the way down, a deer hunt was held in order to replenish supplies. The Indians formed a beaters' line inland from a lake, behind some point. Then, making a great racket, they drove the animals before them into the converging peninsula. Any deer that tried to evade the arrows by taking to the water was killed by men posted offshore in canoes. The French muskets claimed several head and the feat astonished those Indians who had never before seen firearms. Canada's first recorded hunting accident occurred when an Indian walked into the line of fire and was shot.* Along the sheltered reaches of the Bay of Quinte, by modern Belleville (as pretty a town as its name implies), Champlain noted the good fishing, the abundant birdlife, nut trees, and grapes, which, as a

man with a taste for Bordeaux, he pronounced too tart.

Emerging into the main lake—Champlain called it the "Lake of the Onondagas"—through the channel below Amherst Island, the convoy cut straight across the open water at the eastern end and touched the southern shore about Stony Point, not far below the present town of Sackets Harbour, New York. They had been joined by Chief Iroquet and a squadron of Algonquins from the Ottawa. All canoes were now concealed amid the chestnut trees that fringed the shore, and the augmented army proceeded on foot. Champlain estimated the length of Lake Ontario with surprising accuracy, since he was dependent on Indian measurement as converted by his interpreter. He put it at about eighty leagues long (roughly 200 miles). He knew about Niagara Falls and Burlington Bay, but he never saw the western end of the lake.

The expedition, now in enemy country, took an easterly route up the valley of the Salmon River, then swung to the south on a cautious four-day march that brought them to the vicinity of Oneida Lake. They skillfully avoided the people of the villages on the lakeshore, holding the few prisoners taken for later entertainments. The main village of the Onondagas was only about ten miles away, where a creek flowed into the small lake that is now encompassed by the modern city of Syracuse, New York.

Champlain now attempted the impossible—to impose a logical tactical plan on the fight ahead. He asked that all the attackers remain hidden until the next morning, October 11, 1615. The Hurons and Algonquins, however, could not restrain themselves and went whooping into desultory action as soon as any Iroquois were encountered. Having lost the element of surprise, Champlain ordered his men to blaze away with their muzzle-loaders. They got in some telling shots until the Iroquois withdrew into their fort. Five or six of the French had been wounded, and one of them soon died. The Hurons and Algonquins just as promptly "withdrew a cannon shot away." The fort had a 30-foot stockade of double timbers and this easily absorbed a musket ball.

This prompted me to speak out to them, and to use some hard and unpleasant words, to incite them to do their duty. I foresaw that if everything went according to their caprice, evil alone could result, to their loss and destruction . . . I proposed to them the means which should be adopted to capture their enemies, which was to construct a cavelier* *to dislodge the enemies who did us damage . . . and wooden shields to protect our men from the arrows and stones, as fire was laid against the ramparts.*

On the following day, all was carried out . . . except for the wood fuel to burn the palisade of which they collected very little. They were hoping that the five hundred men promised by the Andastes could come . . . but they had not

---

*The author, who lives in the vicinity, affirms that this is still happening every December.

---

*This was a European siege device, a movable platform on scaffolding higher than the palisade from which musketeers could fire into the compound.

The Indian fort shown in this drawing may well be modelled on the fort of the Onondaga, with whom Champlain did battle following his trip of exploration through what is now Ontario. The original fort, a drawing of which appears in his works, was larger, stronger, and much more complex.

kept the rendezvous and this troubled our savages greatly.
Seeing that they were numerous enough to take the fort
without other help, I urged them to attack . . .

But Champlain was crying into the wind. His undisci-
plined, disorganized mob milled about, lighting fires
in the wrong places, firing wasted arrows over the
walls, and shouting and hollering at such a pitch that
he could not make himself heard. The skillful, cool-
headed Iroquois had water ready to quench any fires
and they kept up a steady sniper fire with their arrows.
The four Frenchmen on the platform of the *cavelier*
"killed and maimed many of them," but Chief Ocha-
tequin and another important leader were wounded
and Champlain himself was hit twice–one arrow in
the leg and another in a knee. Seeing the blood of their
chiefs, the warriors immediately retreated, "for no
reason [Champlain adds] except this freak of disorder."

The battle really ended there. The braves would not
respond to Champlain's pleas for a fresh assault based
on obedience to his orders. "They follow their own
inclination and do as they please," he sighed, "and
this ruins all their endeavours." They waited four
days for the laggard Andastes and then on October 18,
as the burnished leaves of autumn were hastened down
by an early flurry of snow, they set off glumly for
Huronia. Brulé arrived with the southern reinforce-
ments two days later and they returned home without
a fight. Even the vaunted guns of the French had not
beaten the Iroquois–a sharp and significant lesson
taken to heart by Huron and Iroquois alike.

Trussed like a baby in swaddling clothes, the
wounded Champlain was carried sixty miles to where
the canoes were cached on the shore of Lake Ontario.
"The pain I suffered from the wound in my knee," he
wrote, "was nothing in comparison with what I en-
dured tied and bound on the back of one of our Indians." He was lucky at that–when some bands were
faced with a hard march, they unceremoniously killed
anyone who could not keep up on the trail.

At the Thousand Islands entry of the St. Lawrence,
he asked for a canoe and paddlers to take him downstream to Montreal so that he could rejoin his people
at Quebec for the winter. The chiefs would not release
a canoe and Champlain soon grasped that their plan
was to keep the French in Huronia in case of reprisals
by the Iroquois. However politely it was all stated,
Champlain was virtually a prisoner–although certainly a privileged one–and remained so until the end
of the following June, when he was delivered back to
the trading meadows under the lee of Mount Royal.
There to greet him stood the indestructible Pontgravé.

From this time forward, Champlain left discovery
to other, younger, men and concentrated on the tooth-
and-nail struggle to keep his colony alive, and then,
with agonizing slowness, to build its strength. With
the government of France in turmoil, he doggedly
countered half a dozen attempts to break up the settlement and permit the fur trade to resume its old suicidal
competition. When he was notified of his discharge as
lieutenant to the Viceroy, he simply sailed again for
Quebec, as though nothing had happened.

He fought for his Canada right to the throne, sending a personal petition to Louis XIII in which he painted a glowing picture of the wealth that could be won
from Canada's forests and waters. He asked the Crown
to send fifteen *Récollets*, twelve hundred colonists, and
three hundred soldiers. He offered to build a fortified
city ("almost as large as St. Denis") at Quebec and
call it Ludovica, and another on the opposite side of
the Narrows. Between them, they would constitute a
tollgate at which all traffic up or down the St. Lawrence would have to pay tribute. This traffic would
soon include heavily laden ships trading to the Orient,
because he undertook "to discover the South Sea passage to China and to the East Indies by way of the
fleuve Saint-Laurent." He came to believe that his "fresh-
water sea" (Lake Huron) was drained on its western
extremity by a river that led to the Pacific. In a memo-
randum to the Paris Chamber of Commerce, he pulled
out all the stops and estimated the annual potential
value of Canada's exports at more than five million
livres. Since the value of the fur trade in a good year
was only 400,000 *livres*, he was counting heavily on
such things as "several types of mines . . . silver, steel,
iron, copper."

Princes and dukes succeeded each other as viceroy,
and the King confirmed that six priests and six families
must be established in New France. But the partners
in the company never lived up to their promises to
support the peopling of the colony. Champlain himself recruited Louis Hébert, his wife, their two daughters, and their small son as Canada's first true colonists
–against the active discouragement of his own associates. The Héberts, of course, had already sampled life
in Acadia on the Poutrincourt seigniory at Port Royal.
Hélène Champlain had come out with three servant-
women for her short stay, and Champlain had taken
on a foster family in the shape of three Indian girls,
aged eleven, twelve, and fifteen, whom he named
Faith, Hope, and Charity. By 1628, the population
had inched up to fifty-five souls.

In the personal saga of Samuel Champlain, small
advances almost always brought large reverses.
Cardinal Richelieu had fired the Viceroy and taken
Canada under his personal supervision. He confirmed
Champlain as "commander" and as his own personal
representative. He set up the *Compagnie des Cent-
Associés*, which was committed to sending out four
hundred settlers. The first detachment of two hundred
settlers departed in a fleet of four ships with everything
needed for their support. The sun seemed to be rising
over the St. Lawrence. But England was now at war
with France in support of the persecuted Huguenots,
and Sir David Kirke was lying in wait off the Gaspé
for Richelieu's convoy. In the first naval battle in

European artists who had not visited Canada tended to depict Indians as half-witted classical heroes with feathers in their hair. Champlain's own drawing (in the bottom right-hand corner), though crude, contains details that could only have been drawn from life.

203

Indians living on the shores of the falls of Niagara.

Canadian waters, a number of French ships were captured and the others dispersed.

This disaster committed the colony to a winter of near-starvation and when the Kirke brothers, Lewis and Thomas, sailed their gunboats up to Quebec on July 19, 1629–guided by none other than Etienne Brulé–Champlain sensibly submitted without a fight. He had just eighty-five people gathered for protection within Fort St. Louis, and only sixteen of them were regular fighting men. Among them, of course, was the gouty but doughty Pontgravé, now in his seventies. The Kirkes treated their captive courteously–they had been raised in Dieppe and Champlain knew their father. But when they shipped him to England, they refused him permission to take two of his Indian girls with him. Thirty-four settlers opted to remain in Canada. For nearly four years, Quebec was an English colony–in name, at any rate.

At the nadir of his fortune, Champlain, with a fortitude that is really beyond praise, began the long fight back. At sixty-three, he lobbied everyone in authority whom he could reach–both in England and in France –for the return of his beloved colony. "Few besides himself," wrote Professor Wrong, "seem to have had any hope."

Ironically, the war had already been over in Europe before the Kirkes took Quebec. But Charles I was, at first, deaf to the arguments of the French Ambassador. Champlain spent five weeks in London without result. Back in Paris, he importuned his fellow associates in the Company of One Hundred, Cardinal Richelieu, and Louis XIII himself. He condensed and revised his earlier books into the *Voyages* of 1632, making shrewd additions which explained the potential value of Canada "four times the size of France." He overlooked no bets, dropping all favourable references to the poor *Récollets* in favour of the rich and powerful Jesuits, who had taken over the missions in 1625. Eventually, England's Charles, who was having trouble getting money from a refractory Parliament, remembered that he was still owed 400,000 crowns of the dowry of his Queen Henrietta Maria, Louis' sister, and he offered to return Canada for this sum. There were other adjustments, including £20,000 for the Kirkes. The Treaty of St. Germain-en-Laye confirmed the deal.

On May 22, 1633, Champlain ended his last voyage. He slowly climbed the steep road to the summit of Quebec–past the spot where his statue stands today– and resumed command of Canada as the direct representative of Cardinal Richelieu. He rebuilt the ruined warehouses, repaired the fort, and raised the Church of Notre Dame-de-la-Récouvrance. Genuine settlers arrived to take up farms on the river bank at Beauport, and the outpost of Trois-Rivières was established. As his days slipped away, he divided his hours between formulating plans for yet another campaign to put down the Iroquois and in preparing for himself a place in the next world. Each evening he had someone read to him from the *Lives of the Saints*.

The discovery dream engrossed him to the end, and at Christmas, 1635, as he lay in a semicoma, he still hoped to hear news that a way had been opened to Cathay. He had sent Jean Nicolet to press to the furthest reaches of the "fresh-water sea," taking in his baggage a robe of Chinese damask to wear in the court of the Ming emperors. Nicolet got as far as Wisconsin. There was, of course, no passage to the Orient by the "River of Canada," but in the selfless striving of Samuel Champlain of Brouage to bring reality to his impossible dream, this country came to be.

BARRIER OF ICE

For European sea captains and their backers, the world of the Americas was an obstruction. There must be a way round it! Magellan soon found the southern way, but it was only hundreds of years later that the northern route was negotiated. Even in the twentieth century this voyage requires the most careful preparation, and those who try it may still be turned back by the icy barrier. But in those days when the first crews saw the whales and tried to breach the barrier, feelings of fear and wonder must have been uppermost.

MARTIN FROBISHER:

For five hundred years and more, men dreamed and worked and froze to find a northwest passage from the Atlantic Ocean, across the top of North America, to what lay beyond. The first Englishman to be obsessed by this dream was Martin Frobisher (1539?-94) – sometime buccaneer, pirate, soldier, gold-seeker, and discoverer, but one whose favourite sport was fighting the Spaniards. After fifteen years' search for backers, he made his first voyage to Canada's Arctic in 1576, bringing back bits of ore which some thought contained gold. Two more voyages followed in 1577 and 1578, but these were in search of gold, not new lands or waters. His exploring

Below, Frobisher is soldier more than sailor–eager to draw on the Spaniard.

Below, the frontispiece of Martin Frobisher Historia Navigationis, *showing an Eskimo in a kayak harpooning birds, and a view of family life on shore.*

"A Most Valourous Man"

career ended in disgrace when samples of the ore proved to be worthless. But he later received a knighthood for his deeds in helping to repel the Armada in 1588. Frobisher and his men were the first Europeans to make contact with the Eskimos: their relations were hostile and bloody from the beginning. On one occasion Frobisher lost five of his crew who strayed too far from the main ship. He retaliated by taking hostages, and he also took natives back to England, who soon died of civilization. He learned to respect the Eskimos for their skill and strength, but neither side was able to understand the ways of the other. The fabled passage remained barred.

After a terrible storm on the third voyage, blacksmiths and carpenters repair the fleet. Miners (left) look for "gold."

HUNTERS AND THE HUNTED

For many years (after the era of Frobisher, Hudson and Baffin) interest in the northern seas shifted from exploration to exploitation. In 1607 Henry Hudson first noticed the whales and "sea horses" (walruses); in the following centuries hundreds of ships went out to hunt these creatures. Despite their entirely commercial objective, the whalers did acquire knowledge and experience that assisted future discoverers. Later, the main whale hunt shifted to the Antarctic, and in the Arctic attention turned to metals and other minerals.

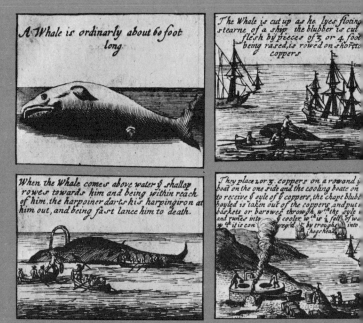

Below, "Clubbing the Great Auk." This flightless bird, slaughtered for its flesh, feathers, and oil, was extinct by 1850.

From early times the polar bear fascinated Europeans. Largest of all bears, they were taken alive in the middle ages to serve as gifts to royalty. Jacques Cartier presented one "as big as a cow and as white as a swan." The polar bear's whole life was a constant search for food to supply his huge frame (up to ten feet long and 1600 pounds); his usual food was seal meat but an occasional unwary explorer or hunter provided an interesting change of diet.

Below, an engraving by A. Meyer showing bartering along the shores of Davis Strait. The traders are exchanging fish for pelts.

THE FABLED QUEST

After Frobisher, the search for the Northwest Passage went on. The world knows the tragedy of Henry Hudson's last attempt. In 1610, he discovered the huge bay that bears his name, but mutiny left him and part of his crew to perish in its desolate waters. Yet his ship, *Discovery*, made several more attempts to find the Passage. The exploration of Hudson Bay was carried forward by many sea captains, including the Dane Jens Munck and the Bristol mariner Thomas James. Each of these expeditions wintered on the shores of the Bay and made successful returns. James spent a particularly miserable winter at the lower end of the bay later named for him, and the published account discouraged exploration for some years. There was, of course, no passage here to the Orient, and another two hundred years would pass before Robert McClure discovered the last link much higher in the north.

One artist's conception of the tragic scene, as Henry Hudson, his young son, and the sick crew members are set adrift.

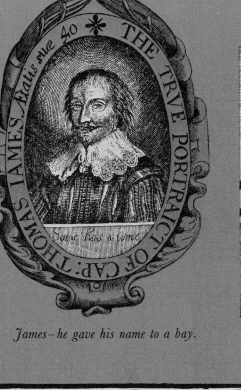

James—he gave his name to a bay.

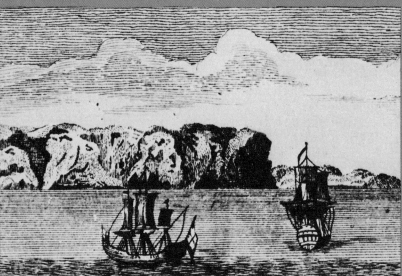

Cape Walsingham, Baffin Island — the stark view that greeted the discoverers.

Caught by an early winter, Captain Jens Munck's crew hastily prepares shelter at the mouth of the Churchill River, 1619.

TOWARDS THE ERA
OF SCIENTIFIC EXPLORATION

After the pioneering and heroic voyages of the sixteenth and seventeenth centuries there was a pause. The official search for the Passage was shelved. During this time, whalers, fur traders, and others were gaining more understanding of this environment. With the accumulation of this useful information, the next stages could begin: the scientifically oriented search for the North Pole and the study of the ecology.

Part V
James Cook - The Humble Hero

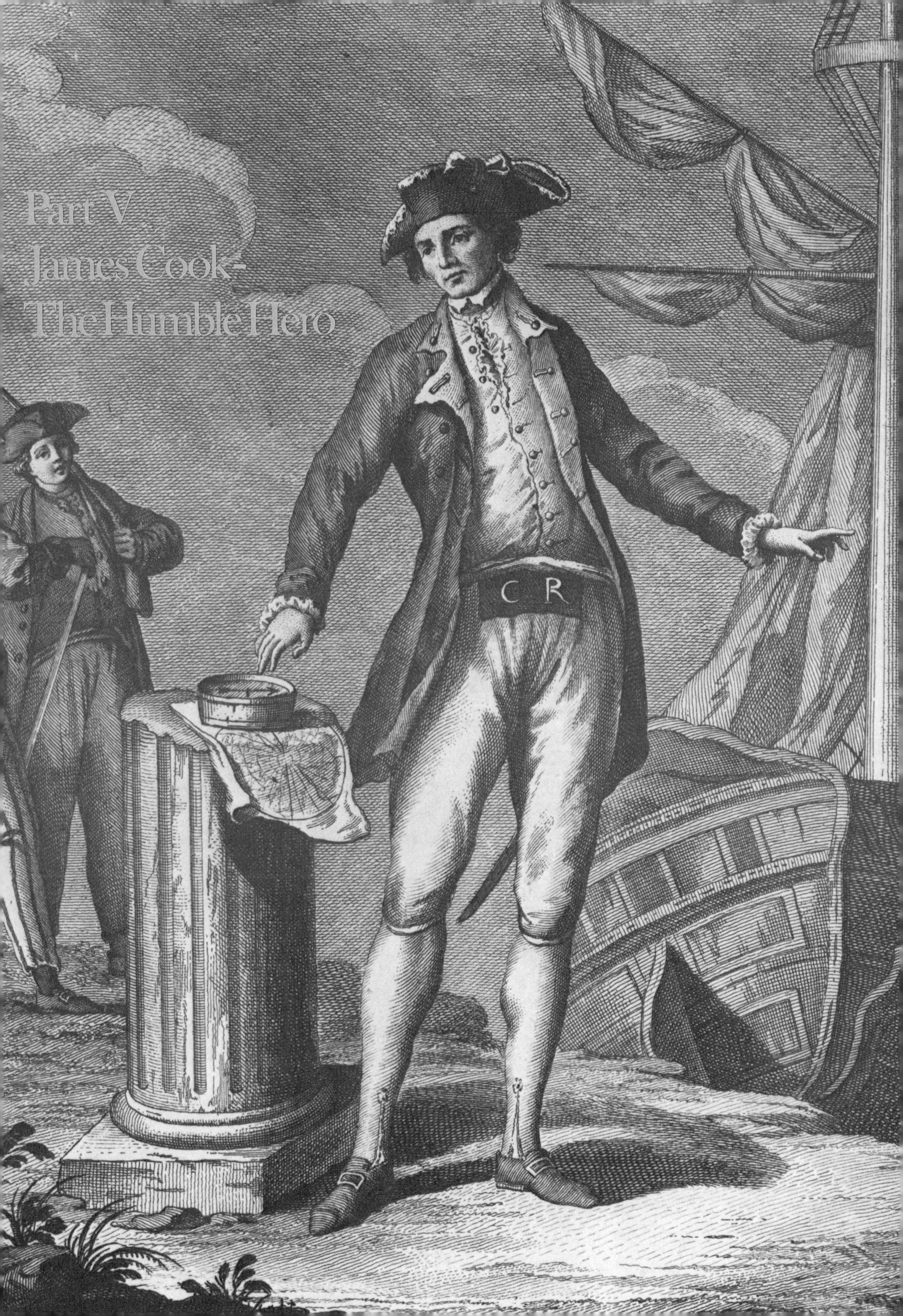

CHAPTER SIXTEEN

The Master of the River

URING the two and a half centuries in which the eastern coasts and waterways of Canada were brought into modern knowledge by Cabot, Cartier, Champlain, and their contemporaries, the magnificent western seaboard remained hidden under the rain clouds blowing in from the high Pacific. A remarkable tribal life, rich and intricate, teemed unknown in the forests that flowed down the mountains to the very edge of white beach and deep fiord. In seashore villages, in cedar mansions up to three hundred feet long and sixty feet wide, wealthy Indian nobles ruled slave societies and proved their status by what they ostentatiously gave away. They hunted the whale in dugout canoes paddled by fifty heavily muscled men. This secret world was guarded from the fatal impact and intrusion of Europe by the snow-capped chains of the Cordilleras and the unmeasured breadth of a continent. The sea approach was concealed in the vastness of the Pacific Ocean, covering one-third of the globe.

A handful of valiant captains, in 1520, led by Ferdinand Magellan clawed their way west across the mostly empty sea. They stayed, however, in southern latitudes, drawn to the Spice Islands. The Spaniards, industriously and mercilessly exploiting the lead given them by Columbus, had spread from Mexico to the Inca kingdom of Peru by the 1530's, and had a colony in the Philippines by 1565. Andrés de Urdaneta solved the problems of the prevailing ocean winds, and a fairly regular shipping service was established between Acapulco and Manila. Spain still claimed all of North America – by the terms of the Treaty of Tordesillas and by virtue of Balboa's declaration as he stood knee-deep in the Pacific (he called it the South Sea) in 1513 that all the lands washed by it belonged to King Ferdinand V. But Spanish power was never broad enough to hold the huge territories which were marked out by her brilliant discoverers, and the swiftly rising strength of Elizabethan England sent men like Drake to contest the new ocean.

The Spanish had fingered the central western coasts of America, with Juan Rodrigues Cabrillo and Bartholomew Ferrelo pushing north from Acapulco in 1542-43 to the vicinity of San Francisco Bay. Like many who followed, they looked in vain for the Straits of Anian, the waterway through the continent at about 40° north latitude, which, they hoped, would save them the long and scurvy-wracked journey by Cape Horn. This dream soon merged into the search for the Northeast Passage – a Pacific entry into the ocean route across the top of Canada, hopefully connecting with the Northwest Passage that now seemed to be opening to the heroic efforts of Martin Frobisher. Sir Richard Grenville planned a voyage that would circumnavigate the Americas, defying the Spanish claims and returning to England via the mythical straits. This was the task given to the Devonshire sea dog who was, according to taste, either the worst pirate who ever lived or the most gallant captain in an age of intrepid commanders. Under either hat, he was the first to claim an English stake in the Americas.

Francis Drake, son of a lay preacher, was in his lusty mid-thirties when he took his convoy of three ships into the Pacific in 1578. His private war against Spain had already brought him fame and wealth from his raids on the West Indies and the Isthmus of Panama – he had hijacked burro trains carrying thirty tons of silver. He dined in his cabin on the *Golden Hind* on gilt plate emblazoned with his own coat of arms, serenaded by musicians. He told even the cabin boys that they would become rich with their share of Spanish loot, and when his old comrade and partner, Thomas Doughty, spoke out against the dangerous passage of the Strait of Magellan, Drake had his friend's head struck off as a warning to waverers or traitors.

The gales of the Horn defeated two of the ships, and the *Golden Hind*, only 100 tons, coasted alone up the long pointing finger of South America. With brazen impudence, Drake sailed into every promising harbour from Valparaiso to Callao and Guatulco (Mexico), carrying off precious metals, porcelains, linens, and silks. He took several ships as prizes, including the *Cacafuego*, which was carrying gold, gems, and no less than twenty-six tons of silver. Incredibly, only token resistance seems to have been offered anywhere, and a few rounds from the guns of the *Golden Hind* settled all arguments. Once word of Drake's depredations reached high Spanish authority, a trap was set to catch him at the Strait of Magellan, where, it was assumed, he must pass on his return trip to England.

But Drake had no plans to retrace his steps. With his ship well ballasted with silver and gold, he pressed northward, keeping a sharp lookout to starboard for the Straits of Anian. In mid-1579, he was, according to the contemporary reports quoted in Hakluyt's *Voyages*, in a climate zone where his rigging froze, where the trees on the coast were leafless, and where the natives lived in houses covered with earth.* Behind the shore rose ridges of snow-capped peaks. He is said, however, to have reached only 48° north latitude – about the southern end of Vancouver Island.† And, although all those conditions *could* be imagined along the rugged coast of the State of Washington, it seems likely that there was an error, common in those times, in shooting the sun with the astrolabe. He may have been ten degrees further north, among the Tlingit of the Alaskan Panhandle – the time available in the records would easily allow this. In any event, when he found himself in "vile, thick and stinking fog," Drake turned south and put into a harbour at 38° north latitude for a five-week stay. This was, almost certainly, San Francisco Bay, and here, Drake claimed the territory for the Virgin Queen, naming it New Albion.

With fog blocking any hope of finding the Northeast Passage back to the Atlantic and Plymouth Hoe, and with the Spaniards doubtless waiting in the south, Drake set off into the western sea with only some stolen Spanish pilot charts of the Philippines to guide him. Fourteen months later, he was back in England, with loot worth a million and a half pounds, and the added fame of being the first Englishman to sail around the world. As every admiring schoolboy knows, Queen Elizabeth knighted him on the deck of the *Golden Hind*.

Two hundred years now passed before another, even more illustrious, Englishman saw those same wooded coasts with their marching mountains through a veil of rain. This was James Cook, the Yorkshire farm labourer's son, risen to be the British navy's most renowned captain, already acclaimed the greatest discoverer of his or any age from his two epic voyages across the southern Pacific. From this time forward – it was the spring of 1778 – the western coasts of Canada

and of all northern America were clearly on the map of the world and their fascinating peoples entered the written story of the human race. In Cook's crisp and workmanlike journals, the far western reaches of Canada, the British Columbia of today, take shape and draw their boisterous breath.

There had been, since shortly after Drake's time, the unconfirmed chronicle, first published by Samuel Purchas in his anthology of early voyages, of the discovery by Juan de Fuca of "a broad inlet of sea" lying between 47° and 48° north latitude which he had explored for twenty days. The Basque, Sebastian Vizcaino, had returned suggesting California was an island. Sir John Narborough was sent out by the British Admiralty through the Straits of Magellan in the 1660's to survey the coasts above New Albion, but he didn't get any higher than Chile. The roistering piratical William Dampier (who remains, curiously, a concealed hero of the late Age of Discovery) reopened Grenville's scheme for a western entry to a direct sea passage in the north from Cathay to Europe. The Dutch were always in the van in the Pacific, and Jacob Roggeveen, Abel Tasman, and others crossed and recrossed the tropics – but did not venture north. When the British admiral, George Anson, made his sensational round-the-world voyage in 1740-44, he too ran before the westerlies of the Capricornian latitudes.

John Byron, leveller of Louisbourg and grandfather of the poet, was sent out in 1764 to check on various Spanish discoveries, including those of the nonexistent Admiral Bartholomew de Fonte. He was ordered to "go to Drake's harbour in New Albion . . . and as far to the northward as you shall find it practicable . . . If you find any probability of exploring a passage from the said coast of New Albion to the eastern side of North America through Hudson's Bay, you are most diligently to pursue it and return to England that way." He got nowhere near New Albion before he decided "to run for India by a new track."

The French were brilliantly represented in the Pacific by Louis-Antoine de Bougainville, who had so recently been the Marquis de Montcalm's aide-de-camp in the losing battle for Canada. The sophisticated Bougainville fell in love with Tahiti and its open-armed girls (who didn't?) and named it *la nouvelle Cythère*. But on his route back to St. Malo, he was never above the equator in the Pacific. The north still held its secrets.

Cook and Bougainville were on opposing sides in Canada in the Seven Years' War, but in the greater challenge of breaking the watery tundra of the Pacific to the service and uses of man they were colleagues and respected allies. They could hardly have been more different. When he began his voyage around the world, Bougainville was thirty-seven, a Chevalier of St. Louis, highly educated in law and the sciences (already elected to Britain's Royal Society), a man of aristocratic tastes (he would later be made a Count of

---

*These were common in the Aleutians and Alaska. Also, the winter house of the B.C. Salish was a pit roofed with saplings upon which earth was thickly banked.

†Mount Golden Hind, 7,219 feet, on southern Vancouver Island was named by enthusiasts of this persuasion.

the Empire by Napoleon), a colonel with an extensive war record, and a colonizer of the Falkland Islands. James Cook, a year younger than Bougainville, was, at thirty-seven still uncommissioned in the British navy, had never fought a battle, was highly regarded as a surveyor (he was then charting the coasts of Newfoundland), but was unhonoured and unknown to the public at large. He was, moreover, a steady, bluff Yorkshireman with very little formal education, a man of the plainest tastes. A full decade later, James Boswell, always a-twitter at the wits and swells of eighteenth-century London, described his meeting with Cook: "It was curious to see Cook, a grave steady man, and his wife, a decent plump Englishwoman, and think that he was preparing to sail around the world."

The rise of Cook into the select company of the world's truly great men can, of course, be charted, giant step by giant step, but it nevertheless remains a thing of wonder. It would be almost as unlikely today as it was then. In the strictly stratified society of his time, it took men of wide humanity, sharp discernment, and experience in the field to see the ripening genius in Cook and allow it room to grow. Fortunately, such men were plentiful in that marvellous age. They included John and Henry Walker, Quaker ship-owners of Whitby, Sir Hugh Palliser, captain of HMS *Eagle* (and later Governor of Newfoundland), the Earl of Sandwich, First Lord of the Admiralty, Benjamin Franklin, and others in a spiral of talent and title that included, lastly, King George III.

Cook was the second of Grace and James Cook's seven children. He was born on October 27, 1728, in a cottage at the hamlet of Marton, in the North Riding of Yorkshire, close to the ocean port of Middlesbrough. His Scottish father was a day-labourer who later became foreman for squire Thomas Scottowe on his farm

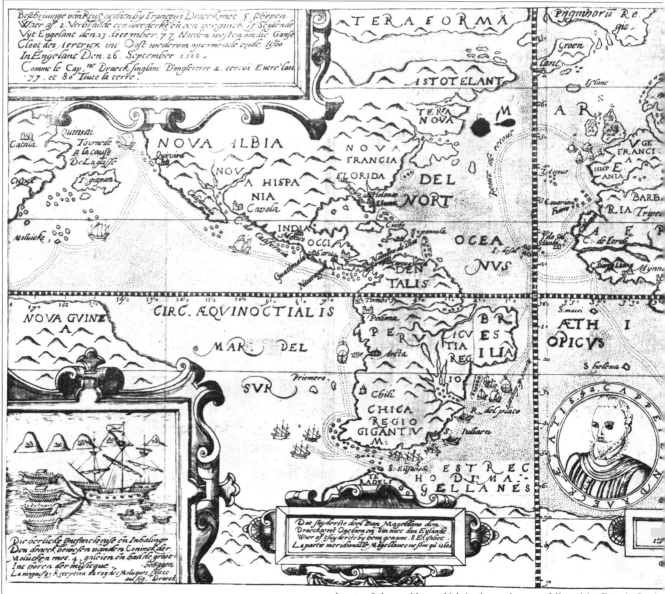

A map of the world on which is shown the route followed by Francis Drake in his circumnavigation of the globe. Being the first Englishman to perform

"Airyholm" at nearby Great Ayton. Young James was raised within smell of the North Sea, and it can be assumed that he grew hardy at farm chores on those bleak Cleveland Hills. The scant schooling he received came from *Dominie* Pullen at Ayton, but the legend has it that he showed "a remarkable facility in acquiring the science of numbers."

This is probably true, because at seventeen, James left the stone cottage to serve a four-year apprenticeship to William Sanderson, Dry Goods and Groceries, in the little fishing port of Staithes. (The cottage, incidentally, was bought by an Australian philanthropist in 1934 and moved–stone by stone–to Melbourne, where it is today regarded as one of Australia's treasured historical shrines.) After eighteen months amid the starched collars and artichokes, James sought his release and moved ten miles down the coast to the prosperous port of Whitby, a port known since Nor-

this feat, he was knighted on April 4, 1581, on the deck of the Golden Hind. *He brought back a fortune in plunder.*

man days. It was a Whitby ship that in 1709 rescued Alexander Selkirk, the prototypal Robinson Crusoe; and a century later, William Scoresby sailed from here on his whaling and discovery voyages to the Arctic.

Despite his advancing age, Cook was accepted into an apprenticeship by the Walker brothers, ship-owners of Grape Lane–poor boys of that day usually went to sea at thirteen. These kindly men put him into the big collier, *Freelove*, trading between Newcastle and London. And when the winter storms kept the shallow-draught "cats" in harbour, John Walker had his eager protégé hard at work on mathematics and navigation. The attic where young Cook studied, and shivered, to candles sneaked in for free by the Walkers' housekeeper, is still preserved–and shown, by hopeful fathers, to unwilling mop-haired sons who have been bewitched by lesser idols.

Cook's rise was never swift. The thing about it, though, is that it never stopped. He was to demonstrate the inevitable triumph of an all-encompassing knowledge and deeply tested skill over the flash and fizzle of more incandescent talents.

For two years, he served before the mast on the *Freelove*, and he never lost his respect for the type. These sturdy, commodious 400-ton oaken ships earned the name "cat" from their hull-shape–the naming of ships by standardized rigging came later. Alan Villiers, who writes as well as he sails, explains that they were "apple-cheeked forward but fine aft, flat-floored to sit on the bottom and stand up with minimum ballast." It was to the Whitby "cat" that Cook turned for his discovery ships. They may have been colliers, but not a speck of dust was allowed to mar the decks–the 'prentices saw to that. In the frequent storms that blew up fast in the shallow waters of the North Sea, when the changing winds could quickly drive a ship onto the sandbanks, the crew would leap into the shrouds at the order: "Aloft and furl!" As the "cat" leapt from crest to trough, the masts seemed to dip to the cutting spume, the Whitby men and boys hanging on to the rigging for life itself.

When his time was served, Cook stayed with the Walkers as able seaman, and then, for two years, as mate. He made voyages into the Baltic, and to French and Irish ports. New Zealand Professor J. C. Beaglehole, the ranking expert on Cook and South Pacific discovery (to whom these chapters owe considerable debt), notes that Cook was probably better equipped technically than any of his Pacific predecessors. So many others, in all oceans, were ambitious aristocrats or entrepreneurs first, and mariners and navigators only second.

In 1755, when nearly twenty-seven, Cook was offered the command of the coaster *Friendship*. However, instead of accepting this post, he volunteered at Wapping for the navy as a lowly seaman. He wasn't crazy. The climactic conflict between Britain and France was shaping up–an ominous year had passed since Louis Coulon de Villiers had turned Colonel George Washington out of Fort Necessity in the disputed Ohio country–and there was opportunity in a fast-expanding navy for an ambitious well-trained seaman. In peacetime, a working-class boy could never hope for an officer's commission; but in wartime, ability and courage could sometimes carry away the class barriers. British men-of-war were already blockading French channel ports and Cook's steady eye was already on wider waters.

A week later, he joined the 60-gun ship of the line, HMS *Eagle*, at Portsmouth. He began to keep a log, his personal journal, from the day that he began naval service, and he kept it up until shortly before his tragic death, twenty-four years later, on a Hawaiian beach. His journals of his three discovery voyages are available in many editions–the first biography appeared in 1788–but those readers who, hopefully, will pursue the story of Cook beyond these pages should discover for themselves the pleasures of the volumes edited and annotated for the Hakluyt Society in 1955 by Dr. Beaglehole. He weighs and examines every crumb from the wardroom table.

The *Eagle* tacked so close to Cherbourg that she was fired upon by the guns of the fort. She seized some prizes on the Bay of Biscay and was badly damaged in the duel in which the 1,500-ton Indiaman, *Duc d'Aquitaine*, was taken. Cook had been quickly raised to master's mate, a minor petty officer, but when Captain Hugh Palliser (whose name Canada would later come to know) took command, he was raised to boatswain, a noncommissioned rank of real substance. When several cutters were sent out as a screen for the valuable man-of-war, Bo'sun Cook was given command of a forty-footer. After two years, Palliser, who had by now taken over from Walker as Cook's patron, procured for him a master's warrant in the 64-gun *Pembroke*, bound for the Canadian front. In that time, a noncommissioned master commanded the seamen aboard, but sailed the ship wherever ordered by the senior military officers–a master chauffeur, if you like.

The battle for Canada had opened with the land and sea assault in June 1758, on the fortress of Louisbourg, which controlled the entry to Cabot Strait from its strategic site on the northeast coast of Cape Breton. The *Pembroke* was still in Halifax when the assault opened, but she soon joined the blockading ships, and was present at the surrender on July 26. This marked the beginning of James Cook's 20-year relationship with Canada–an association signally uncelebrated in this Dominion, so careless of its heroes.

William Pitt's grand strategy to throw the French out of North America called for three hammer-blows: one through the Virginian colonies under Major-General Edward Braddock to crush Fort Duquesne at the Ohio forks; the second up the Champlain Pass (the Hudson-Richelieu river route); and the third straight down the throat of the St. Lawrence at Quebec. The

Sir Hugh Palliser did much to help Cook in his early naval career.

Second from the top in the left-hand column of this muster role is the name of James Cook, First Mate aboard the Friendship.

first came to bloody defeat; the second trundled along for two years; but the third, as all the world knows, succeeded brilliantly in 1759 under Major-General James Wolfe and Vice-Admiral Charles Saunders.

The important part played in that victory by the 31-year-old sailing master of the *Pembroke* has remained in shadow, although it was acknowledged by the surviving principals. It is the opinion of the experts that without the preliminary charting of the river's rocks, shoals, and currents that was carried out under the direction of James Cook, it would have been impossible to bring the invasion fleet into the Quebec Basin without serious loss. Pitt had sent a quarter of the Royal Navy's strength to Canada: forty-nine men-of-war and one hundred transports and store ships. No ship of the line had been up the St. Lawrence as far as Quebec since Sir William Phips' nervy entry in the 44-gun *Six Friends* nearly a century and a half earlier, and the forewarned French had now removed all buoys and markers from the river's intricate channels.

Before Wolfe's first landing attempt on the shore in front of the heights of Montmorency, the shallow river approach had to be charted thoroughly, with soundings by handline right to the strand. This task was assigned to Cook and it was carried out in the dark on successive evenings "to the entire satisfaction of his superiors." Although operating directly under the guns of Brigadier François Lévis, Cook evaded detection until the job was almost done. When his small boats were spotted and pursued by Indians in canoes, Cook had his sailors pull hard for the Island of Orleans, and – so the tale goes – jumped off the bow as the natives clambered over the stern.

The most difficult passage in the whole river approach to Quebec was the channel around Orleans, the portion known as "the Traverse." It was studded with rocks, small islets, and shoals, the whole conditioned by the state of the 18-foot tides, and by the steady downstream winds of the season. The British had to pass two hundred ships – nineteen of them front-rank battleships – up this obstacle course, in the dark and against the strong stream. They fully expected that Montcalm would have batteries mounted on commanding heights (such as Cap Tourmente), but as it happened, Montcalm had been unable to convince Governor Vaudreuil to take such precautions. Even Point Lévis, well within cannon range across the river from Quebec itself, was left undefended. Cook took charge at the Traverse and so accurate was the chart which he produced that every one of the British ships passed up safely. (When published later, his surveys of the river remained in use for a century.)

After the victory had been taken on the Plains of Abraham, Cook was transferred to the *Northumberland*, the flagship of Rear Admiral Lord Colville, who was remaining as commander-in-chief of the North American station. On Colville's personal order, Cook continued working on his charts of the river, as far upstream as Montreal. In his dispatches to the Admiralty from his base at Halifax, Colville referred to "Mr. Cook's genius and capacity" and Cook was granted a bonus of £50 for "making himself master of the pilotage of the river." The admiral had joined the growing group of men, all solid professionals, who were watching with admiration the forging progress of the self-taught Yorkshireman. Colville told the Lords of the Admiralty – who would shortly be joined by Sir Hugh Palliser – that he considered Cook "well qualified... for greater undertakings of the same kind." General Wolfe had consulted Cook personally about approach problems to certain possible assault points.

In the *Pembroke*, two other notable men had influenced Cook's career and were themselves to play some part in the development of Canada. During the uneventful days in the blockade at Louisbourg, and at Halifax, Captain John Simcoe guided Cook's study of astronomy and trigonometry, leading him through the more difficult pages of Leadbitter's mathematical works. Captain Simcoe died at forty-five at sea off Anticosti before the triumph at Quebec, but his son, John Graves Simcoe, became the first lieutenant-governor of Upper Canada in 1791, and gave his father's name to the largest inland lake in southern Ontario. When the new lieutenant-governor reached Canada, his first home was the tent which he had purchased in London at a sale of Cook's effects.

Major Samuel Holland, who was to survey so much of Ontario, Quebec, and the Maritimes – leaving his own name on the Holland River and marsh, forty miles north of Toronto – gave many hours of instruction in map-making to Cook in the main cabin of the *Pembroke*. He was Cook's own age, but had the great advantage of having obtained a classical education in the Netherlands before entering the British army in 1754. Holland left a memoir describing Cook's fascination with the plane table, and how quickly he mastered its use.

For a while, Cook acted as the surveyor's assistant, spending spare evening hours with Euclid's *Elements*. "Whenever I could get a moment from my duties," Holland wrote, "I was on board the *Pembroke*, where the great cabin dedicated to scientific purposes, mostly taken up with a drawing table, furnished no room for idlers. Under Captain Simcoe's eye, Mr.

Cook and myself compiled materials for a chart of the Gulf and River of St. Lawrence." Holland was later appointed Surveyor-General of Quebec and was mainly responsible for laying-out the lands alloted to the fifty thousand Loyalists who chose Canada and the monarchy after the American Revolution.

In 1762, when he was a steadying thirty-four – near to middle age for the eighteenth century – Cook was paid off from the *Northumberland* with handsome savings of £291. The Thames-side bordellos, the parlours of Drury Lane, and other places of amusement were on the lookout for returning sailors with pay in pocket. The six-foot sailing master had, no doubt, become rather accustomed to the company of gentlemen and he might well and properly have sought associations in line with his rising position. What he did, though, was to swiftly court and marry a working-class girl named Elizabeth Batts, of Wapping. She was thirteen years younger than Cook, the only daughter of John and Mary Batts. Cook may have known her before he left England in 1758, but in his reserved manner, he revealed in his journals practically nothing of his private life. They were married at St. Margaret's Church in Barking, Essex, on December 21, 1762, and Cook took a small house in Shadwell, in the sprawl of London's East End.

A few years later, when he had been presented to the King and promoted after his voyage around the world in the *Endeavour*, he did move his home – to the Mile End Road in equally humble Stepney. Here, Mrs. Cook remained, despite the mounting fame of her husband, and here their six children were born. One son, Joseph, the father never saw – he was born after Cook's departure on a voyage and dead and buried before his return. Another son, George, lived only four months. Two of the surviving sons, Nathaniel and James, went into the navy as boys. Nat was drowned at sixteen when the *Thunderer* foundered in a hurricane in West Indian waters, and James Junior met a similar fate at thirty while in command of the sloop *Spitfire*. The other son, Hugh, had his father's brains and became a scholar at Christ's College, Cambridge, but died of a fever at seventeen. He had been named after Captain Palliser.

Elizabeth Cook outlived all of her family, and just about all of her contemporaries as well. When her husband's death was announced, King George III wept and granted the widow a pension of £200 a year, which she was to draw for fifty-six years. She became wealthy on a half-interest in the profits from the publication of Cook's journals and always wore a ring that contained a lock of the discoverer's hair. For the rest of her life she would state as an expression of ultimate disapproval: "Mr. Cook would never have done so."

CAPTAIN JAMES COOK

Cook as he looked at the age of forty-eight, painted by John Webber.

On the coasts of Canada, east and west, James Cook left his imperishable mark. Renowned for his great voyages into the South Pacific, he first made his name in the St. Lawrence and then brought the British Columbia of today into the bright light of modern knowledge.

The bark *Endeavour*, Cook's ship on the first voyage of discovery, is seen here as the collier *Earl of Pembroke* in Whitby Harbour in Thomas Luny's painting. It was at Whitby that Cook first went to sea as apprentice to John and Henry Walker. The son of a farm-labourer, he was born at Marton, Yorkshire, in 1728. After rudimentary schooling, he served eighteen months as a grocer's apprentice, but by 1746 he knew he wanted to be a sailor. In eight years with the Walkers, Cook rose to the rating of mate; they also encouraged him to study mathematics and navigation. His memory of the merits of Whitby ships led him to choose four of them in later years for his voyages round the world.

MASTER COOK
AT HIS CALLING

James Cook's later fame stemmed from his years of charting the St. Lawrence and the shores of Newfoundland and Labrador. Already known to sailors for many years, these waters had to be sounded with the lead line, their currents observed, and exact latitudes and longitudes confirmed. Cook's charts are topographical portraits of the bottom, showing depths, contours, submerged rocks, shoals, and distances. His genius in marine surveying would be tested in the unknown waters off New Zealand and Australia.

A sextant from Cook's era, maker unknown. It was used by navigators to measure altitudes of celestial bodies.

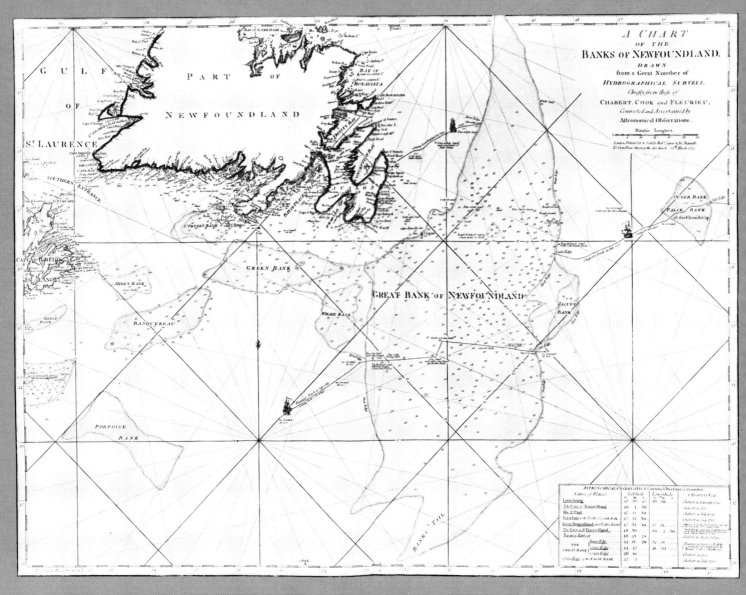

This chart shows coastlines and water depths and was based on observations made by Cook and others. Cook also surveyed rivers and harbours.

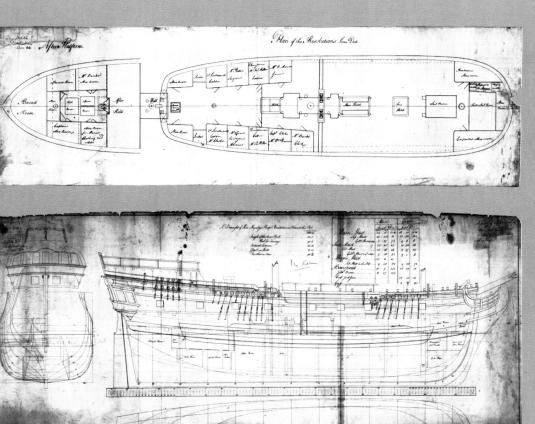

SHIPS
OF
DISCOVERY

His experience with Endeavour *convinced Cook that ships of the Whitby type were unexcelled for exploring and charting. He reported that she steered well, had a top speed of eight knots, and could be careened without danger—an important consideration when the crew had to clean and caulk the hull. Thus when Cook was to set out again, he asked for a Whitby ship and a sister ship, for safety's sake.* Resolution *and* Adventure *were both former colliers. Proposed changes that Cook rejected are shown at left on the plan.*

A scale model of the Endeavour *in the National Maritime Museum at Greenwich. She was a bark of 368 tons and in 1768 carried a crew of 71.*

The sailors shown in the drawing by Cook at right belonged to the crew of *Endeavour*, and are busy filling water casks at Tolaga Bay, New Zealand. Cook landed at this pleasant spot late in 1769 after leaving Tahiti on his first voyage. Here he encountered Maoris who were eager to trade, tattooed their faces, and decorated their house posts and canoes with rich carving. They shocked the English, however, with their cannibalistic practices. It was during this voyage that Cook established that the main area of New Zealand was composed of two large islands – no large southern continent was to be found here. Sailing on, he explored the east coast of Australia, at one point going aground on a shoal of the Great Barrier Reef. Only an emergency measure called "fothering" enabled the crew to stop the leaks until the ship could be beached and repaired. At Cooktown, the crew first saw kangaroos.

EXOTIC ANCHORAGES

One of the aims of Cook's second voyage was to sail into the high latitudes of the southern hemisphere on a further search for the supposed continent. In January of 1773, *Resolution* crossed the Antarctic Circle; Cook was sure his was the first and only ship ever to have done so. The crew put some of the icebergs they encountered to good use—pieces chopped from them were taken aboard ship and melted for fresh water. After a summer of exploring the island area northeast of New Zealand, Cook returned to searching the Antarctic for the non-existent continent. Turning north in February 1774, the ship reached Easter Island the next month. The strange stone idols roused the curiosity of the crew and were sketched by Hodges, the expedition's artist. In his thorough way, Cook returned to his circumnavigation of the globe in the high southern latitudes the next winter. When he reached Cape Town in March 1775, he was able to say that there was no southern continent except perhaps under the South Pole. The bark *Resolution* was away from England three years and eighteen days in all. Thanks to Cook's care, only one crew member had died of sickness during the long voyage.

Captain Cook must have dropped anchor gratefully in the peaceful inlet at Nootka. His ships had been buffeted severely since the west coast of North America (the shore of Oregon) was first sighted early in February 1778. In spite of the rains of April, he would use this shelter to repair his ship and continue his usual keen examination of new peoples and places. When William Ellis painted the anchorage, both *Resolution* and her sister ship *Discovery* were present. Tents to serve as observatories were set up on the point at the right which was named Astronomers' Rock. Cook called the large island in the inlet after his shipmaster, William Bligh, who prepared many of the charts made on the voyage.

LANDFALL AT NOOTKA

A Nootka woman in a woven cedar-root hat. | *Nootka man with nose jewel and bark cape.* | *An ornamented beauty from the northwest.*

COOK'S CANADIAN HOSTS

The clever and colourful people of B.C.'s Nootka Sound swarmed out chanting in their dugout canoes to greet the English ships in hospitable fashion. Though friendly to Cook's men, they carried on bloody warfare with their neighbours. The generosity of nature provided them with food, fish, and furs in profusion, and the massive cedar trees from which to make hats, cloth, and vast plank houses. They were eager to buy any metal tools. In the Aleutian Islands, Cook found equally cordial natives who wanted to trade furs for tobacco.

The interior of a house in Unalaska. With a timber and whalebone frame, it was roofed with sod and entered from above via a rough ladder.

John Webber's impression of Nootka Sound, showing the typical rough, hilly country. The Indians at the left are sitting in a dugout canoe.

THE LAST EFFORT

It was late summer when Resolution *and* Discovery *sailed past Bering Strait.*
Blocked by the ice-field seen in Webber's painting, they turned back.

After leaving Nootka, Cook followed
the coast northward, giving names to
many mountain peaks and promontories
as he passed them. Turning west with
the shore, he spent some time probing
inlets that might be the much-sought
passage to the east. Then parallelling
the Alaska Peninsula and its dribble
of islands to Unalaska, the ships
turned north and proceeded along the
the west coast to Bering Strait.
Pressing on, they crossed the Arctic
Circle and on August 18, 1778, reached
their farthest north at latitude
70° 44'. Here their way was blocked
by ice. Doggedly Cook pursued the
search for an opening to the east,
but the wall of ice was beyond the
strength of his ships to penetrate.
It was time to turn back. Undeterred
by his own ill-health and a limping
ship, Cook was determined to winter
in southern waters and return to his
task the next summer. But man only
proposes; this was to be his final
valiant reconnaissance.

*Cook's murder at Kavarua Point by
the Hawaiians, based on evidence of
witnesses. In order to destroy the
illusion that Cook was a god, the
priests believed he must be killed.*

EXALTATION
OF A HERO

Designed by H Ramberg Engraved by J Neagle and Ornamented by W Grainger.
NEPTUNE raising CAPT^N COOK up to Immortality, a GENIUS crowning him
with a Wreath of Oak, and FAME introducing him to History. In the Front Ground are
the FOUR QUARTERS of the WORLD presenting to BRITANNIA their various Stores.

Published as the Act directs by J Cooke N°17 Paternoster Row.

CHAPTER SEVENTEEN

North Atlantic, South Pacific

NEWS of the French counter-invasion two years after the surrender at Montreal didn't reach the British fleet at Halifax for some weeks. (In fact, there are probably millions of Canadians who haven't heard about it even yet.) The Comte d'Haussonville sailed from Brest with five ships, easily evaded a slack blockade, and landed eight hundred troops near St. John's, Newfoundland, on July 24, 1762. Three days later, the small British garrison surrendered, and the French fleet under Admiral de Terney sailed through the Narrows into that already-ancient harbour. The real purpose of the attack was to give France some stronger cards to play in the extended peace negotiations following the Seven Years' War.

When word of this impudence reached Admiral Lord Colville, he quickly put together a small expeditionary force, with land units under the command of Colonel William Amherst, brother of the all-conquering general. James Cook, as sailing master, brought the three-decker flagship *Northumberland* from Chebucto Harbour, ready for action; and other units converged from Placentia and New York. Troops fought their way ashore at Torbay, nine miles north of St. John's, and pushed towards the famous port. At Quidi Vidi, the French made a spirited stand and then retreated into the fortifications on Signal Hill. Taking advantage of a thick fog, Admiral de Terney slipped his ships out to sea, leaving his compatriots to British mercies. By September 20, it was all over.

In this dramatic fashion, the surveyor of the St. Lawrence now began his five years of unglamorous but highly regarded labours on the charting of the Newfoundland and Labrador coasts. Cook had already completed the first professional survey of Halifax's four miles of harbour and its inner Bedford Basin. Now he charted the harbours of St. John's and Placentia, and the islands of St. Pierre and Miquelon. While the British fleet remained for a time in Placentia, Cook made a deep impression on Captain Thomas Graves, Governor of Newfoundland.

The highly competent Graves was the son of an admiral and he was to reach that rank himself – and to be raised to the peerage as well. Examining Cook's surveys of Placentia and the surrounding terrain, he petitioned London for a special surveying budget and asked that James Cook be appointed to the task. Graves was succeeded by none other than Palliser of the *Eagle* – perhaps Cook's most consistent booster – and the eight-year-old schooner, *Sally*, sixty-eight tons, was bought in Massachusetts and handed over to Cook as His Majesty's survey vessel *Grenville*.

Though he was to remain in noncommissioned rank for another six years, Cook now had his own lively little ship and was doing just the kind of solid work he seemed to enjoy most. No word or inference in his detailed journals ever suggests that he thought himself ill-used in the matter of rank. As a matter of fact, with his special rate of ten shillings a day as a master surveyor, he was better off financially than a man holding a lieutenant's commission. The one dark spot on his experiences aboard the *Grenville* was an accident in which a flask of powder exploded in his right hand. As a result of this mishap, Cook carried scars for the rest of his life.

Seamen say that in Newfoundland waters there are three seasons: July, August, and winter. But a stormy coast was a routine risk to a man used to bringing the Whitby "cats" down past the Dogger Bank to the Thames. Cook now spent as long as the season would allow on the Atlantic coast, then sailed the *Grenville* back to England. In the winters, he would work up his charts, patiently cross-checking every calculation, and deliver them to the Admiralty. They were universally admired when published in the *North American Pilot*, and his reputation – that slow-motion avalanche that would eventually sweep him to fame – gained ever more momentum.

The job he did at "York Harbour on the Coast of Labradore" is typical of his Canadian work. This is the place now known as Henley Harbour, in Chateau Bay, at the northeastern entry of the Strait of Belle Isle.

Four years after Cook charted it, the British erected York Fort on this inhospitable shore to protect the garrison and seal-fishermen against the Eskimos and against the occasional French who refused to accept their diplomats' cession of the coast. Close examination of this chart reveals that the canny Cook named one bay "Pitt's Harbour." He gave the name of his schooner to another.

While Governor Palliser was having his troubles trying to discourage settlement in Newfoundland – the British wanted to use the island principally as a training ground for seamen – Cook was trudging inland to survey the central highlands, pinpointing the positions of some of the large, barely-known lakes which brim the glacial valleys. His maps were the first to attempt an accurate description of the incredibly ragged and rocky northeastern and western coasts.

In the Canadian vernacular, Yorkshire's Jim Cook may well have been the very first "eager beaver" – and his stolid delight in expanding and demonstrating his accomplishment was now inevitably moving him toward the breakthrough which the student of his career always senses has been approaching. In August 1766, he had been in the navy for eleven years and was now almost thirty-eight. On August 5, he observed an eclipse of the sun from one of the islands off Burgeo, on the southwestern coast of Newfoundland. His detailed report, allowing the most exact computation of longitude so far, was sent to the Royal Society by Dr. John Bevis and published in the *Philosophical Transactions* the following year.

Chartered by Charles II in 1662, the Royal Society of London for Promoting Natural Knowledge had become the dynamo of the scientific world. Christopher Wren and Isaac Newton had served as presidents, and the British Museum was now being established on the basis of the collections of Sir Hans Sloane, a more recent president. The fellows of the society included many of the most polished and progressive minds of the eighteenth century, among them a rich young landowner and amateur botanist named Joseph Banks. The society now heard of James Cook and noted Dr. Bevis' remarks that the marine surveyor of Newfoundland was "very expert in his business."

When the Royal Society petitioned the government to send a ship to the South Seas in order to observe the transit of the planet Venus across the sun in 1769, it was Cook who was chosen to command. The Lords of the Admiralty, however, had a second and secret purpose in mind for the voyage – to try to clear up the mystery of *Terra Australis Incognita*, the continent which many believed lay across the southern Pacific latitudes "to balance" the huge land masses of the northern hemisphere. Marco Polo had begun the legend with his Land of Locach. And when Ferdinand Magellan went through his 400-mile-long strait at the tip of South America in 1520, he thought that the bleak mountains of Tierra del Fuego, to the south, were probably part of that continent. Early maps showed the supposed *Terra Australis* reaching all the way from Cape Horn to Van Diemen's Land (Tasmania), which had been discovered by Tasman in 1642. As the Solomons, New Hebrides, Marquesas, and other island groups were discovered (and sometimes lost again),

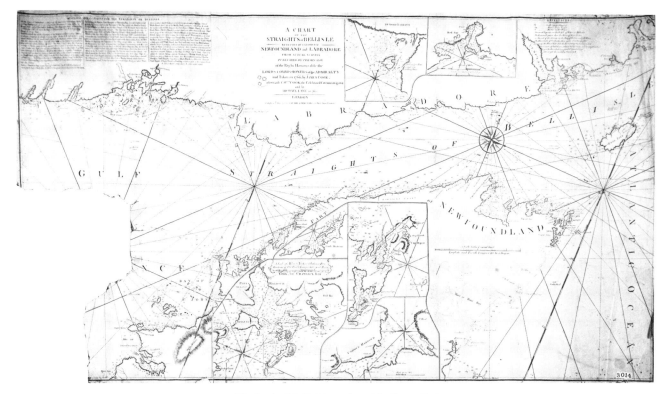

The Strait of Belle Isle as charted by James Cook.

each was hailed at first as the coast of the long-sought continent. When Tasman ran into the mountainous west coast of the South Island of New Zealand, he thought that *that* was the edge of it. But when the hostile Maoris came out in canoes and clubbed a boatload of Dutchmen to death, he named it Murderers' Bay and made off northwards, where he stumbled across the more kindly Fijians and Tongans.

The most ardent British advocate for *Terra Australis* was the geographer, Alexander Dalrymple, a member of the Royal Society, who had made some voyages to the East Indies. Dalrymple, a Scotsman, had been chosen to superintend the forthcoming astronomical observation, and the Marquesas had been selected as the best site. Dalrymple, however, was both big-headed and pig-headed, and when he demanded that the over-all command of the navy's ship be vested in him also, Admiral Hawke, First Lord of the Admiralty (the hero of Quiberon Bay), refused just as dogmatically. Dalrymple seems to have imagined himself the Columbus of the Pacific, destined to add vast territories to the realm of the British Crown; and once he had accepted the existence of a southern continent as fact, nothing could budge him from that conclusion. Dalrymple's family held the old Earldom of Stair, he counted the celebrated Dr. Johnson as friend, and he would not concede superiority in command to anyone. In fact, he finally withdrew from the entire expedition – which was just fine with James Cook.

With Sir Hugh Palliser, Baronet, now among the Lords of the Admiralty, Cook was swiftly commissioned first lieutenant and given command of the bark *Endeavour* for the Pacific voyage. His commission was dated May 25, 1768; but it seems quite likely that Palliser had inside information on the appointment, because before the end of March, negotiations were underway to purchase a Whitby "cat" of the type familiar to Cook.

The one that was found by the Admiralty's surveyors was the *Earl of Pembroke*: 106 feet long; 29 feet, 3 inches wide; of 368 tons; built by Messrs. Fishburn at Whitby in 1764; 15-foot draught; square stern; square-rigged; deep and ample store space – a slowish but utterly reliable sailer. Since this was the prototype of the ships which Cook would later take to the western shores of Canada, his views on the "cats" are of special interest. They were, he wrote, "of the safest kind, in which officers may with the least hazard, venture upon a strange coast...She is a good Roader and careens easily [allowing easy repairs to the hull] and no sea can hurt her laying to under a mainsail or mizzen balanced." The sturdy colliers could make seven to eight knots with the wind "a point or two abaft the beam." The government paid exactly £2,840. 10s. 11d for the *Earl of Pembroke* and changed the name to *Endeavour*. They fitted her with ten carriage guns and twelve swivels, and filled her eleven-foot hold with an astonishing heap of stores for a two-year voyage. Con-

version work was held up by a traditional British phenomenon – a dock strike.

In addition to the planned crew of eighty-five (including a platoon of twelve marines), they also manned her with the botanist Banks and his suite of eight, including his four personal servants, the Swedish naturalist, Dr. Daniel Carl Solander (a librarian at the British Museum), and two artists. Banks also took along two greyhounds – he could easily afford such gentleman's toys, as the income from his lands was £6,000 a year, a very considerable sum for the times. One can compare with Banks' income the Royal Society's "gratuity" to Cook of 100 guineas and his navy pay of £84 a year. Banks was reported to have spent £10,000 on his staff and scientific equipment for the voyage.

Five men who had been with Cook aboard the *Grenville* moved with him into the *Endeavour* – and so did a milking goat that had already been around the world with Captain Samuel Wallis in the *Dolphin*. Wallis, too, had been looking for *Terra Australis*, but he had done little but follow the tracks of his predecessors. He had, though, found a delightful island which he named King George's Island – although the handsome and hedonistic natives appeared to call it "Otaheiti." Wallis returned to England on May 20 with an accurate fix on the new island. Since nobody had seen the Marquesas for 173 years, the site for the observations was switched, almost at the last minute, to Tahiti. It turned out to be the perfect place to observe Venus.

It is difficult to convince oneself today that when Lieutenant Cook took the *Endeavour* out of Plymouth on August 26, 1768, more than half the Pacific, north and south, was unseen by European eyes. Nearly three centuries after Cabot claimed North America for England, with Quebec already a respectable 160 years old, the Pacific was still cast in baffling shadow. Ten thousand miles by ten thousand, it could swallow the Old World at a gulp, and leave not a ripple. Although a dozen crossings had been made – by Portuguese, Spanish, Dutch, French, and British – the navigators had almost all followed the safety-first "diagonal course" from Cape Horn via the trade winds to the northern passage around New Guinea and into the welcoming havens of the Moluccas and Java, where the Dutch had established Batavia (now Djakarta) in 1619. Tasman's sketchily-known New Zealand – he called it Staten Land – could, for all anyone knew, stretch all the way east to Easter Island, south to the Pole and north to the Fijian group.

It was to be Cook's role in two voyages to unravel all the major mysteries of the South Pacific, to so expertly quarter the vast wastes of that ocean as to disprove any possibility of there being any major lands north of Antarctic ice, to perform a like service in the North Pacific, and, while retrieving Drake's New Albion and seeking the Northeast Passage, to bring the future British Columbia into the world's eye. As a discoverer, he changed the face of the globe. Charles Darwin said Cook added a hemisphere to the civilized world.

And yet Cook was much more than a navigator. One of his shipmates on his last voyage, David Samwell, surgeon of the *Discovery*, left an appreciation that has not been surpassed by any of the writers who have since produced many volumes on the man whom his colleagues called "our great and excellent commander":

Nature had endowed him [wrote Samwell] with a mind vigorous and comprehensive, which in his riper years he had cultivated with care and industry. His general knowledge was extensive and various; in that of his own profession he was unequalled. With a clear judgment, strong masculine sense, and the most determined resolution; with a genius peculiarly turned for enterprise, he pursued his object with unshaken perseverance, vigilant and active in an eminent degree; cool and intrepid among dangers; patient and firm under difficulties and distress; fertile in expedients; great and original in all his designs; active and resolved in carrying them into execution. In every situation, he stood unrivalled and alone; on him all eyes were turned; he was our leading star, which at its setting left us involved in darkness and despair.

This is a man Canada must know. The long gap between the discovery of Canada's eastern and western coasts—it approached three hundred years—causes most of our national histories to skip hurriedly over the maritime events of the Pacific. From an historical point of view, they are awkwardly out of balance with Atlantic and Laurentian development. A century of nationhood *a mari usque ad mare* has not yet brought the great men of British Columbia's beginning a fame equal to that of the heroes of eastern Canada. To make closer acquaintance, then, we look now into Cook's first two voyages. The achievements are well-enough known; here, we pursue the man.

For a picture of the captain who ordered anchors aweigh on the *Endeavour* in late summer of 1768, we can look at several portraits which differ considerably. The most famous is the study in oils which shows Cook seated, chart in lap, wearing gilt-edged coat, white vest (several buttons undone), and white breeches. Painted by the Italian-trained Englishman, Nathaniel Dance, this portrait hangs in the National Maritime Museum, Greenwich, on the south bank of the Thames, opposite London. It was painted in 1776, at the urging of Joseph Banks. The steady, even gaze, strong nose, broad, determined shoulders, all bespeak the commander of men, a no-nonsense Yorkshire resolution about him—not a man to trifle with, or to love. In the National Art Gallery, Wellington, New Zealand—a country where Cook is venerated—there is the standing portrait by John Webber. Also executed in 1776, it was done, at Cook's request, as a present for his wife. The rig is the same, but there is some humour to the face, almost a twinkle in the eye. The Mitchell Library at Sydney, New South Wales, has a portrait

which is attributed to William Hodges, official artist on the second Pacific voyage—although it is possibly by Johann Zoffany, the painter of Garrick, who was once contracted to go on that same voyage (he went to Italy and India instead). The author personally prefers the Australian version, which shows a man who just possibly *could* be worried or wrong once in a while. The heroic bronze statue in London by Sir Thomas Brock is, well, a fine bronze. Surgeon Samwell has left us this account of Cook's disposition:

His constitution was strong, his mode of living temperate. He had no repugnance to good living and always kept a good table, though he could bear the reverse without murmuring. He was a modest man and rather bashful; of an agreeable lively conversation, sensible and intelligent. In his temper he was somewhat hasty, but of a disposition the most friendly, benevolent, and humane. His person was above six feet high, and though a good-looking man he was plain both in address and appearance. His head was small, his hair, which was a dark brown, he wore tied behind. His face was full of expression, his nose exceedingly well-shaped; his eyes, which were small and of a brown cast, were quick and piercing; his eyebrows prominent, which gave his countenance altogether an air of austerity.

Samwell was writing here under the emotional impact of Cook's recent death, but other records don't quarrel basically with this assessment. Cook was probably at times a bit more irascible than indicated. For instance, he suffered from stomach ulcers after nearly twenty years of navy salt pork (or salt horse), although his journal admits only to "bilious colic." Beating up from the Antarctic towards Easter Island, Cook was racked with hiccoughs and unable to keep down any of the usual rations. The ship's naturalist offered his pet vegetarian dog from Tahiti, and, made into soup, this helped Cook back to precarious health.

Certainly, Cook's equanimity was tried at the outset of his first voyage by the demands made by Banks and the other supernumeraries who had been dropped in his lap. The *Earl of Pembroke*, now the *Endeavour*, was built to carry as many coals as possible from Newcastle, and not to provide private cabin accommodation for fastidious passengers. Decks had to be subdivided and the ship's officers (except the captain) were relegated below to allow the Royal Society's party what privacy there was. The "great cabin" which normally served as chart room, library, mess room, and bar for the officers now had to serve also as workroom and recreation room for all the gentlemen-scientists and their artists and technical writers—to say nothing of the greyhounds. Cook had not only to suffer this horde in the sanctum which, after so long a wait, was his by right, but also had the daily reminders of the social gulf that yawned between the Yorkshire farm lad, however risen, and the wealthy Lincolnshire landowner, of Eton, Harrow, and Oxford, a member of the Royal Society, kin to the Cecils and Stanhopes, among the noblest and richest families in England. In writing to Banks on one occasion, Cook referred to himself as "a man of my station in life."

Banks had already made a botanizing trip to Newfoundland in 1766, where Cook had once glimpsed him being rowed on pretty cushions to the man-of-war *Niger*, in which he had travelled from England. Banks had, in fact, almost died ashore from typhoid. Now, in 1768, Banks was only twenty-five to Cook's forty. Yet the self-taught, uncommunicative professional seaman and the gay, sophisticated darling of fortune got along very well together–for neither was exactly what he seemed. Cook had the kind of mind that could not resist science of any discipline, and he could spot a phoney at the nether end of a gangplank. Banks was a dedicated and highly intelligent amateur from the original mold, arrogant no doubt, but humble before the mysteries of the universe. Born to a life of ease, he was to make further exhaustive expeditions, to inaugurate Kew Gardens, and to hold the presidency of the Royal Society for forty-two years. Cook suffered the botanists' bulky apparatus and the invasion of his private quarters, and his journal entries soon began to show that he was speculating upon zoology, entomology, anthropology, and other studies new to him. For his part, Banks held to his dying day that Cook was the greatest man he had ever met.

Banks was granted a baronetcy, and so was the portraitist Dance. But Cook was never elevated from his humble station. There was plenty of opportunity for honours, too, after the first and second voyages–but apart from his promotion to captain, he received only the Copley Medal from the Royal Society, which also elected him a fellow. It is likely, though, that the medal outweighed a title in his estimation; it was awarded for his paper on the combating of scurvy at sea. Thus, it recognized Cook's obsessive interest in the health of his crews and his unique contribution to the welfare of seamen everywhere.

For twenty years, James Lind, a Scottish surgeon, had been trying to interest the navy in his experiments with citrus juices in the treatment of the vitamin-deficiency disease which attacked, with horrible certainty, every crew on long voyages. Cook was willing to try all the new-fangled ideas and his men glumly worked their way through barrels of sauerkraut, brewer's malt, breakfasts of "portable soup boiled with wheat," "marmalade of carrots," and all the strange but fresh vegetables (like Tahiti's yams and New Zealand's "wild celery") that Cook and the botanists came up with. Every man was issued twenty pounds of onions bought at Madeira. The result could be measured at Batavia, where the *Endeavour* arrived–after more than two years at sea–without one death from scurvy. The *Resolution* had no deaths due to scurvy in just over three years. Cook had men flogged for refusing to eat what was given them–though he usually gained his

purpose by more subtle means, as this entry in his journal for Thursday, April 13, 1769, attests:

At this time we had but a very few men upon the Sick list and these had but slite complaints, the Ships compney had in general been very healthy owing in a great measure to the Sour krout, Portable Soup and Malt . . . Wort was made of the Malt and at the discition of the Surgeon given to every man that had the least symptoms of Scurvy upon him . . .

The Sour Krout the Men at first would not eat untill I pout in practice a Method I never once knew to fail with seamen, and this was to have some of it dress'd every Day for the Cabbin Table, and permitted all the Officers without exception to make use of it and left it to the option of the Men either to take as much as they pleased or none atall; but this practice was not continued above a week before I found it necessary to put every one on board to an Allowance, for such are the Tempers and disposissions of Seamen in general that whatever you give them out of the Common way, altho it be every so much for their good yet it will not go down with them and you will hear nothing but murmurings gainest the man that first invented it; but the Moment they see their Superiors set a Value upon it, it becomes the finest stuff in the World and the inventer an honest fellow.

The spelling, capitalization, and punctuation in the above are, of course, Cook's and they fairly represent his normal style–haphazard even in a century which placed no great stock in convention. His handwriting was rather schoolroom-large, but clear and forthright –with even some flourishes on the capitals and some of the perpendiculars. He would at times flow along for several pages without paragraphing, or without punctuation. When he did use stops, he often used a period in the way that we would use a comma. His spelling had him swapping his *i*'s and *e*'s with unconcern and producing "clowdy," "beeds," "pyrmid," "clifts," "danceing," and so on. The excerpts from his journals which appear in the following pages have been edited by the present author, with some words and phrases altered to their equivalent in modern usage.

When Cook brought back his *Endeavour* journal in 1771, he was instructed to hand it over to Dr. John Hawkesworth, a crony of Dr. Johnson, who had wangled himself a fat fee of £6,000 to prepare the story for the press. The achievements of the expedition had preceded the *Endeavour's* return and public interest in the Pacific was intense. For this reason, the Commissioners of the Admiralty would not consider leaving it in Cook's rough-and-ready prose. Hawkesworth also had Joseph Banks' notebooks and he melded the comments and descriptions of the two men, plus a lot of flourishes of his own, into a bulky best-seller at five and a half guineas (the equivalent of $50 to $60 today). He dwelt lovingly on the loving girls of Tahiti– their smiling price of a common nail for their most

As Cook's men soon learned, the women of the South Seas were possessed of both great beauty and remarkably amorous dispositions.

intimate favours set loose a wave of wanderlust in Britain. In a Stone Age society, iron was miraculous – the Polynesians planted their nails in the soil and watered them carefully, hoping to raise the trees that provided these wonders. With no knowledge of weaving, they used only beaten bark as cloth.

Cook had not been able to check Hawkesworth's text before publication, but he was probably not as much mortified by its flights of fancy as some biographers imagine. To the tight-lipped mariner, his mind fully taken up with questions of sober complexity, the arcane world of the writer and the dilettante was of little concern. The literary luminaries of the London of his time were men like Walpole, Sheridan, Sterne, and Goldsmith. But who today would measure their fame against that of the humble navigator from Whitby? After his second voyage, Cook's journals were edited by Dr. John Douglas, Canon of Windsor, who allowed them to run as a much simpler narrative.

When all of the concrete achievements of the *Endeavour*'s three-year voyage had been admired and digested – the exploration of New Zealand, the examination of Australia, the Society Islands, the virtual elimination of *Terra Australis* – it was the apparent paradise of Tahiti that claimed the public imagination. Here, surely, was Arcady, the promised land. The marines Webb and Gibson of Cook's crew had run away with their girls to the island's high mountains to try to stay in a land where food dropped from the trees or leaped from the lagoons, where the sex guilt of the Christian world caused only ripples of suppressed laughter. The comparison between the glades of Tahiti and the slums of English or French cities in the eighteenth century can be easily imagined, and several men from Samuel Wallis' crew of the *Dolphin* had volunteered to return to the South Seas with Cook. He had taken four of them, including Richard Pickersgill, who was later to seek the Northwest Passage in the brig *Lyon* from Baffin Bay. How did the men of the *Endeavour* (and later of the *Resolution* and the *Adventure*) enjoy Tahiti? In short, in the same measure as did the sailors of Captain Bougainville, when that veteran of the Canadian campaign visited the island the previous year:

It was very difficult to keep four hundred young French sailors at their work [wrote Bougainville] when they had not seen a woman for six months. In spite of all precautions, a young girl came on board and placed herself on the quarterdeck near one of the hatchways, which was open to give air to those who were heaving at the capstan below. The girl casually dropped a cloth which covered her, and appeared to the eyes of all beholders such as Venus showed herself to the Phrygian shepherd, having, indeed, the celestial form of that goddess. Both sailors and soldiers scrambled to the hatchway and the capstan was never spun with more alacrity . . .

When our men went ashore, they were invited to enter the houses; nor did the hospitality end with food – they offered them young girls. The hut was immediately filled with a curious crowd, who made a circle around the guest . . . The ground was strewn with leaves and flowers and their musicians sang to the tune of their flutes.

Here, Venus is goddess of hospitality, her worship does not allow any mysteries and every tribute paid to her is a feast for the whole nation. They were surprised at the confusion which our people appeared to be in as our customs do not allow of these public proceedings. However, I would not say that every one of our men found it impossible to conform to the customs of the country.

The Britishers in Cook's crews fell victim just as happily. The veterans of the *Dolphin* warned Cook of the value of a nail, and to save his ship from being taken apart, he issued orders that "no sort of iron or cloth or other useful or necessary articles are to be given for anything but provisions." How well this rule was observed can be judged by the number of times that weary men jumped into their hammocks only to fall to the deck with a thump—the nails supporting the hammock rigging had been extracted quietly by their comrades. One seaman, Archibald Wolf, was given two dozen lashes for being caught with hundreds of nails stolen from the ship's stores. Some of the more desirable girls were now demanding two and even three nails, instead of just one. The handsome young Mr. Banks soon succumbed. The reporter here is Cook himself:

Mr. Banks was as usual at the gate of the fort [where the transit of Venus was observed on June 3, 1769] trading with the people when he was told that some strangers were coming . . . They had with them about a dozen young plantain trees; these they laid down about twenty feet from Mr. Banks . . . Several pieces of cloth were spread upon the ground. One of the young women then stepped upon the cloth and, with as much innocency as one could possibly conceive, expose herself entirely naked from the waist downwards. In this manner, she turned herself around once or twice, I am not certain how many times, then stepped off the cloth . . . The cloth was then rolled up and given to Mr. Banks and the two young women went and embraced him, which ended the ceremony.

The fate of Banks can be surmised. He once wrote of Tahiti: "On the island of Otaheite where love is the chief occupation, the favourite, nay, the sole luxury of the inhabitants, both the bodies and the souls of the women are molded into the utmost perfection." With Solander, though, Banks did take time to assemble a magnificent collection of 1,000 previously unclassified plants, five hundred fish, five hundred bird skins, and "innumerable insects."

Cook himself seems to have been rather of the stuff of Samuel Champlain—an interested and even close observer, but seldom a participant in the tender battle man was born to lose. In the well-named Friendly Isles, a group of matrons presented to him a welcoming company of young, beautiful, willing maidens—

and he rejected the lot, to the consternation of the donors. He did not apply his own rules to his men, however, and at one stage, laughing Tongan girls were virtually living aboard. On May 14, 1769, Cook recorded "an odd scene at the gate of the fort at Matavai Bay on Tahiti where a young fellow more than six feet tall lay with a little girl of about ten or twelve years of age, publicly before several of our people and a number of the natives. What makes me mention this is because it appeared to be done more from custom than lewdness." Cook once described Obarea, who seemed to be the Queen of the Polynesians, as "like most of the other women, very masculine"—a conclusion with which few of his shipmates would have concurred. His eye was taken more by the Marquesans, of whom he wrote: "For a fine shape and regular features, they perhaps surpass all other nations."

The honours of the first voyage, to read the English papers of the time, belonged overwhelmingly to Banks and Solander. To the ignorant, the role of Cook was, apparently, that of the capable ship-chauffeur. It was difficult—as difficult then as it is now—to make a survey sing. After the second voyage of the *Resolution* and the *Adventure* (1772-75) had stitched a pattern across the southern Pacific and southern Indian oceans which left no possible doubt of the nonexistence of *Terra Australis*, but added several new features to the world map (for example, New Caledonia), Cook was overdue, at forty-eight, for a well-earned rest. Almost incidentally, he had also accomplished the first west-to-east circumnavigation of the world. He was not a well man, suffering from rheumatic pains and recurring stomach upsets. After he had been congratulated by his king, he was handed the sinecure of a captaincy of Greenwich Hospital. But, as he wrote to his old Whitby patron, John Walker: "Whether I can bring myself to ease and retirement, time will show."

Time, of course, soon showed that he could not. The Admiralty reward of £20,000 for the man who could find a passage around the top of Canada from Atlantic to Pacific—or the other way round—still stood, and the outbreak of the American Revolution had sharpened the search. Fifty voyages had tried—and failed—to penetrate from the east. The Danish captain, Vitus Bering, had found a strait between America and Asia in the northernmost Pacific. Was it possible that his passage would lead at last to the magic avenue between Europe and China which had been sought since Cabot's time? Maybe. At any rate, there was one man whom the Admiralty would trust to find out.

In February 1776, John Montague, the fourth Earl of Sandwich, First Lord of the Admiralty, gave a dinner party in London to which he invited Sir Hugh Palliser (now Comptroller of the Navy), Phillip Stephens (Secretary to the Admiralty), and Captain James Cook. They were looking for someone to lead yet another Pacific voyage. At that table, to no one's surprise, a great man volunteered.

CHAPTER EIGHTEEN

The Secret World
of Nootka

A T nine o'clock on the morning of Sunday, March 29, 1778, when Captain Cook first saw Canada from the west from the quarterdeck of HMS *Resolution*, he made some notes for his journal: "The country had a very different appearance to what we had seen before. It was full of high mountains whose summits were covered with snow; but the valleys between them and the land on the coast, high as well as low, were clothed with forest ... Between two points, the shore forms a large bay, which I called Hope Bay, in which, from the appearance of the land, we hoped to find a good harbour – and events proved that we were not mistaken."

With these words, the future British Columbia came into our ken. Cook was approaching the entry to the wide inlet, halfway up the western side of Vancouver Island, that he would first name King George's Sound and then courteously change to Nootka Sound, under the mistaken impression that this was its name in the native tongue. Trailed closely by the smaller *Discovery*, under Captain Charles Clerke, Cook warily entered the inlet. When the wind dropped at 5:00 P.M., all boats were lowered to tow the 462-ton *Resolution* into sheltered anchorage by sheer muscle power. It was a back-breaking moment in a voyage that had already opened up the centre of the Pacific Ocean, from far Tahiti, discovering the Hawaiian Islands on the way.

For exactly four weeks, Cook stayed at Nootka "refreshing" the 180 men of his ships, cutting new masts and spars, caulking seams, repairing storm damage to the rigging, always surveying, examining the new land, and striking up acquaintance with an entirely new people. These short, strong, body-painted whale hunters, with their great dugout canoes and wooden houses, were entirely different in looks, temperament, and life style to the languorous, fun-loving Polynesians of the lower Pacific. Cook was at first uncomplimentary: these Canadians were "slovenly and dirty to the last degree."

It was not Cook's first look at northwest America.

That had come at dawn on March 7, at 44° 33′ north latitude, 235° 20′ east longitude, a spot about halfway up the coast of Oregon. He had closed to within about twenty miles of the coast, but gale-force westerlies made up and the ships were in danger of being blown ashore. Sleet and rain squalls harried the navigators, and in fact they tacked off to the southwest, losing ground on the master sailing plan for Bering Strait in the high north. Cook named the first point he had seen Cape Foulweather, a label which has stuck for the same good reason that it was first given. He was on the fringe of Francis Drake's New Albion, merely a way station on an itinerary which was to lead him, hopefully, into the Northeast Passage, or – from the European viewpoint – a Pacific entry to the Northwest Passage which had baffled, beaten, and broken many of the world's best mariners for three hundred years.

Thus, Cook's discovery of Canada's west coast was, in a way, almost accidental. His instructions from the Lords of the Admiralty were to "fall in" with New Albion at 45° north latitude – and James Cook was nothing if not precise. He was asked not to give any "umbrage or offence" on the way north to any subjects of His Catholic Majesty of Spain whom he might find. He was then to push north "to latitude 65° or farther ... there to search for and explore such rivers or inlets as may appear to be of considerable extent and pointing towards Hudson or Baffin Bay."

After battling past the 1,000-foot Cape Foulweather, Cook inspected the land again from a respectable distance on Monday, March 9, and on the succeeding two days. He named Cape Perpetua and Gregory Point after obscure saints. In hail, sleet, and wild winds, he saw "nothing like a harbour" – he had been swept past the mouth of the Columbia. "It is really rather a lamentable business," wrote Captain Clerke in the *Discovery*, "that we can neither forward our matters by tracing the coast nor have the satisfaction of getting into a harbour to take a look at the country. While this weather continues, we dance about in the offing and make the best we can of it."

As they bucketed about above the forty-eighth parallel, Cook thought he saw "a small opening in the land which flattered us with hopes of finding a harbour," and he held off the coast until dawn on March 23 to get a better look. In the midst of a new gale and rainstorm which blew directly onto the land, he decided there was no opening and moved further out to sea, and safety. He called the point which he had seen "Cape Flattery." Here, his discoverer's luck was out, as the cape was the southern entrance to the magnificent waterway which today leads to the safe harbours and fine cities of Vancouver and Seattle. Cook was actually looking for the Strait of Juan de Fuca, as the "legend" of its existence had persisted in marine chronicles for a century and a half. But he had crossed the fifteen-mile entrance during the storm-tossed darkness and had thus lost the almost-certain discovery of the Gulf of Georgia and the thready channels behind Vancouver Island to the northwest. Nevertheless, George Vancouver, a midshipman on the *Discovery*, would return to these waters in his own ship in 1792 and make good all omissions.

Lieutenant James King, of the *Resolution*, remarked in his own diary: "This part of the continent has not, so far as we know, ever before been seen, for there is no certain account of any navigators being so high as latitude 44°, excepting Drake and Vizcaino, and both were stopped from proceeding farther to the north by the rigour of the climate." The evidence strongly suggests that Drake was higher, but neither Lieutenant King nor Captain Cook–nor just about anyone else outside of Madrid–seems to have known that the Spanish had sent Don Juan Perez up that coast to the top of the Queen Charlottes in 1774 to discourage the Russians in Alaska, and Bodega y Quadra with the 36-foot *Sonora* and two other ships the following year. But as far as is known, these Spaniards never set foot on the present territory of Canada. Cook had read "some account of the Spaniards having visited this coast" before he left England in 1776, probably garbled translations of items which appeared in the Madrid press.

The Spanish voyages are loyally recalled in place names such as Estevan Point outside Nootka Sound (Estevan José Martinez was Perez' pilot) and Quadra Island. But the Spanish contact was slight and the impact on world knowledge next to nil. When controversy, and nearly bloody war, flared over ownership of the territory later, the Spanish declared that Martinez had gone ashore at Nootka (they called it San Lorenzo) in a longboat from Perez's *Santiago* four years before Cook's arrival. For evidence, they offered in part a few lines from Cook's own journal wherein he reported that a native who had come into Nootka with a group of tribesmen from some other area to see and trade with the whites was wearing around his neck as an ornament two silver table spoons. From the shape of these spoons, the crews supposed them to be of Spanish manufacture. Cook himself said that there was no hallmark on the spoons and that he had never seen any like them before. In any case, they could just as easily have been acquired by trade, passing through many hands. These famous spoons were bought by Lieutenant Gore–later to take command of the whole expedition–and eventually presented to Sir Joseph Banks.

It is a fortunate legacy that Cook's last journal is particularly rich in reference to his visit to the western coast, the furthest reach of the great prize wrested from the French on the St. Lawrence nearly twenty years earlier. With his depth of scientific knowledge, he was probably the first to know accurately the massive breadth of the continent. He was the major surveyor to that time of eastern Canada, and his instruments told him he was now four thousand miles, seventy degrees of longitude, west from Newfoundland's Cape Race. To a boy from Yorkshire's narrow fields, it was indeed a whole new world.

After his first two epic journeys into the South Pacific, Cook was the most renowned Englishman of his time, and translations of his narratives had spread his fame abroad. He was nearly forty-eight when he led his ships out of Plymouth on July 12, 1776, on this third voyage. And although he had been ashore for almost a full year, he was not his former rugged self. He had been at sea for thirty years, in storms without counting, in often unknown waters washing submerged rock and coral, his clothes wet, his sleep short, the surcease of quiet family bliss too thinly spread, and, above all, deeply worn by the etching acid of sole command. As he drove the *Resolution* once again around the Cape of Good Hope, across the empty vastness of the southern Indian Ocean, through the stormy strait, between the two main islands of New Zealand, that now carries his name, and up into the island group that also honours him, he showed occasional signs of deep fatigue, flashes of uncharacteristic behaviour, a world-weariness perhaps.

Before he left Plymouth, he had paid his compliments to Admiral John Amherst, the younger brother of Lord Jeffery Amherst, the conqueror of Canada, in the 90-gun man-of-war *Ocean*, and noted a huge fleet, sixty-two sail, bound with troops to put down the tragic revolt in the colonies. Having shared so importantly in the securing of British America, he was probably doubly saddened at the outset of his journey by this fratricidal strife.

In New Zealand, he had rested in his favourite anchorage in Queen Charlotte Sound, off Cook Strait, where he had made friends previously with the intelligent but aggressive Maoris. Here, place names like Gore, Palliser, Stephens, and Endeavour denote Cook's several visits. There was, though, some underlaying menace here this time. During the second voyage in 1774, John Rowe, the master of the *Adventure*, and a party of nine men sent to gather greens had been ambushed by the natives, and eaten. The Maoris expected retribution and the main culprit, an unpopular brute named Kahure, was pointed out. Cook, however, turned the other cheek and allowed the murderer to come aboard and sit for his portrait by John Webber. The puzzled Maoris no doubt regarded this as being eccentric, womanish behaviour, and they may well have suffered from Kahura's spear after the British departure. A man who could kill Europeans without punishment would meet little resistance among his own people.

The same Cook, soon afterwards in the Friendly Islands, ordered the ears sliced off an insolent native thief, had several lashed–including a chieftain (a degrading punishment in Polynesian eyes)–and had another man branded. At idyllic Moorea, he ordered the smashing of canoes and the burning of houses because of a stolen goat (which was later returned). Dr. Beaglehole, whose career has been devoted to Cook, wrote of this period: "One can see a change coming already in the humane man, as if the multitudinous demands of the preceding years, the anxious struggle with the winds after leaving New Zealand, had at last begun to try his fundamental equanimity." Men who had been with Cook on both of the earlier voyages–there were six of them–were perplexed and worried about him.

When the islands of Owhyee raised their dramatic volcanic shapes out of the bluest of seas in mid-January 1778, Cook seemed to shake off his dolour. He wrote admiringly of these "open, candid, active" people, both sexes going naked above the waist, and marvelled at how the Polynesians could have spread over such a vast space, from New Zealand to the new archipelago–a distance of 1,200 leagues. (That puzzle has not yet been entirely solved.) It was a happy landfall, with no premonition of the tragedy that would be enacted a year hence. Cook was revered as the god Lono, fresh meat and fruit were plentiful, and the Hawaiian girls were not only eager for dalliance with the sailors but indignant if their advances were refused. All the Britons were awed by the natives' swimming ability; even women carrying nursing babes swam through the mountainous surf with flashing smiles. Cook named the islands for Lord Sandwich, and the name stuck until, in Queen Victoria's time, the British refused to annex the chain and it drifted under American control as the Territory of Hawaii.

Understandably, the coves of Canada's Nootka Sound, steep under the slanting rain, its phlegmatic people wresting a living from the fringes of a boisterous ocean in the March gales, provided a raw contrast to the tropical paradise which Cook had left behind seven weeks earlier. When he first raised the western coast above 48° north latitude, Cook must have known that, notwithstanding the reports of the Strait of Juan de Fuca, there could be no through passage by water for sailing vessels across the land before him. Everyone who approaches British Columbia today by ship enjoys the impressive sight of range after range of snow-capped mountains, marching into the interior. Plane travellers can see the Cascades merging into the Coast Mountains and running a thousand miles of jagged peaks to join the Cassiars of the Yukon, and perhaps they are able to glimpse the eastern surges of the Columbias and Selkirks of the Rockies. Cook knew that no matter how promising any bays or river mouths might look, there could be no penetration by sail of that mountain wall. But both of his ships badly needed repairs and fresh water, and the shelter of Nootka Sound beckoned.

Once inside the sound, Cook anchored for the night at the entrance to the present Zuciarte Channel in

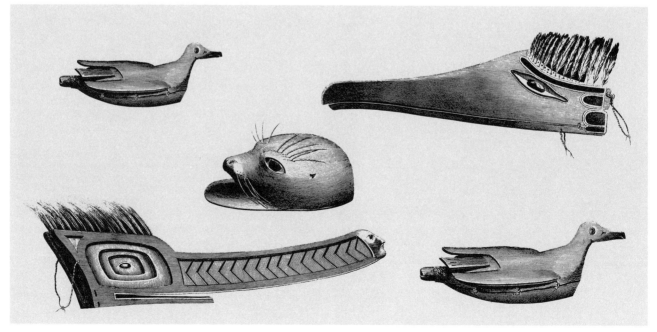

These drawings showing articles made by the Indians of Nootka Sound were drawn by Webber, one of the artists on Cook's third voyage.

eighty-five fathoms (500 feet) of water within hawser-length of the shore. Thirty canoes of "a mild, inoffensive people" milled about the ships and a dozen of them kept vigil all night. In the morning, Cook sent out armed longboats to look for better anchorage and eventually chose Resolution Cove, at the southeast end of the sizeable island in the middle of the sound which was later named for his sailing master, William Bligh. In the fickleness of fame, Bligh—a fine and courageous seaman, though harsh of temper—was to become one of the world's most notorious captains when he was put out of his ship, the *Bounty*, by Fletcher Christian and his mutineers a decade later. But Bligh survived all hardships and subsequent enquiries, became a colonial governor, and died a vice-admiral.

While his carpenters and iron-founders toiled on the ships, Cook set up an observatory for his astronomical research ashore, then turned his all-embracing curiosity to the natives of Nootka. He found them as fascinating in their way as his South Sea friends—indeed, the Canadians were to treat him kindly and hospitably throughout his stay, and no Indian hand was raised seriously against the Europeans. Which was just as well, as the Nootka showed not the slightest fear of firearms. They had, of course, exactly the same disregard for property rights as did the South Sea islanders. Cook found them "as light-fingered as any people we had before met with...One fellow would amuse the boat-keeper at one end of the boat while another was pulling her to pieces at the other."

The Nootka were proud of their oratory, although their language was in the beginning completely unintelligible to any Europeans. Cook ordered William Anderson, his talented surgeon-naturalist, to collate a simple vocabulary, the first effort ever made to give written form to the Nootka-Kwakiutl language. Cook coined the term "Wakashan," still in use, from the natives' frequent use of the term "*Wak'ash*"—meaning friendship. The Nootka were distinguished by the ornate ceremonial cedar masks they wore, carved to represent eagle, whale, bear, and other animals. By April Fool's Day, 1778, Cook was writing:

They generally went through a singular ceremony. They would paddle with all their strength completely around both ships while a chief or other principal person stood up with a spear, or some other weapon in his hand, speaking or rather shouting, all the time. Sometimes this person would have his face covered with a mask, either that of the human face, or some animal, and sometimes instead of a weapon would hold a rattle in his hand. Very often they would give us a song in which all joined with a very agreeable harmony ...

All who visited us, men and women, were of a small stature. Hardly one of the women, even the younger women, had the least pretensions to being called a beauty. Their faces are rather broad and flat, with high cheekbones and plump cheeks. Their eyes are small, black, and devoid of sparkle. In general, they have not a bad shape—except in the

legs, which in most of them are crooked, probably from sitting on the legs too much.

Their hair is black or dark brown, straight, strong, and long. They generally wear it flowing, but some tie it up in a bunch on the crown, and others twist it into large locks and add false hair to it so that their heads look like mops. On special occasions, they sprinkle their hair with white downy feathers from birds, which they carry in a bag. Some men have long beards, while others pluck out all facial hair.

Some of their clothes are made from the skins of land and sea animals, with very little art or trouble. They do no more than form them into a kind of cloak which is tied over the shoulders with a string and reaches as low as the knees. Besides these, they have other clothes, made from a mixture of bark and a coarse kind of wool or hair. They also have another cloak, which resembles a round dish-cover, with a hole in the middle just big enough to admit the head. On most of these dresses, they work borders of different colours, the collar being edged or lined with beaver, and the skirts fringed. For a head-dress, they have a strong straw hat which is shaped like a flower pot and is as good a covering for the head as can possibly be invented. The men seldom wear anything about their middles and are not ashamed to appear naked, but the women are always decently clothed and seemed to be bashful and modest.

The journal of David Samwell, then surgeon's mate aboard the *Resolution*, offers an amusing corollary to Cook's remarks, as they apply to the eternally-important matter of the sailor and his girl. Here, it was the young Europeans who had to take the initiative. But once the Indian men got their meaning, they brought girls to the ships—the usual price being one pewter plate for the night. Soon, so many girls were provided that "many of us left this harbour not being able to muster a plate to eat our salt beef from."

To make themselves as desirable as possible, the girls had heavily greased their bodies and painted their hair and faces with black, white, and red ochre mixed with whale oil. The British, showing the initiative that was winning them an empire, got out a large tub and had great fun giving the mystified girls a bath with soap and warm water. "They called it the Ceremony of Purification," Samwell wrote, "and it must be mentioned to their praise that they performed it with much piety and devotion." He added that the girls were very modest and timid, in contrast to the girls of the South Sea islands, who "in general are impudent and loud." Indian experts today are convinced that the girls who were hired out were drawn from the ranks of the slaves, captured in the incessant raids on other tribes or bands. Later arrivals who thought that all Nootka women were promiscuous sometimes paid for this error with their lives.

After nearly three weeks of hard work in almost continuous rain—in which new masts were cut from standing timber—the ships were again in good repair and Cook decided to make an excursion through the

The Indians of Nootka, living in dank longhouses and dressed in heavy garments, were a far cry from the nubile natives of Hawaii.

sound. He ordered his "middies" into two longboats and had himself and fellow officers rowed for thirty miles on an inspection. Beginning at Yuquot Point, at the western entrance to the sound, they passed up the west side of Bligh Island through what has since been known as Cook Channel. At the top of the main inlet, Cook noted two arms running further inland (Kendrick and Tahsis Inlets) around the bulk of Canal Island. He did not enter them, as brackish water informed him that they did not penetrate very far. He must have been taking notes on his knee as he gives us the dimensions of wickerwork fishing weirs at the head of the sound, and of huge trees (possibly Douglas fir) growing close to the water's edge.

The midshipmen pulled lustily across the top of the sound, passing the entrance to Tlupana Inlet, on the way to another village. Here, the local panjandrum would not allow Cook to enter any of the houses and made unmistakable signs for him to depart. "Some young women," Cook records, "more polite than their surly lord, dressed themselves in a hurry in their best clothes, got together and sang us a song which was far from being harsh or disagreeable." The party rowed down the Zuciarte Channel, along Clerke Peninsula of Bligh Island, back to Resolution Cove. One of the middies, James Trevenen, weary but happy after this pleasant day, composed a few lines of verse:

> *Oh Nootka, thy shores can our labour attest,*
> *For thirty long miles in a day are no jest.*
> *Oh day of hard labour! Oh day of good living!*

> *When Toote* was seized with the humour of giving!*
> *When he clothed in good nature his looks of authority*
> *And shook from his eyebrows their stern superiority.*

Cook's written instructions from the Admiralty ordered him to observe at any new places he might touch – apart from all the usual recordings of latitude and longitude – "the nature of the soil and the produce thereof; the animals and fowls that inhabit or frequent it; the fishes that are to be found," and enough other questions to keep a modern company of pollsters at work for months. He was to "observe the genius, temper, dispositions and number of the natives...and to endeavour to cultivate a friendship with them, showing them every kind of civility and regard but taking care nevertheless not to suffer yourself to be surprised by them." In what time he had left, in the few quiet hours he found on the open sea as he pursued his mission into the Arctic ice, he did his usual excellent best to comply. His account is also our first report on the "Canadian Riviera":

> *Whenever it rained with us, snow fell on the neighbouring hills. But the climate is, however, infinitely milder than on the east coast of America under the same parallel of latitude. The mercury in the thermometer never even in the night fell lower than 42° and very often in the day it rose to 60°. No such thing as frost was perceived.*
> *The only quadrupeds we saw were a raccoon and an*

---

*A nickname for Cook, not used within his hearing.

animal like a polecat. But the inhabitants also had the skins of bears, foxes, wolves, wild cats, deer, martens, ermine, squirrels, and of seals and sea beaver [otter]. We saw few land birds and few water fowl, and all species except ravens and crows were extremely shy and fearful, probably from being often hunted. Among the land birds is a very beautiful hummingbird. Fish seemed to be in plenty, though we got none except by trade with the Indians, who supplied us with a small fish like the sardine, fish like bream, and now and then cod.

Of the vegetables the place produced, we benefitted by none except for the spruce tree of which we made beer* and the wild garlic. This with some nettles that grew about the villages were the only vegetables I saw fit for the pot. The only fruit trees I met with were raspberry, currant, and gooseberry.

The inhabitants are a docile, courteous, good-natured people but are very passionate and quick in resenting what they look upon as an injury, and, like most other passionate people, as soon forget it. I have often seen a man rave and scold for more than half an hour without anyone taking the least notice of it, nor could any one of us tell who it was he was abusing. In these fits, they act as if they had not enough words to express themselves. At other times, they are uncommonly grave and silent and are by no means a talkative people.

In trading with us, some would betray a knavish disposition and would run off with our goods without making any return, if there was an opportunity. But in general, most of them acted with different principles. Their passion for iron and brass, and indeed any kind of metal, was so strong that few could resist the temptation to steal it whenever an opportunity offered.

When some members of the Cook expedition were offered (and bought) human skulls and severed hands with flesh still adhering, they assumed that the Canadians were cannibals. The astronomer, William Bayly, wrote: "They made signs that they were good eating and seemed to sell them to us for that purpose, or at least all of us understood them in that light." Not quite all of them. Thomas Edgar of the *Discovery*, trying to clinch the matter, bought a hand from one native and then tried to bribe him to eat it offering "more iron and brass than would have purchased one of their most elegant dresses." The man refused with contemptuous gestures, and when Edgar persisted, he departed angrily. Captain Clerke noted in his diary that a girl of three or four years of age was brought to his ship for sale. "To enhance her price," he added, "they gave us to understand that she was very good to eat . . . The price demanded was a small hatchet." Clerke, however, was not convinced that this was clear evidence. Cook himself noted the sale of skulls and hands, and left the matter there – he was well acquainted with cannibalism, ritual and otherwise.

It was too early for the salmon run, but the British saw bales of dried fish stored in the huge split-cedar houses. Cook entered one that was 150 feet in length, 24 to 30 feet wide, and 7 to 8 feet high. There were no native buildings to compare with these north of Mexico. The officers were full of admiration for the skill and patience required to split a 1½-inch board, 30 feet long and up to 5 feet broad, from the whole tree, using axes and adzes of stone and wedges of wood or deer antler. To lever the roof trees into position on the stout pilings – and they were literally *whole* trees – called for considerable knowledge of engineering. Many of the wider houses contained a central passageway, with family apartments, each about 16 feet by 12 feet, opening off on each side. An open fireplace surrounded by raised banks for sleeping was placed in the centre of each apartment, the smoke escaping through the loose boards of the roof. Cook speculated that the frequent rains must find their way in just as easily, and suggested that the houses were meant to be used only in the summers, when the tribe was on the sea coast.

Nothing seems to have escaped Cook's probing gaze. He noted that both men and women pierced their ears and used pine resin as a kind of chewing gum. He described how their song rattles were made in the shape of a hollow bird, with small stones in its belly; how one man created an instant mask by dropping over his head a tin kettle purchased from the ships; how food was boiled in a wooden trough by adding heated stones to the water with a pair of wooden tongs.

When the serious dispute arose between Britain and Spain over possession of the northwestern coast following Estevan Martinez's seizure of John Meares' ships at Nootka Sound in 1789, Cook's on-the-spot notes became especially important. On July 16, 1778, he had sent Lieutenant John Williamson ashore at Cape Newenham on Bristol Bay, in today's Alaska, to formally claim "the country" for Great Britain. In 1786, Captain James Stuart Strange, a godson of Bonnie Prince Charlie, had enacted another such ceremony on the inland heights of Vancouver Island, leaving an inscribed copper plate as evidence. Cook had written that he personally did not regard the possession of some crude metal knives or copper ornaments by the Nootkas as evidence of earlier Spanish discovery. "Indeed," he wrote, "one cannot be surprised at finding iron with all the nations in America, since they have been so many years in a manner surrounded by Europeans and other nations who make use of iron, and who knows how far these Indian nations may extend their traffic with one another? I

---

*The *Resolution* had left England with no less than nineteen tons of beer (and 1,397 gallons of spirits). Spruce needles and branches were boiled, and the liquor fermented to make, in Cook's words, "a very good and well-tasted small beer." In New Zealand, they had used local trees, adding a little rum for flavour. The "beer" was recommended as an aid against scurvy – as Jacques Cartier had learned in the St. Lawrence nearly 250 years earlier.

George Vancouver as an older man. He was an officer on Cook's last voyage.

cannot therefore look upon iron as a mark of the Spaniards having been at this place." Nothing else of significance was seen, except the two silver spoons which we have already noted.

The British Parliament thundered for war over Nootka, but with the French Revolution causing re-alignments in Europe, Spain was neither ready nor eager for a major confrontation with Britain's sea power. After three years of sabre-rattling, claim and counterclaim, Senor Juan Francisco Bodega y Quadra and Captain George Vancouver met at Nootka. In an amicable ceremony, Spain ceded her supposed exclusive rights and paid a grossly inflated indemnity to Meares. Both nations retained the right to visit the harbour as they pleased and to erect temporary buildings. But, in fact, when formal war broke out between the parties in Europe in 1796 (resulting in the Spanish naval defeat at the hands of Admiral John Jervis off Cape St. Vincent), the Spaniards abandoned the northern coasts and retired to their Californian capital at Monterey.

In Cook's last hours on Canadian soil, on Sunday, April 26, 1778, as his ships were being towed out of the cove to catch a promising wind, all petty thievery and unsettling native habits were forgotten and the Britons took a genuinely fond farewell of their hosts. Lieuten-

ant James Burney, brother of the famous novelist Fanny Burney and an admiral-to-be, wrote: "As we hove up the anchor, all the canoes in the cove assembled and sang us a parting song, flourishing the saws, swords, hatchets, and other things they had got from us." Cook's journal entry for that day includes:

Our friends, the Indians, attended upon us till we were almost out of the sound, some on board the ships and others in canoes. A chief [Cook left a blank here to be filled in later, but didn't get around to it—no doubt it was the great Maquinna] who had attached himself to me was one of the last to leave us. Before he went, I made him a small present and he gave me a beaver skin of greater value. I then made some addition to my present, upon which he gave me the valuable beaver cloak he was wearing. I did not want him to be poorer because of his friendship and generosity to me so I made him a present of a new broadsword with a brass hilt, which made him as happy as a prince.

The *Resolution* and the *Discovery* were no sooner out of the shelter of the sound than they were scudding before a squall with driving rain so dark that the officers could not see the length of their ships. For four days, they were blown out of sight of land, thus passing the Queen Charlotte Islands and the remainder of the Canadian coastline. Cook did come back to the coast to name Cape and Mount Edgecumbe and to see Mount Elias, named by Vitus Bering, which rears its 18,000-foot peak at the southwest corner of the Yukon. He left his own name on the great inlet which today leads to the Alaskan metropolis of Anchorage. He was now following his final instructions to investigate any likely passage that might lead toward Hudson Bay, some 1,500 miles or more to the east.

The chilling barrier of the Chugach and Alaska Ranges, all too visible from his quarterdeck, told him —as he must have expected all along—that his chances of success were minimal. Now he had to beat *south* around the long rocky finger of the Aleutians, before he turned north again in the Bering Sea beyond latitude 65° to pass Bering Strait, the fifty-mile channel separating America from Asia. Beyond, in the vicinity of Point Barrow, Cook forced his uneasy men right to the edge of the ice barrier, and not until August 29 did he issue orders to turn back.

He had been further south than any other man, and now he stood at the edge of the Beaufort Sea, the twelve-foot wall of ice stretching north to the pole, rising higher in the eye-stinging distance, grinding to the incessant restless pressure of the oceans. Even so, he told his shivering crews that he would bring them back the following summer to search again for that open-water passage to the Atlantic.

For James Cook, that summer never came. He ran his ships to Hawaii for the winter and there, on the beach at 8:00 A.M. on St. Valentine's Day, 1779, he was murdered.

The Last Coast
Conquered

WHEN the pitiful remains of James Cook–his skull, leg bones, and hands–were delivered by penitent Hawaiians at Kealakekua Bay, they were identified by the scars on the hands which Cook had suffered from powder burns while serving in Canada's eastern waters. He was just fifty years of age, and had he survived to claim his due position and rewards, it seems certain that he would have directed attention to the further and closer examination of the northwestern shores of this land. For one thing, the sea otter furs which the British had got cheaply in trade caused a sensation in the Russian ports, bringing as much as £7 per skin– some of Cook's men made more than a year's pay. Chief Maquinna had promised to lay in big supplies of furs if the British would return. Moreover, the poker-straight trees, bigger than any Cook had seen before, offered all the masts and spars that a seafaring nation might need–especially with war again ravaging the eastern Americas.

Cook wrote that it had blown "a perfect hurricane" the day after he left Nootka in 1778, and even though the *Resolution* had sprung a dangerous leak, he had to keep his ships well off the coast. In his journal, he "regretted very much" his inability to remain close-in. Had he been able to do so, he would, without doubt, have added the 180 miles of the Queen Charlottes to his discoveries and would most likely have entered the ocean gap of the sound to make some contact with the true mainland, near today's Ocean Falls, British Columbia.

On Cook's death, Charles Clerke, who had been a shipmate on all the discovery voyages, took over. With a resolution not a whit weaker than Cook's, Clerke endeavoured to carry out the plan for a second look for the Northeast Passage, even though he was certain that the journey into the ice would kill him. He was suffering from advanced tuberculosis and died at Kamchatka on the way home. When he first knew he was ill, Clerke had thought briefly of resigning his commission at Tahiti and spinning out his remaining years in the sun. Then he decided, without ever mentioning it, to spend what time he might have in adventure and discovery. But there was another man in those ships, bent to the public service by Cook, who would survive long enough to return to the coasts of forest and mountain to do exactly the job which the great discoverer would have demanded. He was then only twenty-one and his name was George Vancouver.

Today, of course, the name of Vancouver graces the handsome city and thriving seaport, and the massive land–an island only by virtue of some streams of salt water–which protects it. But the man himself still waits in the shadows for his call to the national hall of fame. In a remarkable survey voyage between 1791 and 1795, Vancouver took the *Discovery* and the *Chatham* first to Australia, New Zealand, and the Sandwich Islands, then across the North Pacific to New Albion, and finally into the Strait of Juan de Fuca. For three summers, he pushed into practically every cove from Peter Puget's sound (naming the majestic Mount Rainier, 14,408 feet, in the hinterland after his friend Admiral Peter Rainier), to Sir Harry Burrard's fiord, to James Cook's own inlet striking into the heart of Alaska. He named a point for Horatio Nelson, another for George Grey, and an archipelago for William Pitt the Younger. He found that Kitimat already had a perfectly good name. All these, and every other discernible feature, he had drawn into a set of meticulous charts which won worldwide admiration.

Apart from his task to superintend the departure of the Spanish from Nootka, Vancouver was also to look for "any water communication which may tend to facilitate the purposes of commerce between the north-west coast and the country on the opposite side of the continent which is inhabited or occupied by His Majesty's subjects." Those British just wouldn't give up the dream of the Straits of Anian! Before he sailed home to die in Surrey at a tragically early forty, Vancouver was able to finally quash the myth. "I

247

trust the precision with which the survey has been carried into effect will remove every doubt and set aside every opinion of a Northwest Passage or any water communication navigable for shipping existing between the North Pacific and the interior of the American continent, within the limits of our researches."

A passage, of course, did exist across the very top of Canada. But it ran mostly through practically permanent ice that closed it to all shipping until our own times (and even now it resists "the purposes of commerce"). In the century and a half between Champlain and Cook, while French and English kings lost their thrones (and sometimes their heads), while Peter the Great built one vast empire and the Americans began to build another, that third ocean coast of the Canadian north reluctantly gave up a few of its secrets.

By the end of the eighteenth century, the mariners had broken their hearts, and often their ships, against the ice of Foxe Basin and Davis Strait, and in the bewildering *cul-de-sacs* opening off Baffin Bay. Most of that deadly island-strewn coastline was not charted until the mid-1800's, at which time the forty ships searching for the lost Franklin expedition fought their way into every possible open channel—and into some that closed upon them forever. The true eastern entry through Lancaster Sound had been found (yet not totally penetrated) by Lieutenant William Parry in 1819, and it was not until 1944 that the Royal Cana-

dian Mounted Police vessel, *St. Roch*, became the first ship to go through the Northwest Passage in a single season.

Overland, Samuel Hearne had reached the mouth of the Coppermine River on an arm of the Arctic Ocean, in 1771, and it was his report to his employers, the Hudson's Bay Company, of a narrow margin of ice-free water in Coronation Gulf in July that spurred the Admiralty to propose Captain Cook's last voyage. Other heroic figures had struck out from the St. Lawrence and the Great Lakes to explore the vast Canadian hinterland—men like Radisson, Albanel, Jolliet, La Salle, Kelsey, the La Vérendryes, Henday, Fidler, Pond, and Mackenzie. The latter reached the Pacific by land, on Cascade Inlet, near today's Bella Coola, on July 20, 1793. If he had made it exactly fifty-one days earlier, he would have surprised and astonished George Vancouver who surveyed that very cove from the ocean on May 31.

The nineteenth century added the illustrious names of Thompson, Fraser, Howse, Clouston of Ungava, Campbell of the Yukon, Franklin, Back, Pallister, Dawson, Hind, Butler, the indomitable Tyrells, and many others. They went into unknown places, lightly bearing risks which we should think horrendous today, and left us a more perfect and secure knowledge of the great land that we now hold in trust. But the overland exploration of Canada is another story, and it will be told in a subsequent volume.

It is no wonder that the tiny ships of the past failed to traverse the Northwest Passage, when the specially constructed tanker, Manhattan, *made the journey with great difficulty.*

Acknowledgements & Bibliography

One of the larger problems facing a writer attempting a work in the distant historical field is that he has to take someone else's word for it all. If he were writing about "Quebec Today," he could go to Salaberry-de-Valleyfield and see for himself. But, although H. G. Wells gave us *The Time Machine* back in 1895, even the inspired mechanics who have put man into space haven't been able to carry any one of us backwards a single hour. The writer must thus approach the sometimes-dismaying pile of books on the subject that have preceded his own, sifting back to the original journals, diaries, letters, notebooks, and public records where he can.

Of course, he intends to add a fresh perspective, to create a new, entertaining and useful structure from the materials, but he may come to fear that so many of the books already gathering dust on library shelves are so much better than anything he could publish that he should turn to another task. He may, on the other hand, take heart from such as Morris Bishop, who wrote in his life of Champlain, "In reading history one must always be impressed by the fact that our knowledge is only a collection of scraps and fragments that we put together into a pleasing design, and often the discovery of one new fragment would cause us to alter utterly the whole design."

If he proceeds, then, the writer must come to the page where, in his *Acknowledgement*, he tries to express his gratitude to those, dead and alive, upon whose shoulders he is standing, without actually confessing how much he pillaged from each. One time-honoured way, used in many of the two hundred books I studied in researching this present volume, is to say that one has a debt beyond computation to this or that authority—and then attempt over many inches of type to compute it. My method will be to list in the *Bibliography* (which is, in a way, an advertisement for those books still in print) all of the volumes I drew upon for ideas, illustrations, quotations, confirmations or contrary opinions, and to publicly thank the authors and publishers, one and all. Although I did draw much of my material from this considerable reading, all opinions (except where labelled) and all errors and omissions in the text are my own.

The scholar or specialist who will seek more depth in some subjects that I have given will find his needs satisfied in the appended select library on the discovery of Canada. If hackles rise at my use of the word "Canada" to describe the country from the earliest days, I can only say it was a term used on this soil centuries before any European dared the Atlantic and that no apology is offered. I would particularly draw attention to the journals of the discoverers themselves –from Cartier to Cook–published by learned societies and edited by dedicated men sheltered from raucous commerce by the public purse. Nothing can supplant the descriptions and comments (even if sometimes hasty) of the men who were there when it happened, who often *made* it happen, notwithstanding that they were much better seamen than scribes.

James Cook, not yet admitted by many into the Canadian pantheon, wrote, "I have given the best account of things in my power. I have neither had an education, nor have I acquired abilities for writing. I have been almost constantly at sea from my youth and have dragged myself ... through all the stations, from 'prentice boy to commander." Bringing him into the thin ranks of our heroes could, charitably, be considered my "one new fragment."

For the extended loan of such valuable volumes I wish to especially thank Miss Olive Delaney, of the Corby Library, Belleville, and her colleagues within the inter-library loan service–particularly the Douglas Library of Queen's University, Kingston.

To my children, Hilary, Trevor, Maureen, and Shelagh, heart-felt thanks for turning down the volume on those cacophonic records; to my wife, Barbara, my debt is, as they say, "beyond computation." L.F.H.

Arbman, Holger. *The Vikings, Ancient Peoples and Places.* New York: Praeger, 1961.

Armstrong, Richard. *The Discoverers.* London: Ernest Benn, 1968.

Averill, Esther. *Cartier Sails the St. Lawrence.* New York: Harper & Row, 1937.

Baird, P. D. *Expeditions to the Canadian Arctic. The Beaver,* Winnipeg: 1949.

Bakeless, John. *The Eyes of Discovery.* New York: Lippincott, 1950.

Baker, J. L. N. *A History of Geographical Discovery.* London: Harrap, 1948.

Banks, Joseph. *Journal, 1768-1771.* (Beaglehole, J. C., Ed.). (2 vols.). Sydney: Angus & Robertson, 1962.

Barrow, John. *A Chronological History of Voyages into the Arctic Regions.* London: 1818.

~ *Captain Cook's Voyages of Discovery.* London: J. M. Dent (reprint), 1906.

Beaglehole, J. C. *The Exploration of the Pacific.* London: A. & C. Black, 1934.

Begg, Alexander. *History of British Columbia from its Earliest Discovery to the Present Time.* Toronto: Briggs, 1894.

Bennet, C. L. *et al. The Face of Canada.* Toronto: Clarke, Irwin, 1959.

Bettex, Albert. *The Discovery of the World.* New York: Simon & Shuster, 1960.

Biggar, H. P. (Editor). *A Collection of Documents Relating to Jacques Cartier and the Sieur de Roberval.* Ottawa: King's Printer, 1930.

~ *The Precursors of Jacques Cartier, 1497-1534.* Ottawa: King's Printer, 1913.

~ *The Voyages of Jacques Cartier.* Ottawa: King's Printer, 1914.

~ *The Works of Samuel de Champlain* (q.v.)

Bishop, Morris. *Champlain, The Life of Fortitude.* New York: Alfred Knopf, 1948.

Blacker, Irwin R. *Hakluyt's Voyages.* New York: Viking Press, 1965.

Boland, C. M. *They All Discovered America.* New York: Doubleday, 1961.

Boucher, Pierre. *Canada in the Seventeenth Century.* Montreal: G. E. Desbarats, 1883.

Bougainville, Louis-Antoine de. *A Voyage Round the World.* London: 1772.

Bourne, E. G. *Voyages and Explorations of Samuel de Champlain.* (2 vol.). New York: Allerton, 1922.

Brebner, J. B. *The Explorers of North America, 1492-1806.* Garden City: Doubleday, 1955.

Brendon, J. A. *Great Navigators & Discoverers.* Toronto: George G. Harrap, 1929.

Brøgger, A. W. *Ancient Emigrants.* London: Oxford University Press, 1929.

~ *The Viking Ships.* Oslo: Dreyer, 1951.

Brøndsted, J. *The Norsemen in North America Before Columbus.* Washington: Smithsonian Institution, 1953.

Burpee, L. J. *The Search for the Western Sea*. Toronto: Musson, 1908.

~ *The Discovery of Canada*. Toronto: Macmillan, 1944.

Burt, A. L. *The United States, Great Britain, and British North America*. New Haven, 1940.

Champlain, Samuel de. (Biggar, H. P., Ed.). *The Works of Samuel de Champlain*. [Includes: *Brief Discours*, 1859; *Des Sauvages*, 1604; *Les Voyages*, 1613; *Voyages et Decouvertures*, 1619; *Les Voyages* (revised collected edition), 1632]. (6 vols.). Toronto: Champlain Society, 1922-1936.

~ *Oeuvres de Champlain* (Laverdiere, C.-H., Ed.). (6 vols.). Quebec: 1870.

Charlevoix, P. F. X. *History & General Description of New France*. (6 vols.). London: 1902.

Chubb, Thomas Caldecot. *The Venetians: Merchant Princes*. New York: Viking Press, 1968.

Churchill, Winston S. *History of the English Speaking Peoples*. (4 vols.). London: Cassell, 1957.

Colby, Charles W. *The Founder of New France*. Toronto: 1915.

Collier, John. *The Indians of the Americas*. New York: Norton, 1947.

Cook, James (Beaglehole, J. C., Ed.). *Journals*. I. *The Voyages of the Endeavour, 1768-1771*. II. *The Voyage of the Resolution and Adventure, 1772-1775*. III. *The Voyage of the Resolution and Discovery, 1776-1780*. Hakluyt Society. Cambridge: Cambridge University Press, 1955-1967.

~ *An Account of a Voyage Around the World by Lieutenant James Cook, Commander of His Majesty's Bark The Endeavour*. (Hawkesworth, J., Ed.). [From "Hawkesworth's Voyages," Vols. II and III]. London: 1773.

~ *A Voyage to the Pacific Ocean* Volumes I and II by Cook; Volume III by James King. London: 1784.

~ *Cook's Voyages of Discovery*. Edinburgh: Adam and Charles Black, 1879.

~ *The Three Voyages of Captain James Cook*. London: William Smith, 1842.

Creighton, D. G. *Dominion of the North*. Toronto: Macmillan, 1944.

Crone, G. R. *Maps and their Makers*. New York: Hillary House, 1953.

Curran, J. W. "Here Was Vinland." Sault Ste. Marie: *Sault Daily Star*, 1939.

Dalvell, Kathleen E. *Queen Charlotte Islands*. Vancouver: Evergreen Press, 1968.

Dasent, Sir G. W. *The Story of Burnt Njal*. London: J. M. Dent, 1911.

Davies, Blodwen. *Gaspe, Land of History and Romance*. Toronto: Ambassador Books, 1949.

Debenham, Frank. *Discovery and Exploration*. Garden City, N.Y.: Doubleday, 1960.

Denys, Nicholas. *The Description and Natural History of the Coasts of North America*. (Ganong, W. F., Ed.). Toronto: Champlain Society, 1908.

De Volpi, Charles and Winkworth, P. S. *Montreal, a Pictorial Record, 1535-1885*. Montreal: 1963.

Diereville, Sieur de, *Relation of the Voyage to Port Royal in Acadia or New France*. Toronto: Champlain Society, 1933.

Dionne, N. E. *Champlain*. Toronto: Morang, 1906.

Dodge, E. S. *Northwest by Sea*. London: Oxford University Press, 1961.

Dollier de Casson, F. *A History of Montreal, 1640-1672*. (Flenley, R., Ed.). Toronto: 1928.

Donovan, Frank R. *The Vikings*. New York: Harper & Row, 1964.

Doughty, A. G. *Quebec of Yester-year*. Toronto: Thomas Nelson, 1932.

Douville, Raymond and Casanova, Jacques-Donat. *Daily Life in Early Canada*. New York: Macmillan, 1968.

Driver, Harold E. *Indians of North America*. Chicago: University of Chicago Press, 1961.

Du Bois, Jay. *Travellers' Tales*. New York: Everybody's Vacation Publishing Co.

Duff, Wilson. *The Indian History of British Columbia*. (Vol. 1, The Impact of the White Man.) Victoria: 1964.

Dunmore, John. *French Explorers in the Pacific*. London: Oxford University Press, 1965.

Ferguson, Robert D. *Man from St. Malo*. Toronto: Macmillan, 1959.

Galbraith, J. S. *The Hudson's Bay Company as an Imperial Factor*. Toronto, 1957.

Ganong, W. F. *Crucial Maps–In the Early Cartography and Place-nomenclature of the Atlantic Coast of Canada*. Toronto: University of Toronto Press, 1964.

Gjerset, K. *History of Iceland*. New York: Macmillan, 1925.

Graham, G. F. *Empire of the North Atlantic*. Toronto: 1950.

Grattan, Hartley C. *The Southwest Pacific to 1900*. Ann Arbor: University of Michigan Press, 1963.

Hakluyt, Richard (Editor). *The Principal Navigations, Voyages, Traffics and Discoveries of the English Nation, Etc.* London: 1589-1600; New York (reprint): 1962.

Hale, John R. *Age of Exploration*. New York: Time Incorporated, 1966.

Hallberg, Peter. *The Icelandic Saga*. Lincoln: University of Nebraska Press, 1962.

Hampden, John. *New Worlds Ahead*. London: Kaye & Ward, 1953.

Hannon, Leslie F. *Canada at War, The Record of a Fighting People*. Toronto:

McClelland & Stewart, 1968.

Harrison, Alec. *With Cartier up the St. Lawrence*. London: Muller, 1967.

Hart, Henry H. *Sea Record to the Indies*. New York: Macmillan, 1950.

Hayward, A. L. *Explorers & Their Discoveries*. New York: Abelard-Schuman, 1955.

Hearne, Samuel. *A Journey from Prince of Wales Fort in Hudson's Bay to the Northern Ocean, 1769-72*. (Glover, R., Ed.). Toronto: Macmillan, 1958.

Herrman, Paul. *Conquest by Man*. New York: Harper, 1954.

~ *The Great Age of Discovery*. New York: Harper, 1958.

Hoffman, Bernard G. *Cabot to Cartier*. Toronto: University of Toronto Press, 1961.

Innis, H. A. *The Cod Fisheries: The History of an International Economy*. Toronto: Ryerson Press, 1940.

Jane, Cecil. *The Journal of Christopher Columbus*. New York: Potter, 1960.

Jenkins, Kathleen. *Montreal, Island City of the St. Lawrence*. Garden City, N.Y.: Doubleday, 1966.

Jenness, Diamond. *Indians of Canada*. Ottawa: King's Printer, 1932.

Jewitt, John Rodgers. *Adventures & Suffering Among the Savages of Nootka Sound*. Edinburgh: Constable, 1824.

Johnston, Sir Harry. *Pioneers in Canada*. London: Blackie and Son, 1912.

Jones, Gwyn. *The Norse Atlantic Saga*. London: Oxford University Press, 1964.

Josephy, Alvin, M. *The Indian Heritage of America*. New York: Alfred A. Knopf, 1968.

Kendrick, T. D. *A History of the Vikings*. New York: Scribner's, 1930.

Kerr, D. G. G. *Historical Atlas of Canada*. Toronto: Thomas Nelson, 1961.

Kirwan, L. P. *A History of Polar Exploration*. New York: Norton, 1959.

Koht, Halvdan. *The Old Norse Sagas*. New York: W. W. Norton, 1931.

Lamb, Harold. *New Found World*. Garden City, N.Y.: Doubleday, 1955.

Landstrom, Bjørn. *The Quest for India*. New York: Doubleday, 1964.

Laut, Agnes C. *Pioneers of the Pacific Coast*. Toronto: Glasgow, Brook, 1916.

Leacock, Stephen. *Adventures of the Far North: A Chronicle of the Arctic Seas*. Toronto: Glasgow, Brook, 1914.

~ *Canada, the Foundation of its Future*. Montreal: Privately printed, 1941.

~ *Dawn of Canadian History*. Toronto: Glasgow, Brook, 1915.

~ *Mariner of St. Malo*. Toronto: Glasgow, Brook, 1915.

~ *Montreal Seaport and City*. Garden City, N.Y.: Doubleday, 1942.

Leithauser, J. C. *Worlds Beyond the Horizon*. New York: Knopf, 1955.

Lescarbot, Marc. *The History of New France*. (Grant, W. L. Ed.). Toronto: Champlain Society, 1907-14.

Lorant, Stefan. *The New World*. New York: Duell, Sloan and Pearce, 1946.

Lower, A. R. M. *Colony to Nation: A History of Canada*. Toronto: Longmans, 1946.

McFeat, Tom. *Indians of the North Pacific Coast*. Toronto: McClelland & Stewart, 1966.

McInnis, Edgar. *Canada, A Political & Social History*. New York, Holt, Rinehart & Winston, 1963.

MacKay, Douglas. *The Honourable Company*. Toronto: McClelland & Stewart, 1949.

MacNutt, W. S. *The Atlantic Provinces*. Toronto: McClelland & Stewart, 1965.

Major, R. H. (Editor). *The Voyages of the Venetian Brothers, Nicolo and Antonio Zeno, to the Northern Seas in the* XIV*th Century*. London: Hakluyt Society, 1873.

~ *Christopher Columbus, Four Voyages to the New World*. New York (reprint), 1961.

Marshall, James and Carrie. *Vancouver's Voyage*. Vancouver: Mitchell Press, 1955.

Matthews, Wm. *Canadian Diaries and Autobiographies*. Los Angeles: University of California Press, 1950

Mawer, A. *The Vikings*. Cambridge: Cambridge University Press, 1913.

Milton, Viscount and Cheade, W. B. *The Northwest Passage of Land*. London: Cassell, Petter & Galpin, 1875.

Mitchison, Naomi. *The Swan's Road*. London: Naldrett Press, 1954.

Moorehead, Alan. *The Fatal Impact*. London: Hamish Hamilton, 1966.

Morison, Samuel Eliot. *Admiral of the Ocean Sea*. Boston: Little, Brown, 1942.

Morton, W. L. *The Kingdom of Canada*. Toronto: McClelland & Stewart, 1963.

Mowat, Farley. *Ordeal by Ice*. Toronto: McClelland & Stewart, 1960.

~ *Westviking, Ancient Norse in Greenland and North America*. Toronto: McClelland & Stewart, 1965.

Neatby, Hilda. *Quebec, The Revolutionary Age, 1760-1791*. Toronto: McClelland & Stewart, 1966.

Oakley, Amy. *Kaleidoscopic Quebec*. New York: Appleton-Century, 1947.

O'Donoghue, Denis. *St. Brendan the Voyager*. Dublin: 1893.

Oleson, Tryggvi J. *Early Voyages and Northern Approaches*. Toronto: McClelland & Stewart, 1963.

Oxenstierna, Count Eric. *The Norsemen*. Greenwich, Conn.: New York Graphic Society, 1965.

Parkman, Francis. *Francis Parkman's Works*. (16 vols.). Toronto: Morang, 1897

~ *Romance of Canadian History*. Toronto: Morang, 1902.

~ *The Parkman Reader* (Morison, S. E., Ed.). Toronto: Little, Brown, 1955.

Pearson, Hesketh. *Henry of Navarre*. London: Heinemann, 1963.

Penrose, Boies. *Travel and Discovery in the Renaissance, 1420-1620*. Harvard University Press, 1952.

Pohl, F. J. *Atlantic Crossings Before Columbus*. New York: Norton, 1961.

~ *The Lost Discovery*. New York: Norton, 1952.

Pope, Joseph. *Jacques Cartier, His Life and Voyages*. Ottawa, 1890.

Raddall, Thomas H. *Halifax, Warden of the North*. Toronto: McClelland & Stewart, 1948.

Rand, Silas Tertius. *A Dictionary of the Micmac Language*. Charlottetown: 1902.

Rich, E. E. *Hudson's Bay Company*. Toronto: McClelland & Stewart, 1960.

~ *The Fur Trade and the Northwest to 1857*. Toronto: McClelland & Stewart, 1967.

Riddell, W. R. *The Life of John Graves Simcoe*. Toronto: McClelland & Stewart, 1926.

Rienits, Rex and Thea. *Voyages of Captain Cook*. London: Paul Hamlyn, 1968.

Ritchie, C. T. *The First Canadian, the Story of Champlain*. Toronto: Macmillan, 1961.

Roberts, Lynette. *The Endeavour*. London: Peter Owen, 1954.

Rowse, A. L. *The Elizabethans and America*. London: Macmillan, 1959.

Rugoff, Milton (Editor). *The Great Travellers*. (2 vols.). New York: Simon & Shuster, 1960.

Saint-Clair, R. W. *The Saint-Clairs of the Isles, Being a History of the Sea-kings of Orkney and their Scottish Successors of the Surname of Sinclair*. Auckland, N.Z.: 1898.

Sanceau, Elaine. *Henry the Navigator*. New York: Norton, 1947.

Sawyer, P. H. *The Age of the Vikings*. New York: St. Martin's Press, 1962.

Simons, Eric N. *Into Unknown Waters*. London: Dennis Dobson, 1964.

Sinclair, Alexander. *The History of Roslin and its Possessors*. Irvine, 1856.

Smith, C. M. *Northmen of Adventure*. London: Longmans, Green, 1932.

Stanley, G. F. G. *New France, The Last Phase 1744-1760*. Toronto: McClelland & Stewart, 1968.

Stefansson, Vilhjalmur. *Great Adventures and Explorations*. New York: Dial Press, 1947.

Stenton, F. M. *Anglo-Saxon England*. London: Oxford University Press, 1947.

Story, Norah. *Oxford Companion to Canadian History & Literature*. Toronto: Oxford University Press, 1967.

Swift, S. C. and Marquis, T. G. *The Voyages of Jacques Cartier in Prose and Verse*. Toronto: Thomas Allen, 1934.

Sykes, Sir Percy. *A History of Exploration*. London: Routledge & Kegan Paul, 1934.

Symington, Fraser. *The Canadian Indian*. Toronto: McClelland & Stewart, 1969.

Thomas, Lowell. *The Untold Story of Exploration*. New York: Dodd, Mead, 1935.

Thomson, D. W. *Men and Meridians. History of Surveying and Mapping in Canada*. Ottawa: Queen's Printer, 1966.

Thwaites, Reuben G. (Editor). *Jesuit Relations and Allied Documents*. (73 vols.). Cleveland: Burrows, 1896-1901.

Tillotson, John. *Adventures in the Ice*. London: 1869.

Toye, William. *The St. Lawrence*. Toronto: Oxford University Press, 1959.

Trudel, Marcel. *Atlas Historique du Canada Francais*. Quebec: Laval University Press, 1961.

Tytler, Patrick. *The Northern Coast of America & the Hudson Bay Territories*. London: 1853.

Van Steen, Marcus. *Governor Simcoe and his Lady*. Toronto: Hodder & Stoughton, 1968.

Villiers, Alan. *Captain James Cook*. New York: Scribner's, 1967.

Wallace, W. Stewart. *By Star & Compass*. Toronto: Ryerson Press, 1953.

~ *Dictionary of Canadian Biography*. Toronto: Macmillan, 1926.

Wallis, W. D. and Wallis, R. S. *The Micmac of Eastern Canada*. University of Minnesota Press, 1955.

Walsh, A. *Scandinavian Relations with Ireland during the Viking Period*. Dublin: Talbot Press, 1922.

Warkentin, John. *Canada, A Geographical Interpretation*. Toronto: Methuen, 1968.

Williams, Archibald. *Romance of Early Exploration*. London: Seeley, 1909.

Williamson, James A. *The Cabot Voyages and Bristol Discovery under Henry* VII. Cambridge: Cambridge University Press for the Hakluyt Society, 1962.

~ *Cook and the Opening of the Pacific*. New York: Macmillan, 1948.

~ *The Ocean in English History*. London: Oxford University Press, 1941.

Wilson, Edmund. *Apologies to the Iroquois*. New York: Farrar, Straus & Cudahy, 1959.

Wrong, George M. *Rise and Fall of New France*. Toronto: Macmillan, 1928.

Picture Credits

Order of appearance in the text of pictures listed here is left to right, top to bottom. Numbers refer to the page on which the picture appears.

1
British Museum /
American Heritage
2
Royal Ontario Museum /
Rolph-Clarke-Stone
Royal Ontario Museum /
Rolph-Clarke-Stone
Royal Ontario Museum /
Rolph-Clarke-Stone
National Maritime Museum,
Greenwich /Michael Holford
4
National Maritime Museum,
Greenwich /Michael Holford
8 /9
British Museum
10
New York Public Library,
Astor, Lenox & Tilden
Foundation
13
John de Visser
14
Ray Webber
15
John de Visser
16
John de Visser
17
John de Visser
18
Freeman Patterson
John de Visser
John de Visser
Metropolitan Toronto Central
Library
John de Visser
John de Visser
19
John de Visser
20
Miller Services
21
John de Visser
Don Newlands
John de Visser
Don Newlands
22
John de Visser
23
John de Visser
24
Miller Services /
Peter Tasker
25
Culver Pictures Inc.
26
British Museum
28
Radio Times Hulton Picture
Library

29
Radio Times Hulton Picture
Library /Culver Pictures Inc.
30
Culver Pictures Inc.
30 /1
Radio Times Hulton Picture
Library
32
Culver Pictures Inc.
34
Metropolitan Toronto Central
Library /Tuttle
37
Metropolitan Toronto Central
Library /In Northern Mists
39
Newfoundland & Labrador
Tourist Development Office
41
Universitets Oldsaksamlung,
Oslo
42
Arctic Institute
43
Universitets Oldsaksamlung,
Oslo
44
Universitets Oldsaksamlung,
Oslo
Royal Ontario Museum
Universitets Oldsaksamlung,
Oslo
National Museum of Iceland
45
Antikvarish-Topografiska-
Arkivet, Stockholm
Universitets Oldsaksamlung,
Oslo
Antikvarish-Topografiska-
Arkivet, Stockholm
Antikvarish-Topografiska-
Arkivet, Stockholm
Antikvarish-Topografiska-
Arkivet, Stockholm
46
National Museum of Scotland
Universitets Oldsaksamlung,
Oslo
Antikvarish-Topografiska-
Arkivet, Stockholm
47
Antikvarish-Topografiska-
Arkivet, Stockholm
Universitets Oldsaksamlung,
Oslo
Antikvarish-Topografiska-
Arkivet, Stockholm
Universitets Oldsaksamlung,
Oslo
Antikvarish-Topografisak-
Arkivet, Stockholm
Universitets Oldsaksamlung,
Oslo
48
Antikvarish-Topografiska-
Arkivet, Stockholm
50
Public Archives of Canada

51
Culver Pictures Inc.
52
Metropolitan Toronto Central
Library /A Voyage to Hudson's
Bay
54 /5
Public Archives of Canada
56
Radio Times Hulton Picture
Library
58
Radio Times Hulton Picture
Library
59
Radio Times Hulton Picture
Library
61
Radio Times Hulton Picture
Library
63
New York Public Library
Public Archives of Canada
New York Public Library
65
Library of Congress
66 /7
Library of Congress
68 /9
Library of Congress
70 /1
Bibliotheque Nationale,
France /Giraudon
72
The Huntingdon Library,
San Marino, California
74
Ontario Science Centre
75
Radio Times Hulton Picture
Library
77
Metropolitan Toronto Central
Library
78 /9
Giraudon
80
Public Archives of Canada
82
Culver Pictures Inc.
85
New York Historical Society
88
Radio Times Hulton Picture
Library
89
Metropolitan Toronto Central
Library /Art Bulletin
90
Royal Ontario Museum
91
The Masters & Fellows of
Magdalene College,
Cambridge
92
Science Museum
93
Science Museum

94
Metropolitan Toronto Central
Library
Metropolitan Toronto Central
Library
Museo di Storia della Scienza,
Florence
National Maritime Museum,
Greenwich
British Museum
National Maritime Museum,
Greenwich
95
National Maritime Museum,
Greenwich
96
National Maritime Museum,
Greenwich
97
Radio Times Hulton Picture
Library
99
Giraudon
100
Radio Times Hulton Picture
Library
102
Radio Times Hulton Picture
Library
103
Quebec Archives
104
Public Archives of Canada
108
Public Archives of Canada
109
Public Archives of Canada
113-120
Royal Ontario Museum /
Lee Warren
122
Public Archives of Canada
123
Public Archives of Canada
122 /3
Royal Ontario Museum
125
Giraudon
127
Public Archives of Canada
128
Public Archives of Canada
129
Royal Ontario Museum
130
Arctic Institute
131
Metropolitan Toronto Central
Library /Topsell
132 /3
Public Archives of Canada
134
Metropolitan Toronto Central
Library /Gesner
Metropolitan Toronto Central
Library
Public Archives of Canada
Metropolitan Toronto Central
Library

Public Archives of Canada
Arctic Institute / *Voyage de la Baie Hudson*
135
Metropolitan Toronto Central Library
136
Metropolitan Toronto Central Library
The Metropolitan Museum of Art, Harris Brisbane Dick Fund, 1932
138
Public Archives of Canada
141
Webster Canadiana Collection
143
Royal Ontario Museum
144
Public Archives of Canada
146
Radio Times Hulton Picture Library
147
Culver Pictures Inc.
149
Public Archives of Canada
150/1
Metropolitan Toronto Central Library / *Biggar*
153
Bodleian Library, Oxford
154
National Portrait Gallery
Metropolitan Toronto Central Library / *The Cabot Voyages & Bristol Discovery*
155
Victoria & Albert Museum
Victoria & Albert Museum / Michael Holford
British Museum, Royal 16F II f23
156
Service de Documentation Photographique
Lord Chamberlain
157
Bibliotheque Nationale, France
158
Guildhall Library
Mansell Collection
Mansell Collection
159
Mansell Collection
160
Giraudon
Bibliotheque Nationale, France
161
Ashmolean Museum, Oxford
Bibliotheque Nationale, France (marginal drawings)
162
London Museum
Art Gallery of Ontario
163
Museum of Fine Arts, Boston
Art Gallery of Ontario
London Museum

164
National Maritime Museum, Greenwich
The Huntingdon Library, San Marino, California
167
Webster Canadiana Collection
168
Webster Canadiana Collection
172
Webster Canadiana Collection
176
Metropolitan Toronto Central Library / *Biggar*
177
Metropolitan Toronto Central Library / *Biggar*
178
Webster Canadiana Collection
181
Public Archives of Canada
182
Public Archives of Canada
183
Quebec Archives
Public Archives of Canada
New York Public Library
184
Public Archives of Canada
185
Public Archives of Canada
Webster Canadiana Collection
186
National Museum of Canada
Quebec Museum
Quebec Museum
187
Metropolitan Toronto Central Library / *Biggar*
Quebec Museum
Quebec Museum
188
Bibliotheque Nationale, France
190
Public Archives of Canada
193
Metropolitan Toronto Central Library / *Biggar*
195
Culver Pictures Inc.
Radio Times Hulton Picture Library
198
John Ross Robertson
199
Public Archives of Canada
201
Royal Ontario Museum
203
Public Archives of Canada
Royal Ontario Museum
Public Archives of Canada
204
Royal Ontario Museum
205
Arctic Institute
206
Bodleian Library, Oxford
Arctic Institute

207
Arctic Institute
208
Metropolitan Toronto Central Library
Royal Ontario Museum
209
Metropolitan Toronto Central Library / *Arctic Exploration*
Public Archives of Canada
210
Royal Ontario Museum
211
Webster Canadiana Collection
Arctic Institute / *Voyage de la Baie Hudson*
Metropolitan Toronto Central Library
212
Arctic Institute
213
British Museum
216/7
New York Public Library, Rare Books Division
218
National Maritime Museum, Greenwich
219
Whitby Literary & Philosophical Society / Axel Poignant
221
New Zealand Art Gallery
222/3
National Library of Australia
224
National Maritime Museum, Greenwich
Public Archives of Canada
225
National Maritime Museum, Greenwich
226
British Museum
Metropolitan Toronto Central Library / *Cook's Voyages*
Metropolitan Toronto Central Library / *Cook's Voyages*
227
Metropolitan Toronto Central Library / *Cook's Voyages*
National Library of Australia
228
Metropolitan Toronto Central Library / *Cook's Voyages*
229
British Museum / Paul Hamlyn
230/1
National Maritime Museum, Greenwich
231
Metropolitan Toronto Central Library / *Cook's Voyages*
232
Paul Hamlyn
234
Webster Canadiana Collection

238
Metropolitan Toronto Central Library / *Cook's Voyages*
242
Metropolitan Toronto Central Library / *Cook's Voyages*
244
Metropolitan Toronto Central Library / *Cook's Voyages*
246
Vancouver Archives
248
Metropolitan Toronto Central Library

Every reasonable effort has been made to ascertain ownership of the illustrations used. Information would be welcomed that would enable the publisher to rectify any error.

Index

254